SERVICE OPERATIONS
MANAGEMENT

Pearson
Education

We work with leading authors to develop the
strongest educational materials in management studies,
bringinng cutting-edge thinking and best learning
practice to a global market.

Under a range of well-known imprints, including
Financial Times Prentice Hall, we craft high quality
print and electronic publications which help readers
to understand and apply their content,
whether studying or at work.

To find out more about the complete range of our
publishing please visit us on the World Wide Web at:
www.pearsoneduc.com

SERVICE OPERATIONS MANAGEMENT

Robert Johnston

Graham Clark

FINANCIAL TIMES
Prentice Hall

An imprint of **Pearson Education**

Harlow, England · London · New York · Reading, Massachusetts · San Francisco · Toronto · Don Mills, Ontario · Sydney
Tokyo · Singapore · Hong Kong · Seoul · Taipei · Cape Town · Madrid · Mexico City · Amsterdam · Munich · Paris · Milan

PEARSON EDUCATION LIMITED

Edinburgh Gate
Harlow
Essex CM20 2JE
United Kingdom

and Associated Companies throughout the world

Visit us on the World Wide Web at:
www.pearsoneduc.com

First Published 2001

ISBN 0 273 63922 6

British Library Cataloguing in Publication Data
A CIP catalogue record for this book can be obtained from the British Library.

10 9 8 7 6 5 4 3 2 1
05 04 03 02 01 00

Typeset by 30
Printed by Ashford Colour Press Ltd., Gosport

Contents

· ·

Preface

The focus of this book

This book is concerned with the management of service operations. Its key focus is on how organisations deliver service and the operations decisions that managers face in managing their resources and delivering service to their customers. How well a service is delivered is the acid test of an organisation's ability to put together an effective strategy, motivate its employees, and manage its resources.

The book also focuses on the service sector. This sector encompasses many types of organisation: public sector, voluntary, mass transport services, professional services, retailers, Internet services, tourism and hospitality, for example. We do not focus on any particular type of service but seek to cover the many decisions that operations managers in all of these organisations face.

We also refer to many aspects of 'business performance', not simply 'profit'. Although many organisations are motivated by profit, most operations are also assessed on their costs, revenues and adherence to budgets, customer loyalty and technological leadership, for example. We have sought to provide examples and illustrations from many different organisations and many countries to reflect the diversity of service organisations.

Who should read this book?

This book is intended as a textbook for those who want to build on knowledge of the basic principles of operations management. It will also serve as a handbook for operations managers in service organisations as they seek to develop and implement operations strategies. Specifically it is intended for:

- *Undergraduates* on business studies or joint studies degrees or those specialising in hospitality, tourism or the public sector, for example, who wish to enhance their understanding of service operations management.
- *MBA students* who are managing service organisations and want to stretch their understanding of the area and assess and improve their operations.
- *Executives* who want to focus on certain aspects of service delivery, such as design, capacity, recovery, performance measurement or service strategy development for example, in order to challenge and change their own organisations.

Distinctive features

- **Operations focused**. This text has a clear operations focus and is concerned with *managing* operations. It explores operational issues, problems and decisions. It exposes undergraduates to the problems faced by service operations managers and helps practising managers deal with those issues.

- **Frameworks and tools**. Each chapter provides tools, frameworks and techniques which will help students not only analyse existing operations but also understand better how they can deal with the issues that operations managers face. The frameworks, approaches and techniques will vary from topic to topic and will include, for example:

  - a list of key points to bear in mind when making decisions in a particular area
  - a diagram or chart showing the relationship between two variables or sets of variables to help position an operation or help identify the nature of the relationships
  - a list of questions, checks or tests that can be applied to a situation
  - ways of quantifying or assessing qualitative variables
  - the key stages in undertaking a particular activity.

- **Real-world illustrations**. Operations management is an applied subject so each chapter includes a number of short illustrations from around the world which show how organisations have either identified or dealt with the particular issues being discussed.

- **Underpinned by theory**. Appropriate theoretical underpinning and developments are included and we have tried to explain them in an unobtrusive and accessible way. References are provided for anyone wishing to undertake more work in a particular area.

- **Managing people**. A key task for operations managers is managing people and so this book contains a significant 'managing people' element. This includes not only employees but also customers, as well as managing and changing the culture of the organisation as a whole.

- **e-service**. Information technology, e-service and virtual operations are integrated into the book and their operational implications explored in detail.

- **State of the art**. The book contains some of the most recent ideas and information, covering in particular world-class service, performance management, service concept, service recovery, guarantees, satisfaction and service processes.

- **Summaries**. Each chapter concludes with a bullet-point checklist summarising the key points in terms of the chapter's objectives.

- **Questions for managers**. At the end of each chapter there are some questions aimed at practising managers which they can ask of their/an operation. We hope that these questions will encourage you to apply the material in the chapter to real situations and will allow you to better understand, challenge and improve your service operations.

- *Discussion questions and further reading.* We have also provided some general discussion questions, aimed at undergraduates, to help them both assess the material and apply it to a variety of situations. These are followed by some suggestions for further reading.

- *Case exercises.* Each chapter, with the exception of the final chapter, concludes with a case exercise suitable for class discussion. The cases are short but focused on the topic and are a rich source of material for debate and development.

- *Instructor's manual.* An Instructor's Manual is available to lecturers adopting this textbook. It includes OHP masters of the figures in the book, which are also available on disk. It provides additional detailed questions to go with the cases and bullet-point answers to the questions.

Acknowledgements

Many people have helped us in the writing of this book. Academic colleagues from around the world have provided encouragement and contributions including important ideas and material, useful feedback, illustrations and case studies. We would like to express our gratitude to all of them, but especially Colin Armistead of Bournemouth University, Len Berry of Texas A&M University, Guenther Botschen of Aston Business School, David Bowen of The American Graduate School of International Management, Stan Brignall of Aston Business School, Stephen Brown of Arizona State University, Dick Chase of University of Southern California, David Collier of Ohio State University, Simon Croom of Warwick Business School, David Crowther of Aston Business School, Carole Driver of Plymouth Business School, Bo Edvardsson of Karlstad University, Lin Fitzgerald of Warwick Business School, Jim Fitzsimmons of the University of Texas at Austin, John Haywood-Farmer of the University of Western Ontario, Jim Heskett of Harvard University, Kim James of Cranfield School of Management, Sheryl Kimes of Cornell University, Bob Lillis of Cranfield School of Management, David Lyth of Western Michigan University, Steve Macaulay of Cranfield School of Management, John Mackness of The Management School, Lancaster University, Jan Mattsson of Roskilde University, Maureen Meadows, Warwick Business School, Andy Neely of Cranfield School of Management, Elaine Palmer of the University of Auckland, Parsu Parasuraman of the University of Miami, Adrian Payne of Cranfield School of Management, Aleda Roth of the University of North Carolina, Roland Rust of Vanderbilt University, Mike Shulver of Warwick Business School, Rhian Silvestro of Warwick Business School, Nigel Slack of Warwick Business School, Bernd Stauss of Ingolstadt Katholische Universität Eichstätt, Bridgette Sullivan-Taylor of Warwick Business School, Mike Sweeney of Cranfield School of Management, David Tansik of the University of Arizona, Chris Voss of London Business School, and Jochen Wirtz of the National University of Singapore.

Our colleagues at Cranfield and Warwick have helped us greatly by not only providing ideas and encouragement but also creating the stimulating environment in which we work. We are particularly grateful to our secretaries, Sue Gregory and Mary Walton, whose efforts have kept us focused on the task and as organised as is possible.

Practising managers from around the world have also been kind enough to provide some rich material about their activities and organisations, past or present. Our grateful thanks go to Colin Brown from Anglian Water, Roger Clark, independent consultant, Stuart Cross from Boots the Chemist, Mike Day from Pegasus, Keith Edwards from Anglian Water, Nicholas Georgiades from TLC Ltd, David Good from the Central Samui Hotel, Thailand, Sean Guilliam from Lombard Direct, Bernard Harrison from Singapore Zoological Gardens, Doug Henderson from DHA, Tony Hughes from Bass Leisure Retail, Lawrence Lim from Singapore General Hospital,

Marilyn Merriam, Jean Neumann from the Tavistock Institute of Human Relations, Jan Nowell from Oxfam, Vincent O'Farrell from adabra.com, B K Ong from Singapore Airlines, Bruce Rance from The Customer Service Network, Kirit Shah from the GP Group, Bangkok, Roy Staughton from Shape International, Michael Tay from the Institute of Forensic Science and Forensic Medicine, Singapore, Catrin Weston from BUPA, and Laurie Young from PriceWaterhouseCoopers.

We are particularly grateful to the book's reviewers whose considerable efforts and expertise provided us with comments, ideas and suggestions, all of which have had a significant influence on the text. The reviewers included Ian Holden of Bristol Business School, Lesley Kimber of Southampton Business School, Geoffrey Plumb of Staffordshire University, Mike Shulver of Warwick Business School, Rhian Silvestro of Warwick Business School, Remko Van Hoek of Erasmus and Cranfield Universities, and Jan de Vries of the University of Groningen.

We have greatly benefited from the guidance, encouragement and support of the very professional team at Pearson. Our thanks go to all of the staff at Pearson, with special thanks to Penelope Woolf, Alison Kirk and Emily Pillars.

It is appropriate also for us to thank all of our students, both past and present. They have, over many years, been a source of great stimulation and development. Each one of them has had an influence on this book.

Last, but not least, we would like to thank our wives, Marilyn and Shirley, and our families for their support and patience and for allowing us to dedicate a significant amount of our time to this project. They have been our major source of encouragement and without their support, and also their direct involvement in the book, we would never have completed this task.

Graham Clark and Robert Johnston

About the authors

Robert Johnston is Professor of Operations Management at Warwick Business School. Bob has a management degree from the University of Aston and a PhD from the University of Warwick. Before moving to academia Bob held several line management and senior management posts in a number of service organisations in both the public and private sectors. Bob continues to maintain close and active links with many large and small organisations around the world through his research, management training and consultancy activities. Bob's research interests include service quality, performance measurement and strategy and he has written numerous

texts, papers and case studies. Bob has served as associate dean at the Business School and as programme director on two MBA programmes. He is the founding editor of the *International Journal of Service Industry Management* and he also serves on the editorial board of the *Journal of Operations Management* and the *International Journal of Tourism and Hospitality Research*.

Graham Clark is Senior Lecturer in Operations Management at Cranfield University. He has a degree in mechanical engineering and a Master's degree in management from Imperial College, London. Graham has considerable experience in managing operations. Since moving to Cranfield in 1986, Graham has focused on research and teaching in service management and he is involved in a wide range of consultancy assignments. He has written a book on customer support for manufacturing companies and a second book, *Inspired Customer Service*, was co-written with David Clutterbuck and Colin Armistead. He is also the director of the Cranfield

Service Operations Research Club. Graham's research interests include the management of customer relationships, organisational flexibility, the strategic management of call centres and the management of service performance. He has held the appointment of Director of Quality for the School of Management and has recently completed three years as Director of the Executive MBA Programme where he was fully involved in the School's personal development work. He is also part of the tutor team for the Group Dynamics Programme for MBAs.

Part 1

INTRODUCTION

1

Introduction to Service Operations Management

1.1 INTRODUCTION

We all come into contact with service operations every single day. We are customers or users of a wide range of commercial and public services, for example childcare services, hospitals, shops, educational establishments, holiday firms, police services, restaurants, television and the Internet. Indeed, many of us are responsible for delivering service not only as part of our jobs, in organisations such as those above, but also as part of daily life: delivering catering, taxi services, organising holidays or providing emotional support services to our friends and families.

Service operations management is an activity that is concerned with both *what* service we deliver and *how* it is delivered to our customers. It involves understanding the needs of our customers, managing the processes that deliver the services, ensuring our objectives are met, whilst also paying attention to the continual improvement of our services. As such, operations management is a central organisational function and one that is critical to organisational success.

The objectives of this introductory chapter are:

- to identify the nature of service operations management and the problems in defining 'service'
- to provide a definition of service and service operations management
- to introduce a classification of service operations in order to provide an understanding of different service processes
- to discuss the challenges facing operations managers
- to explain the structure of the book.

In this book we will attempt to provide a detailed coverage of service operations issues and we will provide many tools and frameworks that managers can use to understand, assess and improve the performance of their operations. Whilst the development of operations management as a discipline has its roots in production management (for a discussion of this see Johnston 1994 and 1999), this text seeks to concentrate on the service operations issues, though many of the concepts are equally relevant to manufacturing organisations. In this introductory chapter we want to introduce some definitions, frameworks and themes that will continue throughout the book and identify what we think are the significant problems and challenges facing many service operations managers. We will then link each of these challenges to chapters in the text to provide a 'road map' for its use and explain the book's structure.

1.2 OPERATIONS MANAGEMENT AND THE NATURE OF SERVICE

1.2.1 Operations management

Operations management (OM) is a particularly important discipline to study, concerned as it is with the management of processes, people and resources in order to provide the required goods and services to a specified level of quality, doing so in the most cost-effective way. OM is also critical because it is responsible for the successful implementation of corporate strategy, whether this is an implicit or explicit strategy.

There are three main tasks for the operations manager (see Figure 1.1):

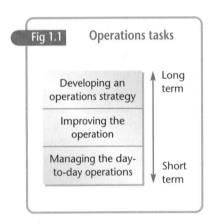

Fig 1.1   Operations tasks

- To develop an operations strategy for the future to ensure that the organisation has the appropriate mix of processes, control systems and people skills in order to compete and/or continue into the future.
- To find ways to continuously improve processes and motivate people in order to carry out operations more effectively, thus increasing quality of service and/or productivity.
- To manage day-to-day operations in such a way as to achieve the required performance targets, balancing service delivery, quality of service and resource productivity.

These three tasks must be achieved together. It is pointless running a cost-effective operation and trying to improve the quality of service provided if the operation does not meet the long-term needs of the organisation as a whole. Operations managers must pay attention to both strategy and the detail of process and resource management to create and sustain a successful organisation.

A significant component of the excitement of operations management is its immediacy. By this we mean the constant challenge of dealing with the needs of a stream of customers, making operational decisions to ensure the delivery of an appropriate quality of service at an appropriate cost. The danger of this immediacy, however, is that it can lead to a short-term focus and managers who, understandably, spend their time on managing the day-to-day operations for the following reasons:

- The pressure on the organisation to perform in the short term leaves little time for longer-term strategic planning.
- The contrast between the tangible, rational nature of many short-term operational decisions and the intangible, more intuitive processes required for strategic

thinking may mean that the individual manager's style may contain a bias towards the tactical implementation of strategy rather than its formulation.

● Poor management of internal interfaces, in particular between marketing and operations, may mean that either party takes up entrenched positions, impeding the communication required for effective strategy formulation.

As a result the strategic aspects of operations management are frequently neglected and so a disproportionate amount of time is spent on managing the day-to-day operations (see Figure 1.2).

Operations management must integrate thinking about the future as well as the effective operation of the present and provide a way of bringing together all the various management disciplines to help create a realistic strategy capable of effective implementation.

1.2.2 Service and service operations management

In this book we are concerned about operations management associated with the provision of service. When we talk to groups of managers, a frequent problem arises. It is clear that the word 'service' conjures up a wide variety of images. Some will consider the output of a service organisation as 'the service'. Examples might be the provision of a train service, an insurance policy, or a public service such as refuse disposal. Manufacturing organisations often use the term 'customer service' in a particular way to describe the logistics or distribution function, the activity of ensuring that customers receive their orders in a timely fashion. Indeed this is not an insignificant activity; for such companies the logistics function may constitute as much as 15 per cent of product cost.

A common (inaccurate) assumption is that service relates solely to the way that the organisation deals with its customers. In this sense, service means little more than customer care or dealing with customer complaints. There is no doubt that this activity too may be central in an organisation's policy or competitive strategy, but we must make it clear that our definition of service is not limited to this aspect alone. More importantly, service organisations must work to integrate value-adding activities in terms of outcome and experience, as we discuss in the following section.

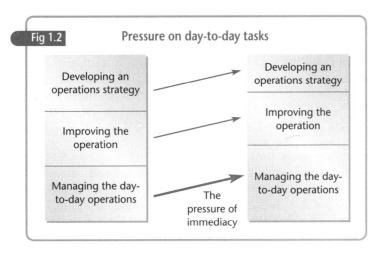

Fig 1.2   Pressure on day-to-day tasks

Indeed, it could be argued that most of the activities of an organisation, be it in the service or manufacturing sector, fall under the classification of service operations. Much of what is discussed in this book applies equally to internal services, such as human resource or marketing functions, as to organisations dealing with consumers, such as financial or leisure services.

The problem in trying to define 'service' is that it means so many different things in many different contexts. Haywood-Farmer and Nollet (1991) neatly summarised this problem:

> *Despite more than 25 years of study, scholars in the field of services management do not agree on what a service is. Indeed, instead of coming closer to a definition they seem to be less certain ... the problem is trying in a few words to describe 75 per cent of the economic activity of developed nations. Is it any wonder that there are exceptions for all definitions?*

1.3 SERVICE OPERATIONS: MANAGING EXPERIENCE AND OUTCOME

One of the most complex service organisations is a hospital, and managing a hospital is an extremely complex task. Hospitals employ vast numbers of people and provide numerous services for large numbers of customers. Like many service organisations they comprise many different operations that deliver those services to their customers. These include reception services, diagnostics, pharmacy, theatres (where operations *on* people are carried out!), restaurants, physiotherapy, security, and so forth. In addition, there are the internal services such as information systems support and finance. Box 1.1 about Singapore General Hospital contains a description from the Chief Executive Officer who explains what is meant by 'service' and how he tries to achieve it.

Box 1.1 Singapore General Hospital

The Singapore General Hospital (SGH) is the country's largest acute tertiary care hospital. It has a total of 1,612 beds and 22 clinical departments providing a comprehensive range of medical services. The hospital employs around 5,500 staff, from clinical and research directors to hospital attendants. SGH is structured as a private limited company for flexibility of operations, but is a not-for-profit organisation owned by the Government of Singapore.

The hospital's mission is to provide excellence in health care through cost-effective methods for the benefit of the patient, community and staff. Lawrence Lim is the hospital's Chief Executive Officer and he explains how they deliver their mission. 'The hospital has three "pillars" supporting our mission statement. Service, that is taking care of our patients, is our number one priority. The second pillar is teaching and nurturing the next generations of care-givers, doctors, nurses, physiotherapists, etc., and the third area is undertaking clinical research to expand our knowledge and skills in medical science.

'In terms of service we aim to offer our patients "best outcome, best experience". We want to provide the best outcome by providing the best clinical care. I know people do not wish to come to a hospital but if they have to, we want to provide them with the best experience possible. This idea was derived and drawn up by the doctors and administrators together and provides a common purpose, mind-set and language that permeate the whole hospital. There are four key principles underlying this:

- Assure best outcomes (i.e. clinical quality)
- Create seamless service (i.e. operational quality)
- Build relationships
- Delight with personalised care (i.e. service quality).

'We have a quality council comprising doctors and administrators that come together to chart the strategies and programmes for quality in the hospital. They discuss clinical quality, which has to do with getting doctors, nurses, physiotherapists, etc. to produce the best outcome for the patient. We also talk about operational quality, that is how we move a patient around and how we organise our services around the patient. These activities mainly concern operational processes which we try to "engineer" in order to create a seamless service for the patient. We are also concerned with service quality, which is about the individual; building a relationship with the patients and showing that we care. From the patients' perspective all these three types of quality, i.e. clinical, operational and service, are intertwined but we need to ensure that our staff are focused on all of them too.

'We have worked with all the different people in the hospital to try to get everybody to think how they can improve the service. We get them to think about communication skills, even grooming, dress and body language. We are a government hospital and people's concept of a government hospital in the past is that it is bureaucratic, officious, and slow to respond. I always tell my staff, let's surprise the patient!'

Questions

1 *How has Mr Lim focused his staff on providing 'best outcome, best experience'?*

2 *From whom do you think he encountered most resistance and why?*

It is helpful to consider 'service' from two overlapping perspectives (see Figure 1.3): the customer perspective (the dotted box), which includes what Mr Lim refers to as best experience and best outcome, and the operational perspective, i.e. how it is delivered.

1.3.1 The customer perspective

The service product

The primary reason customers are paying for, or using, an organisation's services is to receive a service product (sometimes referred to as the service package) – for example:

- car insurance
- consultancy advice
- a restaurant meal
- computer maintenance
- public healthcare.

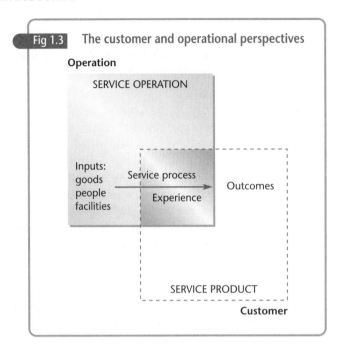

Fig 1.3 The customer and operational perspectives

Within each of these products there are two key ingredients: the outcomes of the service and the service experience. Although we describe these two aspects separately below, it should be noted that there may be considerable overlap between outcome and experience. It is also important to realise that a customer's evaluation of one component may influence their perception of the other. A service experience that exceeds customer expectations may give rise to a better evaluation of service outcome than might otherwise have been expected.

The service outcome

We use the term service outcome to describe the result for the customer of the service. Examples of this might be the ability of a recipient of a software training course to construct a spreadsheet, or for a patient in a hospital to enjoy full mobility after a hip operation.

The service experience

The service experience is the customer's direct experience of the service process and concerns the way the customer is dealt with by the service provider. It contains aspects of how customer-facing staff deal with customers and also the customer's experience of the organisation and its facilities.

It should be noted that the customer's experience of the organisation as a whole will probably start before this point as expectations are shaped by sales and marketing activities and by word-of-mouth advertising from existing customers.

Aspects of the 'service experience' include:

● the extent of personalisation of the process

● the responsiveness of the service organisation

● the flexibility of customer-facing staff

- customer intimacy
- the ease of access to service personnel or information systems
- the extent to which the customer feels valued by the organisation
- the courtesy and competence of customer-facing staff.

We define 'service' as the combination of outcomes and experiences delivered to and received by a customer. Customers therefore judge the quality of the service on the experience as well as the outcome. Students on a business administration programme or executives on a training course are buying both the experiences – the time in the lecture room, the process of learning, and the interaction with other people – as well as the outcomes, which will include increased effectiveness at work, better prospects in the job market and a qualification. The role of service operations managers is to manage both aspects together, though long-term success, and competitive advantage for companies in competition, may come from either or both, dependent on the nature of the service and the competition.

The fact that service operations managers are providing an intangible experience as well as the usually more tangible outcomes, creates a particular challenge for operations managers because it can be difficult to define and control the service. It is additionally difficult because the customer is frequently an integral part of the production process. In a restaurant, for example, customers are not just walking away with a meal inside them (the tangible outcome), they have also received a service in which they too have played a part. Their mood or attitude may well have an impact not only upon their own experience but upon that of other diners and the general atmosphere of the restaurant. This means that a critical part of the service product is outside the direct control of the service manager.

1.3.2 The operation's perspective

The service operation

The operation is the configuration of resources and processes that create and deliver service to the customer. We have used the traditional input–process–output model (see Figure 1.3) to show this. Operations managers manage the specification and co-ordination of the input of goods and materials from suppliers. They have to manage the people, staff and managers and also the customers themselves. Other resources include the facilities, equipment and buildings that provide not only the means of service delivery but also the 'set' or backdrop against which the service is delivered. This is sometimes referred to as the 'servicescape' (Bitner 1992) (see Chapter 9).

The service process can be thought of as having two component parts, the front office and the back office. The front office is the interface between the organisation and the customer or user. The front office contains the part of the process that 'processes' customers and is the part that the customers directly 'experience'. Back office operations contain processes carried out remotely from the customer/user interface.

Front office versus back office focus

Figure 1.4 compares two types of service operations. Some organisations are heavily front office focused (the shaded part of the diagram) in the sense that a significant amount of the service product is delivered whilst the customer is present. A restaurant again provides a good example in that much of the service product rests for customers in being in the restaurant, enjoying the atmosphere, and enjoying the company. In some cases the possible outcome of not being hungry might be relatively unimportant compared to the opportunity of being able to socialise with friends.

At the other extreme there are organisations with very little direct customer processing and that therefore provide little experience of the organisation and its processes for the customer. Mail order companies and indeed many manufacturing companies might be described in this way: there is limited interface between the company and its customers, and the service experience is limited to a simple transaction of supplying goods.

As an aside, it is interesting to note that many manufacturing companies are attempting to compete by differentiating themselves through increasing the service experience, whilst the opposite is true for some service companies who have recognised that in some cases the customer wishes the outcome, not the experience. An example of this would be some furniture and DIY warehouses, IKEA for example, that don't provide 'customer service' in the form of cheerful and helpful staff, but simply 'value for money' goods.

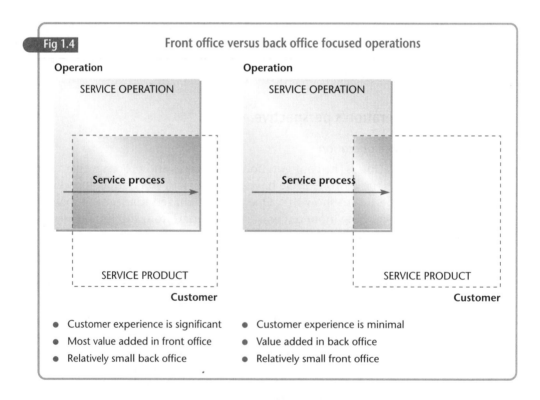

Fig 1.4 — Front office versus back office focused operations

- Customer experience is significant
- Most value added in front office
- Relatively small back office

- Customer experience is minimal
- Value added in back office
- Relatively small front office

1.4 UNDERSTANDING DIFFERENT SERVICE PROCESSES

The service process is the central element of a service operation and most service operations managers are primarily concerned with managing their process or processes. It is helpful therefore to recognise that there are many different sorts of processes with different implications for customers, managers and the organisation as a whole (this point is developed further in Chapter 6). There are many ways of classifying service processes and here are some of the common classifications:

- 'professional' services vs. 'mass' services
- services delivered to businesses (business-to-business) or services delivered to consumers (business-to-consumer) or services selected and enacted by the customer, such as electronic services, e-service (consumer-to-business)
- services that have the customer as the focus of delivery, as compared with those services that are directed to equipment or information
- services segmented by sector such as leisure, financial, hospitality, and government.

Throughout this book we will try to provide examples from a variety of service sectors and both business-to-business and business-to-consumer services. However, we will tend to concentrate on services where the customer is the focus of delivery. We will also include organisations from the professional to mass continuum on the

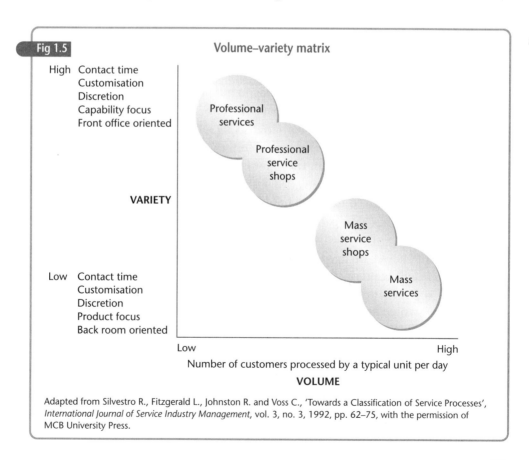

Fig 1.5   Volume–variety matrix

High   Contact time
Customisation
Discretion
Capability focus
Front office oriented

Professional services

Professional service shops

VARIETY

Mass service shops

Mass services

Low   Contact time
Customisation
Discretion
Product focus
Back room oriented

Low   High

Number of customers processed by a typical unit per day

VOLUME

Adapted from Silvestro R., Fitzgerald L., Johnston R. and Voss C., 'Towards a Classification of Service Processes', *International Journal of Service Industry Management*, vol. 3, no. 3, 1992, pp. 62–75, with the permission of MCB University Press.

volume–variety matrix. This approach provides us with four basic types of service processes (see Figure 1.5).

Early service operations management texts (for example Sasser *et al.*, 1978) identified that a spectrum of service operations exists ranging from professional services to mass services. It was recognised that this classification was not complete in describing all aspects of service operations, not least because many – if not the majority of – service organisations fall between the extremes. This middle ground was occupied by a range of service organisations designated as 'service shops', having something of the volume of the mass service, yet providing a degree of customisation that requires some of the capability of professional services.

Clark and James (1997) describe an adaptation of this classification which proposes that there are professional service shops born out of the desire for some professional service firms to grow their business in terms of volume. Likewise, there are mass service shops arising from commodity services attempting to differentiate themselves by increasing their range of service products.

Although this classification has merit, we feel that it is unhelpful for this text to try to 'force' all service operations into these four service types. So where it is appropriate we will describe the issues, challenges and some of the appropriate service operations tools for two extreme cases: high-volume/low-variety service operations and low-volume/high-variety service operations.

1.4.1 High-volume/low-variety service operations

Many consumer services fall into this category, and are frequently termed 'mass services'. Some of the key characteristics are:

- High volumes of customer transactions per individual provider or service unit. A call centre, for example, may handle several thousand phone calls each day, with individual agents possibly dealing with over one hundred transactions.
- Standard processes, with increasing reliance on information systems.
- Short customer transactions with the 'technical core' of the service operation carried out away from the organisation/customer interface.
- Clear service propositions, often replicated across many service delivery units, often linked to global brands.
- Emphasis on gaining process consistency with units often dealing with thousands of transactions per day.
- A key challenge is to increase flexibility or customer personalisation without forfeiting productivity.
- Innovation in service concept design takes place largely as a central staff activity, which may lead to problems relating to employee ownership of service processes at the unit level. A key challenge lies in the need to motivate large numbers of customer-facing staff in what may be a geographically dispersed network of service units.
- The capability of these services is linked to the development of a tightly controlled service product, and the design of service processes required to deliver it. Large numbers of people are recruited to tight specifications to play their part in these processes, and are often trained to high levels to carry out a specialised task in what is a small part of the total process.

Examples of these services would include many of the call-centre operations, dealing with routine enquiries, order taking and customer complaints. Much of the financial services sector is of this type, as are services within distribution, transport and leisure.

As we will discuss further in Chapter 6, the focus of these services is on developing and delivering a tightly specified service product. Customers are buying a clear service proposition, often having the capacity to compare a range of competing services as in fast food or motor insurance.

1.4.2 Low-volume/high-variety service operations

These services are frequently based on the skill or professional expertise of the individuals in the organisation. Examples of this type of service operations include such professional services provided to individuals by lawyers and accountants, or services provided to businesses by consultants, software developers and corporate financial advisers. Some key characteristics of this type of service are:

- The key 'assets' of the organisation are frequently the skills and knowledge of the individuals who work for it, and these may be highly specialised.

- The emphasis of the organisation is on providing 'solutions' for its customers or users, and as such, its service concept may be less tangible than that for a high-volume/low-variety service.

- The organisation values innovation both in providing new solutions for its customers, and also in generating new ways to deliver them. A significant challenge for these operations lies in 'managing the detail', it being common for them to deliver an excellent service outcome or solution, but to do so in a way that annoys the customer.

- The organisation may have a number of contact points with its customers in the period from service request to completion. An individual service employee may have a wide variety of service transactions to complete in the course of a typical week. Some customer or client contacts may last for several hours, whilst the same employee may spend numbers of days with very little customer contact.

- A major challenge facing these organisations is that of growth. A trade-off might be that of building a strong brand through consistent processes and standard solutions that may threaten the perceived autonomy of individuals and risk stifling creativity.

- The capability of the professional service organisation is closely linked to the competence and reputation of the individuals it employs. A key challenge is to develop the individual employee or partner, but then to ensure that these skills are retained for the firm and not lost if the individual should leave.

In contrast to high-volume/low-variety operations, these services typically do not have such a tight service specification to market to potential customers. These organisations are generally selling their capability to meet a wide range of customer needs through skills, expertise and knowledge. A characteristic of professional services is that the individual professional is frequently both 'designer' and 'deliverer' of the service. In fact, the client may be 'buying' the individual professional, rather than the firm itself. As such, these professional service providers have a great deal of individual autonomy as to what they do.

1.4.3 The service shops

As we indicated earlier, many organisations do not lie at the extremes of the continuum between high-volume/low-variety operations (typified by mass services) and low-volume/high-variety operations (typified by professional services). Professional service shops are those which have grown in size, perhaps becoming global in scale. The major consultancies provide good examples of professional service shops, and these experience many of the challenges for this type of organisation:

- increasing standardisation of product and delivery processes
- organisations sell and implement standard solutions
- limited individual autonomy, particularly for junior staff
- the development of a 'house style', a distinctive organisational culture and brand
- the development of 'semi-professionals' able to perform many routine tasks carried out by professionals in smaller firms, but at lower cost
- increased importance of revenue as opposed to margin
- a change in the management of client relationships, being managed by people responsible for this task, rather than being owned by individual working professionals.

The move towards higher volumes and greater standardisation brings with it a change in management style. The focus in professional services is on the autonomous professional, with management providing the environment for effective working relationships. The move to the professional service shop frequently brings a more directive style of working, with specialist managers or partners more concerned with business development than professional competence.

In contrast, the move to the mass service shop brings more freedom to customer-facing staff. The organisation is concerned to offer a greater choice of products to its customers. This may require staff to be able to offer advice to enable customers to make appropriate choices of product, requiring these employees to have greater levels of skill than previously. Many financial service organisations have developed much wider product ranges, but need to provide more customer assistance as a result. This may mean moving skill or expertise that was previously located in a specialist back office function into the front office. This is commonly achieved, not by moving technical experts, but by investing in information systems and specialist training which allow the customer-facing staff to act 'as if' experts, able to deal with the vast majority of customer requirements.

The challenges of moving from a mass service to a mass service shop include:

- increasing the product range without relinquishing tight cost controls. A key issue here is that it becomes more difficult to generate accurate figures as to how much each service product costs to deliver
- increasing the range of discretion of customer-facing employees may mean that service consistency deteriorates

- high-calibre customer-facing staff may be in short supply
- mass service shops must be more careful in eliciting information from the customer to ensure that the most appropriate service is selected.

In Chapter 6, these differences between service processes are explored in more depth. In addition, we provide a profiling tool to enable service managers to diagnose possible mismatches between the requirements of the service product and the capabilities of the service process.

1.5 THE CHALLENGES FACING SERVICE OPERATIONS MANAGERS

1.5.1 The challenge of service operations

In this section we outline some of the key issues to be addressed by service managers. We will not deal with them in detail here, but provide chapter references to enable the reader to identify where to look for concepts and frameworks to aid understanding.

Operations management is primarily concerned with the 'how' of the organisation: in other words 'how' the service product can be produced and delivered to specification and in such a way as to achieve the organisation's objectives. Operations managers are not usually directly responsible for deciding 'what' the organisation is delivering, that is, the nature of the service product to meet market requirements – although clearly if the 'how' is managed with little or no reference to the 'what', it would be surprising if this were particularly effective. This leads to a number of challenges variously faced by service operations managers.

Knowing who is the customer

Knowing who your customer is should be straightforward but for many organisations this is not the case. The nurseries referred to in Box 1.2 have as consumer, not only the child for whom they are providing an education and social experience, but also the parents for whom they are providing a 'parental substitute' service. There are other customers, education authorities and health and safety officials for example, for whom the nursery provides information and related services. Understanding who are the various customers (Chapter 3), understanding their needs (Chapter 4), developing relationships with them (Chapter 3) and managing the various customers (Chapter 8) are key challenges for operations managers.

Knowing what the organisation is selling/providing

There may be differing views about what an organisation is 'selling' and/or the customer is 'buying'. Some parents may see the nursery as simply a baby-sitting service, others may see it as a critical educational experience for their offspring. Articulating and communicating the service concept (Chapter 2) is critical for clarifying the organisation's product to all of its customers and in ensuring that it can be delivered (Chapters 6–9) and that it is delivered to specification (Chapter 10).

Box 1.2 Cybernurseries

In 1991 a group of Cambridge University students from the School of Computer Science set up the first website camera (webcam). They focused it on the faculty coffee machine so that members of staff could see a 'live' picture, updated every few minutes, of the machine on their desk computer. This allowed them to check that the coffee jug was not empty before they went to use the machine.

A higher-profile use of webcams was made in 1996 when Jennifer Ringley, a web-page designer from Washington, DC, trained a camera on her life and broadcast 24 hours a day from her flat. Because webcams are relatively cheap and easy to set up, with basic systems only requiring a PC with a camera, a video capture card and a phone line into the Internet, they are now found in a wide variety of situations. Now there are over 10,000 webcams worldwide relaying images every few seconds 24 hours a day. Anyone connected to the Internet can now see some breathtaking and bizarre sights, including the conditions at 3,880 metres on Mount Everest, the view of the top of the ski run at Lake Tahoe, sights in the African Bush, views from the Palazzo Senatorio in Rome, weddings at Las Vegas' Little White Chapel, even the contents of a Swedish family's fridge!

One recent innovation has been the arrival of webcams in nurseries so that anxious parents can use their computer at work, or home, to 'look in' on their children. Security is tight, with pictures being encrypted and passwords required for access. The pictures they receive are single frames, updated every minute, but the quality is enough for parents to see their child, relaxed and happy, and remind them what life is about!

Whilst parents and grandparents are revelling in this innovation, others are queuing up to condemn it. Some psychologists are concerned that it becomes an on-screen substitute for involvement in a child's upbringing that simply assuages the guilt of working mothers. Other people worry about it fuelling the current paranoia about child safety. However, at a time when childcare is needing an injection of trust and with more and more working parents, cybernurseries could soon be commonplace.

Questions

1 *What are the advantages and disadvantages of having webcams in nurseries?*

2 *How do you think the service has changed as a result of the webcam?*

This illustration is based on material in 'Big Mother is Watching You', *London Evening Standard*, Friday 5 November 1999, pp 10–11, and 'Around the world in 10,000 webcams', *Daily Mail*, Tuesday 15 February 2000, p. 53.

Managing the outcome and the experience

One of the challenges for the service operations manager is that, for many services, there is no clear boundary between 'what' and 'how' at the customer interface. A customer in a restaurant is buying both the meal and the way that s/he is served. The education and the educational experience, likewise the childcare and the child care experience, are inseparable. This is rather different from most manufacturing operations where the production of the product may be separated from how it is delivered to customers. A critical challenge for service operations is managing both outcomes and experiences simultaneously (Chapters 6–9).

The intangible nature of the experience provides particular problems for both specification and indeed control. Some call centres, for example, use scripts to ensure conformance and clarity but such scripts lose out on flexibility, development of rapport and maybe also opportunities for cross-selling (see Chapter 8). This requires a clarity about the experience the organisation is selling (Chapter 2) supported by appropriate performance measurement (Chapter 10).

Some service organisations try to manage the intangible parts of the service by attempting to make them more tangible. At the nursery the intangible experience for the child has now been captured as a television product, visible and available to the parent (Chapter 2).

Managing the customer

Many service managers face a challenge not shared by their manufacturing counterparts, that of the presence of the customer, often as an essential part of the service production process. This requires careful design of the processes that handle back office activities but especially those that handle the customer. The design must manage the customer through the process with an awareness of the moods and attitudes of individual customers. The latter may affect not only the service for that individual, and the attitude of the provider, but also other customers in the process (Chapters 6–9). A key task for the nursery attendant is managing the children in their care and recognising that tears or tantrums can easily affect the others in the group.

The presence of the customer also renders the operation visible to the customer, so the servicescape needs to be designed to create the right atmosphere for the service (Chapter 9). In the nursery, the facilities and activities are visible not only to the child but also to the parents when dropping off and picking up the child and during the day as they 'drop in' via the Web. As such the servicescape is an important part of the service.

Service is real-time

Many services happen in real-time, they cannot be delayed or put off. A passenger wanting to purchase a ticket for immediate travel may not be willing to return tomorrow if the agent is busy. Streams of aircraft coming into land cannot easily be put on hold whilst equipment is serviced or controllers take a break. A child screaming for attention or in danger from hurting themselves in the nursery likewise cannot be ignored. Furthermore, during a service encounter it is not possible to undo what is done or said – things in the heat of the moment or promises that cannot be kept. In service there is no 'rewind button'. Smacking a child in the nursery is inexcusable and will not go unnoticed with webcam 'spies' in the room. Managing capacity (Chapter 7), managing staff and employees (Chapter 8) and creating an appropriate culture (Chapter 14) are key challenges in managing real-time services.

Co-ordination

The management of service operations is extremely demanding, requiring an integration of marketing, resource management, people management and so forth (Chapter 15). The operations manager is responsible for co-ordinating the various parts of the organisation in the delivery of the service product; this includes not only understanding the needs of their customers (Chapter 4) but also overseeing the logistics of the supply chain to ensure that all materials and equipment are in the right place at the right time (Chapter 5). A nursery without staff and the right materials will not only provide a poor experience for the child but could be potentially dangerous. At the same time as delivering service the operations manager has to ensure that the operation is viable (Chapter 11) and supports the strategic intent of the organisation (Chapter 13).

Knowing the relationship between operations decisions and business success

Making the right decisions that will lead to business success, is a major challenge for many service operations managers. Business success may mean satisfying and retaining customers, attracting new customers, entering new markets, making profit, reducing costs or meeting budget targets. The problem is in knowing the effect of pulling operations levers on business performance (Chapters 10 and 11) and in knowing which improvements are appropriate (Chapter 12). Nursery managers using webcams believe that their introduction provides a highly valued service for their parents, giving them an edge in the market and maybe even allowing them to charge more for their services.

Knowing, implementing and influencing strategy

Operations, besides being the 'doing' part of the business, is also thereby responsible for the implementation of strategy (Chapter 13). It is the nursery operation and its staff that deliver childcare, not its marketers or financial managers, though in a small organisation like this these roles may be undertaken by the same people. It is therefore critical for service operations managers to understand their role not only in implementing strategy but also in contributing to it. Operations managers can have a significant effect in developing and sustaining a strategy (Chapter 13) by knowing what they can, or could, deliver (Chapters 6–9) and by driving change through the organisation (Chapter 12).

Improving the operation

A challenge faced by all service operations managers is how to continually improve and develop their processes and products (Chapter 12), ensure that the outcomes are real improvements (Chapters 10 and 11) and that there is a culture that is supportive of service and change (Chapter 14). An important management challenge in this area is in managing the increased complexity resulting from change (Chapter 15).

1.5.2 The economic challenge

At a macro level service organisations are a vital and significant part of most developing and developed economies. In most developed countries services account for in excess of 70 per cent of gross domestic product (GDP), and for over 50 per cent of GDP in developing economies. They also provide employment for a significant number of people. The challenges facing service operations managers throughout the whole range of service organisations – such as financial institutions, government bodies, retailers, wholesalers and personal service providers – need to be taken seriously and managed well to support economic success and development.

We can see that from the standpoint of economic value alone we should pay attention to the service sector, and to service operations in particular as this is where the service, and therefore wealth and value, are created. Services also have an important economic role in non-service organisations. Many manufacturing companies have significant revenue-earning service activities, such as customer support, and also many service activities internal to the organisation, such as payroll, catering, information and IT services etc. Indeed it has been estimated that around 75 per cent of non-service organisations' activities may be directly or indirectly associated with the provision of services (Quinn and Gagnon 1986).

Service companies provide employment for the vast majority of the working population in most developed and developing countries. Some service organisations are indeed people intensive in the sense of utilising large numbers of relatively low-skilled employees to deliver service. However, many service sectors, such as financial services, have begun to implement large information technology projects to reduce headcount and increase productivity. In many economies, the service sector is the only area where new jobs are being created, notably in tourism and leisure.

Finally, we cannot ignore the vast numbers of people employed in the public and voluntary sectors. Managing services such as education, health, fire, police, social services, famine relief organisations, churches and charities, requires as much expertise as their private-sector counterparts. For example, governments increasingly are 'subcontracting' to the voluntary sector many services that were previously provided directly by the state. In so doing, governments are applying commercial approaches to supplier assessment, and there is therefore a growing pressure on the voluntary sector to apply commercial improvement methodologies such as Total Quality Management and Business Process Re-engineering. Although there may not always be as clear a definition of 'customers' and 'customer satisfaction', there is no doubt that there is ever-increasing pressure to provide higher levels of 'value for money' with the same or reducing resources.

1.5.3 A quick guide to the book – matching challenges to chapters

A key challenge for us in writing this book about service operations is that not all services, and therefore challenges, are the same. So we will try to highlight some of the key differences that will influence the operations manager's decision-making. For example, managing a business-to-business service with relatively few corporate accounts will have some significant differences from those who deal with large numbers of consumers at multiple sites. The business-to-business service with few corporate accounts may have greater clarity about its customers, though be less specific about what it is selling. The key levers for financial success may be manpower

Table 1.1 Linking challenges to chapters

Challenges	Chapters
Knowing who is the customer	3, 4, 8
Knowing what the organisation is selling/providing	2, 6, 7, 8, 9, 10
Managing the outcome and the experience	2, 6, 7, 8, 9, 10
Managing the customer	6, 7, 8, 9
Service is real-time	7, 8, 14
Co-ordination	4, 5, 11, 13, 15
Knowing the relationship between operations decisions and success	10, 11, 12
Knowing, implementing and influencing strategy	6, 7, 8, 9, 12, 13
Improving the operation	10, 11, 12, 14, 15

utilisation for one organisation but equipment utilisation for others; managing customers in real-time may be an issue for one but not another.

What we can say at this point is that it is vital for operations managers to understand the particular demands of their own service or services to ensure that the appropriate service concept, customer relationships, service processes etc. are applied. Table 1.1 provides a summary of the challenges we have discussed in this section and indicates the chapters which deal with them in more depth.

1.6 THE STRUCTURE OF THE BOOK

Figure 1.6 shows the structure of the book. We have organised its contents around five key tasks that are covered in four parts of this book – two of the tasks (customer and supplier relationships) have been combined into one section because they are both part of the supply chain.

Part Two – Customer and Supplier Relationships

Operations management plays an important part in developing and maintaining relationships with both suppliers and customers. Most operations must pay attention to the management of a wide range of supplier and customer relationships. Whilst Chapter 4 focuses on customer satisfaction and service quality, the themes of quality management and quality improvement are interwoven throughout the whole text. The reason for this is that we believe that quality should be an intrinsic part of service delivery, clearly defined and managed, rather than a separate aspect. In the same way, resource productivity must also be managed as part of service delivery. Key aspects of managing customer and supplier relationships include:

- managing different types of customers
- developing an understanding of the range of customer relationships, and the issues in developing and maintaining such relationships

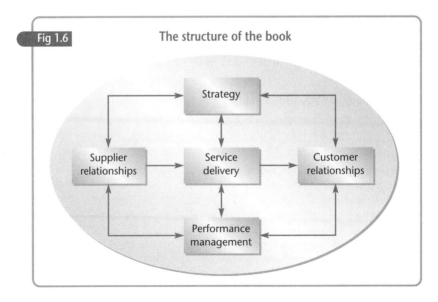

Fig 1.6   The structure of the book

- building customer satisfaction by understanding expectations and managing perceptions
- understanding supply chains and supply chain management
- understanding the use and management of intermediaries
- identifying the main types of supply partnerships and how they can be managed effectively.

Part Three – Service Delivery

The prime focus of this book is that of service delivery. The ultimate test of service operations management is at the point of delivery to customer. In a sense, it may be relatively easy to provide a service which will satisfy (or delight) customers, but very much harder to do this within budget or at a profit! The key aspects of this task include the following:

- managing service processes
- managing capacity
- managing people – both staff and customers
- managing physical or virtual operational structures and technology
- exploring the opportunities and issues provided by e-service.

Part Four – Performance Management

Performance management covers the measurement of service operations perfor-mance, the development of performance measurement systems and structures, and the task of driving changes in performance. Issues covered include:

- assessing the purposes and types of performance measures
- developing interlinkages between the various types of measures
- benchmarking, target-setting and links with improvement and rewards
- understanding the cause–effect relationships between operational decisions and business performance
- understanding world-class service and its key characteristics
- using service recovery and service guarantees to drive improvement.

Part Five – Managing Strategic Change

This part of the book deals with the process and content of developing service strat-egy. The success of a strategy is clearly influenced both positively and negatively by organisational culture. Equally, operations managers have the opportunity to influ-ence the culture of their organisations, in particular by changing the nature of processes, the organisation structure, and by altering the performance measurement and reward systems. This part also tries to show the complexity faced by service operations managers, that is the interrelationships between all of the tasks which create a complexity that is at the same time both fascinating and frustrating. Issues covered include:

- developing service as a competitive weapon
- identifying operational priorities

- developing and sustaining a service strategy
- managing evolutionary and revolutionary change
- understanding organisational culture and how to influence it
- the types of culture and the implications for service delivery systems
- managing change and the pitfalls to avoid
- the nature of complexity and the operational consequences of complexity.

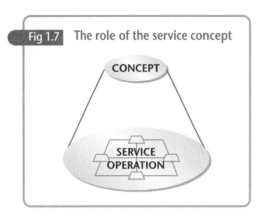

Fig 1.7 The role of the service concept

CONCEPT

SERVICE OPERATION

The service concept

The service concept provides cohesion and context for these core operational tasks. The next chapter of this introductory section, Chapter 2, will describe the overarching role of the service concept and will explain how the service concept provides organisational alignment and strategic direction for the various elements of the service operation (see Figure 1.7).

1.7 SUMMARY

Operations management and nature of service

- Operations management is a central and critical task.
- Service operations management is concerned with the management of processes, people and resources in order to provide services to a specified level of quality, doing so in the most cost-effective way.
- 'Service' can mean many different things depending on context.

Operations: managing experience and outcome

- Service is the combination of outcomes and experiences delivered to and received by a customer.
- The service operation is the configuration of resources and processes that create and deliver service to the customer.

Understanding different service processes

- There are many ways of classifying services.
- The volume–variety matrix is a useful way of understanding different service processes and their management implications.

The challenges facing operations managers

- The challenges faced by service operations managers include:
  - ➤ knowing who is the customer
  - ➤ knowing what the organisation is selling/providing

➤ managing the outcome and the experience
➤ managing the customer
➤ service is real-time
➤ co-ordination
➤ knowing the relationship between operations decision and financial success
➤ knowing, implementing and influencing strategy
➤ improving the operation.

● At a macro level services are a critical part of most economies, accounting for a significant proportion of GDP and employment.

1.8 DISCUSSION QUESTIONS

1. Describe the service experience and outcomes for a fast-food restaurant, a doctor's surgery and an Internet-based fashion clothing retailer. Compare and contrast the services of these three organisations.

2. What are the similarities and differences in terms of the challenges faced by a large house-and-contents insurance firm compared to a small commercial insurance broker providing insurance for stately homes?

3. Select a service organisation and identify the key back office and front office tasks. What activities have most impact on outcome and experience? Could any task move from one area to the other and what would be the implications?

1.9 QUESTIONS FOR MANAGERS

1. For operations managers in your organisation what is the balance between day-to-day, improvement and strategy tasks? Is this deliberate? Is it appropriate?

2. Describe your service in terms of experience and outcomes from both a customer and organisation perspective. Assess the mismatches between these perspectives.

3. With Internet access the customer may have greater access through a web site to people who previously might have worked in back office functions. On the other hand, customers no longer see the people they are dealing with. What are the implications of this for your organisation?

4. Select a process and plot it on the volume–variety matrix. What are the pressures to change and in which direction? What are the issues and challenges facing this process?

1.10 SELECTED FURTHER READING

Johnston R., 'Service Operations Management: Return to Roots', *International Journal of Operations and Production Management*, vol. 19, no. 2, 1999, pp. 104–24.

1.11   REFERENCES

Bitner M.J., 'Servicescapes: The impact of physical surroundings on customers and employees', *Journal of Marketing*, vol. 56, April 1992, pp. 57–71.

Clark G. and James K., 'The "Coping" Zone: Stress and quality', in Ribera J. and Prats J. (eds), *Managing Service Operations: Lessons from the service and manufacturing sectors*, IESE, Barcelona, 1997, pp. 385–90.

Haywood-Farmer J. and Nollet J., *Services Plus: Effective service management*, Morin, Boucherville, Quebec, 1991.

Johnston R., 'Operations: From factory to service management', *International Journal of Service Industry Management*, vol. 5, no. 1, 1994, pp. 49–63.

Johnston R., 'Service Operations Management: Return to roots', *International Journal of Operations and Production Management*, vol. 19, no. 2, 1999, pp. 104–24.

Quinn J.B. and Gagnon C.E., 'Will services follow manufacturing into decline', *Harvard Business Review*, vol. 64, no. 6, November–December 1986, pp. 95–103.

Sasser W.E., Olsen R.P. and Wyckoff D.D., *Management of Service Operations*, Allyn and Bacon, Boston, 1978.

Silvestro R., Fitzgerald L., Johnston R. and Voss C., 'Towards a Classification of Service Processes', *International Journal of Service Industry Management*, vol. 3, no. 3, 1992, pp. 62–75.

CASE EXERCISE

Sky Airways

This case was co-written by Bridgette Sullivan-Taylor, Warwick Business School

Sky Airways is a major European airline with routes predominantly in Europe but offering daily flights to New York, Johannesburg, Mumbai and St Petersburg. At the last meeting of the board of directors the airline's owner and chief executive, Bernie Williamson, expressed concern at the growing number of complaints his airline was receiving. His analysis of the increasing trend revealed a strong link between number of complaints and minutes' delay. This did not surprise him. What did surprise him was the large number of underlying complaints which were, in the main (around 72 per cent), about the on-board catering.

Given his desire to increase RPK (revenue passenger-kilometre), which had declined by 5 per cent over the past three years, he was keen to hear ideas from his team as to how they could deal with the problem. This was an opportunity seized upon by Angela Carter-Smith, Sky's recently appointed marketing director. She suggested that the airline should consider moving away from pre-packed and reheated meals in tourist class to the business-class style of service, whereby food is pre-cooked but heated, assembled and served in front of the customers. She explained: 'Many international airlines are attempting to enhance their competitive edge by differentiating their in-flight service offering across their global network.' The food costs, she suggested, would be little different but simply require more time by cabin attendants, which they have on the longer flights. If this proved to be successful on the long hauls, it could then be considered on the short hauls. When Bernie reminded her that they needed to provide an upgraded service for the premium-fare passengers, she added that the answer here was to provide 'culturally sensitive' meals: flying to and from Mumbai, the food should be Indian, while to

Johannesburg it should have a distinct African flavour. All eyes then turned to Peter Greenwood, the operations director, who had his head in his hands and was groaning. He promised to 'look into it' and report back at the next meeting.

The next day Peter made time to talk about the rising trend in complaints to Christina Towers, the catering subcontract manager, Justin Maude, a senior cabin attendant, and David Goh, senior gate manager.

Christina Towers: 'The problem we have, like all other catering companies, is consistency. Although we can specify menus, portions and costs there are inevitably wide variations in quantity and quality loaded at various airports around the world. We have the biggest problems at the furthest destinations. You also put us under pressure to maintain costs, so we only try to load the precise number of meals required in order to reduce wastage and space required. It is not easy making pre-flight predictions about both numbers and choices, and you cannot expect it to be right 100 per cent of the time without substantially increasing the number of meals loaded over and above passenger predictions. It is not cost effective and it is weight prohibitive to load two of every meal option, even for a business-class passenger who would expect, more than anyone else, to receive their first choice. I think we would get less complaints if we reduced choice of menus.'

Justin Maude: 'You would not believe the difficulties we face in providing something as simple as meals to passengers. We frequently have to explain to passengers, in all of the cabins, why they can't have their first choice of meal. This creates a great deal of stress for crew. There is just no room for more meals on board, the galleys are really tight for space. The biggest problem we have is over passengers who order special meals for religious, dietary or health reasons. I reckon one in five is not loaded onto the aircraft. Sometimes we have passengers on board who ask whether the food contains nuts and we have no idea. We can only offer them water and bread rolls to be safe. I think we should ensure the caterers let us know the contents of every meal and always provide extra vegetarian and kosher meals because passengers don't always remember to pre-book them. Another problem is caused by the last-minute passengers whom you want us to take to fill seats, so we often have to ask for more meals shortly before take-off. I know this causes problems but, unlike a restaurant, during flight there is nowhere to find additional supplies. I think it would help if we could have meals which needed less preparation time and take less space so we can load more meals in anticipation of an increase in passengers and also load additional special meals, just in case.'

David Goh: 'The main problem I have is ten minutes before take-off when we find that the incorrect quantity, quality and meal type are loaded and the crew request extra meals. We often end up delaying a plane and missing a slot whilst the caterers rush over half a dozen extra meals. We should let the plane go. I am sure not everyone actually wants a meal. They only eat because they are bored. I think we should stop providing meals altogether, certainly on the short hauls. Tourist-class passengers often eat at the airport anyway and we already provide food for business class in the executive lounges.'

Peter had not dared raise the idea of changing the methods of service in tourist class and increasing the range and type of meals to business-class passengers. His thoughts turned to how he could explain to the board the difference between what might be desirable and what is deliverable and appropriate.

Questions

1 *What problems does Peter Greenwood face?*

2 *If you were Peter Greenwood what would you say to the board?*

2

The Service Concept

2.1 INTRODUCTION

In Chapter 1 Mr Lim from Singapore General Hospital said, 'people's concept of a government hospital in the past is that it is bureaucratic, officious, and slow to respond'. This is what he thinks some of his customers believe the service will be like; a view he hopes to dispel.

The service concept is a critical element in knowing and defining what the organisation is selling and the customer buying or using. The service concept (and its development) is a core task in managing service operations. It can be used as a central tool in the design, delivery and improvement of services, yet its potential is underutilised.

The objectives of this chapter are:

- to define the service concept
- to demonstrate the power of the service concept as a strategic tool
- to use the notion of 'focus' to define four types of service concept
- to examine how unfocused organisations can gain the benefits of focus.

Surprisingly little has been written about the service concept, yet it is critical and central to service organisations. This chapter will explain the service concept and show how this powerful yet simple idea can help integrate the various functions of a service organisation. We will also explain, using an example, how by concentrating on the service concept an organisation can develop strategic advantage. Service concepts focused on either a market segment and/or providing a limited range of services offer advantages for both the consumer and the operation, yet many services are unfocused, doing 'everything for everyone'. We will explain how such organisations can gain the benefits of focus.

2.2 THE SERVICE CONCEPT

From an organisational perspective the service concept is the way in which the 'organisation would like to have its services perceived by its customers, employees, shareholders and lenders' (Heskett 1986); in other words, the service concept is the business proposition. From a customer perspective it is the way in which the customer perceives the organisation's services (see Figure 2.1). In theory, and in the minds of some managers, these two views are the same; in reality this is often not the case. Customers don't always know what an organisation is trying to provide (Collier 1994) or they see it in their own, sometimes irrational, idiosyncratic way. Likewise organisations don't always understand how their customers view their services. The example in Box 2.1 about the trading giant Daewoo, provides an example of a company with a revolutionary approach to car retailing

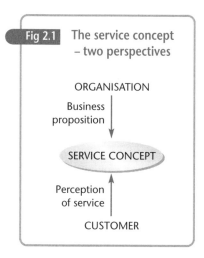

Fig 2.1 The service concept – two perspectives

ORGANISATION

Business proposition

SERVICE CONCEPT

Perception of service

CUSTOMER

Box 2.1 Daewoo – a revolutionary concept in car retailing

Daewoo Corporation is a major multinational trading company based in Korea. It exports over 3,500 different products including steel, car components, industrial plants, electronics, textiles and chemicals to over 165 countries around the world through its network of over 200 branch offices and subsidiaries. It also provides services such as international financing and project management. The Daewoo Corporation was established in 1967 by its current chairman, Mr Kim Woo Choong, with just five employees and a capital of US$10,000. Thirty years later, in 1997, it had a turnover of over $30 billion and assets valued in excess of $22 billion.

Daewoo has broken the mould of car retailing in the UK by becoming the first manufacturer to sell its cars directly to the public through its own showrooms. It has further challenged the traditional car retailers, sometimes characterised by the car-buying public as pushy, manipulative and interested only in earning commission, by having staff who are paid fixed salaries, fixed-price cars with no hidden extras, and a comprehensive aftersales package. With no high-pressure sales staff – a recent advert claimed 'Our car salesmen only speak when they're spoken to' – customers are encouraged to browse at leisure. The showrooms have family-friendly facilities, including children's play areas, video walls, refreshments and interactive multi-media display screens giving all the information a prospective purchaser requires. In recognition of its revolutionary, hassle-free approach to car retailing, Daewoo has been granted Millennium Project status by the UK's Design Council.

Questions

1 *How does Daewoo's concept differ from that of a traditional car retailer?*

2 *What do you think are the key operational challenges in delivering this concept?*

This illustration is based on material from http://dwc.daewoo.com and http://www.daewoo-cars.co.uk.

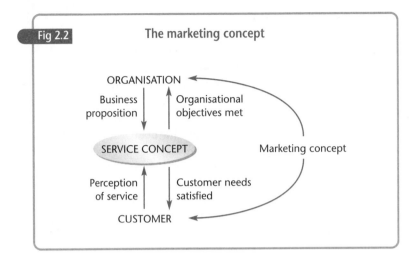

Fig 2.2 The marketing concept

ORGANISATION

Business proposition

Organisational objectives met

SERVICE CONCEPT

Marketing concept

Perception of service

Customer needs satisfied

CUSTOMER

which uses major advertising campaigns to explain their concept to a sceptical but receptive public.

What is sometimes referred to as the 'marketing concept'(see, for example, Dibb *et al.* 1997) attempts to reconcile these views. The marketing concept is a management philosophy that encourages organisations to understand and then satisfy customers' needs and fulfil the objectives of the organisation (see Figure 2.2).

In Chapters 3 and 4 we look in more detail at the needs of customers and in Chapter 8 we take a more organisational perspective. In this chapter we want to get right inside the service concept and understand it in detail, and then explore its power in uniting the organisation.

2.2.1 The 'DNA' of the service concept

The service concept is often defined (in operations texts) in terms of the service product, all the different constituent parts that form the service, the outcome and the experience, including the servicescape. This has also been referred to as the 'customer benefit package' (Collier 1994), the things that provide benefit and indeed value for the customer. This approach, defining the nature of the service in terms of its constituent parts, has also appeared in the marketing literature. Lovelock and Wright (1999), for example, use the '8Ps' of marketing which encompass the elements of the service product – Product, Process, Place, Physical evidence, People, Productivity and quality – plus additional marketing elements: Price and Promotion (the '8Ps' are based on the '7Ps' by Booms and Bitner 1981, which were developed in turn from the '4Ps' by McCarthy 1960).

Deconstructing a service in this way is helpful in that it allows us to identify the various elements of a concept, check them against customers' needs (see Chapter 4), design and deliver those elements (Chapters 6, 7, 8 and 9) and measure our performance against them (Chapter 10). However, this 'bits and pieces' approach belies the complexity of many services and also ignores the fact that customers' perception of service is integrative. For example, 'A day out at Disney's Magic Kingdom is more likely to be defined by its designers and its visitors as a magical experience rather than six rides and a hamburger in a clean park' (Clark *et al.* 2000).

2.2.2 The service concept – service in the mind

Whilst the elements of the rides, hamburgers and facilities are all expected by customers and all have to be delivered by the operation, it is important to recognise that when customers are buying a service they are not simply purchasing the bits and pieces. Customers are buying something greater and also less tangible: a magical experience from Disney, an educational experience at a university, an evening out at a restaurant.

The *Concise Oxford Dictionary* (1996) defines a concept as a 'mental picture of a group or class of objects formed by combining all their aspects'. A service concept is thus more than the DNA of a service, the elements of the service product, it is the mental picture that is held by customers, employees and shareholders about the service provided by the organisation. It is 'service in the mind' (Clark *et al.* 2000).

LASTING MEMORY

The terminology 'service in the mind' has been adapted from thinking about the psychoanalysis of organisations. The phrase 'organisation in the mind' has been used to express the idea that employees may have very different mental pictures and assumptions about the real purpose of their organisation (Armstrong 1991), which may be rather different from the version designed for public consumption! When we apply this thinking to service organisations, there is the added dimension of the customer, who may have assumptions or 'service in the mind' which are radically different from either what is intended or what is experienced.

In section 2.3 we will explore the use of the service concept in creating 'alignment of perception' between the organisation and its customers. *EXPECTING + GETTING THE SERVICE*

2.2.3 Concept v. mission v. vision v. idea

Before explaining in more detail what the service concept is, it is appropriate to say what it is not. The service concept is not necessarily the same as an organisation's vision or mission. An organisation's vision is usually concerned with where it expects to be at some time in the future. The service concept is concerned with the present, what the organisation does now and what its customers think it does today. Indeed, the service concept is more likely to be tied to the past based on past marketing or previous experiences or what people have communicated about past experiences.

It is not usually the same as a mission statement. Organisations' mission statements cover many notions from 'vision statements' to 'company philosophy' (Campbell and Yeung 1990). Like vision statements, mission statements may be concerned with the future rather than today's reality. On the other hand, if they define the organisation's philosophy it is ·possible that they tend to be more concerned with organisational values rather than the detail of the service that is delivered.

Finally, the service concept is more than an 'idea'. An idea is an initial notion of a service. A service concept is a more complete picture, which includes some details about what the service will be like, the outcomes and the experience.

2.2.4 The service concept – a means of communication

An organisation's service concept may be an explicit statement made by the organisation or it may be inferred from marketing information, either direct marketing by the organisation or indirect marketing through experience and word-of-mouth. We find it helpful to think of the service concept as a succinct statement that encapsulates the nature of the service business. Here are a couple of service concepts extracted from the marketing literature of two well-known organisations:

Club Med

A fully paid vacation package where you make your arrangements and pay the bill in advance in return for a well-managed programme in which you don't need to worry much about money, transportation, food, activities or clothes.

American Express

A wide range of services, including card, financial and travel, to support the international traveller.

We believe there is an opportunity for many service organisations to take control of their service concept and make it explicit. This is the first step in gaining alignment (see next section). If you ask a group of individuals, customers and staff, to define the service concept of a particular organisation you will invariably find a range of views. Organisations need to eradicate such inconsistency. They must take responsibility for making the nature of their service explicit by ensuring a clear and appropriate marketing message to both employees and customers. Only in this way will they help ensure appropriate service delivery.

To help with this challenge there are four key elements that should be covered in a statement of service concept (see Figure 2.3). They are:

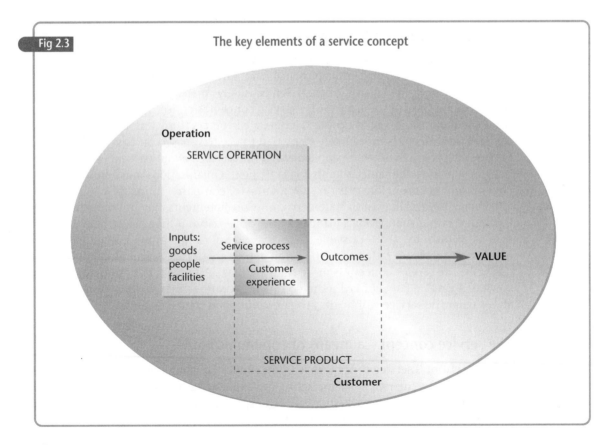

Fig 2.3 The key elements of a service concept

- the service experience – the customer's direct experience of the service process concerns the way the service provider deals with the customer
- the service outcome – the result for the customer of the service
- the service operation – the way in which the service will be delivered
- the value of the service – the benefit that customers perceive to be inherent in the service weighed against the cost of that service.

Whilst three of these elements were discussed in Chapter 1, the term value deserves some additional treatment here.

2.2.5 Service value

An important element of the marketing mix is price. Price is the value placed on the service. This could be its monetary value, the financial price, or its comparative value if the service is bartered. The 'price' of a service may be referred to in many different ways: the price of money is called 'interest', the price of poor motoring may be, in financial terms, a 'fine', the price for use of equipment is 'rent'.

The cost of a service to a customer is a combination of the financial price together with the cost, or inconvenience, of making the purchase, sometimes called the sacrifice (Zeithaml and Bitner 1996). For example, the cost of buying the weekly groceries involves not only the monetary value of the goods but also the cost of going to the shops to make their purchase – this is not only the bus or train fare but also the sacrifice of effort and time involved which could have been put to other uses. The cost of poor driving is not only the fine, but also loss of 'no-claims bonus', higher insurance premiums and possibly injury or even death, with the mental 'cost' that follows.

THE 'COST' OF CARRYING OUT AN ACTION CHOICE

To understand value these costs to the consumer have to be weighed against the benefits consumers perceive in the service. This may not only be the outcome and the experience but also psychological factors such as a feeling of well-being or being recognised in a restaurant. Value does therefore not necessarily mean 'low price'. Value is the customer's assessment of the benefits of the service weighed against all the costs involved.

A key role of marketers is to try to assess these issues to understand what customers value in order to help the organisation make pricing decisions. Operations management, on the other hand, is the art of creating and delivering value. The task for operations is to find the balance between maximising the value for customers and minimising the cost to the organisation; that is, striking a profitable or in-budget balance between:

- maximising the benefits to the consumer
- minimising the financial and sacrificial costs to the customer
- minimising the cost to the organisation.

The service concept is therefore a key tool which can communicate the set of benefits (outcome, experience, operation, together with the psychological benefits) to the customer in order to demonstrate the potential value of the service.

Operations delivers and creates value by playing a part in the supply chain (Chapter 5); adding value to the supply chain to create its services and value to its customers.

Some organisations go further – indeed the more successful organisations 'do not just *add* value, they *reinvent* it' (Normann and Ramirez 1993). Many services have been reinvented over the last few years. Internet banking has challenged and radically changed the value delivered by banks and received by their customers. From a customer's point of view new approaches to banking have provided 'a new kind of value. In particular, it eliminated traditional constraints of time and space' (Normann and Ramirez 1993). Now customers can manage their accounts and withdraw cash at any time of day or night, almost anywhere. Internet banking has not only reinvented value for customers but also changed the nature of value creation by the operation. Managers are now concerned with the design and maintenance of customer-interaction technology (web sites, plastic cards and computer networks to support the machines), and in dealing with the inevitable disadvantages of automation, such as trying to maintain a relationship with customers they rarely see.

2.2.6 Making the intangible tangible

Because many services have a high degree of intangibility contained in their service concept, a key task for service designers is to find ways of giving physical cues to the customer, that reinforce the value of the concept. For example, a five-star hotel contains within its concept much more than high-quality service and food. It wishes to create an environment for its guests where they feel pampered and their every wish can be responded to quickly. Some tangible cues to support this concept include thick carpets and ornate decorations, telephone hotlines to ask for help or report problems, bold staff uniforms that make members of staff easily recognisable and therefore approachable.

The key issue here is that a high degree of intangibility is frequently linked to premium pricing as in the luxury hotel example above. A management consultant charges high fees to her/his clients and, particularly if the client is a new one, will provide evidence to give reassurance that the expenditure is justified. This evidence might include professionally generated scoping documents and reports, the provision of client reference lists, expensive clothes and jewellery (obligatory cufflinks for a man) and an expensive car. Of course, as the relationship strengthens, these cues are less important as the client assesses the effectiveness of the consultant in the light of experience.

Whilst the competitive advantage for many services, indeed the core of their concept, derives from intangibles and the service experience, significant support can also be gained by using appropriate cues from tangible elements of the service.

2.3 THE SERVICE CONCEPT AS A STRATEGIC TOOL

Besides helping us define and understand the nature of the service we experience or deliver and the value it provides, the service concept can – and we believe should – be used as a strategic tool (see also Van Looey *et al.* 1998). It can be used to:

- create organisational alignment
- assess the implications of design changes
- drive strategic advantage.

2.3.1 Using the service concept for alignment

The problem is that different parts of an organisation may have differing perspectives and priorities about the nature of the service. For example, operations may be concerned about managing the process, staffing problems and operational costs. Customers may be concerned about the experience, price and value. Marketing may be concerned about brand development, new opportunities and revenue generation. Accounting may be concerned with cash flow and budget projections. Human resource managers may be concerned about staff skills and competencies, attitudes and recruitment. These valid, but none the less differing, perspectives and priorities often result in functional myopia leading to actions which are functionally appropriate but internally inconsistent. SHORT SIGHTEDNESS

By articulating the nature of the business and capturing the value proposition we would argue that the service concept can act as an alignment tool that links together different organisational functions with a common purpose and 'standard' against which their actions can be checked. 'In this respect the service concept acts as a lens and filter through which internal functions may see each others' roles and contributions to the service delivered to the customer' (Clark *et al.* 2000). The articulation and agreement of a service concept is a means not only of identifying the nature of the business but also of providing it with a sense of purpose and common direction. It also provides a means of assessing the contributions and interrelationships amongst the various functional groups.

We would therefore suggest that in order to share, communicate and evaluate a concept it needs to be written down, discussed and indeed agreed. This allows a check to be made internally to reach agreement about what is being provided and why. It also provides explicit signals to customers, existing and potential, about what the service will be like and the benefits they should expect. 'Even when written down, the service concept does not have an objective reality in the same way that a manufactured product has, however, it is a means by which organisations can gain internal and external alignment – by ensuring that all constituencies have the same or at least similar "service in the mind" (Clark *et al.* 2000).

2.3.2 Using the concept to assess design changes

The service concept can be used as a driver for long-term service development. By defining the concept, service designers can compare it to alternatives, proposed or already provided by other service suppliers, to help operations managers identify the implications of change. Whether the changes are deliberate changes to the concept or an evolutionary approach with modifications to process or procedures, changes to service concepts have implications for all parts of the organisation. 'There is substantial evidence to suggest that significant changes to service concepts expose the weaknesses in the organisation, its ability to co-ordinate all the various constituencies, and its capacity to communicate effectively both internally and externally' (Clark *et al.* 2000).

Such a 'concept audit' can be achieved by using a simple profiling tool. Box 2.2 describes a change of concept in the Natural History Museum in London which is then profiled in Figure 2.4.

Box 2.2 The Earth Galleries at the Natural History Museum, London

Michael Shulver, Warwick Business School

In 1985 the Geological Museum merged with its neighbour, the Natural History Museum, in Cromwell Road, London. The merger was cemented in 1988 by the construction of new gallery space linking the two sites.

From the mid-1930s to the early 1990s the Geological Museum consisted largely of taxonomic displays of rocks, gems and minerals and was a place for quiet study of 'rocks in boxes' by specialist geologists. This contrasted sharply with the noisy, lively and enthusiastic atmosphere of its neighbour. In the 1970s the Natural History Museum had begun a programme of exhibition renewal, using advanced and innovative methods of display to interest and entertain visitors, to support its mission 'to maintain and develop its collections and use them to promote the discovery, understanding, responsible use and enjoyment of the natural world'. The resultant 'Life Galleries' are very popular and have won awards for excellence in design.

In 1985 the Geological Museum adopted the Natural History Museum's mission and a new name, the Earth Galleries, together with a duty to communicate the natural world to the general public in a way that they could understand.

Operationalising that mission was not going to be easy. A survey of museum-goers found that they were less than enthusiastic about geology as a subject. It was perceived as dry, dull and had little to do with everyday life – in short, it was just about rocks. The perception was that the only reason you would visit something called the Geological Museum was because you had to pass an exam in geology.

The museum took up this challenge, as Dr Giles Clarke, Head of Department of Exhibitions and Education, explains. 'Surely volcanoes are interesting, fascinating things, and earthquakes are really significant, fascinating and important, gems are beautiful, especially in jewelry, and fossils, they are interesting too. So, there is a whole range of topics there that don't immediately come to mind when people say geology, but nevertheless are perceived as being fascinating. What we can then do is take the breadth of the subject that we want to display and talk about in the galleries, and to shuffle it around so that the high-profile ones come early, and so they will be an attraction to visitors to come in to the subject, and we can use those as a leader to collect people and move them around the exhibitions.'

Value, hitherto defined as access to a superlative reference collection of gems and minerals, was now to be reflected more in the degree to which the museum educated, enthused and entertained the public in the earth sciences. The target consumer was now a 15-year-old intellect who would already have had significant exposure to television and film of volcanoes, earthquakes, mining and so on. If the museum was to 'promote the discovery, understanding, responsible use and enjoyment of the natural world' to this consumer group, then it could not rely on the collection alone.

Such consumers would need to be helped by staging devices that moved them from the world they knew into the unfamiliar world of geology and inspire engagement with the subject. The exhibits would also have to educate the consumer gradually, and gently guide them through the museum's narrative. The museum would also have to cater for groups, in particular children, who would be more inclined to sample 'chunks' of galleries rather than the whole, so the galleries had to be structured to accommodate short attention spans. Mini-exhibits or galleries, each with a complete story, were created but the logic of the story was integrated with the overall museum theme. Some displays became interactive, encouraging visitors to experiment with geological processes through hands-on engagement with both hard and soft exhibits, such as minerals, molten surfaces and water, for example.

To support the social and family groups in which the public visited the museum, facilities such as restaurants, shops and restrooms had to be developed to be at least as good as those at a theme park.

When the museum completed its work in 1998, geologists still had access to a world-class reference collection, although in very different surroundings. However, the material was now used to enthuse and educate a much wider audience about the secrets of the earth.

Questions

1 How would you describe the concept of the Geological Museum and of the new Earth Galleries?

2 What do you think were the key problems faced by the designers in creating the new concept?

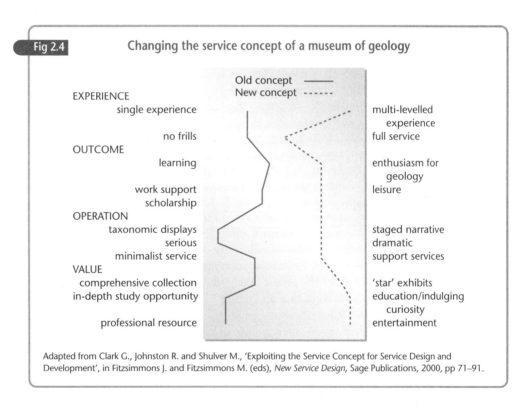

Fig 2.4 Changing the service concept of a museum of geology

Adapted from Clark G., Johnston R. and Shulver M., 'Exploiting the Service Concept for Service Design and Development', in Fitzsimmons J. and Fitzsimmons M. (eds), *New Service Design*, Sage Publications, 2000, pp 71–91.

A key point here is that of alignment. It is rare that a change to experience, outcome, operation or value can be made in isolation. Changes in one element will have consequences in others. Sometimes these represent opportunity, sometimes the potential for conflict. The use of the service concept and a profiling tool allows the people involved in the design or re-design of a service to understand what is required and to assess and therefore manage the implications of change.

Capability mapping

One enhancement of the profiling tool is the identification not only of the old concept and the new requirement as in Figure 2.4, but also the capability map of the existing service, i.e. its current potential. This capability envelope can be used by organisations which perhaps do not have a specific new or revised service in mind but can use it to explore what opportunities there might be for using operational potential.

Box 2.3 explains how one organisation used the capability envelope to identify the areas where the company needed to develop new capabilities.

Box 2.3 TECLAN Translation Agency

Michael Shulver, Warwick Business School

TECLAN provided a one-stop shop for language translation. The company used 35 in-house translators for most European languages, Japanese and Chinese. Translation to and from other languages was subcontracted to a network of some 3,000 translators. Though the company would handle just about any translation work, over time they had developed a distinctive competence in translating technical documentation, particularly computer software. The majority of software translation was the 'localisation' of software written in English, this localisation being the conversion of hypertextual help-files. However, TECLAN often encountered help-files that lacked sufficient flexibility, and in localising they had to resort to developing completely new help-file structures. Thus developed a new competence in help-file authoring and rudimentary programming.

By themselves these new competencies were not particularly distinctive, but coupled with the company's translation capability, they provided the potential for a highly competitive resource-set. TECLAN's service concept profile is mapped in Figure 2.5. The profile shows where the company started from and the shaded portion represents the new operations potential that TECLAN developed. The dotted line indicates an idealised service concept for a new service that exploits the newly developed potential. This also highlights the gaps between current capability and that required for the new service. The main areas requiring attention and development were in quality performance and the company's ability to manage relationships with its new class of customers. Although translators had developed the ability to manage relationships with clients' own technicians, TECLAN's account managers lacked the technical knowledge to market and sell the new capabilities.

Questions

1 *Summarise TECLAN's current service concept.*

2 *How does this compare to where they are trying to go and what do you think will be the operational problems in making this change?*

This illustration is taken from Clark G., Johnston R. and Shulver M., 'Exploiting the Service Concept for Service Design and Development', in Fitzsimmons J. and Fitzsimmons M. (eds), *New Service Design*, Sage Publications, 2000, pp 71–91.

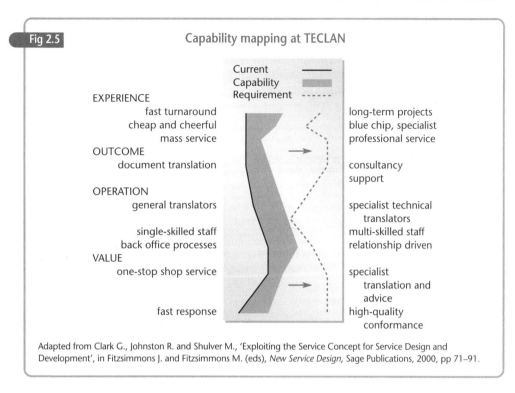

Fig 2.5 Capability mapping at TECLAN

Adapted from Clark G., Johnston R. and Shulver M., 'Exploiting the Service Concept for Service Design and Development', in Fitzsimmons J. and Fitzsimmons M. (eds), *New Service Design*, Sage Publications, 2000, pp 71–91.

2.3.3 Using the service concept to drive strategic advantage

Thinking about the service concept not only helps managers understand their business but also challenges them to view it in ways that can make it stand apart from other organisations. Lord Marshall, Chairman of British Airways, made the point:

There are different ways to think about how to compete in a ... service business such as ours. One is to think that the business is merely performing a function – in our case, transporting people from A to B, on time and at the lowest possible price. That's the commodity mind-set, thinking of an airline as the bus of the skies. Another way to compete is to go beyond the function and compete on the basis of providing an experience. In our case, we want to make the process of flying from A to B as effortless and pleasant as possible. Anyone can fly airplanes but few organisations can excel in serving people. Because it's a competence that's hard to build, it's also hard for our competitors to match. (Prokesch 1995)

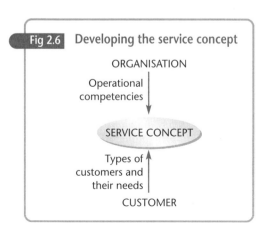

Fig 2.6 Developing the service concept

ORGANISATION

Operational competencies

SERVICE CONCEPT

Types of customers and their needs

CUSTOMER

By thinking carefully about the market, the different customer segments and the needs of the customers in those segments, together with a dispassionate understanding of the core competencies of the operation, managers may be able to develop totally new and innovative concepts that have great appeal to customers and give the organisation a significant competitive edge (see Figure 2.6)

Box 2.4 describes the development of a new concept at Singapore Zoo which could be difficult for other organisations to follow. You will see that this development springs from the current operational competencies together with a realisation why the zoo did not attract foreign visitors, a very large and lucrative market.

Box 2.4 Singapore Zoological Gardens – a new service concept

Singapore Zoo is no stranger to innovation. In 1982 the Zoo started offering a new service: breakfast or tea with an orang-utan called Ah Meng. Since then she and her companions have played host to some 50,000 guests a year. So well known is the Zoo for its innovation that a spoof article in the *Straits Times* on 1 April 1998 offered a new 30-minute low-impact aerobic work-out with Ah Meng before breakfast. Mr Bernard Harrison, the Zoo's Chief Executive, said he was amazed by the flood of interest in the 'new service', the authenticity of which most people did not seem to doubt!

Singapore Zoological Gardens is a public limited company owned by the Government of Singapore and has been in existence since 1983. Its aim is to be a world-class leisure attraction striving to provide excellent exhibits of animals displayed in their natural environment for the purposes of recreation, education and conservation.

The Zoo is situated on a 28-hectare site about 30 minutes to the north of the city of Singapore. It houses a collection of 2,800 animals representing 216 species, using an 'open zoo' concept. The animals are kept in spacious, landscaped enclosures, separated from the visitors using psychological restraint techniques based on the animals' natural instincts for defining a territory as their own, or by a natural fear of some elements such as water. The water moats, for example, are concealed with vegetation or dropped below the line of vision. The more dangerous animals, such as leopards and jaguars, are housed in beautifully landscaped glass-fronted enclosures. Oppressive cages, which typify 'old' zoos, are absent. Stimulation is provided by trying to re-create the natural stresses of the wild and bring out the animals' natural instincts and reflexes. For example, instead of throwing neatly chopped chunks of meat to the big cats, the keepers hang a large hunk of meat up high, forcing them to leap for it and grasp it with their claws, much as they would when hunting in the wild.

Despite having a successful world-class zoo, Mr Harrison and his colleagues know that it has limited appeal, in that the majority of the Zoo's visitors are local residents. For the large numbers of tourists on short stopovers, visiting a zoo, which they could easily do at home, was a low priority. The Zoo needed a new concept.

After four years of planning and three years of construction Singapore Zoo's Night Safari was opened in May 1994. The Night Safari is the world's first night-time wildlife park. It occupies a 40 hectare site adjacent to the Open Zoo, with its own entrance and facilities, from which guests can explore the wildlife in the natural tropical jungle. Over 1,000 nocturnal animals of 100 species can be seen in large naturalistic habitats. Given most animals are nocturnal, a night safari offers the best chance to see them.

The Night Safari is nothing like an ordinary zoo, but a real safari experience. Quiet electric trams provide guided safaris for visitors around a 3.2 kilometre trail, which takes about 45 minutes to complete, though there are stop-off points. The ride provides the Zoo's staff with a chance to educate and inform, and its guests time to relax and enjoy the ride. The same 'open concept' as the day zoo is used, to tremendous effect. Indeed, under the cover of darkness, the moats can be very effectively camouflaged using netting and shade. Other less dangerous animals, such as deer, are roaming freely in large areas bounded by cattle grids. Occasionally the tram has to stop and wait for an animal to move out of its way. During the ride the landscape changes to provide appropriate settings for its animals, from the rocky outcrops of the Himalayan foothills, to the grassy plains of equatorial Africa, and ending with the forests of South-east Asia. Information boards at intervals provide facts about the animals nearby. Indeed the impression of free-roaming wild animals is so realistic that one visitor was overheard asking his partner how come all the animals were in the right places – could they read?

Three walking trails are well marked and provide opportunities to see all of the animals at close range. The dark jungle paths create an eerie atmosphere, and guests come face to face with many animals. Because it is dark, the glass-fronted cages which house the big cats are not noticeable – nor are the visitors to the cats because of the lighting differences, so they carry on as normal with their night-time activities.

Lighting is provided by a combination of mercury and incandescent lights, mounted on tall poles to provide a soft bluish moonlight which neither detracts from the ambience nor disturbs the animals. Only certain areas are 'moonlit' as the dark background adds to the atmosphere and lighting the foreground would spoil the effect of the appearance of freedom. Flash photography is forbidden to ensure the animals are not disturbed.

All the facilities are consistent with the safari theme. The walkways from the car parks to the tram station are constructed from wooden boards with wooden handrails. The central 'rooms' have high ceilings, wooden beams and ceiling fans but no walls and so are open to the dark jungle. Around the restaurant and shops, and the bongo burger bar with food aimed at the younger visitors, there is no piped music, just the quiet chattering of the wildlife. Even the toilets have a safari feel: they are open to the sky with sinks set in stone outcrops surrounded by jungle.

Questions

1 *Compare and contrast the service concepts of the Night Safari and a traditional zoo by identifying their key characteristics and drawing their profiles using the profiling tool (Figure 2.4).*

2 *Why do you think that other zoos will find it difficult to copy this concept?*

This illustration is based on visits to the Zoo, discussions with staff and material from the Zoo's web site http://www.zoo.com.sg.

2.4 FOCUS AND THE SERVICE CONCEPT

The notion of 'focus' was introduced into the manufacturing literature by Skinner in 1974 and it has now become one of the central pillars of the subject of manufacturing strategy (see, for example, Hayes and Wheelwright 1984, Hill 1993, Skinner 1985, Slack 1991). Skinner (1974) claimed that 'A factory that focuses on a narrow product mix for a particular market niche will outperform the conventional plant which attempts a broader mission. Because its equipment, supporting systems, and procedures can concentrate on a limited task for one set of customers, its costs and especially its overheads are likely to be lower than those of a conventional plant.'

2.4.1 Service focus

The idea of focus – concentrating on providing a particular segment of customers with a narrow range of products – applies equally well to service industries (see, for example, Heskett 1986, Kimes and Johnston 1990a and 1990b, Van Dierdonck and Brandt 1988) and is indeed what many service organisations do. Young children are not welcomed at some high-class restaurants and children's menus are not available. Some banks and credit/charge card companies focus on providing dedicated and personalised services to high-wealth individuals. Some consultancy companies focus on providing specialised services to particular types of client.

Indeed service focus makes good sense: 'tight focus is imperative because you can't provide great service unless your business system is optimized to the needs of a certain segment' (Davidow and Uttal 1989). Focus provides benefits both to the organisation such as simplicity of operation and to the customer, high value at low costs (see Table 2.1).

Table 2.1 The benefits of focus

Benefits to the organisation	Benefits to the customer
● Simplified operation	● Ease of use
● Predetermined service	● Customers can select a service according to their specific needs
● Dedicated operation	
● Dedicated facilities	
● Tight process control	● Low price
● Ease of training	
● Lower costs	

2.4.2 Four service concepts

Using the two traditional dimensions of focus – number of markets served and range of services provided (see Figure 2.7) – service concepts can be categorised into four broad types: service focused, market focused, service and market focused, and unfocused. For example, an organisation that focuses on providing a narrow range of services to a niche market (bottom left) will have a 'service and market focused' concept, for example a structural engineering consultancy. An organisation that serves many markets with a wide range of services, such as a leisure centre, has an unfocused concept (top right), that is 'provide a wide range of services for a wide range of people', in other words providing (almost) everything for everyone.

The traditional view of focus is that it can be achieved through either limiting the range of services provided and/or limiting the number of markets served. For example, Barclaycard, where the service concept is to provide credit facilities through the use of a card accepted in retail outlets throughout the world, serves many markets, but has a relatively small range of services. American Express on the other hand, whilst providing a greater range of services than Barclaycard – Global Assist, a range of insurance services, travellers cheques and airline tickets – focuses its concept on supporting the international traveller. It is interesting to note that both of these organisations are slowly losing their focus. Barclaycard is adding on more services,

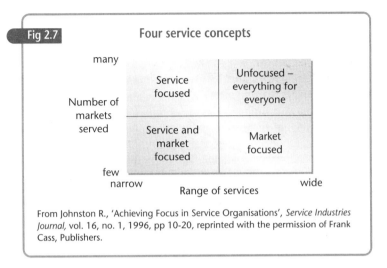

Fig 2.7

Four service concepts

From Johnston R., 'Achieving Focus in Service Organisations', *Service Industries Journal,* vol. 16, no. 1, 1996, pp 10-20, reprinted with the permission of Frank Cass, Publishers.

such as insurance, and Amex is trying to broaden the appeal of its card (see Figure 2.8). Internet banks such as Egg are focused on regular Internet users (a rapidly growing market) and offer either one main product (service and market focused) or, as in Egg's case, a range of services including credit card, mortgages, loans and travel insurance. Telephone-based credit companies such as Lombard Direct tend to be both service and market focused, with service concepts focused on clear market segments and providing a limited range of services. Through a 24-hour dedicated call centre Lombard Direct mainly provides unsecured loans from £800 to £15,000. These account for 90 per cent of its business. The organisation is in a position to consider expanding its product range. (More information on Egg and Lombard can be found in Chapters 9 and 10.)

There is possibly a natural tendency for organisational growth to come through first increasing the range of services, then expanding the market, or by market expansion and then through product or service proliferation. Focus is then achieved by separating out the organisation into distinct operations or organisations focused on providing a particular service or on a particular market segment (see Figure 2.9). Indeed this is what has happened in the case of Lombard Direct, which is a subsidiary of National Westminster Bank.

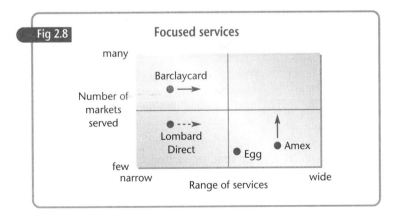

Fig 2.8

Focused services

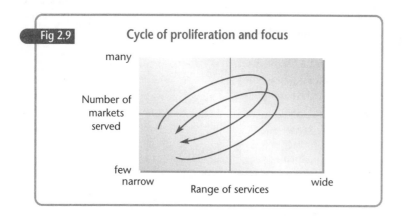

Fig 2.9   **Cycle of proliferation and focus**

2.5   UNFOCUSED SERVICE OPERATIONS

Through either a strategy of growth and development or strategic positioning many successful service organisations are unfocused and are doing 'everything for everyone' – Disneyworld, supermarkets, hypermarkets, the Internet, police services ... all serve a very wide range of customers with a very wide range of services. What these organisations do, however, is achieve the benefits of focus (simplicity and lower costs) in different ways. There are three main ways in which organisations that wish to 'do everything for everyone' can achieve the benefits of focus (developed from Johnston 1996):

- business focus
- operational focus
- encounter focus

2.5.1   Business focus

If it is possible to split the market into segments with similar needs and expectations the organisation may be able to split its businesses to deal with those different customer types. Holiday Inn's businesses are described in Box 2.5. The company is seeking to 'do everything for everyone' by providing a whole range of services – long stay, short stay, full service and limited service – to a wide range of customers. It has developed several different businesses to focus on particular services for particular market segments – business focus (see Figure 2.10).

2.5.2   Operational focus

For some organisations each business or site provides the same range of services to a wide range of customers and they are unable to focus on particular services or segments at each site or business. Such organisations can gain the benefits of focus by splitting their operation into several parts so that each caters for a set of needs. Either customers then choose their channel and therefore their experience, or the organisation assists or makes the decision and designs fixed delivery channels for its customers.

Box 2.5 Holiday Inn

Holiday Inn claims to be 'The World's Most Global Hotel Company' and has created several different business brands for a number of identified market segments. 'Our continued focus on guest preference has resulted in development of a range of brands, each serving a different market segment of the international hotel market ... providing a variety of services, amenities and lodging experiences catering to virtually every travel occasion and guest need.'

The service concept at Holiday Inn Express hotels focuses on value for money, offering competitive rates and limited service aimed at both leisure and business travellers. Holiday Inn Express provides, for example, a free continental breakfast bar, rather than table service, to reduce costs but meet the needs of guests wishing a light and fast breakfast. Holiday Inn's new Staybridge Suites focus on the long-stay guest, providing a variety of suites (from studio to several bedrooms) together with a variety of on-site services, such as laundry rooms, library and breakfast room. Crowne Plaza Hotels and Resorts provide 'upscale lodging' to international discerning travellers, and the recently acquired Inter-Continental Hotels focus on providing five-star service and facilities.

Question

1 *Summarise what you consider to be the concepts of Holiday Inn's different businesses. Assess the type of focus of each of them.*

This illustration is based on material from http://www.basshotels.com.

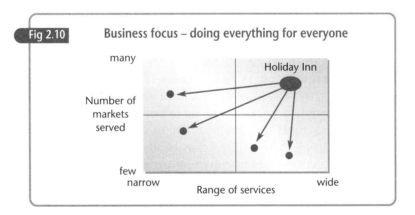

Fig 2.10 Business focus – doing everything for everyone

Hypermarkets are unfocused organisations and provide 'everything for everyone' at each site, but few of their customers want 'everything'! Hypermarkets deal with this by having 'shops-within-shop'. Many hypermarkets, or large shopping malls, include many different types of shops, retailers, cinemas and a range of eating-places for example, allowing customers to create their own service experience. For some the service concept will be a great day out using many of the facilities; for others it could be a retail-based 'shop-'til-you-drop' experience, or maybe just a trip to the cinema.

Other service organisations design different service channels for their different customer segments. In hotels premium-rate customers are escorted to their rooms and

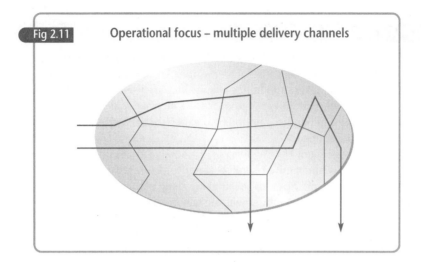

Fig 2.11 Operational focus – multiple delivery channels

provided with spacious accommodation in 'executive' or 'club' rooms. They may have their own dedicated lounges and complimentary breakfast bars. In these cases the operation is split into different sections, 'shops' or channels and guests then choose, or are guided through, the appropriate sections (see Figure 2.11).

2.5.3 Encounter focus

Some organisations wish to 'do everything for everyone'. Yet where all the businesses or sites are the same and the delivery channels are identical they can still achieve some degree of focus at the service encounter. This level of focus is achieved by encouraging staff to recognise and deal with the varying needs of their customers by adapting the encounter to focus on their particular needs. Reception staff at an hotel, for example, could be encouraged to try and assess the needs of the customers as they approach the front desk. A business executive may appreciate a brisk service whereas a family may appreciate more time being spent explaining the facilities, the children's meal options and where to find information about local attractions, for example. The facilities may be identical for every customer but the service encounter is customised by the front-line staff.

Many service organisations are neither focused on a market niche nor provide a narrow range of services, yet, using a variety of means, they can gain the many benefits of focus, not just for their operations but also to the benefit of customers.

2.6 SUMMARY

The service concept

- A service concept is the mental picture that is held by customers, employees and shareholders about the service provided by the organisation.
- A service concept embraces the service experience, the service outcome, the service operation and the value of the service.

The service concept as a strategic tool

● The service concept can be used to create organisational alignment, assess the implications of design changes, and drive strategic advantage.

Focus and the service concept

● Focus means providing a particular segment of customers with a narrow range of services.

● There are four basic service concepts based upon levels of focus: service focused, market focused, service and market focused, and unfocused.

Unfocused service organisations

● Many service organisations are, by nature, unfocused but they can gain the benefits of focus by adopting a business focus, operational focus or encounter focus.

2.7 DISCUSSION QUESTIONS

1. Select four service organisations and define their concepts and levels of focus. Evaluate the options facing them.

2. Assess how the following operations try to tangibilise the intangible: a lecture, an Internet retailer, a music concert.

3. Bernard Harrison, the Chief Executive of Singapore Zoo, is keen to continue developing the Zoo: can you develop a new service concept for him?

2.8 QUESTIONS FOR MANAGERS

1. What is your organisation's service concept? How does this compare with your colleagues' view of its concept?

2. Profile your process and assess areas of weakness (non-alignment) and any opportunities to use it to drive strategic advantage.

3. Assess the ways in which your organisation achieves the benefits of focus.

2.9 SUGGESTIONS FOR FURTHER READING

Fitzsimmons J. and Fitzsimmons M. (eds), *New Service Design*, Sage Publications, Thousand Oaks, California, 2000.

Normann R. and Ramirez R., 'From Value Chain to Value Constellation: Designing interactive strategy', *Harvard Business Review*, July–August 1993, pp. 65–77.

2.10 REFERENCES

Armstrong D., 'Thoughts Bounded and Thoughts Free', Paper to Department of Psychotherapy, Cambridge, 1991.

Booms B.H. and Bitner M.J., 'Marketing Strategies and Organisation Structures for Service Firms', in Donnelly J. and George W. (eds), *Marketing of Services*, American Marketing Association, Chicago, 1981, pp. 47–51.

Campbell A. and Yeung S., 'Do You Need a Mission Statement?', *Economist Special Report No. 1208*, Economist Publications, London, 1990.

Clark G., Johnston R. and Shulver M., 'Exploiting the Service Concept for Service Design and Development', in Fitzsimmons J. and Fitzsimmons M. (eds), *New Service Design*, Sage Publications, Thousand Oaks, California, 2000, pp. 71–91.

Collier D.A., *The Service/Quality Solution: Using service management to gain competitive advantage,* Irwin and ASQC Quality Press, New York, 1994.

Davidow W.H. and Uttal B., 'Service Companies: Focus or falter', *Harvard Business Review*, July–August 1989, pp. 77–85.

Dibb S., Simkin L., Pride W. and Ferrel O.C., *Marketing Concepts and Strategies* (third European edition), Houghton Mifflin, Boston, 1997.

Hayes R.H. and Wheelwright S.C., *Restoring our Competitive Edge*, Wiley, New York, 1984.

Heskett J.L., *Managing in the Service Economy*, Harvard Business School Press, Boston, 1986.

Hill T., *Manufacturing Strategy – Text and Cases*, Irwin, Homewood, Ill., 1993.

Johnston R., 'Achieving Focus in Service Organisations', *Service Industries Journal*, vol. 16, no. 1, 1996, pp. 10–20.

Kimes S. and Johnston R., 'The Application of Focused Manufacturing in the Hospitality Sector', in the proceedings of the Manufacturing Strategy Conference of the Operations Management Association – UK, University of Warwick, June 1990a.

Kimes S. and Johnston R., 'Four Generic Service Concepts', in the proceedings of the Decision Sciences Institute Conference, USA, November 1990b.

Lovelock C.H. and Wright L., *Principles of Service Management and Marketing,* Prentice Hall, NJ, 1999.

McCarthy E.J., *Basic Marketing: A managerial approach*, Irwin, Homewood, Ill., 1960.

Normann R. and Ramirez R., 'From Value Chain to Value Constellation: Designing interactive strategy', *Harvard Business Review*, July–August 1993, pp. 65–77.

Prokesch S.E., 'Competing on Customer Service: An interview with British Airways' Sir Colin Marshall', *Harvard Business Review*, November–December 1995, pp. 101–12.

Skinner W., 'The Focused Factory', *Harvard Business Review*, vol. 52, no. 3, May–June 1974, pp. 113–21.

Skinner W., *Manufacturing: The formidable competitive weapon*, Wiley, New York, 1985.

Slack N., *The Manufacturing Advantage*, Mercury, London, 1991.

Van Dierdonck R. and Brandt G., 'Focused Factory in Service Industries', in Johnston R. (ed.), *The Management of Service Operations*, IFS/Springer-Verlag, Berlin, 1988.

Van Looey B., Van Dierdonck R. and Gemmel P., *Services Management: An integrated approach*, Financial Times Pitman Publishing, London, 1998.

Zeithaml V.A. and Bitner M.J., Services Marketing, McGraw-Hill, New York, 1996.

CASE EXERCISE

Lilliput Ltd

Reg Turner set up Lilliput as an offshoot of his carpentry business in 1997. Some years before he had been asked by a friend to provide his children with a playhouse for the garden. He made them a Swiss-style chalet covering an area of about four square metres. Within 12 months of its arrival in the garden Reg had received requests for 15 more from friends and neighbours. By 1998 Reg had designed 11 different styles, based on modular sections, which were easy to install. The business was located beside one of the large garden centres on the outskirts of the town. He employed three full-time carpenters, a driver, and a sales assistant (his mother-in-law) to run the retail side of the business. Reg would not compromise on quality. He would only buy good materials and he oversaw the construction of the houses himself. A carpenter would always accompany the delivery van and undertake the installation for the customer. He also managed to keep his costs lower than most of his competitors by doing his own retailing and by keeping overheads low. He did not accept any credit cards. He priced his houses about 20 per cent below those of garden centres, although it was possible to find less expensive products. He added, 'You can't forget how important children are in buying playhouses. It's not enough seeing pictures, they have to get inside and try them out. It is so important that we maintain a family-friendly feel to the business.'

By 2000 Reg had developed a reputation for quality and style and he decided to employ his daughter, Tiffany, who had recently finished art school and was showing an interest in the business. Her first task was to create a brochure for the business and he was delighted with the result. Although it wiped out last year's profit, the professional, full-colour brochure exuded quality and style. It displayed his range of houses with pictures of children playing in and around them. Other pictures showed the clean and tidy site and good parking facilities. It provided useful information about sizes, styles, installation and maintenance, sources of timber and construction methods. Tiffany suggested that she should now set up a web site and said that it was time the business invested in some computers.

The site attracted many customers, particularly at weekends. Several people included a visit to Lilliput with a visit to the garden centre next door. Reg had developed a good relationship with the manager of the garden centre. They both believed they gained from each other. Reg also attracted buyers from some of the other garden centres who were always keen to inspect his latest designs and assess his prices. One large garden centre 80 miles away was in the process of negotiating a contract for Reg to supply it with playhouses.

The site itself was causing Reg some problems. As he made all the houses on site he had to keep an area fenced off from the customers for safety reasons. This was at the back of the site and necessitated delivery lorries moving through the display area. He explained: 'This site was only meant to be temporary. We had to demolish the building that was here before to make space. But it works well being next to the garden centre, so I think we might well stay here.' Reg knew he would need to lay a proper car park, as the existing one was just an open area with a rubble base and no markings. There were no signs except for one at the gate. Few of the houses had information, or even prices, on them – indeed it looked like they had been torn off.

The staff were friendly but the carpenters had little time to deal with the customers. Mavis Williams, Reg's mother-in-law, was based in the portacabin office. She complained, 'I am rushed off my feet with people placing orders and calls for brochures. I hardly get out of the office. Some of the customers get cross because they have been kept waiting but I have only one pair of hands.'

By the end of 2000, the business was so successful that there were now at least five weeks between order and delivery. Reg asked Mavis not to make any promises on delivery dates for all new orders. Mavis replied with uncharacteristic anger, 'You just don't realise how difficult it is for me at the moment. How do you think the customers are going to react when I tell them I don't know when we can deliver and install the house? It's going to take me twice as long to deal with them now and I bet we lose a lot of sales. You have just taken advantage of me over the last three years and I have had enough.'

Reg was keen to grow the business and there was no shortage of interest in his product. He realised he now needed to focus his attention on the operation.

Questions

1 *Evaluate Lilliput's service concept.*

2 *What changes should Reg make?*

3 *How should Reg go about developing his business?*

Part 2

CUSTOMER AND SUPPLIER RELATIONSHIPS

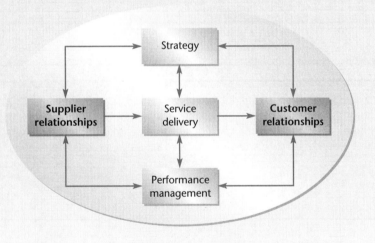

3

Customers and relationships

3.1 INTRODUCTION

It should, perhaps, be self-evident that a text on service operations should include an examination of customers and customer relationships. Indeed, in some organisations, service is virtually synonymous with customer focus, ensuring that service design and delivery recognise the needs and desires of the customer. Sadly, this is often not the case. Organisations start with good intentions to recognise the customer, but often become somewhat arrogant in thinking either that they know best, or that they know what the customers want without having to ask. All companies would do well to review the way that they think about their customers, being prepared to challenge any strongly held assumptions.

The objectives of this chapter are:

- to describe the development of customer relationships
- to identify and understand different types of customer
- to discuss the operation's view of segmentation
- to recognise the benefits of customer retention and identify issues in the calculation of customer lifetime values
- to develop an understanding of the range of customer relationships, and to describe the implications for operations management of developing and maintaining such relationships
- to introduce the concept of customer–provider partnerships
- to describe the challenges of managing temporary relationships.

This chapter discusses the different ways that customers can be segmented or grouped. Just as service marketing will devote attention to segmenting customers in order to understand which groups are prime targets for the organisation, so service operations must be clear as to what is involved in delivering to each customer group. Also, service organisations are often concerned to rebuild relationships with their customers. We will examine the operational implications of relationships and describe how, where appropriate, operations can contribute to strengthening them. Finally, we will examine approaches to customer relationship management in different service operations.

3.2 CUSTOMER RELATIONSHIP DEVELOPMENT

The marketing profession has moved its focus in recent years towards 'relationship marketing'. The emphasis has changed from acquiring new customers to retaining existing ones. For many organisations this has resulted in attempts to strengthen relationships with their customers in the belief that this will lead to loyalty and fewer defections. Customer relationships may take many forms, from the 'temporary relationship' created for the short, limited-scope transaction of the high-volume service, to the long-term personal relationships that may be built between two people in the context of a business-to-business or professional service.

This chapter examines the operational implications of the diversity of approaches to customers. This is a central issue for service operations managers. Knowing customer requirements in depth for each segment enables appropriate service delivery system design to balance short-term resource productivity targets against the benefit of long-term customer retention. Operations managers must manage the detail of differences amongst customers in the selling process (for example, economising customers, 'greys' and empty-nesters); similarly, different customers in the service delivery process (new customers, experienced customers, helpful, and complaining customers) will pose different challenges to managers.

In any given context, it is important firstly to clarify the 'vision' for the relationship. Figure 3.1 illustrates some of the options, starting in each case with a transactional approach which views each encounter as a 'one-off' activity, with providers having little or no memory of previous transactions and no expectation of future business.

Customer relationship development often contains mixtures of the two approaches outlined in Figure 3.1. The customer retention approach is focused on what might be

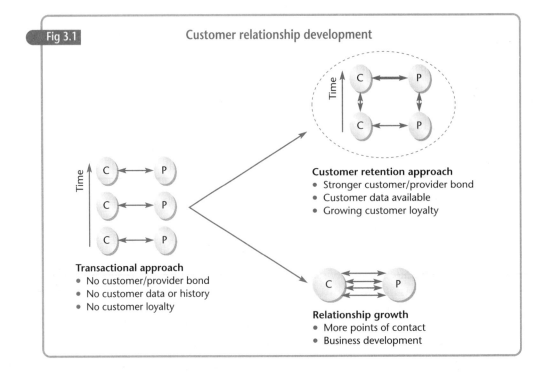

Fig 3.1 Customer relationship development

Transactional approach
- No customer/provider bond
- No customer data or history
- No customer loyalty

Customer retention approach
- Stronger customer/provider bond
- Customer data available
- Growing customer loyalty

Relationship growth
- More points of contact
- Business development

termed an 'enhanced' transaction approach. Usually facilitated by better information on general customer requirements, here the provider concentrates on higher levels of service quality. Increasingly, through better informational exchange, the provider can concentrate on providing what individuals require. Over time this leads to higher levels of customer loyalty with all its attendant benefits.

The relationship growth approach means that the service organisation concentrates on developing more points of contact with their customers. In a business-to-business environment, this might mean that during the course of a project the customer finds more ways for people from equivalent functions (for example design, operations and support services) to meet and work together. In a business-to-consumer service, the relationship grows as the customer buys an increasing range of service products. In either case, the relationship becomes stronger and less susceptible to competitive action.

Organisations with relatively few customers, but with a wide range of capabilities, will tend to concentrate on the relationship growth approach. Organisations with high volumes of customers, but with relatively few 'commodity' products, will tend to use the customer retention approach – though it should be made clear that the approaches are not mutually exclusive.

However, before we discuss relationship management in more detail, we must understand who the customers are, how we segment customers and how we retain them and build relationships with them.

3.3 CUSTOMERS

When we use the word 'customer' it can mean very different things. We could be referring to consumers, or clients, or even internal customers. A first and critical step in understanding customers and then meeting their needs is to understand who is the customer. Customers can be classified in several different ways:

- external versus internal customers
- intermediaries versus end users or consumers
- stakeholders: payers, beneficiaries or participants
- valuable customers versus not-so-valuable customers.

3.3.1 External versus internal customers

In many service sectors, particularly consumer services such as banks and restaurants, it is usually clear who is the customer. Customers are the individuals or groups of people, external to the organisation, who are receiving and often paying for the service. In many of these situations there is a clear time connection in the sense that service will be delivered on receipt of the required price, as in a fast-food restaurant or retail store.

We should also recognise that within organisations there are 'internal customers' to whom services must be delivered. Internal customers are individuals or groups of individuals who are a part of the same organisation but from a different unit or operation. For example, the accountancy department, the personnel department, the IT department, all in their own way provide services to the other parts of the organisation just as they also require services from the rest of the organisation. The recognition of 'internal customers', and the need to provide them with services and information, is one of the key elements of many quality improvement programmes. These programmes are based on the important premise that the quality and cost of service provided to external customers depend upon the quality of the service provided to and by the network of internal customers.

[handwritten margin note: IF SERVICE IS BAD TO INTERNAL THEN BAD TO EXTERNAL]

3.3.2 Intermediaries versus end users or consumers

One of the design issues under debate for many service supply chains is the question of whether or not to use intermediaries, the 'middle-men' who sell a product or service to an end customer on behalf of one or more suppliers. Some financial services, for example, have recently removed the intermediary stage of independent insurance broker to set up their own 'direct' operations. They have done this largely to reduce the transaction costs for commodity-type services such as motor insurance, but also to gain ownership of the end customer. This has been possible to achieve as increasing customer knowledge about industry prices has forced companies and customers alike to re-evaluate the worth of the broker network.

The situation that many organisations face is the need to manage both their direct customers such as brokers or retailers, whilst at the same time being aware of the needs of the end consumer or user, and therefore to encourage the intermediaries to give the desired service to their customers in turn. In theory this should make perfect sense, though as Pegasus Software found, this is not always straightforward (see Box 3.1).

Box 3.1 Pegasus Software

Pegasus Software provides accounting software to a range of customers, from sole traders needing basic bookkeeping software to medium corporates requiring integration of financial systems with other business systems such as sales order processing and inventory management.

Pegasus has traditionally sold through retailers and value-adding resellers (VARs). As part of its competitive strategy Pegasus is concerned about the quality of service it is providing in support of its software. In reviewing its customer service strategy, the Service Director has spent considerable amounts of time with the intermediaries trying to understand how best to deliver high-quality service. A central aspect of Pegasus' strategy is 'customer migration'. By this they mean the process by which their business customers will upgrade their software as the business grows. Providing high levels of customer support is a fundamental requirement. This initiative has been welcomed by many, but with suspicion by other resellers who have fears that Pegasus will try to steal 'their' customers.

While Pegasus remains in the high-volume/low-cost software market, this policy of selling through intermediaries seems appropriate. It would be extremely expensive to develop traditional sales channels. A major problem for Pegasus, though, lies in the development of increasingly complex control systems in a move towards offering products that integrate financial systems with sales order processing and inventory management. It is unlikely that many of their existing intermediaries will have the applications expertise to provide the more comprehensive level of support required by these systems. Perhaps this is an appropriate time to develop 'in-house' applications and implementation resources to be sold as a total package to customers? As such it would represent a major change from the existing approach.

Questions

1 *What are the implications for the software customer support team in dealing with both dealers and end users?*

2 *What attributes will be required for support staff in order to service the more complex software applications?*

3.3.3 Stakeholders: payers, beneficiaries and participants

This categorisation explores the customers' extent of involvement with the service. In many services the customer participating in the service expects benefit from the service and also is required to pay for it. In the case of a restaurant, if there is a problem with the food or the service, the customer is aware of it because s/he participates in the service, and cares about the outcome because s/he is a beneficiary. Because s/he is also paying for the service, s/he is able to take appropriate action.

In many service situations, for example prisons, public health services and voluntary services, there may be a clear distinction between and indeed conflicts amongst payer, beneficiary and participant. This is not only found in not-for-profit organisations. In business-to-business services such as photocopier leasing it is possible that the purchasing department may have cost reduction targets for their overall spend which may conflict with the need for high copy quality in the user functions.

The links between purchaser and beneficiary become extremely difficult to understand when we consider public services. These are funded by taxpayers, but the budget is determined by politicians who (supposedly) represent the views and interests of their constituents. In the case of the police service, the beneficiary is again society at large, though the participants (criminals and offenders) may not see the actions of the police as a benefit! Even the most law-abiding citizens may be annoyed when stopped by the police for what seems to them to be a trivial matter.

The UK Benefits Agency is responsible for distributing money to the unemployed, those receiving disability benefit etc. The Agency has invested heavily in improving its service standards for those who are out of work. This stems from a belief that all members of society deserve to be treated as human beings and also that better service will elicit a less aggressive response from individuals who may be under stress from their difficult circumstances.

This approach can be expanded. We can identify all the stakeholders of a service and understand their different perspectives. Box 3.2 describes the stakeholders for a prison service, and recognises that not all stakeholders will be willing participants. The value of this type of analysis is that it then allows the operations manager to identify the varying (and sometimes conflicting) requirements of each stakeholder group.

Box 3.2 Stakeholder analysis for the prison service

The prison service provides an excellent example of the complexity of stakeholder requirements, to some extent reflecting the mixed task it faces. Society requires the service to carry out potentially conflicting activities:

- to ensure that 'dangerous criminals' are locked up for the safety of society
- to provide a regime that will punish wrongdoers as a means of payment for their crimes
- to support inmates, providing counselling and training to rehabilitate and reform them, to reduce the likelihood of reoffending.

The principal stakeholders and their requirements are as follows:

- Government ministers with responsibility for the prison service will be concerned to fulfil manifesto promises whilst meeting spending targets. At the same time they will be concerned about stories of prisoner escapes or drug abuse that may be damaging to their personal reputation, possibly forcing their resignation.
- Prison governors will seek to provide an appropriate environment for inmates, whilst keeping to strict operating budgets.
- Prison officers will be concerned to strike a balance between building a rapport with inmates and enforcing discipline.
- Offenders will have a wide range of requirements depending on the nature of the offence, length of term, desire to change, and so forth.
- Families of offenders may wish to maintain contact with inmates.
- Members of society at large want to feel safe from criminals, but will also believe that some help should be provided for those who wish to reform.

The relationships between these stakeholder groups are often complex. Clearly, politicians ultimately report to those who elect them, including prison officers and families of offenders. Prison governors with hopes of career advancement may feel that they must satisfy the demands of the current party in power that may be at odds with the requirements of other groups.

Questions

1 *If you were a prison governor, what strategies would you adopt to find out about the needs of the various stakeholder groups?*

2 *What operational problems arise from having to manage this diversity?*

3.3.4 Valuable customers versus not-so-valuable customers

Service marketing literature proposes that organisations prioritise service towards customers who can create the most value for the organisation (see, for example, Gummesson 1999, Payne *et al.* 1995, Reichheld 1996). Given that any operation has finite resources, it would seem sensible to ensure that any prioritisation safeguards long-term business interests.

This view links with the idea of assessing lifetime value of a customer (see section 3.5.2). For organisations that deal with many relatively small (in value) transactions it has been found useful to calculate the lifetime value. So a customer with a weekly supermarket spend of £100 represents annual revenues of £5,000 and lifetime revenue in excess of £$\frac{1}{4}$ million. Some service organisations claim that this understanding helps motivate staff to treat customers with respect! This type of analysis certainly may help justify investment in customer service training.

Equipment-related services have been used to this approach for some years, their customers having understood the difference between lifetime cost of ownership as against the cost of acquisition. Indeed it is common in some industries for companies to make a loss on the sale of original equipment, knowing that 25 years of spares and service contracts would ensure long-term profitability.

The difficulty with this approach is that it isn't always obvious as to who are valuable and not-so-valuable customers. Again, business-to-business services may have a reasonable idea about customer value, perhaps represented by size of contracts. In some cases these organisations may have only one customer, in which case this analysis becomes somewhat irrelevant.

Consumer services may have more difficulty with this. Financial services, for example, may be able to classify customers according to social economic groups and make judgements based on this analysis. However, this may hide the fact that the organisation has just annoyed the son or daughter of the managing director of their largest corporate account. In terms of developing a customer-focused culture, such a 'rational' approach would seem to have some dangers.

The notion of a 'customer' is a complex construct and so operations managers need to:

- understand the value of their different customer types
- understand the different nature of each group and the services they require, and
- recognise the conflicts between different customer groups.

3.4 CUSTOMER SEGMENTATION – AN OPERATIONS VIEW

A clear understanding of segments is fundamental to service operations. It has long been true that a 'one size fits all' approach will not satisfy many customers, who wish to be treated as individuals. It is the key in moving from a transactional approach towards either a customer retention or relationship growth strategy (Figure 3.1). For the former, segmentation is a means of focusing service delivery on aspects of service that are likely to build customer satisfaction (see Chapter 4), and for the latter, segmentation may point to opportunities for upselling or cross-selling other service products.

3.4.1 Market segmentation

Marketing segmentation is traditionally based on customer characteristics. Thus organisations will focus on particular economic groups or target a geographic region. Other marketing approaches will consider lifestyles, family circumstances (for example: single parents, 2.4 children, empty-nesters…) or the reasons why customers buy a service (for example: for its benefits, utility, response to promotion…).

Clearly, service operations managers must be aware of the emphasis behind the marketing approach adopted by the organisation. Not only does it make sense to target marketing effort on people most likely to buy the service, but it also helps operations managers design their facilities appropriately and deliver service in the appropriate way.

A restaurant provides a simple example. If the restaurant is targeting couples for romantic dinners for two, the design of seating and ambience will be rather different from a restaurant that considers families as its prime source of revenue. The type of food served and the way in which it is served – for example speed, manner and information provided – will be different. In the case of a family restaurant, easy-to-clean facilities with flexible seating will be required, together with value-for-money meals served efficiently. The romantic restaurant will require different furnishings, lighting, music, staff competencies and food. Clearly, a wide range of other decisions flows from this initial identification of the customer group to be served. Some restaurants manage to adapt to changing needs, providing classical music and reasonably bright lighting for early-evening family groups and more elderly diners, moving to more upbeat music and dimmer lighting for younger couples as the evening progresses.

Thus decisions about market segmentation may define the target customers, such as families or romantic diners, and drive key decisions such as process and capacity management (see Chapters 6 and 7) and staff competencies (Chapter 8). However, once the operation is up and running, customers can be re-classified to allow the operations manager to identify issues critical to service delivery.

3.4.2 Customer types

We believe that operations managers and their staff need to develop an understanding of the nature of individual customers and their resultant behaviour, particularly when they are the direct recipient of the service delivery process, and may in fact be an integral part of it. The nature of the customer could significantly influence the type of service provided, how they need to be dealt with by staff, and their potential impact on other customers in the operation. Possible categories of customers classified by behaviour or attitude could include:

- *The Ally.* These customers usually arrive in a positive frame of mind, willing to help and give positive feedback to facilitate the service. The most helpful Ally is the customer whose opinion is respected by others. If the Ally is happy, then other customers will infer that the service must be good.

- *The Hostage.* These customers require service, but may be 'locked in' to a particular service provider contractually. An example is the customer who must have his/her car serviced by the dealer appointed by the manufacturer. The service may cost rather more, but if an approved dealer is not used, his/her warranty will be invalid. These customers may not be in the most positive moods and will become very difficult whenever service performance deteriorates.

- *The Anarchist.* This customer dislikes rules and systems. Indeed, notices suggesting what should and shouldn't be done present a challenge. It is tempting to let the customer 'get away' with not following the system, but this may set up problems with other customers who feel that they haven't been treated fairly.

[handwritten margin note: SETTING THE SCENE FOR DIFFERENT CLIENTELE, ADAPTING TO DIFFERENT SEGMENTATIONS]

- *The Patient.* This customer is very similar to the Hostage in that they are locked into the service, such as a hospital patient or a student at a school or university. These customers may be positively or unequivocally oriented towards the organisation and are willing to submit themselves to rules and regulations. However, unnecessary restrictions may turn them into a Hostage or Anarchist.

- *The Tolerant.* These customers may be passive, always waiting patiently for service providers to acknowledge their presence and deliver service. In fact they may be so patient that they become invisible to service staff and get ignored as a result. It may be dangerous to trade on their apparent goodwill.

- *The Intolerant.* These customers are seldom passive or patient, often causing stress and problems within the service for themselves, the service providers and other customers. Although initially they may be positively disposed to the organisation, without careful handling these people can easily turn into Terrorists.

- *The Victim.* When something goes wrong in service organisations, some customers appear to attract bad luck. Some jobs seem to be dogged by ill fortune. Victims may react in a number of ways, perhaps blowing incidents up out of all proportion or alternatively becoming resigned to their inevitable fate.

- *The Terrorist.* The Terrorist is the customer who mounts a damaging attack when you least expect it. An example might be the customer who declares his dissatisfaction loudly in the middle of a crowded restaurant, having told you earlier how good the food was.

- *The Incompetent.* Front-line staff should pay particular attention to this customer. It is possible that new customers may be confused by the organisation's procedures and, if not 'trained' by staff, may find the experience threatening with the result that they do not return. It is possible, of course, that some customers are incapable of being trained.

- *The Champion.* What all organisations want – people who are not only supportive of their staff and its service delivery and helpfully participate in the process but who make a point of providing positive word-of-mouth about the organisation, its services and staff.

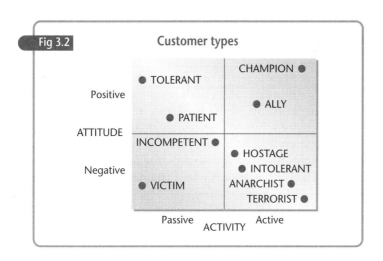

Fig 3.2 Customer types

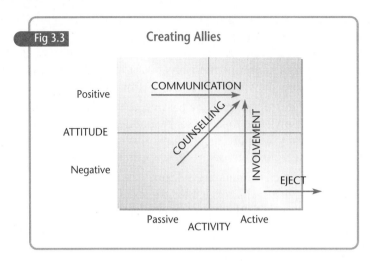

Fig 3.3 — Creating Allies

3.4.3 Creating Allies

Converting customers from the top left quadrant of Figure 3.2 into Allies is the easiest of the tasks. Allies are already positively disposed to the organisation but require engaging in the service delivery. The provision of information, good communication, explanation and involving them in process development through soliciting feedback may easily convert these customers.

The negatively disposed victims in the bottom left quadrant may require counselling and support to turn them into Allies. The risk here is that even after considerable effort Victims can easily turn into Hostages or Anarchists.

Anarchists and Terrorists are the most difficult yet important group of customers for the operation to deal with. De-selection (removal from the organisation) may be the best way out (see Chapter 8). On the other hand if these activists can be employed to the good of the organisation by harnessing their negative energy through personal involvement in the organisation and its processes, they can make powerful Allies, even Champions for the organisation and its cause.

3.5 CUSTOMER RETENTION

A key task for operations managers is retaining their valued customers (Allies and Champions) and valuable customers (high lifetime values). Retaining customers provides significant benefits for the organisation (see Chapter 11). The key benefit of maintaining loyal customers is in capturing the customer's revenue stream calculated as the lifetime spending of a customer (Reichheld 1996, Schlesinger and Heskett 1991). Loyal customers are Allies who are positively disposed to the organisation and use only that organisation when the need arises. This provides many benefits for the organisation. Loyal customers:

- generate long-term revenue streams (high lifetime values)
- tend to buy more than new customers

- tend to increase spending over time
- may be willing to pay premium prices
- provide cost savings since retaining customers is usually significantly cheaper than attracting new ones.

A less direct consequence of customer loyalty has been termed the 'loyalty ripple effect' (Gremler and Brown 1999). This recognises the value of positive word-of-mouth encouragement to other potential customers to use the organisation and its services together with other actions taken by the loyal customers that create value for the organisation. Examples of the latter provided by Gremler and Brown are customers who tidy restaurant tables after they have used them or report messy facilities to staff (see also Heskett *et al.* 1994, Heskett *et al.* 1997 and Peters 1987). So additional benefits from loyal customers are that they:

- provide new opportunities, acting as advocates for the organisation through positive word-of-mouth advertising, at little cost to the organisation (Champions)
- are concerned about the organisation and its services and help the organisation maintain and improve its services (Allies).

The enormous value of retention has been recognised by marketers and senior managers. By building long-term customer relationships, that in turn encourage customers to be loyal, managers and marketers have turned their attention from attracting new customers to retaining existing business (see, for example, Buttle 1996, Gummesson 1994 and 1999, Payne *et al.* 1995).

Marketing alone will not retain customers. The operation must deliver something of value to ensure loyalty. In the introduction (Figure 3.1), we outlined two aspects of relationship development. The first approach we termed 'enhanced' transactional, meaning that the customer–provider relationship is confined largely to a series of transactions, but that the customer becomes more loyal because the service outcome and experience is of a high standard and matches his or her requirement. Central to this approach is a perception that the organisation recognises the customer as being loyal and valued. In other words, there is some capability, often enabled by technology, that carries the memory of the customer from one transaction to another.

By increasing the depth as well as the length of the customer relationship, the second approach, 'relationship growth', is also linked to customer retention. As we shall see later in section 3.5, relationships which are multi-faceted, with multiple links between customer and provider, are far stronger than traditional transactional relationships.

A key problem in changing the emphasis to retention of customers is that many organisations do not have efficient means of calculating the value of loyal customers. 'If companies knew how much it really cost them to lose a customer, they would be able to make accurate evaluations of investments designed to retain customers. Unfortunately today's accounting systems do not capture the value of a loyal customer' (Reichheld and Sasser 1990).

3.5.1 Measuring customer retention

A relatively simple measure to put alongside sales figures is that of customer retention. This may be assessed on an annual basis, for example by tracking the number of customer accounts still 'active' during the year. In practice, of course, this is not always so straightforward. Retail customers frequently shop at more than one store, continuing to make regular purchases in each organisation. In this case the issue is more 'share of the wallet' than customer loyalty. Information systems linked to loyalty cards enable retailers to track trends in spending patterns to assess the 'loyalty' of various customer segments.

For some business-to-business services, customer retention is easy to measure in that the organisation may have only one or two major accounts. Loss of a customer in these cases will mean that the business will probably not survive. This is not the case for many mid-range businesses. One company that supplied chemicals to a wide range of business customers appeared, superficially, to be healthy with reasonable annual sales growth. This hid the fact that of a nominal customer base of over a hundred business accounts, more than 20 per cent had not placed an order in the last 12 months and a further 15 per cent had reduced their order value in the last six months. This analysis prompted the organisation to re-examine the nature of their customer relationships in order to reverse what had become a trend which threatened the business's future profitability.

3.5.2 Calculating the value of a customer

Lifetime value of a customer is of particular interest to high-volume consumer services, for two reasons:

- It provides a degree of motivation for personnel who may deal with high numbers of short customer transactions each day. The customer who makes a regular £4 purchase may not seem that important in the grand scheme of things, but this viewpoint might be changed if this equates to £1,000 annual spend multiplied by the expected loyalty lifetime in years.
- Calculating the lifetime value gives focus to marketing activities.

As indicated above, there are a number of issues to be resolved in thinking about lifetime value. The first is to understand what 'lifetime' really means, and to what extent does this really help in marketing and delivering service. If the argument about lifetime value is followed to its logical conclusion, would this lead service providers to ignore all customers over a certain age? Clearly not, because the direct revenue gained is still valuable, and the value of word-of-mouth advertising and referrals is impossible to calculate.

For the purposes of employee motivation, it may be useful to calculate a value such as annual spend, which makes the point that this £4 transaction customer is someone worth looking after and at the same time does not make potentially exaggerated claims about worth.

Equipment-based service providers have for a long time calculated lifetime revenues based on the economic life of the piece of capital equipment, its original sales price plus expected service, maintenance and repair revenues. This has enabled them to create competitive original equipment-pricing strategies, and to understand that significant resources must be made available to support these revenue streams.

More recently, mobile phone service providers had to use customer value information more defensively. In the rapid growth of the mobile phone market, providers supplied handsets free or at a fraction of their manufacturing cost in a bid to gain a significant market share. They discovered that many customers were not paying line rentals for a sufficiently long period to enable the promotional equipment discount costs to be recouped. As a result, a wider range of tariffs and contracts was introduced to reduce this deficit.

In thinking about the value of the customer it is useful to generate estimates of the following:

- Current and potential annual spend of customer segments, recognising that customers may use more than one service provider.
- The duration and durability of customer relationships. How long do customers remain loyal and is there potential for this to be extended?
- The number of points of contact with customers. How many different service products do they buy? Is there potential for cross-selling of service products?
- What is the current profitability of the customer? Is it costing us more to keep this customer than we are likely to recoup?

Financial services providers are particularly sensitive to this type of analysis. Although the company may offer a number of products from loans and mortgages through to pensions and insurance products, many find that a typical customer only takes one product from the range. They find, though, that once a customer buys two or three products, they tend to stay loyal for rather longer than the single-product customer.

3.5.3 Customer relationship management (CRM)

CRM is a term given to the management of customer relationships in high-volume consumer services, having the objective of growing profitable business. The essential difference between CRM and other approaches to customer retention is that the identification and enhancement of customer relationships is facilitated by technology. CRM attempts to integrate the many communication channels between an organisation's units and its customers, record information about customer preferences for example, and use the information to develop and strengthen the relationship and the profitability of the customer.

The aim of CRM is to collect data from all parts of the organisation to enable tracking and analysis of a single customer relationship as well as the identification of more general trends. For example, until recently it was possible that a customer of a financial services company would have a number of the products – a mortgage, savings accounts, and insurance. Each of these products would be handled by separate parts of the business, with no knowledge of the others. As a result, customers rarely felt that they had a relationship with 'the company'.

In order to redress this, many financial service organisations are turning to data warehousing. A data warehouse is an integrated source of data and it collects, cleans and stores information about customers. Adolf *et al.* (1997) have termed this as 'information-based continuous relationship marketing'. Data warehousing allows the organisation to view relationships and profitability across the organisation.

Companies are now moving to integrated CRM solutions with the advent of e-Commerce. Internet-enabled activity gives rise to the opportunity for companies to give information to their customers and collect data from them in a much more structured manner than previously. A smaller version of the data warehouse is the data mart. This serves a division or department of the organisation and should ideally be integrated with the enterprise's data warehouse. Such integration avoids repetition of the original problem of invisibility of customer relationships across the company.

Finally, these data marts and warehouses are linked to the various forms of technology at the customer interface. Telephone call centres are rapidly being replaced by multi-media contact centres. Customers have a choice of routes into the organisation, whether by letter, phone or Internet. Paper-based transactions have virtually disappeared from most organisations, though companies must guard against devaluing such transactions to the extent that insufficient attention is paid to them. An increasing number of transactions are carried out electronically. Computer telephony integration (CTI) allows the customer to browse the company web site and make contact with a human agent if required.

CRM is therefore aimed at both customer retention and relationship growth approaches as discussed in section 3.2.

3.5.4 Key account management (KAM)

Business-to-business customer relationships tend to be more intense than those experienced in high-volume consumer services. In some cases, a single customer may represent as much as 100 per cent of the business. This should focus the mind on customer retention, though it is surprising how complacent such organisations can be.

An approach appropriate for these situations where companies have a relatively small number of 'strategic' customers is key account management (KAM). In essence KAM recognises that these relationships are complex, with more than one channel of contact between provider and customer. Figure 3.4 illustrates the transition from a traditional ('bow tie') approach to buyer–supplier relationships to the KAM approach represented by the diamond.

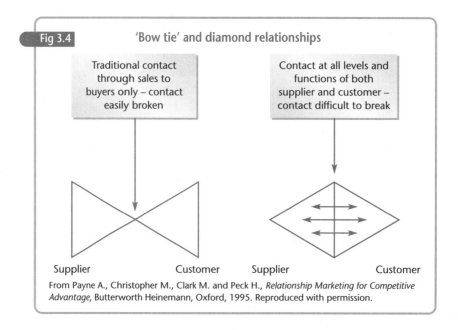

Fig 3.4   'Bow tie' and diamond relationships

Traditional contact through sales to buyers only – contact easily broken

Contact at all levels and functions of both supplier and customer – contact difficult to break

Supplier   Customer   Supplier   Customer

From Payne A., Christopher M., Clark M. and Peck H., *Relationship Marketing for Competitive Advantage*, Butterworth Heinemann, Oxford, 1995. Reproduced with permission.

In the traditional approach, transactions are channelled through one point of contact, a sales or contract manager. As Figure 3.4 indicates, the weakness of this approach is that the relationship is only as strong as the link between a single buyer and the sales or contract manager. This relationship is vulnerable to changes in personnel and some organisations regularly change their buyers in order to maintain 'arm's length' trading conditions. The danger for the supplier is that a change in a buyer might lead to a less favourable environment. The key point to note is that the relationship may be easily broken by competitors who manage to forge a strong contact with other influencers in the customer organisation.

The aim of KAM is to turn the traditional 'bow tie' relationship into a much stronger 'diamond'. In this format, links are encouraged across the boundary between the two organisations. The role of the key account manager is now not to act as a conduit through which all communication must flow, but rather to act as an enabler for the relationship. If the customer has a particular need, KAM is focused on setting up the dialogue between the appropriate parties. Of course, the key account manager must monitor the effectiveness of these relationships to avoid the occurrence of problems that will damage the long-term business.

This approach is particularly useful for professional service firms that contain individuals or groups which are encouraged to be entrepreneurial in business development. It is not uncommon for customers to be approached by numbers of these, all from the same organisation, effectively in competition with each other for the same business, thus giving the customer the impression that the firm does not know what it is doing.

For business-to-business customers, the customer retention approach is so vital, it is almost a 'blinding flash of the obvious' to say that the organisation should focus on customer loyalty. A loss of a customer can threaten the existence of many of these services. The relationship growth approach has to be the main emphasis here, looking to build more links and broadening the base of business connection.

3.6 RELATIONSHIPS

Loyal customers are created by providing a level of service that satisfies or even delights customers. Their loyalty can also be created and/or enhanced by building close 'relationships' with customers. It is important to note that there is a difference between relationship and loyalty and it is possible to confuse the two, particularly in high-volume services delivered to the mass consumer market. For organisations such as train companies, mass transit systems and even financial service providers, customers may be extremely loyal but not have a 'relationship' with the organisation.

Creating customer relationships, or relationship marketing as it is known, is about establishing, maintaining and enhancing relationships with customers for mutual benefit. The emphasis in relationship marketing is on the requirement to develop relationships with individual customers – one-to-one marketing (Peppers and Rogers 1993) – and with groups of like-minded people – affinity groups (Gummesson 1999) – rather than see any and every service as a one-off transaction.

Whilst the notion of relationship marketing appears to be very attractive, it is our belief that this is not appropriate in all situations. For example, in high-volume or commodity-based services, such as retail operations or mass transit systems, many customers may be more influenced by value for money than by a concept as intangible as a relationship. Indeed many customers do not wish for a 'relationship' with some organisations and their staff. This is not to dismiss this idea totally because there is no doubt that people often make decisions based on emotional or unconscious factors, despite thinking that they have been driven totally by logic. Indeed some marketing professionals believe that brands and brand values far outweigh any other factor in customer decision-making.

To try to deal with this apparent mismatch we would suggest that there are essentially two forms of relationship: first, a relationship based on a portfolio of service products frequently found in higher-volume operations; and second, a personal relationship created between an individual customer and an employee, particularly prevalent in low-volume professional organisations.

3.6.1 Product Relationships

Product relationships involve the 'capture' of the customer using a variety of products. Banks, for example, work hard to establish a relationship with their customers by selling (and in order to sell) multiple products, such as current accounts, loans, house loans, insurance and executor services. This provides the customer with benefits such as a single point of contact for their product portfolio, discounts for new products bought, loyalty bonuses etc. The downside for customers who wish to switch is often the difficulty in untying themselves from the set of products. The benefits for the organisation are that product relationships provide higher-value customers, a longer-term revenue stream, and opportunities to cross-sell other products or services to customers who are already engaged with the organisation and also provide valuable information from and about that customer base.

Many service providers, such as retailers, airlines and restaurant chains, actively promote product relationships and loyalty on existing products and service through loyalty schemes such as frequent-flyer programmes or 'club' cards for supermarkets. Most of these are in essence discount schemes encouraging the customer to earn points by spending more money with a particular provider rather than the competition. Such providers are 'buying loyalty' rather than 'building relationships'. However, the relationship can be developed by holding information about a customer's needs: for example, some hotels store information about their card-holding customers so that they are provided with a room that meets their requirements. Customers may also gain certain privileges: airline loyalty customers may be provided with access to executive lounges, free seat reservations, cheque-cashing facilities, company newsletters, opportunities to participate in special events, and opportunities to provide information to the organisation. All of these activities fall into the category of customer retention through the 'enhanced' transactional approach.

Some customers hold several 'loyalty' cards, undermining the very concept! Indeed studies in the behaviour of supermarket customers (e.g. Knox and Denison 1992) have identified large segments of 'promiscuous customers' who switch loyalty to whichever provider is currently offering the best deal.

3.6.2 Building personal relationships

Enhancing the client relationship can easily be overlooked by organisations who are operationally focused and busy delivering services and also by organisations at the other extreme which are 'market' focused and intent on increasing their customer base. Personal relationships can be established and enhanced in four key ways (Maister 1989, Payne *et al.* 1995):

- *Going the extra mile* – providing higher than expected levels of service on a current project such as providing enhanced documentation, analyses, explanations or even presentations, and/or greater accessibility to staff.

- *Increasing the amount of client contact* – frequent visits or telephone calls, creating contacts at different levels in the organisation, scheduling meetings and feedback/development sessions.

- *Building the business relationship* – for example, putting on special seminars for the client, helping them make other contacts, assistance with benchmarking, sending useful articles, even referring business to the client.

- *Building a social relationship* – providing social activities and tickets for events, remembering personal anniversaries etc.

In Box 3.3 the head of a global trading and shipping conglomerate explains how he tries to strengthen relationships with his suppliers and customers.

Box 3.3 GP Group (Bangkok)

The GP Group is a global trading and shipping company based in Bangkok. It is a family firm, which was established 125 years ago in Burma. It now has a turnover in excess of US$2 billion and comprises over 20 companies world-wide, specialising in commodity trading, ship chartering, ship management, rice production, seed research and production, manufacturing and exporting rubber products, chemicals, pharmaceuticals, jewellery and soya bean. It provides services such as property development, tour operations, plastic security cards, port management and project management.

Kirit Shah is the Chief Executive Officer and owner of the Group, and he explained his role in the diversified business. 'I am no longer personally involved in running any of my companies directly. All the companies have managing directors and they run the business on their own. I have good people. For the past 25 years I have been recruiting graduates from business schools. My typical day would involve meeting some of the directors and talking about what they are doing or working on a problem that they might have. I would meet a lot of their customers, their suppliers and their buyers, and I would typically host a lunch or dinner and meet them face to face to help them in their work.

'The way I try to strengthen our business relationships is to have face-to-face meetings with people. I know this is very much against the trend, which is about global communications, mobile telephones and instant communication. But just think about it: if I can sit face-to-face with someone I can see their reaction, which on a fax or email I cannot. As a buyer today you have a choice, the whole world wants to sell to you. So why me? Because you know me, because we had a meeting, had a drink, maybe our families know each other. It is the personal touch that I think is important in today's faceless world. We are all trying to get to a faceless situation but I don't think there is an effective substitute for personal interaction. And it's surprisingly easy to do, it's like an illusion. If you were in London and I was in London and I asked you for a meeting, chances are you would tell me, "OK, let's meet next month," or you might not even accept my call. On the other hand, if I call you from Bangkok, chances are you will take my call as a priority over something else that you were doing. So if I said I was coming from Bangkok and I can meet you the day after tomorrow, chances are that you will see me faster than you would see a guy who is next door or in the next street. It's the perception that he is always there but the guy from Bangkok is not, so I must see him at a time convenient to him, not at a time convenient to me.

'The downside is that we have to travel a lot more than we ever did. Now it's more intense than ever. Before, when I went on a trip it was one week; now, because of frequency of flights, I go somewhere for one day. Even when I go to London I land at six in the morning and I take a flight back at ten in the evening, having spent the day there. With more direct flights we are all burning ourselves trying to get to the farthest point on the globe in the shortest possible time and get back.'

Questions

1 *How does Kirit Shah go about strengthening his company's relationships with clients?*

2 *What are the advantages and problems associated with this approach?*

3.6.3 Attributes of relationships

The following are the key elements of a personal relationship between service provider and customer:

- **Communication.** The extent to which there is two-way communication; the ability to deliver clear messages, and the ability to listen carefully.
- **Trust.** The degree to which one partner depends on the work or recommendation of the other without seeking extra justification or collaboration. In some cases, the partner may commit the other to work without prior consultation.
- **Intimacy.** The extent to which each partner shares their plans, strategies, profits, etc.
- **Rules.** A mutual acceptance of how this particular relationship operates; what is acceptable and desirable, and what is not.

Moving from an 'arm's length', transaction-based approach to a relationship based on partnership clearly has operational implications. In Table 3.1 two organisations are compared, one a professional service (business-to-business), the other a high-volume consumer service (business-to-customer), in order to identify issues that must be dealt with by operations managers.

As we can see from inspection of Table 3.1, there may be considerable resource implications in adopting an approach based on broadening the relationship between customer and provider. Some of these implications are listed below:

- Processes and activities become less well defined and harder to predict.
- Capacity management is less precise, efficiency goals become harder to achieve.
- Processes must be more flexible in order to meet requirements that are ill defined at the start of the relationship.
- Staff will require a different set of competencies.

Table 3.1 Comparison of relationship attributes

	Professional service: management consultant	Consumer service: restaurant chain
Communication	Two-way Free flowing Transfer of knowledge Relates to business possibilities as well as current contracts A significant amount of time is devoted to communication	Largely one-way – from provider to customer, apart from order-taking Formal communication Relates to formal service offer This organisation does not budget for significant informal communication
Trust	Built between individuals (clients and consultants) in the course of the involvement May involve significant amounts of confidential and sensitive information	Built between customer and organisation largely by reliability (delivery to promise) Scope strictly limited to providing value-for-money meals in safe surroundings
Intimacy	Consultants become completely involved with the life of the client's organisation; often regarded as semi-permanent employees Part of the team	Involvement between employees and customers may be limited to order-taking and basic service. Customer intimacy is often linked to fortuitous discovery of common interests
Rules	Rules may be developed as part of the initial relationship-forming process Negotiation as to who does what is often part of initial evaluation, but the brief may change as the relationship develops	Rules are largely set by the organisation or service sector Based on established 'scripts', expected behaviour and assumed knowledge

3.6.4 Risk and relationships

There is often a link between the customer's perceived risk in purchasing or using the service and their desire for a type of relationship with the provider (see Table 3.2). Where the customer doesn't feel that there is much risk, either in making the purchase or in receiving the service, there may be limited opportunity for relationship building. The majority of supermarket customers probably do not have any depth of relationship with Tesco or Wal-Mart, though they may have preferences as to which store they shop in.

Table 3.2 Links between customer relationship and customer perceived risk

	Weak relationship (transaction based)	Strong relationship (partnership based)
High customer perceived risk	OPPORTUNITY	PROTECTED
Low customer perceived risk	BUY LOYALTY	FAMILIARITY

This resistance to relationship only applies, of course, when things are going well. If there is a significant service failure, customers may move quickly from low to high perceived risk. We will discuss this in more depth in the section on service recovery in Chapter 12. Where there is high customer perceived risk, but as yet a weak, transaction-based relationship, there is opportunity for the organisation to build stronger links.

Where there are strong relationships in situations where the customer feels there is significant risk, the emotional switching costs for customers are high. It is likely that these customers will not move unless the relationship is significantly damaged in some way. An example of services of this type is a consultant who may have both a particular expertise and intimate knowledge of the client's company and markets. These relationships are most common in professional services and/or business-to-business services.

Of course, strong relationships may exist where there is low perceived risk, though they are probably rare in commodity services. In many cases these may be one-sided relationships where the customer has a stronger emotional bond to the company than is possible for any one employee to reciprocate. Again, we will return to these customers in our discussion of service recovery in Chapter 12, but it is sufficient to say that if there is service failure, these customers may feel let down, rather than merely angry that something has gone wrong.

An important point to note here is to recognise that in many cases the relationship is formed at the deepest level between individuals rather than with the organisation as a whole. This is particularly true with professional services. When a senior partner leaves to join another firm, his/her clients may follow him/her. The risk for the client in forming a relationship with an unknown quantity, even from the same organisation, may be too great.

In this instance, risk may also have an explicit or implicit cost dimension. The time spent on the client's behalf so that the 'professional' can understand the issues fully in order to make informed judgements will represent a personal investment that will not be undertaken lightly. Cost is clearly not the only issue. If the process demands that client and professional work together for significant periods of time, personal chemistry may well be a significant factor.

3.7 PARTNERSHIPS AND ALLIANCES

Many of the challenges of customer relationships are mirrored by supplier relationships. These are covered in more depth in Chapter 5. It is sufficient to note here that there are many different forms of relationship, covering the spectrum from transaction based on the one hand to full partnership on the other. These include:

● partnerships
● joint ventures
● alliances
● preferred supplier
● sole supplier

- long-term contract
- short-term contracts
- transaction based.

Each of these variants will have its own operational challenges. It is interesting to observe that a number of companies have retreated from 'full partnership' relationships. Indeed Gerry Decker, as vice-president of NCR responsible for overseeing relationships, identified the growth of 'fruit fly' relationships, indicating that partners, particularly in the business-to-business environment, may form a temporary alliance to meet a specific need with no assumption that the partnership will continue.

The management of contractual relationships is often fraught with difficulty. This is particularly true where an aspect of the customer's business has been outsourced to a specialist provider. Examples of this lie in the area of facilities management or information technology support. In order to ensure 'value for money', customer and supplier often enter into service-level agreements (SLAs) (see also Chapter 5). Table 3.3 gives examples of key measures included in typical service-level agreements.

Table 3.3 Examples of service-level agreement measures

Help desk support	
Telephone response	95% within 3 rings
Problem resolution	65% through first line support within 8 hours
	35% through second line support within 24 hours
Complaint escalation	To first line manager after 8 working hours
	To senior manager after 16 working hours
Request for software fix	Initial response within 5 working days
	Outline proposal within 15 working days
Equipment maintenance	
Response to non-critical fault	2 working days
Response to critical fault	2 hours
First time fix rate	95%
Schedule adherence	95% within 2 working days
Spares availability	95% within 48 hours
	100% within 5 working days

The advantage of SLAs is that the measures provide a basis for review of how well the relationship is working. The disadvantage is that it is impossible to describe all facets of service provision through an SLA. If the relationship deteriorates to a 'nit-picking' review of performance against an increasing list of measures, it is likely that it will not continue. Worse still, SLAs are sometimes used to exert undue pressure on suppliers. For example, if a supplier has performed very well against the agreed measures, instead of providing thanks and an extended contract the purchaser may try to reduce the price on the assumption that the supplier had more resources than necessary to meet the performance targets.

3.8 TEMPORARY RELATIONSHIPS

High-volume consumer services often require the formation of temporary relationships, where customer connections are made quickly. Many sales processes depend on the ability of the salesperson to establish common ground with the prospective customer. When the customer is buying something that cannot be readily assessed, part of the purchasing process may include a conscious or unconscious assessment of the competence and honesty of the organisation's representative.

A combination of perceived risk and lack of knowledge on the customer's part will mean that the possibility for relationship will increase, given the need for reassurance on the customer's part. Examples might include purchasing a used car or a personal pension, where the customer is often incapable of making a totally informed decision.

These relationships might, at face value, appear relatively shallow, but there are clear implications for the service operation that recognises their value. The development of information systems to give customer history, training of customer contact staff and allocated time for each customer transaction (performance targets) are examples of areas to be addressed. Some call centres have intentionally relaxed their 'talk time' targets to allow more space for these temporary relationships and have found that although each agent may talk to fewer customers, orders of higher value are being taken as a result of the effectiveness of the temporary relationship.

3.9 SUMMARY

Customer relationships development

- It is important to be clear about the required type of relationship.
- A transactional approach can develop into a customer retention approach or a relationship growth approach.

Customers

- 'Customers' may be external, internal, intermediaries, end users, payers, beneficiaries, participants, stakeholders and valuable or non-valuable.
- Managers need to understand the types of customers, their respective values and recognise conflicts amongst different customer groups.

Customer segmentation – an operations view

- Operations managers need to develop an understanding of the nature of individual customers and their likely attitude and behaviour.
- Operational categories of customers include the Ally, the Hostage, the Anarchist, the Patient, the Tolerant, the Intolerant, the Victim, the Terrorist, the Incompetent and the Champion.

Customer retention

- A key task for operations managers is retaining valued customers (Allies and Champions) and valuable customers (high lifetime values).

- Customer lifetime values depend upon current and potential annual spend, the duration and durability of customer relationships, the number of points of contact with customers and the profitability of the customer.

Relationships

- There are two main forms of relationship, those based on a portfolio of products and those based on personal relationships.
- Customer relationships can be strengthened by going the extra mile, increasing the amount of client contact, building the business relationship and building a social relationship.
- The key attributes of a personal relationship are communication, trust, intimacy and rules.

Partnerships and alliances

- The challenges of customer relationships are mirrored by supplier relationships.
- Service-level agreements are a key way of defining relationships.

Temporary relationships

- High-volume consumer services often require the formation of temporary relationships.
- It is helpful to understand how to generate maximum value from such relationships.

3.10 DISCUSSION QUESTIONS

1. How would you classify yourself and your colleagues/friends in terms of your attitude to a particular service? Could everyone be converted into Allies and if so, how?

2. Calculate your lifetime value for a supermarket, electrical retailer, and bank. What are the problems in assessing lifetime values?

3. Assess the personal relationship you have with a professional service provider. How well is the relationship managed?

3.11 QUESTIONS FOR MANAGERS

1. Is your organisation pursuing a relationship approach? Is this what customers desire?

2. Have you considered the resources required for developing customer relationships?

3. To what extent do your processes take into account the differing needs of your target customer segments?

4. Do you understand the value of a customer? Is it possible to calculate the lifetime revenue that each customer represents?

5. Can you identify different customer behaviours? Can you provide training and/or procedures to deal with these differences?

6. How important is customer retention to your business? How can the customer defection rate be reduced?

3.12 SUGGESTIONS FOR FURTHER READING

Featherstone M., *Consumer Culture and Postmodernism*, Sage, London, 1991.

Gabriel Y. and Lang T., *The Unmanageable Consumer*, Sage Publications, London, 1995.

Payne A., Christopher M., Clark M. and Peck H., *Relationship Marketing for Competitive Advantage*, Butterworth Heinemann, Oxford, 1995.

3.13 REFERENCES

Adolf R., Grant-Thompson S., Harrington W. and Singer M., 'What Leading Banks are Learning about Big Databases and Marketing', *McKinsey Quarterly*, Summer 1997, no. 3, pp. 187–92.

Buttle F., 'Relationship Marketing', in Buttle F. (ed.), *Relationship Marketing, Theory and Practice*, Paul Chapman Publishing, London, 1996.

Gremler D.D. and Brown S.W., 'The Loyalty Ripple Effect: Appreciating the full value of customers', *International Journal of Service Industry Management,* vol. 10, no. 3, 1999, pp. 271–91.

Gummesson E., 'Making Relationship Marketing Operational', *International Journal of Service Industry Management*, vol. 5, no. 5, 1994, pp. 5–20.

Gummesson E., *Total Relationship Marketing*, Butterworth Heinemann, Oxford, 1999.

Heskett J.L., Sasser W.E. and Schlesinger L.A., *The Service Profit Chain,* Free Press, New York, 1997.

Heskett J.L., Jones T.O., Loveman G.W., Sasser W.E. and Schlesinger L.A., 'Putting the Service Profit Chain to Work', *Harvard Business Review*, March–April 1994, pp. 164–74.

Knox S.D. and Denison T.J., *Profiling the Promiscuous Shopper, Evaluating Shopper Loyalty*, Air Miles Travel Promotions Ltd, Sussex, 1992.

Payne A., Christopher M. Clark M. and Peck H., *Relationship Marketing for Competitive Advantage*, Butterworth Heinemann, Oxford, 1995.

Peppers D. and Rogers M., *The One to One Future*, Currency/Doubleday, New York, 1993.

Peters T.J., *Thriving on Chaos: Handbook for a management revolution*, Harper and Rowe, New York, 1987.

Reichheld F., *The Loyalty Effect*, Harvard Business School Press, Cambridge, Mass., 1996.

Reichheld F. and Sasser W.E., 'Zero Defections: Quality comes to services', *Harvard Business Review*, September–October 1990, pp. 105–11.

Schlesinger L.A. and Heskett J.L., 'The Service-Driven Service Company', *Harvard Business Review*, September–October 1991, pp. 71–81.

CASE EXERCISE

The National Brewery

This case was co-written by Dr Rhian Silvestro, Warwick Business School

The National Brewery has over 5,000 pubs in the UK, many of which used to be 'tenanted' houses, i.e. a tenant was appointed to run the pub and s/he was overseen by an area manager. The area managers would pay regular visits to assess the pub's financial position, the success of recent activities and the licensee's plans for the future. Recent legislation, as a result of a Monopolies and Mergers Commission report which found an industry dominated by big brewers which were squeezing smaller real ale brewers out of the industry, forced the big brewers, of which National was one, either to sell a proportion of their pubs or to release them from their tie to the brewery's products.

Some of the big brewers took their pubs back into management and therefore outside the jurisdiction of the legislation, while others sold off their chains of public houses to other companies. Both of these strategies have had the effect of reducing the likelihood of the introduction of guest beers. National decided to change over 2,000 of its tenanted pubs to leased pubs and give the tenants the opportunity to purchase (usually) a 20-year lease. This was seen by many licensees as a golden opportunity to have not only security and control over their futures but also something of value that they could either pass on or sell in the years to come. National recognised that with each of these pubs becoming an independent business in its own right, away from the direct control of the parent company, it needed to create a new body to help and support these pubs in their growth and development. Thus a partnership approach was born through a specially created subsidiary, National Support Services (NSS).

National Support Services

In order to provide the new, extensive and comprehensive range of support and developmental services National have done away with the area managers and appointed NSS managers (NSSMs) to work with licensees to help them develop their businesses. Some of them previously worked as area managers but over 50 per cent were new to the business. The services include sales promotions packages and beer discounts which are delivered directly by the NSSM, together with advice on catering, property, security, financial matters, legal problems, quality standards and training on any aspect of the business, which are provided by NSS consultants. All these services are provided free to lessees. Information about the products is provided in glossy brochures available from the NSSMs.

One NSSM, Richard Jenkins, explained how things have changed. 'In the days before the lease agreements the then area managers had the right to require meetings with their licensees and to demand financial and promotional plans. Now, in the new spirit of partnership, the relationship is much more supportive. It is up to the NSSM to prove to the licensee the need for his or her support. This is achieved in all but a very few instances.' Richard added, 'It's OK for those who are doing well and using our services but what do I do if they then turn round and say that, apart from our beer and lager (which they are required to sell under the terms of the lease), they don't want to sell other National products? Should I continue to offer all of the services or should I withdraw them? Also, what do I do for the lessee who is running a pub in a poor location? These licensees have not been overly receptive to many of the new possibilities – indeed, many of them just want us to reduce their rents, which we don't have the authority to do, or offer unlimited quantities of discounted or free beer for promotional purposes.

'You must realise that delivering the Support Services is not cheap. The payback for these costs comes from the enhanced rental income from our properties. This is achieved by having better-performing businesses because of the support provided by NSS. Some lessees have claimed that their rents have about doubled since the change in agreement. This increase in rents reflects, in part, the increased value that the licensees can now obtain from the premium on the assignment of their business, and their entitlement to take on guest beers.'

National has three types of pub – the community pub, the tavern and the food pub – and it has put out to lease about equal numbers of each type. Examples of these pubs and a summary of their financial position are as follows.

The White Lion, a 'community pub', is a male-dominated, traditional pub in a run-down area of Nottingham, where unemployment has been high for the past 20 years. There are several pubs of similar style in the area. The pub does not have a restaurant but offers bar snacks and sandwiches. The bar offers a limited product range and sells mainly beer. The pub was last refurbished 15 years ago and the decor is now somewhat the worse for wear.

The Oak, a 'tavern', is located in a prosperous working-class suburb in Nottingham. It is a popular family pub, although there are a number of similar offerings in the area. The pub was refurbished at moderate cost five years ago. It remains in good condition and has a friendly atmosphere. The Oak has one restaurant offering a standard menu, and typical spend on food is around £8–9 per head. Pub lunches may be ordered from the bar. There is an indoor family area and an outdoor play area for children.

The Castle, a 'food pub', is a new pub located in an affluent, suburban location in a residential area in Nottingham. The pub is well differentiated in its locality, having a smart, fashionable, 'designer' feel to it, with bright, well co-ordinated furnishings and fittings. The pub targets the business community at lunch times. It is popular with 'yuppies' and 'dinkies' (double income, no kids) in the evenings. There is a 'wayside inn' style restaurant which offers an extensive menu including traditional and ethnic dishes, where typical spend on food is around £15–20 per head. Light meals can be ordered at the bar. Wine and cocktails are popular.

Financial summaries: 1999

	White Lion	The Oak	The Castle
Trading square footage (front of house)	1,000	1,500	2,000
Mix of income (ex. accomm.)			
Liquor sales	90%	83%	35.5%
Food sales	6%	14%	63%
Machine income net	3%	2%	0.5%
Other income	1%	1%	1%
Total annual income	£150,000	£320,000	£450,000
Margin			
Liquor margin	45%	53%	58%
Food margin	40%	54%	67%
Gross margin	43%	52%	63%
Cost ratios to total income			
Wages	11.0%	14.0%	17.7%
Fuel	2.8%	2.6%	2.9%
Trade expenses	1.8%	2.1%	3.4%
Equipment repairs	1.2%	1.3%	1.5%
Promotions	3.3%	2.8%	2.0%
Depreciation	2.0%	2.3%	3.0%
Rates, water, insurance	3.6%	3.4%	3.5%
Building repairs	2.3%	1.5%	1.0%
Overall costs	28%	30%	35%
House net profit	15%	22%	28%
Cumulative profit growth over three years (1997–99, *not* adjusted for inflation)	5%	10%	19%

Questions

1 *Evaluate National Support Services from the point of view of their customers, i.e. the lessees.*

2 *How should the National Brewery go about developing its Support Services to meet the needs of all its lessees?*

4

Customer Expectations and Satisfaction

4.1 INTRODUCTION

The customer is an input resource for many service operations and thus not only do we need to know how to manage the customer (Chapter 8) but also we need to understand what they expect from the operation. Most importantly, they are in most cases the final judge as to how well the quality of the service matches up to requirements, and by their continued support determine its long-term success. This should be more than sufficient motivation for operations managers to ensure that there is a match between expectations and service delivery in order to satisfy or even delight their customers.

The objectives of this chapter are:

- to understand customer satisfaction and service quality
- to discuss customer expectations and how they are created
- to define customer expectations using the service quality factors
- to describe means of finding customer expectations and assessing satisfaction
- to discuss how operations managers can manage perceptions during service delivery.

Although the need to satisfy customers is something that 'goes without saying', this is precisely the problem with many organisations. Assumptions are made about what customers really want and, even if customers have been consulted, it may be such a long time in the past that this information is at best irrelevant, and often positively dangerous. Professional services, in particular, frequently suffer from an attitude of thinking that they know best, because they are the experts. This might be true but this attitude can create blind spots in dealing with customers.

Understanding what satisfies and delights customers is something that must be continually addressed, using a variety of means to ensure that the answers do not fall into well-established patterns simply because the way the questions are asked doesn't vary sufficiently. Customer satisfaction is something that can be managed to some extent by influencing customers' perceptions and expectations of service delivery. This demands in-depth understanding of this subject.

Finally, in this introduction, it is no accident that many of those companies that have a reputation for excellent service spend time and money in listening to customers. Disney, for example, invented a new term for the activity of collecting information from customers. It is called 'guestology', reflecting Disney's approach to treat their visitors as guests rather than mere customers.

4.2 CUSTOMER SATISFACTION AND SERVICE QUALITY

The purpose of trying to understand customers' expectations is to try to ensure that service can be designed and delivered in order to meet those expectations. If the operation meets the expectations, or indeed exceeds them, then customers are satisfied with the service. If they are satisfied they are more likely to use the service again, happily, and may even recommend it to others (their post-purchase intentions).

4.2.1 Customer satisfaction

In simple terms, satisfaction is the result of a customer's assessment of a service based on a comparison of their perceptions of service delivery with their prior expectations (see Figure 4.1) (see, for example, Bitner and Hubbert 1994).

If the customer's perception of the service, the experience and outcomes, matches their expectations then they should be satisfied (or at least satisficed). If their perception of the service exceeds their expectations then they will be more than satisfied, even delighted. If their perceptions of the service don't meet their expectations then they may be dissatisfied, even outraged (Schneider and Bowen 1999). (This is sometimes referred to in the consumer behaviour literature as the disconfirmation theory; see, for example, Cadotte *et al.* 1987, Churchill and Surprenant 1982, Oliver and DeSarbo 1988.)

Satisfaction is the outcome of the consumer's evaluation of a service and can be represented on a continuum from (extreme) delight to (extreme) dissatisfaction, which we have labelled from +5 to –5 (see Figure 4.2).

Thus expectations, and indeed perceptions, are key components in delivering a quality service. Operations managers need to understand and define expectations in order to:

1. Specify, design and then deliver the appropriate service at the appropriate cost.

2. Encourage marketers to try to influence customers' prior expectations so that they can be delivered.

3. Understand how to manage – indeed manipulate – customer perceptions during the service, to achieve the desired level of satisfaction.

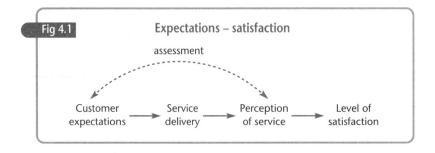

Fig 4.1   Expectations – satisfaction assessment

Customer expectations → Service delivery → Perception of service → Level of satisfaction

Fig 4.2 The satisfaction continuum

4.2.2 Outstanding customer service

Some organisations define their business as exceeding customer expectations in order to continually delight the customers. Some superior service companies such as American Express and Singapore Airlines, for example, maintain their superior market positions by constantly developing and improving their services (outcome and experience), to build loyalty and continually keep them ahead of their competitors.

Less capable organisations that seek to emulate this strategy may find it difficult to do so unless they have the resources to continually develop their services. If you tell your customers that your intention is to delight them, then you may have to ensure your service is even better the next time they use it.

David Good, the General Manager of a high-class resort hotel on the island of Koh Samui, explains in Box 4.1 how he delivers outstanding service to his guests.

Box 4.1 The Central Samui Beach Resort Hotel

The Central Samui Beach Resort Hotel is the leading full-service resort hotel on Koh Samui, a tropical island paradise in the Gulf of Thailand. The hotel is located on the palm-fringed Chaweng beach, the longest and most beautiful beach on the island. The 'new colonial' style hotel has 208 rooms which overlook the tropical gardens, swimming pools and beach. The hotel has excellent facilities including swimming pools, tennis courts, fitness centre, spa and three restaurants.

David Good is the General Manager of the hotel and he explained why guests choose this hotel. 'There are three main reasons why our guests come here: location, space and service. Our location is ideal, a beautiful island with a superb all-year-round climate, but also we are located on Chaweng beach which is the best beach with the best nightlife. Indeed I reckon we have probably the best piece of property on the best bit of the best beach on the whole island. Space too is important. Guests don't like to feel cramped. We have large gardens and common areas so that our guests are able to spread out. They really seem to appreciate that.

'Finally there is our service, which is as good as you will find in the best hotels around the world. It is very traditionally Thai. Our staff are very good-natured and friendly and they provide genuine hospitality and warmth. This has a big impact on our guests. We receive many thank-you letters and guests often send us the photographs they have had taken with the staff, asking us to pass them on with thanks. We also have a large number of returning guests, running at around 5 per cent, and growing, which is amazing given the short length of time we have been open.'

The hotel provides an outstanding level of service and David went on to explain what this means. 'First, we have very few problems or complaints. Indeed, I can honestly say we have no big issues which result in negative feedback. We do, like any hotel, have some minor issues, just small irritations. Right now, for example, we occasionally have problems with water pressure. Some people don't have quite as clear a sea view as they might have hoped, with some trees and bushes in the garden slightly obscuring their view. Some say the curry was a little too spicy.

'Second, high-quality service is about consistency. Consistency is important. When our guests come back they very much expect the same high level of service which delighted them the first time and which continues to delight them. The issue for us is to provide that same level of service – the smiles, the greeting, the helpfulness – day in, day out.

'Third, it's about the little things, personal touches, such as taking time with guests; a few minutes here and there to acknowledge people, or spend a few minutes talking with them. The guest relations staff, for example, sometimes send small gifts to our guests if it's their birthday or if they are a returning guest or if they're on honeymoon or it's their anniversary. We try and track all these things – little surprises here and there – it's these small things that really stick in people's minds.'

Questions

1 *How does the Central Samui Hotel go about providing outstanding customer service?*

2 *By delighting customers on their first visit to the hotel, is David in danger of raising expectations so that they won't be delighted on subsequent visits?*

4.2.3 Service quality

The term 'service quality' is often used to mean different things. Some managers use the term to mean how the customer is treated. This is perhaps more accurately called 'quality of service', as opposed to service quality which could be taken to mean the entirety of outcome and experience. It has been the theme running through this book that service operations must be taken as a whole rather than simply concentrating on the points of contact with customers, important as they are. Other definitions include 'satisfaction', 'a relative impression of the organisation and its services' and 'quality delivered'.

Satisfaction

Sometimes service quality is used to mean the same as satisfaction, i.e. the degree of fit between a customer's expectations and perceptions of a service.

A relative impression of the organisation and its services

Service quality is more often used as a more enduring construct, whereas satisfaction is situation and experience specific (Oliver 1993). Satisfaction has to be experienced (Oliver 1993), whereas customers may have views about an organisation's service quality without ever having experienced the service. Bitner and Hubbert (1994) define service quality as the 'consumer's overall impression of the relative inferiority/superiority of the organisation and its services'. Recent empirical work would also suggest that there is an interactive relationship between satisfaction and service quality, i.e. each can have a moderating effect on the other, and therefore on post-purchase intentions (Taylor and Baker 1994). Patterson and Johnson (1993) suggested that satisfaction judgements decay into service quality, an overall attitude about the service.

Quality delivered

When we talk about service quality from an operations perspective we usually mean the quality of the service we deliver, i.e. does it consistently meet the specification for that service? This, of course, may be different to how a customer sees the service (their perceived service quality), and thus there may be a mismatch between a customer's expectations of a service and their perception of its delivery. This mismatch could be the result of either a mismatch between expectation and delivery and/or a mismatch between delivery and perception (see Figure 4.3). (This is a simplified version of the Gap Model developed by Parasuraman *et al.* 1985.)

There are several reasons why Gap 1 might exist. The service may have been inappropriately specified or designed, or there may be insufficient resources to meet expectations. It is also possible that the customer may have inappropriate expectations. An inappropriate specification or design of the service may be the result of a poor understanding of customer expectations by managers. Managers may have not put enough time and effort into either specifying the service concept and service delivery or getting feedback from customers about what they feel to be an appropriate level of service. Insufficient resources may be the result of a poor understanding of market requirements or demand profiles.

These 'internal' reasons often stem from a lack of determination to deliver consistently high standards. Managers consistently report a view that their organisation does not take the time and trouble to understand what its customers want and therefore the service design process is flawed from the outset. This flows into poor or inappropriate service design and results in poor resource utilisation.

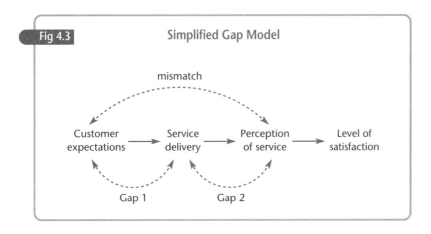

Fig 4.3   Simplified Gap Model

Inappropriate expectations may be the result of inappropriate marketing, promises made by the organisation which cannot be delivered, or inappropriate word-of-mouth or organisational image which may be the result of poor service experiences in the past. Also, there are some customers who have quite unrealistic expectations of some service organisations and can cause a great deal of aggravation and nuisance as a result. These individuals need either their expectations re-shaping before or during service delivery, or removing from the operation, if this is feasible (see Chapter 8).

Gap 2 may be the result of either incorrect delivery of a service or customers inappropriately perceiving the service. Incorrect delivery is not unusual in many service organisations. Service operations are often complex, human-based activities and things do go wrong. A mismatch as a result of poor delivery can be removed or at least reduced through service recovery (see Chapter 12). In service organisations we need to remember that 'reality' is what the customers perceive it to be, and that customers will perceive each service in their own personal, emotional and sometimes irrational way. Customers' perception of the quality of the service may not be the same as the quality of the service delivered because humans tend to filter what they see and experience:

- selective filtering – only noticing what is relevant to current needs
- selective distortion – modifying and seeking information that supports personal beliefs and prejudices
- selective retention – remembering only those things that are relevant to needs and beliefs.

Ideally there should be a match between service quality (the quality of what the operation delivers) and the quality of the service as perceived by the customer. Table 4.1 summarises the reasons for the existence of the gaps and therefore dissatisfied customers.

Table 4.1 Reasons for gaps

	Gap 1	Gap 2
Internal causes	Lack of understanding of customer expectations Inappropriate specification Poor service design Insufficient resources	Incorrect delivery
External causes	Inappropriate expectations of the service experience and/or outcome	Inappropriate perceptions of the service experience and/or outcome

4.2.4 Downsides of the expectation–perception approach to service quality

Whilst the expectation–perception approach to understanding service quality is extremely useful in focusing on the outcome of customer satisfaction and helps focus on mismatches between operational and customer views of quality, it does have some downsides (see, for example, Grönroos 1993).

Service could be perceived to be 'good' when it is 'bad'

If customer expectations are particularly low (and indeed may have been deliberately created that way), poor service may be perceived as highly satisfying because expectations have been exceeded! This may look like a reasonable state, but is clearly one which is extremely vulnerable to competitive threat from higher-quality providers.

Service could be perceived to be 'bad' when it is 'good'

Likewise it is also possible that if expectations are high, due to over-promising for example, then a good service may be seen as inadequate.

Service which was 'good' last time may only be 'OK' this time

If a service was perceived to have been 'good', then the customer's expectations may be raised for next time; thus they may well be less satisfied on subsequent occasions despite the fact that the quality of the service has remained unchanged! This is a problem encountered by Disney. Visitor's first encounter with the Magic Kingdom is often so good – much better than expected – that subsequent visits are sometimes reported to be poorer in quality.

'Satisfied' customers may switch

Even though a particular service may meet customers' expectations and customers are satisfied, customers may still switch suppliers, if there is a choice. Alternative service providers may offer a superior level of service, additional service features, or customers may be naturally disloyal or inquisitive. When it comes to measuring satisfaction, we need to remember also to measure the customers' post-purchase intentions – in particular, will they return? (It is also important to remember that some dissatisfied customers will not switch and they may create particular problems for service employees!)

Nortel, the telecommunications company, surveyed its customers and discovered that those who scored up to 4 on a scale from 1 to 5 (1= very dissatisfied, 5 = very satisfied) were vulnerable to switching. Only those scoring above 4.5 could be thought of as reasonably loyal. Avis Rent-a-Car tracks likelihood to repurchase alongside customer satisfaction. In the early 1990s they developed a 'customer satisfaction balance sheet', estimating the cost to the company in lost sales as a result of poor service.

These issues reinforce the need to link closely the creation of expectations in the minds of customers with the process that tries to deliver service, i.e. to communicate messages to set appropriate expectations and to design and deliver service to meet them and manage them during the service process. We need to see the process of satisfaction formation as a dynamic process (this has been called quality dynamics – Ojasalo 1999).

4.3 CUSTOMER EXPECTATIONS

Organisations need to understand expectations, understand the competition and need to manage expectations. Indeed it may be appropriate to try to rein in customers' expectations in order to keep them at the right level that can be met or just exceeded by service delivery. This is a key challenge for service operations managers.

4.3.1   Levels of expectations

Expectations exist somewhere on a range or continuum, between ideal and intolerable (see Figure 4.4). An intolerable train journey may be one that arrives very late, or even not at all, where the carriages are filthy and the staff abusive. An ideal train journey might be clean, on time, very fast, and include chauffeur-driven transport at either end. The positioning of our expectations, i.e. what we believe to be likely, will vary depending upon which country we are in and the price we are paying, for example.

Some points on this continuum could be defined as follows (see, for example, Zeithaml *et al.* 1993):

- Ideal   the best possible
- Ideal feasible   what should happen given the price or the industry standard
- Desirable   the standard that the customer wants to receive
- Deserved   the level of performance that the customer ought to receive given the perceived costs
- Minimum tolerable   the minimum tolerable standards, those that must be achieved
- Intolerable   the standards the customers should not receive.

It has been suggested that our expectations are not a single point on this scale but a range defined by what customers believe to be likely ('will' expectations) and what they believe 'should' happen, i.e. ideal feasible expectations (Boulding *et al.* 1993). Customers will also be able to differentiate between a 'should' expectation which may be formed as a result of little or no actual experience, and a 'will' expectation based on experience with the service.

The critical point here is that we should be careful when asking customers about their expectations. The questions:

- What would you like?
- What should be provided?
- What would be acceptable?

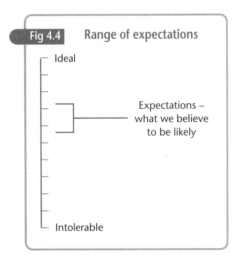

Fig 4.4   **Range of expectations**

Ideal

Expectations –
what we believe
to be likely

Intolerable

may each provide a different response as they refer to different points on the scale.

This range or zone of expectations, as shown in Figure 4.4, is usually referred to as the zone of tolerance and has been defined as the range between desired and minimum acceptable standards (Zeithaml *et al.* 1993). This zone of 'acceptable outcomes' is shown in Figure 4.5.

The importance of this zone of tolerance is that customers may accept variation within a range of performance and any increase or decrease in performance within this area will only have a marginal effect on perceptions (Strandvik 1994). Only when performance moves outside of this range will it have any real effect on perceived service quality.

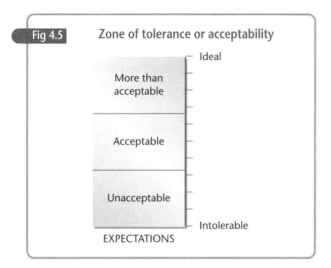

Fig 4.5 Zone of tolerance or acceptability

It has been suggested that the width of this zone of tolerance is inversely proportional to a customer's level of involvement and commitment (Johnston 1995a). This term refers to a customer's level of interest in a service, the importance they attach to it, and their emotional commitment to the service (see, for example, Dibb *et al.* 1997). For example, participants on a training course who have been sent, possibly against their will, may become hypercritical of details of training materials and course content because they have no real commitment to the objectives of the programme. Mature students, on the other hand, who are probably paying for a postgraduate business qualification may be more supportive. This doesn't mean that they will necessarily accept poor quality, but the process by which they raise the issues and seek for a joint solution will often be quite positive. The fact that they have personally invested time and money in the course certainly changes their commitment to it and its success.

4.3.2 Fuzzy expectations

In some instances customers' expectations may be somewhat unclear and they may not be certain what they expect from a service provider, although they may have quite clear views about what is unacceptable. This vague idea about what is required has been called 'fuzzy' expectations (Ojasalo 1999). Ojasalo suggested that expectations, as a whole, are seldom fuzzy but 'that they usually include elements which are more or less fuzzy'. In some cases these expectations may be implicit and are not actively or consciously thought about by customers but they may become explicit when expectations are either not met or exceeded.

Whether customers' expectations are fuzzy or crystal clear, operations managers have to be certain about the expectations they are trying to meet. They need to understand them, define them, and then specify them to ensure that what they deliver meets that specification (this is what operations managers mean by service quality). In many cases this will require providing guidance to customer-facing staff to encourage them to ask questions to clarify the real needs of the customer, rather than to assume that what they are being asked for is actually what is required. Customers are often afraid of looking silly in front of other people (both customers and staff), and may ask for something quite inappropriate, leading to eventual dissatisfaction and defection. In effect, service operations managers need to revisit the service concept (Chapter 2) to identify possible gaps between what is in the mind of the customer and what is in the mind of the service provider.

4.3.3 Influencing expectations

Customers' expectations will be influenced by many things (see Figure 4.6).

Price often has a large influence on expectations. The higher the price, the higher up the continuum towards ideal are customers' expectations. One's expectations of flying tourist class from Paris to Chicago will be at a different level from these flying business or first class. All three customers will have similar expectations about safety and timeliness, but expectations about leg-room, quality of food, attentiveness of the service, ease of check-in may vary considerably. Price is perhaps one of the most important as customers are concerned not just about the service (outcome and experience) but also its value (see Chapter 2).

The *alternative services available* will also help define and set expectations. If you have recently flown business class and the cabin attendants called you by name, you may expect this level of treatment on flights by other carriers.

Marketing can have a considerable influence on expectations. Marketing, image, branding and advertising campaigns help set expectations, often at great cost to the organisation. Also, less controllable *word-of-mouth marketing* can have a profound effect on a customer's expectations. Indeed, in some situations, word-of-mouth may have a stronger influence than organisational marketing.

Previous experience will help shape expectations as prior knowledge makes them not only clearer and sharper but allows customers more accurately to position them on the scale. Previous experience also acts as a moderator on marketing information either from the organisation or by word-of-mouth. It is important to note that previous experience may not be of the service provider in question but of other service providers. Our expectations for how we will be treated when we ring up our electricity supplier with a query will be influenced by our experiences with other call centres such as utilities, retailers and financial services. This aspect is often forgotten by service organisations that continue to think that because they are as good as any other organisation in their sector, this is good enough. This is clearly not true.

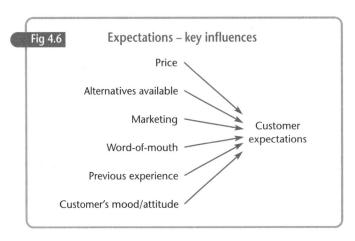

Fig 4.6 Expectations – key influences

Price
Alternatives available
Marketing
Word-of-mouth
Previous experience
Customer's mood/attitude

Customer expectations

Customers' mood and attitude can affect their expectations. Someone in a bad mood or with a poor attitude to an organisation may have heightened expectations; someone less concerned and more tolerant may have a wider zone of tolerance and thus a wider range of expectations.

Expectations are dynamic. They are not fixed at a single point on a continuum between intolerable to ideal and will change over time and indeed during the service itself. Customers are continually experiencing many service situations and consuming services. Their expectations are under continual review and change. What an organisation may have defined as adequate last month may be inadequate this month. As more and more organisations dealing with customer complaints, for example, try to resolve them by phone rather than letter, customers will start to expect similar treatment, whatever the industry.

4.3.4 Expectations of a service never used

Because our expectations can be based on what we believe 'should' happen we therefore do not need to have experienced a service to have expectations about it. People who have not experienced a funeral may have some clear expectations about the nature, mood and style of the event and more fuzzy expectations about the actual series of events. These may be quite clear and explicit if they have, for example, witnessed such events, second-hand, on television or in novels, for example. The problem, for service operations managers, is in trying to meet these unseen and unknown expectations whose formation is to some extent out of the control of the organisation. The key tasks for operations managers are to know how to define expectations (section 4.4), how to discover what customers' expectations are (section 4.5) and then how to manage customers' perceptions during the process (section 4.6).

4.3.5 Providing service cues

Customer expectations are shaped from an early point in their contact with a service organisation. The careful use of service cues will allow the operations manager to influence expectations. For example, the customer entering a restaurant sees the way that it is set out and will draw conclusions about the level of service provided. If the tables and chairs are functional rather than comfortable and customers decide where they want to sit, it is likely that service delivery will be more basic than in a gourmet restaurant. It should be noted, of course, that this says nothing about the friendliness of the service. Service in the gourmet restaurant may contain more direct help for the customer, but if it is delivered in a cold, dispassionate way, it may be judged to be rather poorer than in its more functional cousin.

4.4 DEFINING EXPECTATIONS – SERVICE QUALITY FACTORS

A great deal of work has been carried out recently to help organisations understand the component parts of expectations so that they can operationalise expectations to design and deliver appropriate levels of quality and also to help them create measurement instruments to measure customer satisfaction.

The service quality factors are those attributes of service about which customers may have expectations and which need to be delivered at some specified level. Several sets of factors have been identified (see, for example, Grönroos 1984, Parasuraman *et al.* 1985, Gremler, Bitner and Evans 1994 and Reynoso 1995).

Figure 4.7 provides 18 quality factors (Johnston 1995b, Silvestro and Johnston 1990) which try to capture the totality of service quality. These 18 may be consolidated into broader dimensions (see, for example, Parasuraman *et al.* 1985) and indeed may not capture every aspect of service quality for every organisation. They are at least a starting-point to help us define, deliver and measure service quality.

These factors have been defined as follows:

- *Access.* The physical approachability of service location, including the ease of finding one's way around the service environment and clarity of route.
- *Aesthetics.* Extent to which the components of the service package are agreeable or pleasing to the customer, including both the appearance and the ambience of the service environment, the appearance and presentation of service facilities, goods and staff.
- *Attentive/helpfulness.* The extent to which the service, particularly contact staff, either provide help to the customer or give the impression of being interested in the customer and show a willingness to serve.
- *Availability.* The availability of service facilities, staff and goods to the customer. In the case of contact staff this means both the staff/customer ratio and the amount of time each staff member has available to spend with each customer. In the case of service goods availability includes both the quantity and range of products made available to the customer.
- *Care.* The concern, consideration, sympathy and patience shown to the customer. This includes the extent to which the customer is put at ease by the service and made to feel emotionally (rather than physically) comfortable.
- *Cleanliness/tidiness.* The cleanliness, neat and tidy appearance of the tangible components of the service package, including the service environment, facilities, goods and contact staff.

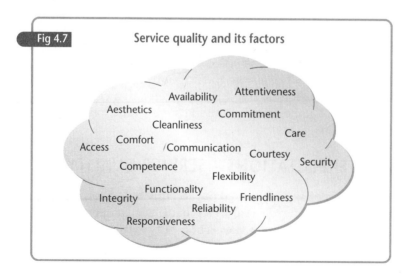

Fig 4.7   **Service quality and its factors**

- *Comfort.* The physical comfort of the service environment and facilities.
- *Commitment.* Staff's apparent commitment to their work, including the pride and satisfaction they apparently take in their job, their diligence and thoroughness.
- *Communication.* The ability of the service to communicate with the customer in a way he/she will understand. This includes the clarity, completeness and accuracy of both verbal and written information communicated to the customer and the ability to listen to and understand the customer.
- *Competence.* The skill, expertise and professionalism with which the service is executed. This includes the carrying out of correct procedures, correct execution of customer instructions, degree of product or service knowledge exhibited by contact staff, the rendering of good, sound advice and the general ability to do a good job.
- *Courtesy.* The politeness, respect and propriety shown by the service, usually contact staff, in dealing with the customer and his/her property. This includes the ability of staff to be unobtrusive and uninterfering when appropriate.
- *Flexibility.* A willingness on the part of the service worker to amend or alter the nature of the service or product to meet the needs of the customer.
- *Friendliness.* The warmth and personal approachability (rather than physical approachability) of the service, particularly of contact staff, including cheerful attitude, the ability to make the customer feel welcome.
- *Functionality.* The serviceability and fitness for purpose or 'product quality' of service facilities and goods.
- *Integrity.* The honesty, justice, fairness and trustworthiness with which customers are treated by the service organisation.
- *Reliability.* The reliability and consistency of performance of service facilities, goods and staff. This includes punctual service delivery and ability to keep to agreements made with the customer.
- *Responsiveness.* Speed and timeliness of service delivery. This includes the speed of throughput and the ability of the service to respond promptly to customer service requests, with minimal waiting and queuing time.
- *Security.* Personal safety of the customer and his/her possessions while participating in or benefiting from the service process. This includes the maintenance of confidentiality.

These factors try to cover many aspects of the service operation, which we defined in Chapter 2, including:

- the service process/service experience – its reliability, friendliness and feeling of security, for example
- the service outcome – the functionality and reliability of the outcome, for example
- the tangible goods used in the service – for example their functionality, reliability and availability
- the staff – their friendliness, responsiveness, appearance, courtesy, competence and communication skills, for example
- the facilities – appearance, aesthetics, accessibility and comfort, for example.

As can be seen some factors may be used to define several different aspects of the service, such as appearance and responsiveness, for example.

4.4.1 Hygiene and enhancing factors

Although they will vary from organisation to organisation and also from customer to customer, the service quality factors can be divided into four groups. These groupings are defined in terms of a factor's ability to dissatisfy and delight – see Figure 4.8 (see, for example, Johnston 1995b, Silvestro and Johnston 1990).

- *Hygiene factors* are those that need to be in place and if they are, they will satisfy; if not, they will be a source of dissatisfaction. They are not likely to be a source of delight. For a bank, security, integrity and functionality, for example, are expected to be acceptable; if they are not acceptable, they will dissatisfy. On the other hand, if they are over-specified, they will not delight. A very large number of security checks will not delight the customer – indeed they could dissatisfy him/her. Having all cash machines in perfect working order all of the time will not delight them either.

- *Enhancing factors* are those that have the potential to delight if they are present, but if they are not there, they are not likely to dissatisfy the customer. Customers of a bank may be delighted with a warm, caring approach by a member of staff or their flexibility in dealing with a problem; however, these things are not necessarily 'expected', so, if they are not provided, may not lead to dissatisfaction.

- *Critical factors* are those that have the potential to both delight and dissatisfy. Responsiveness, communication and competence of bank staff and systems must be at least acceptable so as not to dissatisfy the customer but, if more than acceptable, have the potential to delight.

- *Neutral factors* are the factors that in a given situation will have little effect on satisfaction. The comfort or aesthetics of a banking hall may play no part in customers' satisfaction or dissatisfaction (see Figure 4.9).

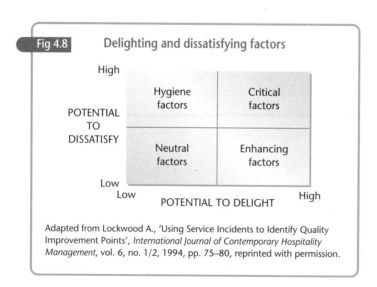

Fig 4.8   Delighting and dissatisfying factors

Adapted from Lockwood A., 'Using Service Incidents to Identify Quality Improvement Points', *International Journal of Contemporary Hospitality Management*, vol. 6, no. 1/2, 1994, pp. 75–80, reprinted with permission.

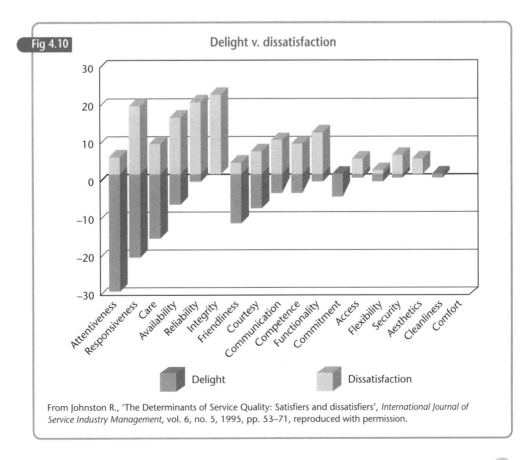

Fig 4.9 — Four types of factors for a bank

High

POTENTIAL TO DISSATISFY

Hygienes
Availability
Reliability
Integrity
Functionality
Security

Criticals
Responsiveness
Communication
Competence

Neutrals
Comfort
Aesthetics

Enhancers
Attentiveness
Care
Friendliness
Courtesy
Flexibility

Low

Low   POTENTIAL TO DELIGHT   High

We believe that managers should not only be aware of the expectations of their customers but should also realise the importance and potential effect of the various factors. We need to know which factors will delight and which will dissatisfy in

Fig 4.10 — Delight v. dissatisfaction

Delight   Dissatisfaction

From Johnston R., 'The Determinants of Service Quality: Satisfiers and dissatisfiers', *International Journal of Service Industry Management*, vol. 6, no. 5, 1995, pp. 53–71, reproduced with permission.

order to better manage the creation of satisfaction during the service process (see section 4.6). How we can find these factors and identify the enhancers, hygienes and criticals is explained in the next section, 4.5.

Whilst factors do not always neatly fall into one category or another, Figure 4.10 shows the relative frequency of mentions made of the factors in a study of UK banks (Johnston 1995b). What is striking is that the factors with the tendency to dissatisfy (hygienes and criticals) are systemic and concern the organisation's ability to deliver its core services: functionality, reliability, competence etc; whereas the factors with a tendency to delight tend to be the more interpersonal factors, such as attentiveness, friendliness, courtesy etc.

Care should be exercised in trying to identify neutral factors, although in the research cited above the fact that few people mentioned security does not mean it is a neutral factor. It simply indicates that there were no instances of security having been the source of dissatisfaction or delight.

4.5 FINDING EXPECTATIONS AND ASSESSING SATISFACTION

The 18 quality factors provide a base to help us understand and define customer expectations (whether internal or external), define appropriate levels (i.e. create the internal quality specification), and also measure customer satisfaction.

There are many different methods available (see Berry and Parasuraman 1997 for an evaluation). The methods divide broadly into those that are primarily used for understanding how customers are satisfied and those that are primarily used for assessing satisfaction.

4.5.1 Understanding how customers are satisfied

The first approach, briefly described by the use of questionnaires and surveys, is the most quantitative approach and can be structured around all or some of the 18 quality factors and analysed by each factor. The other, more qualitative, approaches tend to collect descriptive data and provide the interpretation of events by customers in their own words. This creates more difficulties in their analysis and interpretation in order to extract meaningful summaries. They do, however, have the benefit of providing ideas and examples that managers and employees can use and discuss to understand and improve their services.

- *Questionnaires and surveys*, written or verbal, can be a good means of soliciting opinions about an organisation's services and of identifying what customers find important. Figure 4.11 shows the results of a questionnaire asking customers of an hotel to rate the importance of various aspects of the service. The staff were also asked to do the same. One can see several interesting mismatches between the views of staff and guests (midweek guests only).
- *Focus groups* usually comprise groups of about 15 customers with a trained facilitator brought together to discuss one or a few aspects of a particular existing or planned service.
- *Customer advisory panels* are similar to focus groups but are likely to meet regularly with a more structured agenda.

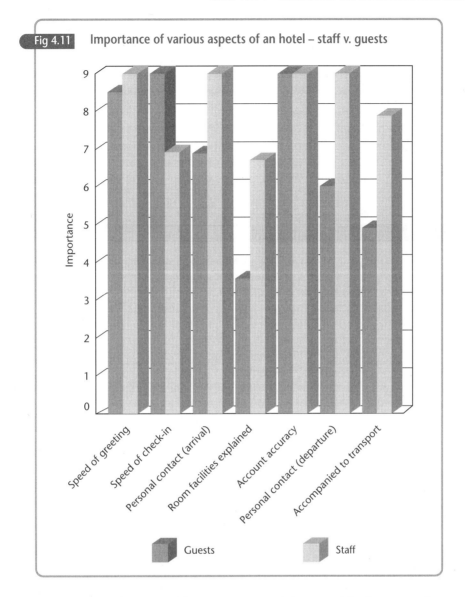

Fig 4.11 Importance of various aspects of an hotel – staff v. guests

- *New/lost customer surveys* are very useful ways of finding out what attracts customers to the organisation and indeed why they left. Whilst many organisations are now conducting exit interviews, the most successful rely heavily upon the direct involvement of senior managers to ensure appropriate access, information and action.

- *Complaint/compliment analysis* can be undertaken upon customers' voluntary contributions; however, these tend to be more negative than positive. They do provide information about the extremes of delight and dissatisfaction. Box 4.2 explains how Singapore Airlines makes use of its complaints and compliments.

- *The critical incident technique* (CIT) attempts to identify the things that delight and dissatisfy customers. Critical incidents are events that contribute to, or detract from, perceived service or product performance in a significant way. The CIT instrument usually comprises two questions. The first question asks customers to think of a time when they felt very pleased and satisfied with the service/product received and to describe, in a few sentences, the situation and why they felt so happy. The second question requires customers to think of a time when they were unhappy and dissatisfied with the service/product they received and to describe, in a few sentences, why they felt this way.

● *Sequential incident analysis* combines CIT, walk-through audits and process mapping (see Chapter 6) (Stauss 1993). Customers are 'walked through' a pre-prepared process map of the service they have recently encountered and asked for their experiences of each stage or transaction in the process. This technique identifies not only critical situations but also potentially critical ones.

Box 4.2 Singapore Airlines (SIA) – listening to its customers

'We constantly monitor passenger feedback, re-examine service procedures and study new technologies to discover ways in which to further improve the service we provide,' said SIA's Managing Director, Dr Cheong Choong Kong. SIA employs varied and systematic methods to obtain information from their passengers, including quarterly passenger surveys and focused group work with their frequent flyers. The company also uses its magazine for frequent flyers, *Priority*, to ask for passengers' reactions to proposed new ideas. They also check out the service for themselves by conducting on-site audits with test calls to reservations, for example, to see how service is being delivered. Also, when any member of staff flies in their aircraft they are asked to submit reports of their travel experiences. Senior staff members must submit a comment sheet on each flight with their expense account. SIA staff also monitor their competitors and often go and check out their services.

Mr B. K. Ong, the Senior Manager for Customer Service Affairs, explained how they deal with complaints and compliments. 'We do get some complaints and pride ourselves in being able to resolve them quickly. We analyse them and try to improve what we do and feed the information back to the people who can make it happen. We really value complaints and see them as opportunities to improve what we do and how we do it. We put a strong emphasis on service recovery, not damage control. We do have many contingency plans in place for when things go wrong and we have a philosophy of 'making good'; trying to provide on-the-spot recovery and fair compensation for anything adverse that has happened.'

SIA also produces newsletters for particular groups of staff. *Highpoint,* for example, is aimed at keeping its 8,000 in-flight personnel informed about the airline's latest offerings and its commitments to passengers. The newsletter also has a regular feature page with about eight or nine extracts from letters, half compliments and half complaints. An example of each follows.

Example compliment

'I noticed the service, although in economy class, was professional and better than any flights I have ever been on. Miss Iris Lee was the most hardworking amongst all the crew. She came round distributing newspapers, drinks, postcards, playing cards, amenities etc. As a director of travel and tours, I fly often and I have never come across such an outstanding cabin hostess .... She loves to fly and it shows.'

Example complaint

'We were sitting close by the galleys and were able to observe the cabin crew at work throughout the flight, and the impression we gained was that they were unable to cope with a full load of passengers. There seemed also to be a lack of leadership and organisation – the cabin crew were rushing back and forth getting in each other's way and not the smooth activity which we have come to expect from Singapore Airlines.'

Higher Ground is a bimonthly newsletter aimed at the ground services staff, including ticketing, reservations, check-in as well as baggage handling, logistics and transportation. *Higher Ground* also contains extracts from letters, usually two complaints and one compliment.

Example compliment

'I would like to pen a note of appreciation for the extra help your staff gave my aged parents when they took your SQ860 from Singapore to Hong Kong. They were told at the check-in counter to come back to see your staff. My brother accordingly brought them to the counter near the check-in time. Then one of your staff very kindly brought them into the restricted area, through immigration and right to the departure room. This was of great help to them as they do not understand the signs in English and may have to look around or ask around for the direction to the departure room. Walking extra distance would also be troublesome for my mother who is recovering from a stroke. Thank you once again to your staff for going out of their way to assist my parents. I am indeed proud of our national Airline.'

Example complaint

'On 26th July we flew Singapore Airlines. Prior to the arrangement being made and also a few days before the actual flight, I reiterated the comment that my mother would require a wheelchair for both embarkation and disembarkation .... She had travelled last year by Singapore Airlines and had no trouble whatsoever. At [embarkation], a wheelchair was provided and we boarded the plane with no problems .... On arrival ... we were not docked at a bridge, but parked in the middle of the airfield. I was then asked if my mother could manage to get down two external steep flights of stairs and to walk to a bus which would then take her to the terminal. As she had come on by wheelchair I would have thought it was patently obvious that this was totally impossible for her. We were told that it was our fault that [the airport] had not been informed. I explained that I had done as much as I could in informing [the station at departure], and they certainly knew she required a wheelchair to get on the plane and therefore, obviously, to get off the plane. It took an hour to get some means of transport to take her off the plane and into the airport terminal.'

Questions

1 *Evaluate the methods used by SIA to understand customer expectations and assess satisfaction.*

2 *What is the purpose of providing both complaints and compliments?*

Extracted from Johnston R., Chambers S., Harrison A., Harland C. and Slack N., 'Singapore Airlines', *Cases in Operations Management*, 2nd edn, Pitman, London, 1997, pp. 508–18.

4.5.2 Assessing satisfaction

Satisfaction can be assessed using some of the more qualitative approaches above but is usually assessed in a more structured way using either questionnaires and surveys or mystery shoppers.

- **Questionnaires and surveys** can be constructed using the 18 quality factors, or those which customers identified as being important in focus groups etc. One of the best-known instruments for assessing service quality is SERVQUAL developed and refined by Parasuraman *et al.* (1988, 1991 and 1994). SERVQUAL is a concise multiple-item scale questionnaire that organisations can use to assess their customers' expectations and perceptions of their service and obtain a single figure for tracking and comparison. The instrument itself is a skeleton questionnaire that asks questions of customers about their expectations and perceptions of the services of a particular company. It uses five consolidated quality factors or dimensions (assurance, empathy, reliability, responsiveness, tangibles) with 22 items for perceptions and 22 for expectations, using a seven-point Likert scale. A perception gap score is then calculated for each pair of statements (expectations and perceptions), the difference being the SERVQUAL score. Different questions relate to the different dimensions which can then be aggregated and averaged to identify perception gaps for each dimension. The scores can also be weighted by getting customers to add weights to each dimension. Repeated administration allows an understanding as to how customers' perceived service quality with each of the dimensions is changing over time (for detailed information see Zeithaml *et al.* 1990).

- **Mystery shoppers** are used by several organisations, in particular retailers, to assess the service that their customers experience. They can be undertaken by managers acting incognito but are usually carried out by external agencies working to an agreed script or scoring system. The problems encountered using this method include whether the expectations implied within the structure are appropriate, as they have been created by managers based on their understanding of what they think customers expect. A particular problem with mystery shoppers is that they are prone to becoming too 'professional' in their analysis. In other words, because they have become sensitised to service quality, they may highlight details which are largely irrelevant to the average consumer.

The challenge for operations managers is to keep enough of the satisfaction measurement process consistent to be able to track improvement over time, but to recognise that it will have to change to reflect the changing nature of the customer. Another problem is that people become increasingly 'survey weary' and do not give as much attention to their responses as the organisation might need, if indeed they reply at all. Tesco, the supermarket chain, meets this problem by taking a 'customer satisfaction pulse'. This means that it selects an aspect of service delivery such as check-out service and concentrates on understanding customer experience in this area before moving on to another aspect at a later time.

4.6 MANAGING PERCEPTIONS

As we suggested earlier in this chapter there should be a match between service quality (the quality of what the operation delivers) and the quality of the service as perceived by the customer. From an operations view it can be all too easy to put aside customers' views or perceptions of the service and focus on operational service quality – i.e. delivery to the specification. We also suggested that managing quality should be a dynamic process and so here we show how perceptions can be managed during the process of service delivery.

4.6.1 Managing perceptions during the service process

Operations managers must become attuned to their customers and understand how perceptions of a service develop during the service process. Figure 4.12 combines Figures 4.2, 4.4 and 4.5 earlier – the levels of expectations and zone of tolerance, and the outcome of a service, level of satisfaction and dissatisfaction – and looks at how expectations give way to perception of satisfaction using the service process (Johnston 1995a). The figure shows the zone of tolerance extending from expectations through the process to the outcome of satisfaction.

Figure 4.12 depicts something similar to a control chart which managers can use firstly to identify customer expectations, what is acceptable, less than acceptable and more than acceptable (using approaches described earlier), and then to assess during the service the impact of each stage or transaction in a single service transaction or encounter or a series of service encounters. This helps managers understand how they can design their service to have the appropriate interventions at appropriate times to achieve the desired outcome, whether satisfaction or delight.

A number of suggestions have been made about the use of this model (Johnston 1995a). Take for example a patient with an appointment to see a

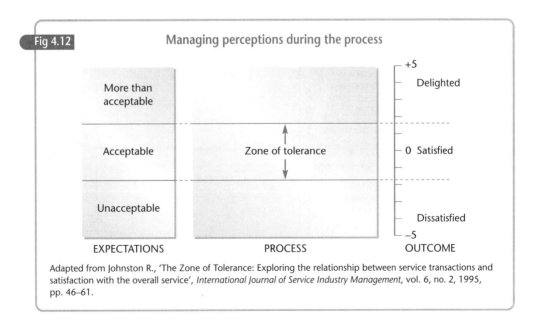

Fig 4.12 Managing perceptions during the process

Adapted from Johnston R., 'The Zone of Tolerance: Exploring the relationship between service transactions and satisfaction with the overall service', *International Journal of Service Industry Management*, vol. 6, no. 2, 1995, pp. 46–61.

doctor for a routine medical examination. We might consider there to be seven transactions here:

1. Arrival at the clinic
2. Reception
3. Waiting for the doctor
4. Introduction to the examination by the doctor
5. Examination
6. Discussion of findings
7. Depart

Expectations may have been managed by the medical practice through its code of conduct, for example, which informs patients that they should have to wait no longer than ten minutes to see the doctor, that they will be treated with care and consideration and all medical facts explained to them in a meaningful way (see Figure 4.13).

1. Performance within the zone of tolerance results in satisfaction.

   Providing the customer's perceptions of the transactions are not greater or less than acceptable, the outcome will be a 'satisfied' customer with a 'score' somewhere within their outcome zone of tolerance (see Figure 4.14). It has been suggested that the quality of a performance within the customer's zone of tolerance may not be consciously noticed, so for an organisation wishing to make an impact they will need to design-in positive (or maybe even negative) interventions.

2. Sufficient incursions above the zone of tolerance threshold will result in a highly satisfying outcome (delight).

   By including one or more enhancing factors the doctor's surgery may be able to delight the patient. For example, the receptionist greeting the patient by name and

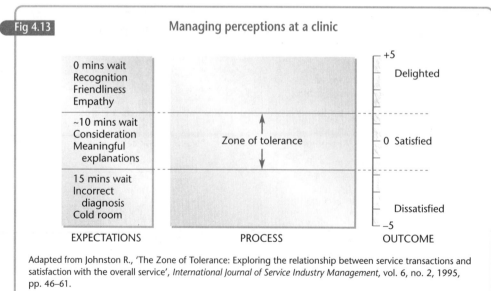

Fig 4.13   Managing perceptions at a clinic

Adapted from Johnston R., 'The Zone of Tolerance: Exploring the relationship between service transactions and satisfaction with the overall service', *International Journal of Service Industry Management*, vol. 6, no. 2, 1995, pp. 46–61.

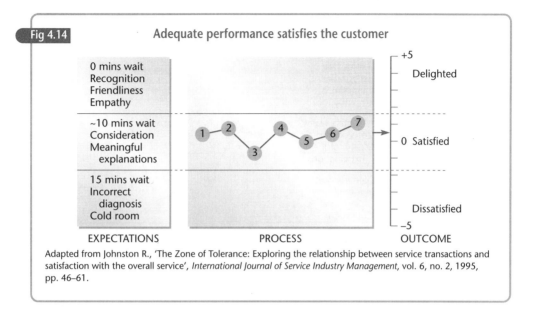

Fig 4.14 Adequate performance satisfies the customer

Adapted from Johnston R., 'The Zone of Tolerance: Exploring the relationship between service transactions and satisfaction with the overall service', *International Journal of Service Industry Management*, vol. 6, no. 2, 1995, pp. 46–61.

inviting them to take a seat whilst s/he brings them a coffee, might be quite unexpected (at least on the first occasion) and delight the customer (see Figure 4.15). The outcome 'score' may not be a mean score but delighting (and indeed dissatisfying) incidents may have the effect of skewing the resulting level of satisfaction.

3. Sufficient incursions below the zone of tolerance threshold will result in a dissatisfying outcome.

A delay of 12 minutes (a hygiene factor) may be forgiven but this coupled with a brusque treatment and a cursory examination may well lead to dissatisfaction (see Figure 4.16).

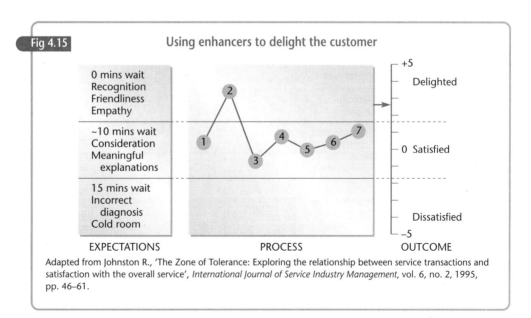

Fig 4.15 Using enhancers to delight the customer

Adapted from Johnston R., 'The Zone of Tolerance: Exploring the relationship between service transactions and satisfaction with the overall service', *International Journal of Service Industry Management*, vol. 6, no. 2, 1995, pp. 46–61.

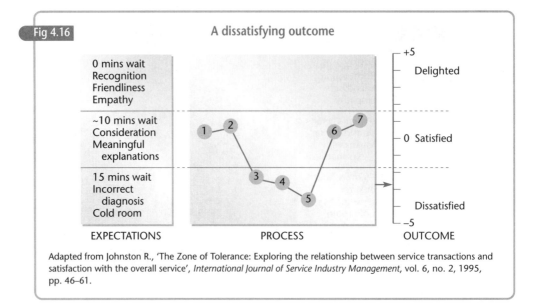

Fig 4.16 — A dissatisfying outcome

Adapted from Johnston R., 'The Zone of Tolerance: Exploring the relationship between service transactions and satisfaction with the overall service', *International Journal of Service Industry Management*, vol. 6, no. 2, 1995, pp. 46–61.

4. Some dissatisfying and satisfying transactions may be compensatory.

Lack of spaces in the car park resulting in a walk of 500 metres in the rain to the surgery will count as a dissatisfying transaction but a profuse apology from the receptionist coupled with particularly caring treatment by the doctor may compensate for the initial problems (see Figure 4.17).

5. Several satisfying transactions will be needed to compensate for a single dissatisfying transaction.

It could be that one dissatisfying transaction will require compensation by more than one delighting transaction (as above).

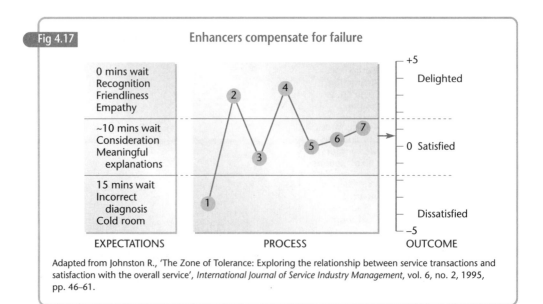

Fig 4.17 — Enhancers compensate for failure

Adapted from Johnston R., 'The Zone of Tolerance: Exploring the relationship between service transactions and satisfaction with the overall service', *International Journal of Service Industry Management*, vol. 6, no. 2, 1995, pp. 46–61.

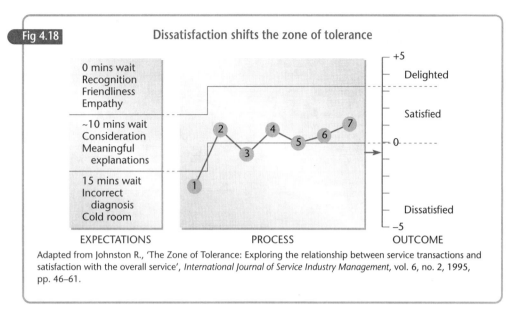

Fig 4.18   Dissatisfaction shifts the zone of tolerance

Adapted from Johnston R., 'The Zone of Tolerance: Exploring the relationship between service transactions and satisfaction with the overall service', *International Journal of Service Industry Management*, vol. 6, no. 2, 1995, pp. 46–61.

6. A failure in one transaction may raise the dissatisfaction threshold.

   A dissatisfying experience may also have the effect of shifting the zone of tolerance upwards, and/or maybe reducing its width. For example, if the patient has
   had to walk 500 metres in the rain, their dissatisfaction with this transaction may
   be such as to negatively dispose them towards the rest of the service. This could
   mean that future transactions that might previously have been within their zone
   of tolerance are now felt to be dissatisfying (see Figure 4.18). This shifting of the
   zone increases the likelihood of the outcome being a feeling of dissatisfaction.

7. Conversely, an enhancing transaction may lower the zone of tolerance (and/or
   widen it) so that further transactions that might before have been within the
   acceptable range are now felt to be delighting. This has also been referred to as
   the 'halo effect' (Wirtz and Bateson 1995). Prompt treatment by the receptionist,
   a feeling of being expected and welcome, and all the forms ready to be signed,
   for example, may not only delight but positively dispose the patient to the rest
   of the service, increasing the likelihood of a delighting outcome (see Figure 4.19).

4.6.2   Design issues

It would seem sensible then for organisations wishing to satisfy the customer to
ensure that there are no failures on hygiene factors throughout the process.
Delighting transactions are unnecessary and the organisation is more likely to satisfy the customer if their zone of tolerance can be made as wide as possible by
appropriate marketing of the service.

For organisations seeking to delight their customers, a narrower zone of tolerance
will increase the likelihood of delighting (and dissatisfying) the customer. Some
delighting transactions are needed and ideally early in the process to affect the level
and possibly width of the zone of tolerance. A delighting transaction at the end
may also serve to put the icing on the cake. Although a delighting early transaction

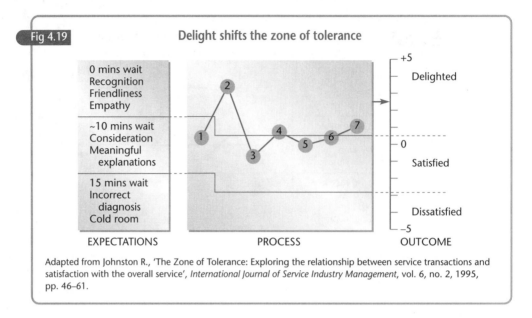

Fig 4.19 — Delight shifts the zone of tolerance

Adapted from Johnston R., 'The Zone of Tolerance: Exploring the relationship between service transactions and satisfaction with the overall service', *International Journal of Service Industry Management*, vol. 6, no. 2, 1995, pp. 46–61.

can have considerable impact, it has been shown that a build-up to a strong end of process results in higher perceived service quality (Hansen and Danaher 1999).

4.6.3 Transaction satisfaction versus overall satisfaction

The above discussion has implied two levels of satisfaction: satisfaction with a single transaction during a service and an overall, cumulative, satisfaction based on the transactions. The question remains as to how exactly do transaction satisfactions develop into an overall satisfaction with the service experience and outcome. We would suggest that there are two key approaches, a rational and an incident-based approach.

The rational approach

The rational approach would suggest that customers consciously or unconsciously use a weighted average, so that a high score on one attribute or factor may offset a low score on another (Sasser *et al.* 1978) to arrive at a rational evaluation of the quality of a service. Indeed many satisfaction surveys, such as SERVQUAL, are based on the assumption that a reasonable way of calculating overall satisfaction is by allocating weights to the various factors of transactions (according to importance as perceived by the customer), multiplying the weight by the score (on a 1–5 scale, for example) for each factor and then cumulating them into an overall satisfaction rating.

The incident-based approach

An alternative view is that customers are less rational and react more to individual incidents, as suggested in the above section. Therefore any single incident, delighting or dissatisfying, could, despite the remaining adequate and satisfying transactions, result in a feeling of overall dissatisfaction or delight. Sasser *et al.* (1978) suggested that either a single factor would determine the outcome, all others receiving nominal or no consideration, or one attribute would determine the outcome, but certain attributes must achieve at least a minimum acceptable level.

The reality is likely to be some combination of these approaches but this question suggests the need to take care when constructing algorithms to assess customers' overall satisfaction with a service. It is certainly a mistake to assume that customers can identify with precision the reasons why they are satisfied or dissatisfied with a service. On a training programme, participants complained about the standard of the accommodation. It was only in discussion with the group that it emerged that the underlying dissatisfaction was with one of the presenters and that the accommodation, although not wonderful, was in fact satisfactory.

4.7 SUMMARY

Customer satisfaction and service quality

- Satisfaction is the result of a customer's assessment of a service based on a comparison of their perceptions of service delivery with their prior expectations.
- Service quality from an operations perspective is about consistently meeting the service specification for that service.
- There may be gaps between expectations, perceptions and service quality delivered.

Customer expectations

- 'Expectations' exist somewhere on a range or continuum, between ideal and intolerable; care needs to be taken when asking questions about expectations.
- Customers may accept variation within a range of performance and any increase or decrease in performance within the zone of tolerance area will only have a marginal effect on perceptions.
- Many factors, including price, will affect an individual's level of expectations.

Defining expectations – service quality factors

- The service quality factors are those attributes of service about which customers may have expectations and which need to be delivered at some specified level.
- Neutral factors have little effect on satisfaction, hygiene factors will dissatisfy but not delight, enhancing factors will not dissatisfy but may delight and critical factors both dissatisfy and delight.

Finding expectations and assessing satisfaction

- There are many different methods for understanding how customers are satisfied and for assessing satisfaction.

Managing perceptions during service delivery

- A key role for operations is to manage customers' perceptions during the service process.

4.8 DISCUSSION QUESTIONS

1. What methods are most effective in identifying the influencers of customer satisfaction, given that some aspects may be unconsciously experienced by customers?

2. For a high-volume/low-variety service (business-to-consumer) and for a low-volume/high-variety service (business-to-business or professional service) identify potential gaps between customer expectation and customer perception of service delivery. What strategies would you suggest these organisations utilise to close these gaps?

4.9 QUESTIONS FOR MANAGERS

1. When was the last time your organisation carried out an exhaustive study of customer satisfaction? Assess the methods used.

2. Who compiled your customer satisfaction survey questionnaire? Have you checked with customers as to how relevant it is, or do you assume you know what customers want?

3. What are the reasons for gaps between customer perception of service delivery and customer expectation? How can they be closed?

4. Do you understand the zone of tolerance for your service delivery? Are customer expectations sometimes fuzzy? What guidance and/or resource is required to clarify these expectations?

5. What is the most effective method of assessing customer satisfaction? How widely have you communicated the findings of customer research?

4.10 SUGGESTIONS FOR FURTHER READING

Schneider B. and Bowen D.E., 'Understanding Customer Delight and Outrage', *Sloan Management Review*, Fall 1999, pp. 35–45.
Zeithaml V.A. and Bitner M.J., *Services Marketing* (international edition), McGraw-Hill, New York, 1996, chapters 4 and 5, pp. 75–132.

4.11 REFERENCES

Berry L.L. and Parasuraman A., 'Listening to the Customer – The Concept of a Service-Quality Information System', *Sloan Management Review*, Spring 1997, pp. 65–76.
Bitner M.J. and Hubbert A.R., 'Encounter Satisfaction Versus Overall Satisfaction Versus Service Quality: The consumer's voice', in Rust R.T. and Oliver R.L. (eds), *Service Quality: New directions in theory and practice*, Sage Publications, Thousand Oaks, Calif., 1994, pp. 72–94.
Boulding W., Kalra A., Staelin R. and Zeithaml V.A., 'A Dynamic Process Model of Service Quality: From expectations to behavioral intentions', *Journal of Marketing Research*, vol. XXX, February 1993, pp. 7–27.
Cadotte E.R., Woodruff R.B. and Jenkins R.L., 'Expectations and Norms in Models of Consumer Satisfaction', *Journal of Marketing Research*, vol. XXIV, August 1987, pp. 305–14.
Churchill G.A. and Surprenant C., 'An Investigation into the Determinants of Customer Satisfaction', *Journal of Marketing Research*, vol. XIX, November 1982, pp. 491–504.

Dibb S., Simkin L., Pride W. and Ferrel O.C., *Marketing Concepts and Strategies* (third European edition), Houghton Mifflin, Boston, 1997.

Gremler D.D., Bitner M.J. and Evans K.R., 'The Internal Service Encounter', *International Journal of Service Industry Management*, vol. 5, no. 2, 1994, pp. 34–56.

Grönroos C., 'A Service Quality Model and its Marketing Implications', *European Journal of Marketing*, vol. 18, no. 4, 1984, pp. 36–44.

Grönroos C., 'Toward a Third Phase in Service Quality Research: Challenges and future directions', in Swartz T.A., Bowen D.A. and Brown S.W. (eds), *Advances in Services Marketing and Management,* vol. 2, JAI Press, Greenwich, Conn., 1993, pp. 49–64.

Hansen D.E. and Danaher P.J., 'Inconsistent Performance During the Service Encounter', *Journal of Service Research*, vol. 1, no. 3, February 1999, pp. 227–35.

Johnston R., 'The Zone of Tolerance: Exploring the relationship between service transactions and satisfaction with the overall service', *International Journal of Service Industry Management*, vol. 6, no. 2, 1995a, pp. 46–61.

Johnston R., 'The Determinants of Service Quality: Satisfiers and dissatisfiers', *International Journal of Service Industry Management*, vol. 6, no. 5, 1995b, pp. 53–71.

Johnston R., Chambers S., Harrison A., Harland C. and Slack N., *Cases in Operations Management* (2nd edition), Pitman, London, 1997.

Lockwood A., 'Using Service Incidents to Identify Quality Improvement Points', *International Journal of Contemporary Hospitality Management*, vol. 6, no. 1/2, 1994, pp. 75–80.

Ojasalo J., *Quality Dynamics in Professional Services*, PhD Dissertation no. 76, Swedish School of Economics and Business Administration, Helsinki, 1999.

Oliver R.L., 'Cognitive, Affective, and Attribute Bases of the Satisfaction Response', *Journal of Consumer Research*, vol. 20, no. 3, 1993, pp. 418–30.

Oliver R.L. and DeSarbo W.S., 'Response Determinants in Satisfaction Judgements', *Journal of Consumer Research*, vol. 14, March 1988, pp. 495–507.

Parasuraman A., Berry L.L. and Zeithaml V.A., 'Refinement and Reassessment of the SERVQUAL Scale', *Journal of Retailing*, vol. 67, no. 4, Winter 1991, pp. 420–50.

Parasuraman A., Zeithaml V.A. and Berry L.L., 'A Conceptual Model of Service Quality and Implications for Future Research', *Journal of Marketing*, vol. 49, Fall 1985, pp. 41–50.

Parasuraman A., Zeithaml V.A. and Berry L.L., 'SERVQUAL: A multiple-item scale for measuring consumer perceptions of service quality', *Journal of Retailing*, Spring 1988, pp. 12–40.

Parasuraman A., Zeithaml V.A. and Berry L.L., 'Reassessment of Expectations as a Comparison Standard on Measuring Service Quality: Implications for further research', *Journal of Marketing*, vol. 58, no. 1, January 1994, pp. 111–24.

Patterson P.G. and Johnson L.W., 'Disconfirmation of Expectations and the Gap Model of Service Quality: An integrated paradigm', *Journal of Consumer Satisfaction, Dissatisfaction and Complaining Behavior*, vol. 6, 1993, pp. 90–9.

Reynoso J., 'Towards the Conceptualisation and Operationalisation of Internal Service Quality: An examination in UK hospitals', Doctoral Thesis, University of Manchester, 1995.

Sasser W.E., Olsen R.P. and Wyckoff D.D., *Management of Service Operations*, Allyn and Bacon, Boston, 1978.

Schneider B. and Bowen D.E., 'Understanding Customer Delight and Outrage', *Sloan Management Review*, Fall 1999, pp. 35–45.

Silvestro R. and Johnston R., 'The Determinants of Service Quality – Enhancing and Hygiene Factors', QUIS II Symposium, St John's University, New York, July 1990.

Stauss B., 'Service Problem Deployment: Transformation of problem information into problem prevention activities', *International Journal of Service Industry Management*, vol. 4, no. 2, 1993, pp. 41–62.

Strandvik T., *Tolerance Zones in Perceived Service Quality*, Swedish School of Economics and Business Administration, Helsingfors, 1994.

Taylor S.A. and Baker T.L., 'An Assessment of the Relationship Between Service Quality and Customer Satisfaction in the Formation of Consumers' Purchase Intentions', *Journal of Retailing*, vol. 70, no. 2, 1994, pp. 163–78.

Wirtz J. and Bateson J.E.G., 'An Experimental Investigation of Halo Effects in Satisfaction Measures and Service Attributes', *International Journal of Service Industry Management*, vol. 6, no. 3, 1995, pp. 84–102.

Zeithaml V.A., Parasuraman A. and Berry L.L., *Delivering Quality Service*, Free Press, New York, 1990.

Zeithaml V.A., Berry L.L. and Parasuraman A., 'The Nature and Determinants of Customer Expectations of Service', *Journal of the Academy of Marketing Science*, vol. 21, no. 1, 1993, pp. 1–12.

CASE EXERCISE

The North County Breast Screening Unit

This case study was written by Dr Rhian Silvestro and Marilyn Merriam

Breast cancer is the most common cause of death from cancer in women in the UK, and women with breast cancer form almost 1 per cent of in-patient admissions. England and Wales have the highest mortality rates for breast cancer in the world, making it a major public health problem which is a national target area in the Government's Strategy for the Health of the Nation. The NHS Breast Screening Programme, set up in 1987, aims to reduce mortality from breast cancer, through early identification of the symptoms, by screening women aged between 50 and 64 every three years. It is possible that the age range will be extended to between 45 and 64 in future.

The North County Breast Screening Unit (NCBSU) was set up in 1989 and serves some half a million residents, with an uptake on invitations for screening of 77 per cent (compared to the national target of 70 per cent and an 'achievable quality standard' of 75 per cent). The NCBSU is part of a hospital Trust. The hospital Trust's Mission Statement is as follows:

We aim to provide high quality acute and specialist services which:
- *are responsive to customer needs*
- *use leading edge and effective medical technologies*
- *are at a cost that compares favourably with the rest of the NHS*
- *have motivated and properly trained staff.*

To this end the Trust supports a number of quality audit and improvement initiatives including ISO 9000 and Investors in People. The NCBSU employs 32 members of staff including part-timers. There are four radiologists, seven full-time radiographers, two breast care nurses, and a number of receptionists and office staff. The unit is also supported by several part-time radiographers and visiting surgeons.

In 1999 a small patient satisfaction survey was conducted to obtain detailed feedback about patient expectations and perceptions of the service and to identify areas for improvement. Staff from the different functional areas were also interviewed in order to identify any gaps between patient expectations and perceptions and staff perceptions of the quality of service provided.

Thirty-two patients were interviewed. These included 16 patients who had come to the NCBSU for screening and 16 patients who had been screened and had been called back to the NCBSU because they were diagnosed with breast cancer. Each patient was asked to assign the relative importance, on a five-point scale, of a series of quality factors. They were then asked to rate, again on a 1–5 scale, their perception of the service levels delivered with regard to each factor. Table 4.2 lists the statements which were used to capture each quality factor and Figure 4.20 shows the mean values assigned for each factor by the staff and patients.

Staff were provided with the same list of factors and asked to rate on a 1–5 scale how important they believed the factor to be to the patients, and what service level they believed the patients perceived themselves to be receiving. This would facilitate identification of any mismatches between staff and patient perceptions.

Table 4.2 The statements used to capture each quality factor

Quality factor	Statements used
Access	Was the NCBSU easy to find? Were there transport problems in getting here?
Availability	Were you given as much time as you wanted with staff?
Care	Were you shown concern, consideration and sympathy? Were you treated with patience?
Communication	Were you provided with enough information in a way you could understand?
Competence	Were you impressed by the skill, expertise and professionalism of the staff?
Courtesy	Were staff polite and respectful? Were staff discreet and unobtrusive when necessary?
Functionality	Did the equipment seem adequate in delivering the service?
Reliability	Was the NCBSU reliable and consistent in performance?
Privacy	Were you given enough privacy?
Responsiveness	Was there much waiting and queuing?
Comfort	Was the unit comfortable?

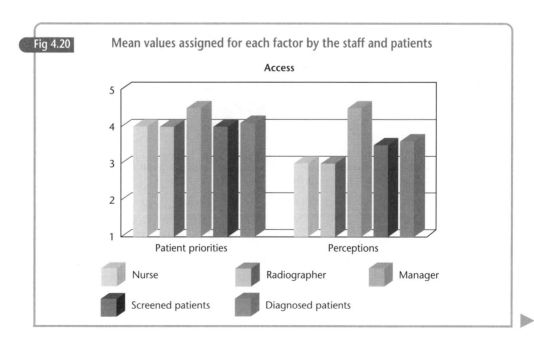

Fig 4.20 Mean values assigned for each factor by the staff and patients

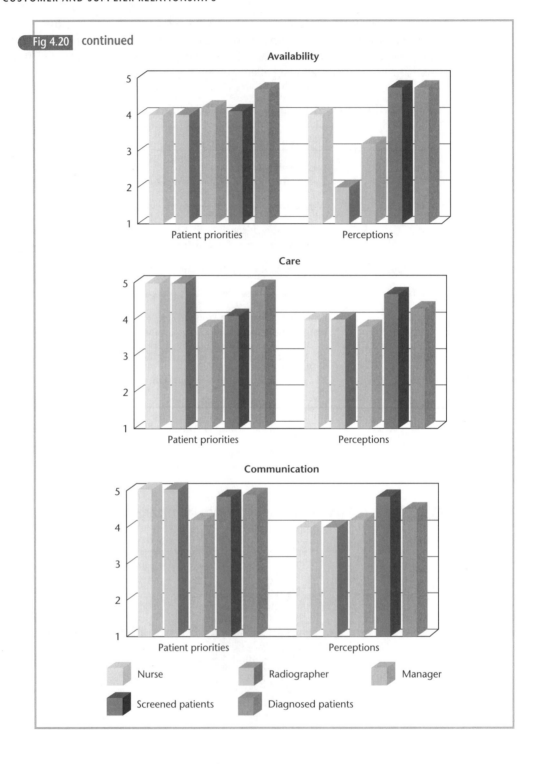

Fig 4.20 continued

Fig 4.20 continued

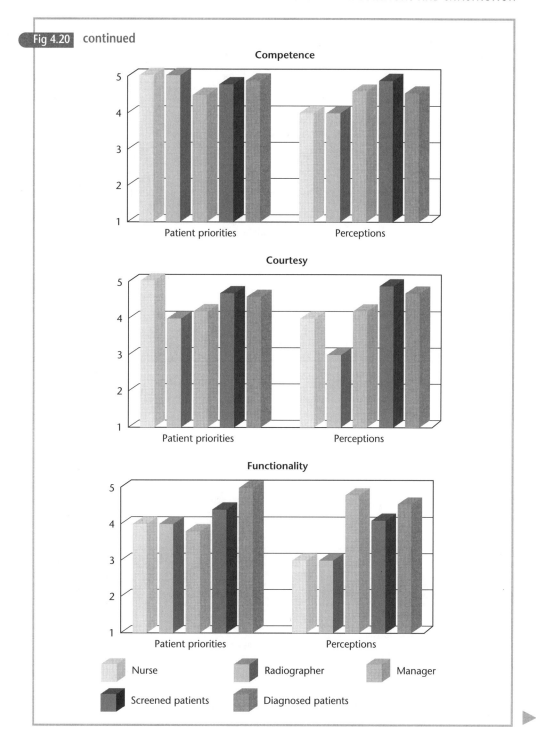

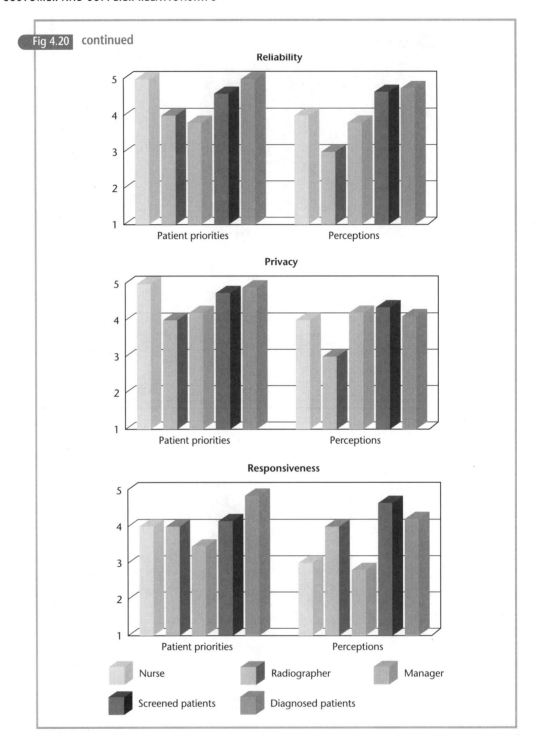

Fig 4.20 continued

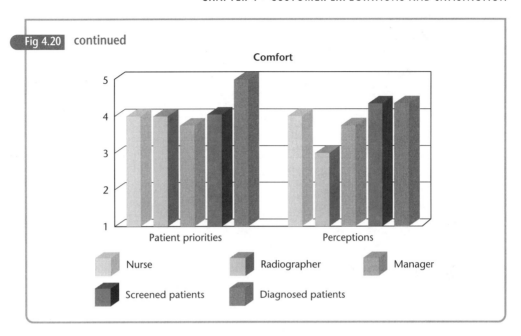

Fig 4.20 continued

Questions

1 *Evaluate the quality of service provided by the NCBSU.*

2 *What recommendations would you make for improvement?*

Managing Supply Relationships

5.1 INTRODUCTION

This chapter describes the management of the relationships involved in service delivery to the end customer. It recognises that the chain or network of activities is frequently rather complex, involving numbers of interrelated participants, each with their own set of priorities and requirements.

The objectives for this chapter are:

- to identify the main types of supply relationships
- to define supply chains, explore service applications and discuss the main issues in supply chain management
- to understand the use and management of intermediaries
- to identify the main types of supply partnerships and how they can be managed effectively
- to evaluate the role of service-level agreements.

Manufacturing companies have been developing their understanding of how to manage supply lines more effectively for many years. The supply chain management approach was born out of an understanding that in order to manage significant increases in product availability combined with greater responsiveness without massive increases in inventory, the various elements of the chain need to operate in synchronisation. These ideas have more recently been applied to service organisations.

5.2 TYPES OF SUPPLY RELATIONSHIPS

This chapter deals with three types of supply relationships: 'simple' service supply chains, management through intermediaries, and supply partnerships (see Figure 5.1).

5.2.1 The service supply chain

Here we address the issues faced by a service provider in ensuring that its own key suppliers meet cost and quality targets required for the effective management of service delivery to customers.

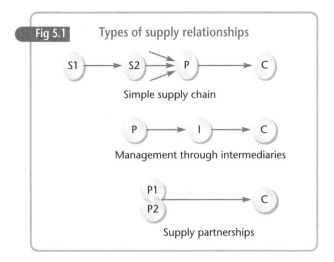

Fig 5.1 — Types of supply relationships

Simple supply chain

Management through intermediaries

Supply partnerships

An example of this type of chain is provided by the service division of a capital equipment manufacturer in the machine tools or construction equipment sector. The economic lifetime of this type of equipment may be in excess of 20 years and the service provider depends on component suppliers to provide proprietary equipment to ensure continuity of service.

5.2.2 Management through intermediaries

Some organisations choose to deliver service to the end consumer through agents or dealers. The reason for this decision varies from a need to provide a sales and service point of contact close to customers but with insufficient volume of demand to support investment in a wholly owned network to provide it, through to a view that providing this type of service is not a core activity for the organisation and is better handled by others.

A capital equipment manufacturer attempting to enter a new geographical market area will not be able to generate sufficient demand to support sales and service activities initially and may choose to use an intermediary in the first instance. Many financial service companies have chosen to sell through brokers, not seeing the customer contact as part of their core business. This approach has been challenged as 'direct' operations have reduced cost and, to some extent, built a sense of greater responsiveness in the eyes of the customer.

5.2.3 Supply partnerships

This aspect of supply relationships relates to the formation of a partnership or alliance to provide a jointly managed service delivery mechanism. These relationships may take the form of joint ventures or, in the retail world, 'in-plants' such as a branded shop within a larger retail store.

Of course there are numbers of combinations beyond the three we have outlined above, but for the most part they are variations on a theme and the principles described below cover the vast majority of situations.

5.3 SERVICE SUPPLY CHAINS

5.3.1 Supply chain definition

A supply chain is the link, or usually the network, which joins together internal and external suppliers with internal and external consumers. Supply chain management (SCM) is concerned with managing the network and the flow of information, materials and customers through the network.

The essential exchange mechanism is information. More accurate information about expected demand passed in appropriate format to upstream suppliers allows them to manage their production with minimum cost. The theory is then that the benefits of increased competitiveness will be shared equitably with the 'partners' in the supply chain. In practice this does not always happen when the organisations with 'muscle' or buying power dominate; however, there are numbers of examples of effective supply chains where purchasers have moved away from adversarial practices.

The concept of supply chains does not translate into all service situations directly. The commodity moving along the manufacturing supply chain or pipeline is inventory, building from raw material to finished and delivered product (see Figure 5.2).

Figure 5.2 is a much-simplified version of a supply chain, but it should be recognised that better information from the point of demand (the supermarket) to the packaging factory allows better co-ordination and potential cost reductions. A simple way of thinking about this is to recognise that there are two reasons for inventory in the supply chain:

1. Processes require work in progress to run. In Figure 5.2, the pet food factory will need several days' worth of inventory for its processes to operate effectively, rather than manufacture a tin at a time!

2. Inventory is put in place because the chain does not operate perfectly. For example, supermarkets require stock on the shelves because they cannot forecast demand with 100 per cent accuracy, and the pet food factory requires more than the minimum inventory because its processes may be inflexible or unreliable.

SCM is targeted primarily at reducing the second of these two reasons for increase in inventory, whilst simultaneously increasing both service level and responsiveness to changing market conditions.

SCM has direct relevance to services that include the provision of manufactured goods as a part of the service concept. For example:

- Retailers who want to combine high levels of product availability with competitive prices and responsiveness to changes in market demand or fashion.

- Equipment service and repair companies who are measured on 'time to fix' need to manage the logistics of spare part availability, frequently across a geographically dispersed network.

- The airline which outsources the production of meals for its passengers needs to manage information flows to ensure that customers receive the choice of meal they require without the airline holding too many extra meals.

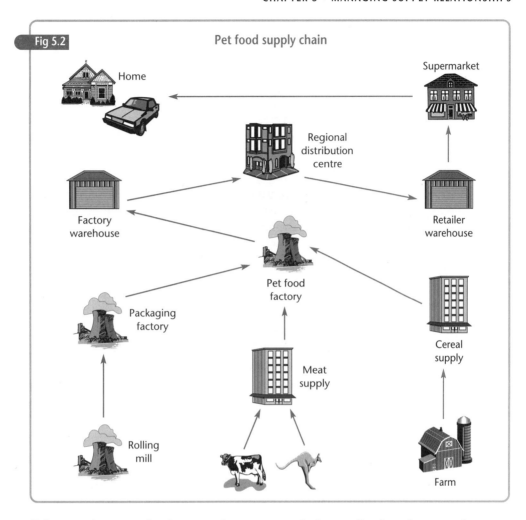

Fig 5.2 Pet food supply chain

Other service organisations need to manage their supplier base because there are significant cost savings to be made. For example, the airlines will watch the price of fuel carefully because marginal savings here will impact the profit line directly. On a smaller scale, the local seafood restaurant will want to develop reliable sources of supply of fresh fish to serve to its customers.

The value of SCM is that it allows for the benefits of vertical integration without the long-term overhead and inherent inflexibility that comes from trying to manage all activities from raw material to final delivery under the umbrella of one organisation. This allows organisations to continue to 'do what they are good at' and to form supply relationships which have sufficient duration to allow for the development of understanding of how to do things better. It is always recognised, though, that as the market demands change, some of these relationships cease to be effective.

Companies in the financial services sector have become interested in the concept of supply chain management, but frequently what is meant in this context is a desire to gain control of the channels to market, a subject considered in more depth in section 5.4.

5.3.2 Supply chain management approaches

The basis of SCM lies in the development of strong buyer–supplier partnerships. Figure 5.3 from the work of Helper (1991) is a useful starting-point to understand the approach.

Helper's work was based on research carried out with suppliers to the large automobile manufacturers in the United States. It is interesting because it views the partnership from the standpoint of the relatively weak suppliers as opposed to that of the buyers, who tend to claim benefits not shared by weaker partners.

Helper's categories are as follows:

- **Voice.** This equates to partnership sourcing. The partners share information as to long-term activity forecasts and in some cases collaborate on R&D. This box is characterised by the expectation of long-term contracts, often linked to placing orders at an aggregate level some months ahead, to be firmed up with more detail as the due date approaches.

- **Exit.** This is what has come be termed 'traditional' or adversarial purchasing. Contracts are generally short, limited to a standard batch size, and there is no sharing of long-term demand forecasts or assistance with process development. It is likely that contracts are placed almost exclusively on price, and buyers will continue to search for competitive bids in order to keep their suppliers in line.

- **Unlikely.** It is unlikely that a supplier will perceive that the buyer is committed to doing long-term business with them in the absence of two-way communication. Of course, it may be that the supplier also chooses to operate at arm's length, not wanting to become too dependent on the one purchaser.

- **Stagnant.** In this scenario, there is a strong sense of commitment, but this has not been turned into a relationship which realises its full potential.

The research was carried out over a period of ten years, during which time many of the automobile manufacturers had moved to just-in-time (JIT) manufacturing and purchasing. At the start of the period, the vast majority of suppliers felt themselves to be in the Exit box, with no real sense of enduring relationship with their cus-

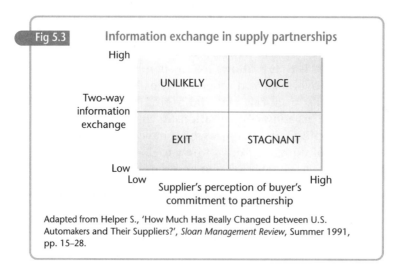

Fig 5.3   Information exchange in supply partnerships

Adapted from Helper S., 'How Much Has Really Changed between U.S. Automakers and Their Suppliers?', *Sloan Management Review*, Summer 1991, pp. 15–28.

tomers. Ten years later, a large number of suppliers reported that they still felt that they were in the Exit box, but that the demands made on them in terms of more frequent delivery and self-certification of quality had increased.

However, there were a significant number of suppliers that reported a move to the Voice box. For these, there was evidence of sufficient confidence to make significant investment in process automation, with resulting improvements in both cost and quality. The conclusion that might be drawn from this is that a relationship approach is not always appropriate or possible. Certainly, one of the aspects of SCM is the reduction in numbers of suppliers, allowing the buyer to concentrate on a relatively small number of 'strategic' partnerships.

The key elements of supply chain management include:

- the management of the supply chain in its entirety, using measures which assess the performance of the total chain
- the development of buyer/supplier partnerships with the expectation of sharing the benefits of increased co-operation over time
- the reduction of the number of suppliers in the chain, with an increase in single or sole suppliers, allowing resource to be focused on the strategic issues
- increasing interchange of information, possibly including long-term demand forecasts, financial costings, process improvements, and research and development
- the possibility of reallocating activities to the most effective position in the supply chain.

The benefits claimed for this approach are as follows:

- reduction in the total cost of inventory held by the chain as a whole
- reduction in administrative overhead involved in managing multiple relationships
- collaboration in scheduling and in process improvement leading to higher service levels and quality improvement
- faster response to changes in market demand.

5.3.3 Supplier selection: multiple, single or sole suppliers?

Selection of suppliers is obviously a key activity, particularly for those who are to undertake critical elements of the supply chain. Some criteria for supplier selection, apart from cost, include:

- financial standing
- people management: skills, training and industrial relations record
- commercial awareness
- productivity
- quality management approach
- focus on continuous improvement activities.

A major consideration is the extent to which the buyer's requirements comprise a significant amount of the supplier's business. A supplier who is totally dedicated to one buyer may seem like a good idea at first sight but may lead to complacency in the relationship. Many buying organisations set targets that limit the proportion of business to be transacted with any one supplier. This has a particular benefit in that if the buyer's business should decline in the short term, their supplier base is more likely to remain viable.

Part of the approach to SCM includes the reduction in the number of suppliers. Concern has been expressed that if the organisation is dependent on a single supplier, that may leave the buyer exposed. Nokia Mobile Phones (IMD case study 1988) has developed an approach to this issue which is typical of many organisations. Nokia has three types of suppliers:

- **Sole suppliers.** These are used for new technologies where there may be only one supplier capable of delivering to the required specification.
- **Single suppliers.** This is the preferred approach for many components. A supplier will be appointed to provide the organisation's total requirements of a component or family of components for a region or possibly globally. Nokia will have other suppliers who are capable of supplying these components in the event of a problem but who are currently providing similar products.
- **Multiple suppliers.** These are used only when necessary, perhaps to develop a supplier's capability or to provide locally specific components.

Nokia's approach to SCM has enabled it to develop the flexibility it requires to meet the demands of a market which has the challenges of rapid growth and shortening product life-cycles.

5.3.4 One-stop shops

A consequence of organisations wishing to reduce their administrative overhead is the rise of the opportunity for service providers to sell a comprehensive package to customers. Facilities management organisations offer full maintenance for organisations which don't wish to employ their own staff to look after their buildings.

The Building Services Limited illustration in Box 5.1 provides an example of a facilities management company needing to develop its own ability to manage suppliers in order to provide a more comprehensive service to its own customers.

Box 5.1 Building Services Limited (BSL)

Building Services Limited was originally formed to provide basic building maintenance services to small to medium companies not wishing to employ their own maintenance team. They were able to employ area teams of mechanical and electrical building engineers to provide a fast response to immediate problems in addition to routine maintenance activities. The speed of response to incidents and frequency of maintenance were laid down in service-level agreements.

BSL realised that they needed to develop new capabilities to manage their customer relationships, and appointed client managers for their largest and most profitable accounts. As a result, the business grew and some of their customers began asking if BSL could take on more of the customer's outsourced requirements. This meant that BSL would now be responsible for servicing more specialised areas such as air-conditioning and clean rooms for semiconductor production.

As an organisation, BSL encourages its regional managers to be entrepreneurial and to develop new service offerings. Their provision of 'energy management' services had been introduced as the result of the initiative of an area team which had seen the opportunity of making use of the information they held for their customers.

As the business grew, so also did the nature and size of the clients. BSL was now providing full facilities management services for national companies that wanted BSL to provide the same level and scope of services to all sites. At the same time, customers wanted BSL to act as a 'one-stop-shop' for all their outsourced services, including IT and office equipment service. BSL saw this as an opportunity to move into the provision of services which commanded higher premiums but recognised that in the short to medium term they would have to act as a services 'broker', buying these services from other service providers now acting as sub-contractors to BSL rather than the final client.

Questions

1 *What are the challenges for BSL in taking on this new role of 'One-stop shop' for its customers' multi-site operations?*

2 *Should BSL continue to develop its own 'in-house' capabilities or increase its own supplier base of 'associated service providers'?*

This illustration is based on a real organisation though all names and places have been changed.

5.3.5 The role of e-procurement

The Internet has seen the advent of numerous web-enabled retail services. It is relatively easy for a retailer to link together a number of suppliers in order to offer a wider range of services for its customers. The excitement about this type of service is that suppliers, whose market was strictly local before, now have access to customers worldwide. However, it should not be forgotten that however fast and easy the ordering process might be, the order fulfilment process still requires the 'old' logistics processes as before (see also Chapter 9).

Croom (2000), in a study of web-based procurement of operating resources supply, found that the participants anticipated a number of benefits:

- reduced procurement cost
- increased procurement control
- enhanced supplier management.

These benefits are realised largely through the possibility of greater co-ordination of activity and greater visibility of information.

5.3.6 Supply chain improvement: lean thinking

Lean thinking is generally held to have originated through the work of Toyoda and Ohno at the Toyota Motor Company in Japan (Womack *et al.* 1990). The Toyota Production System has been studied and copied by manufacturing companies throughout the world who wish to reap the benefits of reduced costs as well as a change in organisational culture that believes in the possibility of continuous improvement throughout the supply chain.

The essence of lean thinking is to drive out *muda*, the Japanese word for waste, defined as anything that creates no value for the customer. Womack and Jones (1996) list five principles of lean thinking:

- *Specify value.* Value must be defined by the ultimate customer. It is so easy to revert to a 'producer' mentality that assumes that because the provider thinks that the product is good, it must represent value. Womack and Jones use airlines as an example of organisations that have not always understood value in these terms, providing executive lounges and extra facilities on flights when passengers really want rapid, safe travel to their destination.

- *Identify the value stream.* The value stream is the set of actions required to bring the product to the customer. The total supply chain from raw material through to final delivery and use by the customer must be understood in order to identify where activities at particular points in the chain in reality create no value for the customer, but have always been carried out because nobody had an overview of the total chain. When analysing the whole value stream, three types of activities can be identified: those which create value for customers, those which create no value for customers but cannot be eliminated given current technology or process constraints, and those which create no value and can be removed.

  It should be noted that the second of these categories of activities, those which create no value but cannot be removed, must be closely examined to see if this assumption is, in fact, correct. It may be that the activity persists simply 'because we have always done it this way', and so the activity may be eliminated.

  Telecom equipment providers such as Ericsson, Motorola and Nortel are working hard to become more involved in their customers' businesses. In order to do this, they must know more about how the customers – the network operators – manage their businesses, and also what the ultimate customers require. This increased customer focus leads to a shortening of the value stream, more focused research and development, lower costs, and greater value for customers.

- *Create flow.* The essence of lean thinking is that work flows continuously and smoothly through a 'pipeline' without stopping. In other words, the tendency to create batches of work that occur when the hand-offs from department to department are not well managed is to be reduced. These discontinuities in the flow of work create the possibility for errors, they slow down the response to customer demand, and create a requirement to manage the work-load which could be avoided. Batched work creates queues with the need to manage priorities and to expedite work which, as it gets later, becomes ever more urgent.

  This thinking has been applied with great success to the back offices of many financial services companies, particularly as many have reorganised around customer processes and dismantled the traditional departmental or 'silo' mentality.

- *Pull not push.* Traditional production systems produce in the hope of selling their wares. This creates *muda* in terms of overproduction and therefore excess cost. The challenge of lean thinking is to have operations schedules governed by demand pull rather than production push. Pull systems are essentially replenishment systems working on the basis of 'sell one, make one'. A good example is provided by McDonald's in the replenishment of burgers as customers buy them. The task for the organisation is to monitor and adjust the replenishment levels as demand patterns vary.

Pull systems require a major shift in operational culture since it means that work in progress is significantly reduced and there isn't the comfort factor of piles of work in progress in the system. The challenge for the service organisation is to find ways to manage the total supply chain in similar ways to the manufacturing examples.

- *Strive for perfection.* This fifth principle of lean thinking flows from the other four. As partners in the total supply chain apply the lean thinking philosophy many of the problems are addressed, but more importantly, a culture of both significant and continuous improvement develops.

Ohno identified seven sources of *muda*:

- over-production ahead of demand
- waiting for the next process step
- unnecessary transport of materials
- over-processing of parts due to poor technology or process design
- excessive inventories
- unnecessary movement of employees
- defective production.

These all apply to many service operations, particularly those which have factory-like back offices, and those which have the supply of physical product as part of the concept. It is also worth applying Ohno's classification to the customer process, considering a customer as the unit of material. This would encourage thinking about the cost to the customer in time or money in dealing with a particular service provider. A reduction in cost for the customer would almost certainly equate to an increase in value which is the essence of lean thinking.

5.3.7 Barriers to supply chain management implementation

Although SCM makes sense in many ways to organisations, there are a number of barriers to successful implementation:

- *Lack of systems capability.* SCM requires the ability to pass information about changing demand patterns through the chain. Not all companies have invested in the capability to achieve this.
- *Complacency.* Where industry sectors have been reasonably stable, organisations may not see the need for SCM and ignore it until a new entrant operates in a different mode. A more dangerous form of complacency exists when organisations feel that they have already fully implemented SCM and have lost the drive for continuous improvement.
- *Information used for a variety of conflicting purposes.* This relates particularly to demand forecasts which may be used on the one hand to create an optimistic picture of the future to manage shareholder expectations, but on the other must

be used for detailed planning activities. The former may bear no relation to reality, leading to over-investment in capacity.

- *Mistrust.* Previous, over-inflated estimates of demand may lead to suppliers reducing capacity allocations to levels less than required.

- *Power games.* Reorganisation along supply chain lines may be resisted by individuals whose power base will be diminished as a result. There may also be resistance on the part of suppliers who fear that they will be overwhelmed by a more powerful partner.

Many of the technical problems can be overcome to make the supply chain more effective. As with most significant change programmes, the major resistance comes from the people involved.

5.4 MANAGING THROUGH INTERMEDIARIES

Many service organisations continue to use intermediaries for the selling process as well as for service delivery to the end customer or user. These organisations have continued to develop support networks of agents, dealers or franchisees for a variety of reasons.

Financial service companies have traditionally dealt through pensions or insurance brokers. This was in part to give the customer confidence that they were being given independent advice, for the same reason that Microsoft uses Certified Solution Providers (see Box 5.2). The problem with this approach is that it often leads to confusion as to who is the 'real' customer – the intermediary or the final consumer.

Of course, the simple answer is that both groups are customers, but it would be wrong to suggest that satisfying both groups is an easy task.

Box 5.2 Microsoft Certified Solution Providers

Microsoft chooses to sell and provide support for its software through a comprehensive worldwide network of partners and associated companies, rather than deal directly with customers. There are a number of channels for Microsoft to manage in order to ensure that its users receive the appropriate level of service.

One of these channels is managed by Microsoft under the Certified Solution Provider Programme. Microsoft Providers are able to receive training, sales support and software, as well as priority information as to the latest upgrades and software patches, to ensure that they are up to date and able to give their customers good service.

For the larger Solution Providers, Microsoft has introduced a Partner Programme. To qualify for this programme, the Provider must demonstrate a number of attributes under the headings of Commitment, Significance, Proactivity, and Effectiveness. To demonstrate their competence the Partner must employ a given number of Microsoft Certified Systems Engineers or Solution Developers. In return, the Partner receives an increased level of support and is allocated the assistance of a Microsoft Business Development Manager. Microsoft requires ongoing evidence not only that their Partners are technically competent, but that they have viable business plans.

The Partners receive significant sales and marketing support. They are linked to the Microsoft.com home page for potential customers looking for Solutions Providers. In the Partner Network, they can search for potential collaborators. Partners receive priority notification of potential sales leads from Microsoft's telesales operation, and they have access to 'customer-critical' technical support.

Microsoft emphasises the independence of their Providers and Provider Partners. They are able to sell and support solutions from other software developers. However, it is apparent that Microsoft offers every incentive to its Partners to proactively sell and support its own solutions.

Questions

1 *How much resource should Microsoft devote to auditing its Partners' continuing ability to meet its criteria?*

2 *What are the costs and benefits for Microsoft in adopting this approach as opposed to developing its own network?*

This illustration is based on material from the Microsoft web site: http://www.microsoft.com.

5.4.1 Why use intermediaries?

Armistead and Clark (1992) suggest the following reasons for the use of agents or dealers in the provision of customer support for products and systems:

- *Closeness to customer.* Many customers prefer to deal with an organisation which is physically close to them. This might be because they prefer to deal 'face to face', have not got access to electronic processes, or the nature of the service requires the presence of the service provider. For example, one of the major drivers for customer satisfaction in the ownership of cars is the ease of access to a recognised dealer for service and repair.

- *Local knowledge.* The parent organisation may have insufficient knowledge of local conditions and culture. In the development of global strategies, much emphasis is placed on 'thinking globally, acting locally'.

- *Focused expertise.* Microsoft (see Box 2.5) has chosen to restrict its activities to software development rather than get involved in the creation and administration of a network of distributors and developers. This allows for a high degree of flexibility as service partners close to the market develop new solutions using Microsoft platforms.

- *Poor service margins.* The volume of service revenue may be too small in some geographical regions for the provision of a dedicated service unit. Capital equipment suppliers may sell only one or two units initially into a region but must provide aftersales support. Rather than recruit and train service engineers for a few service calls per year, the company may use local service agents who may also service competitors' equipment.

- *Insufficient capacity.* A strategy adopted by many call centres is to have 'sub-contract' capacity available through providers set up explicitly for this type of activity. The information systems available to call centre agents enable them to act in such a manner that the customer is unlikely to detect any difference in service delivery.

5.4.2 Managing Intermediaries

The central issue in dealing with intermediaries is that their objectives may not always coincide with those of the parent organisation. Figure 5.4 illustrates a 'military' model for aftersales customer support in which various service delivery mechanisms are outlined. This model suggests that intermediaries may be aligned to 'mercenaries', fighting for the cause, primarily because they are being paid.

The key dimension in Figure 5.4 is that of in-house control. The trade-off which service organisations adopting the intermediary approach are making is between the potential quality cost of poor quality of service and lost customers, against the cost of forming and maintaining a distributed network of service units.

The reasons for maintaining high in-house control of service include:

- using the opportunity to increase the depth and breadth of a customer relationship
- to ensure that customer complaints are effectively dealt with and that rapid feedback for process improvement is facilitated
- the support provided is linked to innovative goods and services for which there is limited resource.

The various service forms are as follows:

- **The Commandos.** These are highly trained service personnel, often used as 'hit squads' able to tackle most problems on their own with little or no management

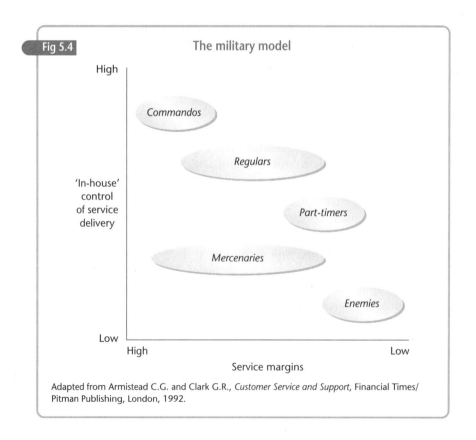

Fig 5.4   The military model

Adapted from Armistead C.G. and Clark G.R., *Customer Service and Support*, Financial Times/ Pitman Publishing, London, 1992.

direction. These are typically used to support complex products such as process automation or innovative information systems. These service providers are often found in professional services, particularly those that provide support services for software or communication systems.

- *The Regulars.* Regulars are less comprehensively skilled than the Commandos and are as less able to work without direction. The tasks they carry out tend to be more specialised and, of course, there are more of them. It is important to note that, because they are employed by the parent organisation, there is still a relatively high level of in-house control. This is diminished slightly by the fact that the Regulars are usually geographically dispersed by region or site.

- *Part-timers.* These service providers are the customers themselves, trained by the parent organisation to carry out service tasks for themselves. An example is provided by the photocopier companies that train key operators to change toner cartridges and free paper jams without using expensive service engineers (Regulars).

- *Mercenaries.* Mercenaries are not part of the parent organisation. The prime reason for 'fighting' on the side of the main organisation is that they are being paid for so doing. They may switch sides if there is sufficient incentive and they do not share the culture of the parent organisation.

- *Enemies.* These are not on the same side. It may be that the parent organisation has decided not to provide service in all circumstances, particularly if the profit margins are small.

In this chapter it is the management and motivation of the 'Mercenaries' which are our prime concern. The challenge is to provide such intermediaries with sufficient financial incentive whilst developing the customer service values required to generate customer loyalty. Strategies include:

- *Financial incentives.* This is particularly relevant when the intermediary is not dedicated to provide service for only one organisation. The parent organisation may provide financial inducements, discounts or credit facilities to encourage the intermediary to favour its service products ahead of its rivals.

- *Punishments.* The ultimate sanction for poor performance is for the parent organisation to withdraw its support. This has become more common in recent years in the automobile industry, with manufacturers removing franchises from dealerships. Generally speaking, though, this approach is only used as a last resort as other dealers, no matter how good they are, wonder if they will be treated in a similar manner.

- *Providing expertise.* One of the most effective ways of motivating intermediaries is to provide support for their business. The parent organisation frequently has considerable resources in areas that are lacking in the intermediary. In Box 5.2 we saw Microsoft providing sales support for solution providers who are stronger in technical skills. Caterpillar, likewise, have created high levels of dealer satisfaction through the support given.

- *Training.* McDonald's Hamburger University is occasionally made fun of, but there can be little doubt as to its value in creating a consistency of approach throughout the network of outlets, company owned and franchisees alike.

- *Information systems and technology.* Provision of process technology will assist in ensuring consistency of delivery. A franchisee generally receives a package of standard equipment and operating procedures to deliver the core service in the manner laid down by the parent organisation. Both Caterpillar and Microsoft provide on-line technical support to their partners and dealers. This serves the dual purpose of ensuring high-quality technical support is given to their customers and also training their partners and dealers in the desired approach.

5.4.3 Selection of intermediaries

The recruitment and training of intermediaries is a critical decision, particularly for those organisations choosing to operate through franchises. Franchisees operate under the company brand and any poor performer will seriously damage it. Criteria for selection should be at least as stringent as for the selection of suppliers, but should also include a review of the potential franchisee's commitment to the brand values of the parent organisation.

5.5 SUPPLY PARTNERSHIPS

As the pace of competition quickens it becomes increasingly common for organisations to enter into partnerships and alliances for a number of strategic reasons:

- to enter a new geographic region, where a partner may have a stronger market presence
- to provide a package of goods and services which require the joint expertise of the partners to deliver them
- to develop new expertise in association with others, sharing resources in order to gain joint benefits.

'Partnerships and alliances' is as vague a term as customer relationships. There are as many forms of partnership in reality as there are types of customers. These range from long-term, formal partnerships, frequently resulting in joint venture companies, through to short-term collaborations which are formed for a specific objective.

Much has been written about strategic alliances (see, for example, Faulkner 1992), but we are concerned in this text with those alliances which are formed in order to collaborate in the development and/or delivery of a specific set of service products.

5.5.1 Types of alliances

Faulkner identifies three dimensions of alliances:

1. *Focused or complex.* A focused alliance has clearly defined aims, and is set up under particular specific circumstances. Generally speaking, the focused alliance deals with a subset of each of the partners' total activities. An example would be a telecommunications system's provider such as Ericsson or Motorola forming an alliance with a software company in China to market a specific communications solution. It is clear that this agreement does not go beyond these boundaries.

A complex alliance would involve a much more substantial part of both partners being involved, perhaps retaining separate brands and marketing identities, but operationally much more interlinked.

2. *Joint venture or working agreement.* A major task for the partnership cannot be handled by semi-formal agreements. It is more likely to be dealt with by the formation of a joint venture company. A significant issue here will be the allocation of power between the two partners.

3. *Partnership or consortium.* Whilst many strategic alliances take the form of a partnership between two organisations, a complex task requiring a wide range of skills and knowledge may be handled using a consortium. The issues involved in the management of these projects are correspondingly more complex.

5.5.2 Conditions for success

Figure 5.5 describes some of the major factors to be considered in assessing the likely success of an alliance.

Criteria for assessing the likely success of an alliance include:

- The extent to which the strategic aims of the partners coincide, but do not overlap. If both partners want the same benefits, there is little point in pursuing the partnership.

- The extent to which the two cultures allow for effective working. Are the values, beliefs and general ways of working compatible?

- Are the two parents ('A' and 'B') in Figure 5.5 able to let the venture work in its own way? The culture of the venture is likely to be different from those of both its parents and may be viewed with suspicion.

- Has there been sufficient discussion and negotiation as to what are the likely benefits for each partner? Is it clear as to which partner is responsible for which activities?

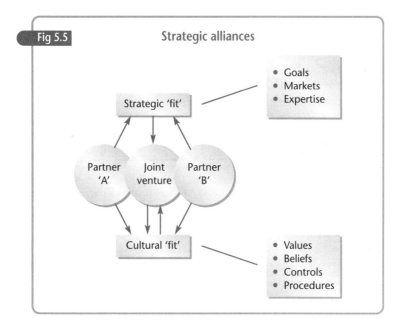

Fig 5.5   **Strategic alliances**

- Is there a dominant partner in the enterprise? Has this been agreed and is the less powerful partner happy with the arrangement?
- Is it clear as to how long the partnership will last and what are the terms of the dissolution of the partnership?

Box 5.3 Sussex Police, UK: Operation Columbus

Police services throughout the UK have undergone a major change in approach to their task in recent years. One obvious sign of this change is that the police is now known as a 'service' rather than a 'force', recognising the need to integrate more obviously into the society it serves rather than simply enforce law.

Sussex Police, in common with others, is facing the issue of dealing with rising levels of crime but with limited resource. Many issues in society today cannot be solved simply by putting more police officers on the streets, even if this were possible to do. Problems of drug dealing or racial unrest require co-operation between society at large, community leaders, and other social agencies. The Sussex Police Way, launched in 1999, sets out five policing principles to support the purpose of Sussex Police, which is 'to reduce the number of incidents which require an intervention by Sussex Police and/or from other social agencies'.

The aim is to address the root cause of problems and to break the vicious cycle of responding to emergency calls in a wholly reactive manner. Principle No. 4 states: 'We will emphasise and develop the partnership approach. This will involve a wide range of official and voluntary agencies as well as the general public.'

One example of this approach is provided by Operation Columbus. Sussex has several language schools attracting students from many countries who are interested in studying English in a location close to the sea but near to London. These students may be vulnerable to attack either because they are naïve or because they provoke jealousy. Months of consultation between police, language schools and student bodies have resulted in a manual available to those involved in student welfare. It covers every aspect of student safety from simple precautions to be taken by the students themselves through to advice for police officers in dealing with students, whether they be victims or offenders. This information is presented in multi-lingual documents, through posters featuring the adventures of Columbus, and through an attractive Operation Columbus web site.

Questions

1 *What benefits can be generated from this partnership approach? How would you justify the investment in time, effort and materials required?*

2 *In extending this approach to more sensitive issues such as drug taking or racial disharmony, what problems could be anticipated in generating the information flows required to build a partnership?*

This illustration compiled from information displayed on the Sussex Police web site http://www.sussex.police.uk and the Operation Columbus site, http://www.sussex.police.uk/columbus/index.html.

The experiences of alliances are many and varied. The key issue is the extent to which senior management is truly committed to the process, rather than paying lip-service to the idea. Hutt *et al.* (2000), in describing the creation of a co-branded service product between a telecommunication company and a financial service organisation, outline the impact of a 'clash of corporate egos'. Each partner was used to exerting its muscle as both were powerful in their traditional markets. The initial lack of compromise between the partners at senior level led to a series of disputes at the operational level, including conflicts as to what company name would be used by customer service representatives.

The study carried out by Hutt *et al.* followed the alliance from inception into its second year. At the end of the first year the alliance was only moderately profitable, but was showing signs of improvement. Both partners found difficulty in generating mutual trust, having been used to adversarial negotiating stances in the past. The study found that this was a major problem in the early life of the project and staff needed continuing social contact to begin to break down barriers raised on day one. The illustration of Sussex Police in Box 5.3 demonstrates that significant amounts of time must be invested in order to generate the levels of trust required to move a partnership approach forward.

5.6 SERVICE-LEVEL AGREEMENTS

Service-level agreements (SLAs) are forms of contracts agreed between a service supplier and the service purchaser or user. These are usually found in a business-to-business context and often between internal suppliers and customers where a traditional contract is not felt to be appropriate. They are an important means of managing the relationship between partners in a supply chain.

Whether for internal use or external use, a service-level agreement goes beyond the traditional remit of a contract, i.e. a statement of a service specification and the price that will be paid for it. Whilst an SLA, like a contract, defines the nature of the goods or services and the level of quality to be provided, the idea of an 'agreement' is that it is a mutually agreed view of what can and will be provided but also, and importantly, exists for the mutual development of both parties. That is, an SLA is seen to be an integral part of the development of a relationship between a supplier and a customer – indeed the SLA attempts to formalise this relationship.

There are three key features of an SLA: setting a service specification, dealing with day-to-day, routine issues, and the development of the relationship.

Service specification

The core of an SLA is the development and agreement of the service specification. This will include:

- Agreeing the key dimensions of performance, such as response times, availability, accuracy etc. This allows for customer and supplier to understand what is important about the service from both points of view.

- Agreeing how each dimension will be measured. Discussion and agreement about the measures to be used reduces the likelihood of disagreements at a later date about performance.

- Setting mutually agreed targets for each dimension. It is possible that standards set by one party may be too high for the needs of the other; clarity and agreement over what is needed and what is possible should lead to a feasible and achievable, and indeed low-cost, outcome.

● Defining where the responsibility lies for the measurement of each dimension. Unlike a traditional contract the responsibility for performance measurement may rest with either the supplier or customer, but such information is made openly available to both parties.

Routinised relationship

The routine part of the relationship formalised by the SLA concerns the day-to-day operation of the agreement. This may include:

● Providing a mechanism for reporting performance against standards at agreed intervals. Underpinning an SLA is the sharing of information, the purpose of which should not be unilateral action as it might be in a traditional contract, but for the purpose of understanding and improvement.

● Setting out the procedures to be invoked if a failure against standard should occur. Routines for dealing with problems should be agreed in advance so that both parties understand their obligations and duties in such event. Failures should not be seen to be negative but as opportunities for supplier and customer to work together to solve each other's problems.

Developmental relationship

A key, though often ignored, element of an SLA is its role in developing a long-term relationship between supplier and customer. This involves:

● Providing a mechanism for routine discussion of the measures and targets and to share ideas for all-round improvements. This 'double loop learning' activity formalises the need to regularly review the agreement, the measures used, the targets applied and the relationship between the parties.

5.6.1 Advantages and disadvantages

Clearly, SLAs require a considerable deal more input of time and effort by both parties than a traditional contract. They have to be tailor-made for each service with each supplier in the supply chain, they can be complex and need an investment of time and effort in the long term to secure the potential benefits.

However, they do have the potentially significant benefits of a closer working relationship and therefore better service between supplier and provider. They can reduce risk for the supplier and the purchaser or user, they create loyalty and reliability by focusing on the development of people and systems rather than focusing on systems of 'punishment'. They also prevent unnecessary and expensive over-provision of quality by defining agreed standards.

5.6.2 Frequent mistakes in SLAs

Sadly, for many organisations, SLAs degenerate into a traditional contract, missing out on the real benefits that can be obtained. The usual mistakes that are made include:

● covers too few or inappropriate dimensions of performance.

● no mutually agreed targets for each dimension

- responsibility for measures is not identified
- no mechanism for reporting and discussion of performance
- no procedures to deal with problems
- mutual benefits not discussed or delivered
- no mechanism for discussion of measures or targets or to share ideas for improvement
- lack of commitment of managers from both parties to derive the benefits from the agreements.

5.7 SUMMARY

Types of supply relationships

There are three main types of supply relationships: 'simple' service supply chains, management through intermediaries, and supply partnerships.

Service supply chains

- A supply chain is the network which joins together internal and external suppliers with internal and external consumers.
- Supply chain management (SCM) is concerned with managing the network and the flow of information, materials and customers through the network.
- The value of SCM is that it allows for the benefits of vertical integration without the long-term overhead and inherent inflexibility that comes from trying to manage all activities from raw material to final delivery under the umbrella of one organisation.

Managing through intermediaries

- The main reasons for using intermediaries include closeness to customer, local knowledge, focused expertise, poor service and insufficient capacity.
- The main trade-off to be managed is between in-house control and profit margins.

Supply partnerships

- It is increasingly common for organisations to enter into partnerships and alliances.
- There are many forms of partnership, the three main dimensions of which are focused or complex, joint venture or working agreement, and partnership or consortium.

Service-level agreements

- Service-level agreements are forms of contracts agreed between a service supplier and the service purchaser or user.
- The three activities involved in managing SLAs are: setting a service specification, dealing with routine issues, and the development of the relationship.
- Many SLAs do not realise the potential benefits.

5.8 DISCUSSION QUESTIONS

1. Compare the approaches of two organisations in the same service sector, one choosing to operate through intermediaries, the other preferring to deal with end customers directly. What are the benefits and challenges of each approach?

2. How can supply chains be managed more effectively to provide more effective service delivery in order to increase customer satisfaction, whilst increasing profitability for all the companies in the chain?

5.9 QUESTIONS FOR MANAGERS

1. Have you reviewed your supplier relationships recently? Are any of these relationships in the 'Stagnant' category? If so, what can you do about them?

2. Could you be more effective in reaching new markets by forming a strategic alliance? What would you require in such a partner?

3. Are you using the potential of e-procurement to manage your supplier base more effectively?

5.10 SUGGESTIONS FOR FURTHER READING

Faulkner D., 'Strategic Alliances: Cooperation for competition', in Faulkner D. and Johnson G. (eds), *The Challenge of Strategic Management*, Kogan Page, London, 1992.

5.11 REFERENCES

Armistead C.G. and Clark G.R., Customer *Service and Support*, Financial Times/Pitman Publishing, London, 1992.

Croom S., 'The Impact of Web-Based Procurement on the Management of Operating Resources Supply', *Journal of Supply Chain Management*, 2000.

Faulkner D., 'Strategic Alliances: Cooperation for competition', in Faulkner D. and Johnson G. (eds), *The Challenge of Strategic Management*, Kogan Page, 1992.

Helper S., 'How Much Has Really Changed between U.S. Automakers and Their Suppliers?', *Sloan Management Review*, Summer 1991, pp. 15–28.

Hutt M.D., Stafford E.R., Walker B.A. and Reingen P.H., 'Defining the Social Network of a Strategic Alliance', *Sloan Management Review*, Winter 2000.

Womack J.P. and Jones D.T., *Lean Thinking*, Simon & Schuster, London, 1996.

Womack J.P., Jones D.T. and Roos D., *The Machine that Changed the World*, Macmillan, New York, 1990.

CASE EXERCISE

The Regional Forensic Science Laboratory

This case was co-written by Tay Ming Kiong, Department of Scientific Services,
Institute of Forensic Science and Forensic Medicine, Singapore

The Regional Forensic Science Laboratory (RFSL) provides a one-stop service to a range of professionals. These professionals include police officers investigating crimes, narcotics officers who want drugs analysing, fire officers concerned to find the cause of a fire, defence counsels who are trying to strengthen the legal case for their clients, hospitals wishing to identify the cause of cases of poisoning, and private individuals who might be considering taking civil action.

Michael Tay is the head of the RFSL and he explains how his unit operates.

'Forensic science is the application of science to the law and our role is to assist our clients in identifying suspects and victims, clearing innocent persons of suspicion and bringing the wrongdoer to justice. Our task is to provide accurate and objective information based on the evidence with which we are provided. We provide both written reports and verbal evidence in legal trials.

'We have seven laboratories here, all under one roof, though often exhibits may well be sent from one lab to another for different specialised examinations. The Toxicology Laboratory examines body fluids and organs to determine the presence or absence of drugs and poisons. The Drugs Analysis Laboratory examines exhibits for drug content and body fluids and hair for drug consumption. The Physical Evidence Laboratory applies the principles and techniques of chemistry and physics to identify and compare a wide range of crime-scene evidence: firearms, gunshot residues, tool marks, shoeprints, tyre prints, paints, fibres, explosives etc. The Biology Laboratory examines exhibits for biological material (dried bloodstains, semen, saliva and other body fluids) and identifies the source using conventional serology or DNA typing. The Document Examination Laboratory examines handwriting, typewriting on documents, some of which may be badly charred, for example, to ascertain authenticity and/or source. The Latent Prints Unit processes and examines evidence for latent fingerprints and identifies the source of lifted prints. And the Forensic Pathology Laboratory investigates sudden unnatural, unexplained or violent deaths to determine the cause of death.

'I know this sounds quite straightforward and scientific but the reality is rather different – it is fraught with problems and confusion. All the police officers, fire officers and hospitals etc. will send exhibits directly to the appropriate lab. This is fine until that lab sends it to another lab and the client no longer knows who has their blood sample etc.

'The sample they give us will have been given to them by someone else. It might have come from a crime scene, from a victim or a suspect or an eyewitness. Because it can take time to get the sample from the origin it means we are under tremendous pressure to undertake the analysis quickly in order to help them complete the investigation. Hospitals, for example, rely on speedy response from the Toxicology Laboratory to ascertain the cause of poisoning so as to be able to quickly administer the right antidote or treatment to save the victim. The other professionals are usually under very tight deadlines imposed by the organisations, such as courts, to which they are responsible.

'Yet we have to be very careful to do a thorough and proper job because at the end of the day the real customer is the suspect, either exonerated or convicted, the families and sympathisers of the suspects, the victims and their families who may have suffered terribly, the public and of course the press and the media. Forensic science carries a heavy weight in the legal system. The judge and jury generally view forensic evidence as objective and impartial when assessing the case against a defendant.

'The forensic expert's testimony must be clear and comprehensible to lay persons. Prosecutors, defence lawyers, judges and juries often have little time or inclination to get to grips with highly technical forensic evidence. We have to provide it in an accessible way. Because we have to make the information accessible and understandable, defence lawyers will use it to try to undermine the quality of the forensic science laboratory, our processes and even our staff. Their job is to interpret the evidence in favour of their clients and so they will look for weaknesses in the forensic findings to discredit the evidence or render it inadmissible.

'We also have a problem with the evidence that is sent to us. We rely on the people, at the scenes of crime for example, to collect the right type and right amount of evidence. There is also the problem of which evidence to believe – it is possible that it may have been 'planted'.

'Furthermore, like many forensic services, our laboratories face significant staff turnover and shortage, which affect capacity, result in loss of expertise and disrupt client relationships. As a result our delivery times can be quite long. The situation is made worse by new technologies that not only are expensive but require a substantial investment in training. Also the people we have are from scientific backgrounds and may be excellent in technical skills but lacking in business sense and customer awareness!

'At the end of the day, members of the public want to see justice done, and the criminal punished. They are alarmed when the criminal and judicial processes are unsuccessful in identifying and convicting the criminal. The public expects the correct culprit to be quickly apprehended and dealt with. Mistakes in the criminal justice systems have wide-ranging impact on the community, victim, victim's family, falsely accused person, investigators, the investigation process, forensic community and the judicial process. In capital punishment cases, the mistake cannot be corrected because the sentence is irreversible. Justice must not only be done; it must be seen as done, and we have a vital role to play in this. Unfortunately, I sometimes feel that the system is against us and we are not doing all that we should.'

Questions

1 *Summarise the problems faced by Michael Tay and the other professionals involved in the collection, analysis and use of forensic evidence.*

2 *How could a 'supply chain approach' overcome some of the problems?*

Part 3

SERVICE DELIVERY

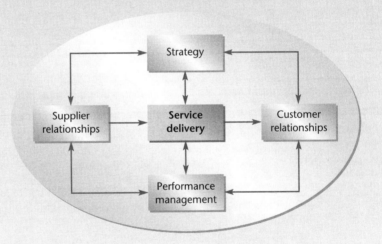

CHAPTER **6**

Service Processes

6.1 INTRODUCTION

In spite of the fact that the service process is the core of service delivery, not only frequently visible to customers but often constituting the very service itself, it is surprising that many organisations devote only limited time and attention to understanding and designing this key aspect of their business. As a result, it is not unusual to find unhelpful and inadequate service processes which have evolved without careful management attention or which are expected to deal with a task for which they were not designed. It is not surprising then that customers are dissatisfied with some aspects of the service, while the operation is not as efficient as it could be and is more costly than necessary.

The objectives of this chapter are therefore:

- to define service processes and their importance
- to understand the nature of service processes
- to identify the attributes and tasks associated with various service processes
- to explain how to reposition service processes
- to provide some tools to help 'engineer' service processes
- to explain how to control service processes
- to introduce some ways of preventing process failures.

This chapter focuses on managing service processes, their design and development. It provides several simple yet powerful tools for managing, assessing, designing and improving service processes and some techniques for managing-out failures that may be inadvertently designed into service processes.

6.2 SERVICE PROCESSES AND THEIR IMPORTANCE

Good service – that which satisfies the customer and meets the strategic intentions of the organisation – is usually the result of careful design and delivery of a whole set of interrelated processes. Services that fail often do so because they have been inadequately designed and executed. Although the service process is only one element of the service operation, it is the part that holds the rest together.

6.2.1 The service process

A holiday consists of many different activities, flights, hotel accommodation, meals, and tours, for example. Whilst these are the elements which come together to create the holiday, it is the way the customer, information and materials are processed and how they link together that creates the experience. Key elements of the experience may involve being met off the plane and being led to transfer coaches, the checking-in at the hotel, the way the reps provide assistance and information etc. The service experience or process is not just the elements of the holiday but also how they link together as the holiday unfolds. Some processes will be highly visible to the customer, such as check-in, while others may be, at least in part, invisible to the customer, such as computerised booking and reservations, cooking and cleaning at the hotel. Some processes will process customers such as the transfer coaches, some processes process information such as reservations systems, and some processes will process materials such as catering services.

A service process links together activities with resources and is defined as the set of interrelated tasks or activities that are required to deliver a service (or product) which together, in an appropriate sequence, create the service. Operations comprise many interrelated processes, some of which predominantly process customers, others information and others materials. Some tasks and activities may be located in the back office away from customers, while other tasks or activities take place in the presence of the customer, either in the organisation's front office or in the customer's home, for example. Together these processes create the service experience and result in the service outcomes. Figure 6.1 shows a simplified diagrammatic representation of some operations processes (see also Armistead and Clark 1993).

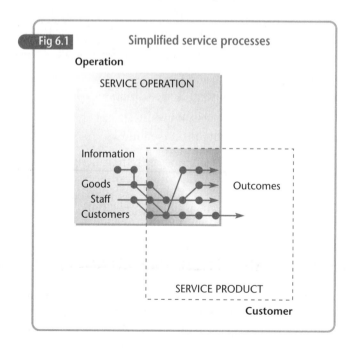

Fig 6.1 Simplified service processes

Operation

SERVICE OPERATION

Information
Goods
Staff
Customers

Outcomes

SERVICE PRODUCT

Customer

6.2.2 Importance of the service process

Customer satisfaction is affected by many, if not all, aspects of the service organisation including, of course, its brand image. That said, the entirety of the service process, from the activities undertaken by suppliers or back office staff through to the handling of the customer interface, must be the most significant element in the customer's assessment of quality.

Most people have 'horror' stories of customer-handling processes, the processes most visible to customers and thus their acid test of an organisation. One of the difficulties we find in quoting examples of excellent service organisations is that in most groups somebody will have a bad experience of most of them. This demonstrates the importance of the design and management of service processes. Whilst some financial service organisations provide their customers with a single telephone number for queries, others provide a large list of numbers, assuming the customer can decide which is appropriate. Being transferred from one department to another is both necessary and often difficult, necessitating the customer ringing several numbers and explaining the problem several times. When checking out at some international hotels the process requires receptionists to page housekeeping staff to go to your room to check that you have not stolen drinks from the mini-bar.

The examples above illustrate the lack of attention to detail in areas which directly impact on the customer's perception of quality of service. In many cases, more damage is done by poor process management 'behind the scenes'. In this chapter we examine the design and management of customer-handling processes (front office), and those of the 'behind-the-scenes' activities (back office). We will also indicate some of the issues in managing co-ordination and communication between front and back offices.

Improving the service process is a key means not only of increasing customer satisfaction, but also of reducing costs, increasing value added and generating higher profits (Collier 1994). This chapter is concerned with how to understand, manage, design and improve service processes.

6.3 HOW TO UNDERSTAND SERVICE PROCESSES

We can gain a great deal of understanding of service processes by asking three questions. How much variety does the process have to deal with, where is the value added for the customer, and how are key tasks allocated?

6.3.1 Process variety

Process variety concerns the variety of activities in the process and is essentially about whether the process is providing standard or non-standard services. This has profound implications for operations managers, as variety has a major impact on cost, complexity and flexibility of operations. A simple yet helpful classification of processes as 'runners', 'repeaters' and 'strangers' (first used by Lucas Industries) can help us understand the degree of process variety required.

Runners

Runners are standard activities predominantly found in high-volume operations, such as the request for the balance of a bank account made to a telephone call centre. From an operations point of view runners:

- are often relatively predictable, allowing the operations manager to match resources to forecast demand with reasonable accuracy
- lend themselves to efficient operations through tight process control or automation.

Repeaters

Repeaters are also standard activities, possibly more complex than runners, but which occur less frequently. Repeaters may be created by default rather than by design when an organisation significantly expands the range of services it offers. This may mean that processes which were designed to handle relatively few standard activities must now deal with much greater variety. Banks have experienced this problem, having moved from providing one or two standard deposit or chequing accounts to offering 'personalised financial packages'. As a result:

- repeaters often absorb more resource than an equivalent runner because lower volumes cannot justify process automation
- there may be some degree of re-learning or readjustment of a process if the previous occurrence was some time in the past.

Strangers

Strangers are non-standard activities, perhaps associated with a one-off project or activity. New service introduction may give rise to 'stranger' activities in the first instance, which usually will migrate to repeaters or runners as service volumes increase. Strangers are the least efficient and indeed the most difficult processes for operations managers to deal with because:

- it may be more difficult to forecast demand
- the resources required to deal with demand may be less certain
- they are least well defined in terms of resource requirements.

However, an organisation that is used to dealing with strangers will be much more flexible and adaptable than one that is used to dealing with repeaters.

Table 6.1 gives some examples of these three types of activities in three different organisations. All three can and usually do exist within the same organisation. It should be noted that the descriptions should be applied to the service process rather than the service outcome. In other words, there may be a wide range of potential outcomes for customers, but the core processes could be 'runner' processes. For example, airlines provide many different outcomes for customers in terms of flight times and destinations, yet the processes by which flights are scheduled and customers dealt with are relatively standard.

We will return to this classification in Chapter 7 where we will examine the problems posed for resource management when the 'mix' of service requirements changes faster than processes. If the mix of surgical procedures in the hospital changed so that there were fewer complex or new operations, and more simple,

Table 6.1 Runners, repeaters and strangers

Service	Runners	Repeaters	Strangers
Car service	Standard oil change and maintenance Replace brake pads etc.	Body panel replacement Gear box repair	Intermittent electrical fault Product recall
International airline	Passenger check-in Baggage handling In-flight service Maintenance Scheduling	Aircraft overdue or replacement required 'Serious' customer complaints	Special charter for VIPs
Hospital	Patient records Standard operations Recovery and rehabilitation Domestic services	Surgery with 'complications' Dealing with difficult or distraught patients and relatives	New surgical procedures

routine procedures, this might mean that some of the more highly qualified (and paid) surgeons would be surplus to requirements and that there might be insufficient junior doctors to carry out the more mundane activities. A possible short-term solution might be to employ the higher-paid consultant surgeons on routine work. This would dramatically affect the cost base and would no doubt seriously reduce the morale of the surgeons!

6.3.2 Adding value for the customer

In operations we must be careful to recognise where value is added and sometimes this may be different to what an organisation does or appears to do. Take a bank, for example. We as customers, and even the bank's staff and management, may say that personal interaction between customers and the bank's staff is important, and indeed it is. But from an operations perspective the bank is essentially a big factory which processes millions of financial transactions every day, most of which we do not see or even think about, such as maintaining standing orders and direct debits (unless there is a problem!). It certainly has to get its customer interaction right but the main value it provides is in handling our accounts and in managing financial movements.

It is therefore important to view service operations in their entirety, i.e. the multiplicity of interrelated processes, both front office and back office, and recognise where the bulk of the activity lies. Although we will look in detail at the customer-processing (front office) activities in some depth later in this chapter, it is a mistake to ignore the back office activities, which may provide the majority of the added value for customers.

Identifying the key decision areas

The key decision area matrix (KDAM) (see Figure 6.2) provides a means of categorising service processes which helps us understand where the prime value is added and therefore what should be the key focus of attention for operations managers. The figure

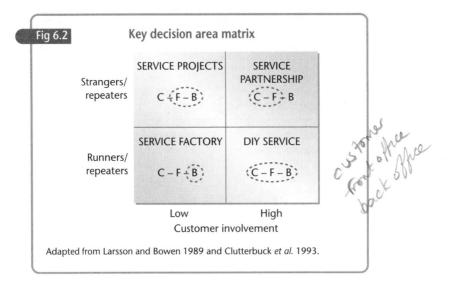

Fig 6.2   **Key decision area matrix**

Adapted from Larsson and Bowen 1989 and Clutterbuck *et al.* 1993.

identifies four types of decision area (the area within the dotted line) in the relation-ship between C–F–B (customer, front office and back office), for runners/repeaters and strangers/repeaters depending upon the level of customer involvement.

Before exploring this further, it is necessary to define 'customer involvement'. By this we mean the extent to which the customer is an intrinsic part of the service deliv-ery process, and thus can be thought of as a resource for the organisation. There is a difference therefore between customer contact and customer involvement. For exam-ple, if you stay in a luxury hotel, the service operation can be described as high customer contact rather than high customer involvement. Customers directly experi-ence the facilities of the hotel, and there are large numbers of staff to attend to their every need. The hotel would move higher on the customer involvement scale if you were required to make your beds and cook your own meals!

The service factory

A service factory is a high-volume, low-variety operation dealing in runners and occasionally repeaters with low customer involvement. Examples include high-volume consumer services such as retail, restaurant chains, and many financial services. The key decision area for these services is in the back office, where the prime task is efficient and consistent, high-volume operations. For example, if a bank wishes to offer a faster cheque-clearing service to its customers, it will exam-ine the capability of the back office first and foremost.

This is not to say that there isn't a role for the front office staff. It is to make this 'service factory' seem friendly and to give the impression that each customer is valued and special. The front office, however, has no ability to offer significantly different services to individual customers.

There is also a role for customers in the service factory. Customers are 'trained' to fit into the service delivery system, filling in the right forms, standing in the correct queues and not making non-standard requests!

The service factory is potentially efficient and consistent (particularly across multi-site operations), but may feel impersonal to customers. There may also be significant problems with low morale in the front office as staff deal with mismatches in customer expectations compared to service delivery.

Do-it-yourself service

DIY services are high-volume, low-variety processes with runners and repeaters but with high levels of customer involvement. We find examples of this type of service in the leisure industry, in tourism and in sports and fitness clubs. Self-service retailing is also moving from the service factory towards the DIY service quadrant. It could be argued that many Internet-based retail services are also found in this quadrant.

We have drawn the key decision area around the total customer, front office, back office chain. This reflects the fact that these services have to balance decisions in all areas. Significant effort lies in the design work for the initial set-up of facilities and networks. Amazon.com has devoted much design time to its Internet service and in setting up back office distribution activities to fulfil customer orders. The capability of the customer must be included in the design brief to ensure that the service runs smoothly. In the case of Amazon.com, the front office decisions regarding the design of the web site and its ease of access and use by customers are also critical.

Some of these Internet-based services rely on significant customer capability in terms of both expertise and equipment. The music sites which allow the customers to download album tracks, creating their own customised collection, currently require a level of sophistication beyond many potential users. It is fair to say that this is not necessarily true of teenagers who are often able to master this technology with terrifying ease!

Service projects

Service projects are processes which involve predominantly strangers with limited customer involvement. A good example of this type of service is provided by a market research company. There is frequently an intensive initial diagnosis/specification phase carried out with the customer by front office personnel. The second phase consists of research work carried out by staff in the back office without the presence of the customer. There is usually a final stage where results are presented and discussed.

In many small market research firms, of course, the front and back offices are one and the same, though this is less common as the organisation grows. The principle remains, however, that service project organisations must have much closer links between front office and back office than is necessary for the service factory, not least because they will be dealing predominantly with strangers and some repeaters, rather than runners.

The front office staff must have more skill and flexibility than in a service factory. When face to face with a potential customer, front-line employees or service professionals must be able to demonstrate considerable technical as well as interpersonal skill. They must have considerable knowledge as to both capability and capacity of the combined front office/back office, often making commitments on behalf of the organisation based on their diagnosis of the customer's requirements.

Service partnership

Service partnerships involve highly customised service processes with high customer involvement dealing in either strangers or repeaters. The key decision area is around the customer (or client) – front office partnership. The theme is very much one of co-development, where the service provider is intimately involved with the client. An example is provided by the sort of consultant who works with a management team in the process of strategy development where there is an expectation that part of the service outcome is that the consultant will mentor management team members as part of their personal development. In this case, the customer is very much part of the service process.

Because customer and service provider are so directly linked, the effectiveness of this service is often a function of the personal chemistry between the individuals involved. Both of the authors have been involved in small consultancies where one of the guiding principles was that we would only work with people we liked.

The challenge for these organisations is to manage the communication link between front office and back office. The back office often provides administrative support and may be perceived to be of lower status than the 'professionals' in the front office.

A mix of decision areas

The challenge for larger, complex service organisations is that all four types may be represented in their operations. To take the example of a bank:

- service factory: retail banking for consumers – high volume, standard accounts
- service projects: business loans for entrepreneurs
- service partnership: managing investment portfolios for large corporate clients
- DIY service: Internet and telephone banking.

It is important to recognise and manage this diversity. It is increasingly true that 'one size fits all' is not appropriate. Each operation will require different performance criteria, technology, management style and, ideally, different processes and people.

6.3.3 Task allocation

Operations managers must make the decision as to which tasks are carried out in the front office, back office, or by the customer. As the service concept extends or changes, it is likely that the positioning of the service as described in Figure 6.2 will also change and thus the allocation of tasks. Figure 6.3 illustrates some examples of task re-allocation which are described below.

- A reinsurance firm operating in the City of London has traditionally based its business on cultivating strong personal client relationships, but is under increasing pressure to demonstrate value and to deliver cost reductions, moving from a service partnership approach to a service project environment. The firm realised that the time spent with individual clients was becoming less effective and contributed to the retention of an ever-decreasing number of clients. This shift required a major culture change to reduce the time spent with clients, and to develop standard ways of working. It also required a significant investment in information systems to support this change.
- High street retailers are moving from a physical presence to providing Internet-based shopping. This represents a move from an organisation largely focused on

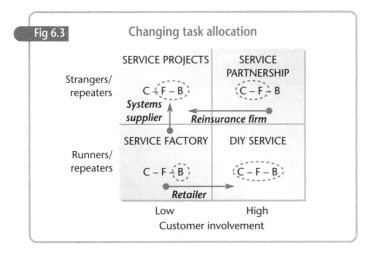

Fig 6.3   Changing task allocation

back office functions such as purchasing and logistics to one which must add to this the ability to design systems which enable the customer to play an increasing role in the delivery system. These systems require a greater sophistication on the part of the customer, perhaps forcing the service provider to give greater thought to the implementation of new technology in terms of initial customer training.

● The systems supplier has largely been concerned with the provision of telecommunications and computer 'boxes'. Its operations have been focused on the production of these systems as efficiently as possible in the back office. As product margins have decreased through competition, the company has recognised the need to provide more customised 'solutions' to its customers. The front office role has moved from being a sales order-processing activity to providing applications consultancy. The major changes for this organisation involve moving expertise that has traditionally been located in a back office role (remote from customers), to a front office activity with significant customer interaction. It is also vital for front office and back office to create more integration in their processes to ensure that greater variation in customer requirements can be dealt with effectively.

The key decision area matrix (KDAM) can give insight into the impact of changes in service concept as they relate to the changing role of the three components of customer, front office and back office. It should be noted that the introduction of new services may mean that traditional distinctions between front and back office may become somewhat blurred. This has been the experience of organisations implementing multi-media contact centres to replace person-to-person service or telephone call centres. The result has been that customers frequently have access to areas within the organisation hitherto 'protected' from customer contact. This clearly poses both a challenge and a significant opportunity for service process design.

6.4 SERVICE PROCESSES: TASKS AND ATTRIBUTES

This section provides more detail on the volume–variety matrix introduced in Chapter 1, where we described the difference between high-volume/low-process variety services and low-volume/high-process variety services. Section 1.4 outlined the principal characteristics of these two extremes of what is a continuum. We indicated that many professional services provide examples of low-volume/high-process variety services, though it is important to note that there are other services which fall into this category which are not thought of as professional services in the strict sense of the term. Companies providing technical services to business customers are an example of this.

Likewise, we noted that mass services generally fall into the high-volume/low-process variety category. Most of the services focused on consumer markets certainly provide good examples of this type of service operation. Equally, many service organisations that might classify themselves as 'professional services' have significant high-volume/low-process variety operations. For example, a company managing out-sourced computer systems will operate many high-volume standard processes.

In Chapter 1, we also discussed the middle ground which, in the classification ranging from professional service to mass service, has been termed the 'service shop'. Also in Chapter 1, we identified two versions of the service shop. The professional service shop relates to professional services which have grown in volumes of customers and transactions. A characteristic of professional service shops is that the solutions they provide tend to be more standardised, designed for one client but then 'rolled out' to as many more clients as possible. We will discuss the implications for the employees and process design in section 6.5.1.

Similarly, mass services, seeking to differentiate themselves on more than price, offer more choice of service product and greater personalisation of the customer experience. As a result, processes may become less well defined, with customer-facing staff acting more like professionals. Again, the implications for organisations undergoing this type of transition are discussed in more detail in section 6.5.2.

A process that deals with runners is likely to be a high-volume/low-variety process and one that deals with strangers is likely to be a low-volume/high-variety process. The key questions are: what should the operation look like, its attributes, and what are its key tasks?

There is a strong link between the classification of service processes introduced in section 6.3.1 and the volume/variety matrix discussed in section 1.4 and summarised above. Rather than use the 'professional' to 'mass' classification, which, although helpful, does not cover all service situations, Figure 6.4 indicates that there are some services which are essentially selling the ability to solve customers' problems, and others which sell a more defined service product. In essence a 'runner' process is concerned with providing a tightly specified service product, a 'commodity', where a consistent outcome and experience is delivered through well-managed processes; whereas a 'stranger' process is primarily concerned with providing 'capability' through particular skills or knowledge. Stranger processes are less well defined, often being designed and redesigned in the course of service delivery.

6.4.1 Capability processes

Processes that lie in the top left-hand corner of the volume–variety matrix (Figure 6.4) are typically focused on providing a capability for their customers or users, rather than a 'pre-prepared' service. As such they do not have the clarity of service

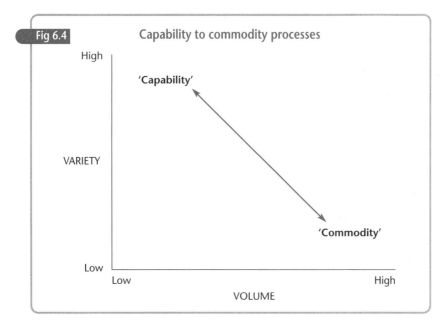

Fig 6.4   Capability to commodity processes

concept that characterises high-volume consumer services, but they have much more flexibility to change service outcomes, service experience and service delivery processes. Examples of this type of service include:

- traditional professional services such as lawyers or accountants, particularly those small firms that deal with a wide variety of work for their clients
- companies that sell their creative ability such as advertising agencies, software developers and engineering design consultants
- organisations that adapt their capabilities to satisfy a wide range of customer needs such as consultants, counsellors and management development providers.

The key task for all of these organisations is to ensure that they maintain their skill base. The firm of lawyers must ensure that it retains its capability to deal with employment or patent law just as the business school must employ professors of the major management disciplines. This points to a number of attributes that generally apply to this type of service operation:

- The service concept is based on the provision of a particular skill set or knowledge base.
- This capability frequently resides with specific individuals, and may be lost to the organisation when the individual leaves.
- Few processes are documented, partly because there is no consistency in types of activity performed, and partly because the individual service providers may resist what appears like an attempt to impose controls on their autonomy.
- Research and development is centred on the individual's capability to deal with a wider range of customer requirements.
- Many professional services are in this category, moving to professional service shops as volume and standardisation increase.

- Such processes tend to be service partnerships or service projects.
- Strangers and repeaters dominate activities, with few runners except in support functions.

6.4.2 Commodity processes

These operations are exemplified by the high-volume consumer services such as fast-food restaurants, general insurance providers, and retailers. The service concept for these organisations is of necessity clear and relatively rigid. This particularly applies when service must be delivered across several service locations, by a wide variety of service employees.

Whereas the 'capability' operations would offer 'solutions' to their customers, 'commodity' operations are much clearer in their definition and marketing of the service concept. They will tend to compete on their ability to provide consistent quality at a competitive price. One of the most significant service dimensions will frequently relate to the availability of service, through the absence of physical queues or rapid telephone response. Examples of these service operations include:

- multi-site services such as restaurant chains, supermarkets or other retail operations
- centralised communication-based services such as 'direct' insurance, telephone banking or catalogue-based selling
- equipment repair services based on simple replacement processes such as car tyre and exhaust centres, domestic appliance repair or computer service.

Central tasks for the majority of these operations include:

- maintaining consistency of service delivery to ensure that customer expectations are met across all encounters
- managing standard service in such a way that individual customers still feel that they are not just a number
- providing an appropriate level of service, managing resource productivity to tight targets.

Contrasts with the attributes of 'capability' services are as follows:

- The service concept is translated into a series of tightly controlled processes, with little opportunity for deviation from standard activities.
- Customer-facing employees are likely to be relatively junior staff and poorly paid.
- The organisation depends on focused training, often of a few days' or weeks' duration for its customer-facing staff, as compared to several years' professional training for key staff in 'capability' operations.
- Capacity is generally well defined, with an emphasis on developing flexibility to deal with rapid changes in demand.
- The operational focus is typically that of the service factory or DIY service.
- The types of service that lie in this area are mass services and mass service shops.
- Activities are typified by runners, with increasing proportion of repeaters as the operation moves towards the service shop.

6.5 REPOSITIONING SERVICE PROCESSES

Many service processes are under pressure to change. High-variety/low-volume capability operations dealing with strangers may be under pressure to increase volumes and/or drive down the high costs of operating such processes. Low-variety/high-volume commodity-type processes dealing primarily with runners may be under pressure to become more flexible and customise their service for customers (see Figure 6.5).

6.5.1 From 'capability' towards 'commodity'

Many innovative organisations have a requirement for growth. The small firm of consultants that has built up a local or national practice may seek to become internationally recognised. Within a global company it may be that an innovative solution developed for an individual customer can be 'packaged' and sold to a much wider range of clients internationally. In order to do this a number of issues must be addressed:

- Customers may require greater levels of consistency across service delivery. For example, a technical consultancy working for a multi-national customer must be able to provide the same solution in all locations, probably at the same price.

- Larger organisations tend to be extremely conscious of their image, which may entail setting stricter guidelines for their staff as to the scope and style of work carried out.

- The 'capability' of the organisation, previously reliant on the skills and knowledge of specific individuals, must be replicated through more specialised resources, tighter process management and specific training if the organisation's growth is not to be limited by scarce resources.

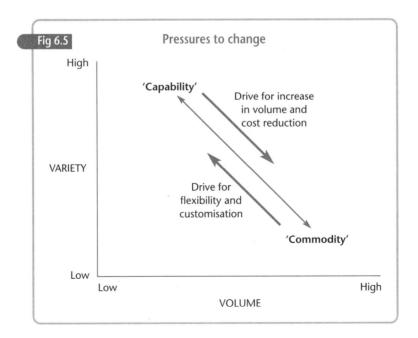

Fig 6.5   Pressures to change

● In order to sustain growth, it is likely that the organisation may have to develop more competitive sales and marketing activities. In some sectors, this might take the organisation into previously non-experienced cost competition.

Perhaps the most significant aspect of this type of transition is the impact on the individual service providers. Many of the individuals in the 'capability' organisations will have joined for the professional autonomy that they offer. It is common for these individuals to enjoy the creativity that frequently is part of their role. As the organisation grows, however, these individuals will not be as motivated to turn their creativity into developing consistent and efficient processes. At the same time, the management task will be changing to become rather more positive in providing direction for the organisation as a whole and for its employees. The Ku-Ring-Gai Vet Hospital (see Box 6.1) demonstrates the increasing pressure for a move from generalist to specialist that comes with increasing volume.

Box 6.1 Ku-Ring-Gai Vet Hospital

The Ku-Ring-Gai Vet Hospital is situated in Sydney, Australia. Opened in September 1966, it is one of the largest veterinary hospitals in the world. Dr Greg Ross, one of the partners, is quoted as saying that their aim in building this hospital was to set a standard for all vets in Australia to follow.

The hospital is on three levels with seven consulting rooms, three operating theatres, two dental stations, two radiology suites, and an intensive care department. The hospital also has a 'grieving room' for distraught owners who wish to be with their pets when they are put to sleep.

This hospital challenges the traditional idea of the local vet dealing infrequently with a wide variety of tasks, but yet building strong client relationships with pet owners. The vet specialist is increasingly the model being adopted as veterinary science follows its human equivalent. Young vets are fast acquiring specialist qualifications, and older vets are being forced back to college to learn new skills.

Despite the 'high-tech' nature of the facilities, the pet owners have not been forgotten in the design process. Glass partitions give visibility for visitors to see what is going on, allaying fears that their pets may not be humanely treated once out of sight of their owners.

The three partners are the veterinarian equivalent of general practitioners. They are able to call on a cluster of specialists which include small animal practitioners, dermatologists and a behavioural psychologist. Just about every part of a pet that can go wrong now has a specialist attached to it.

Questions

1 *How well do you think the hospital has been able to cope with the increase in volume of transactions? What are the potential disadvantages for customers and how could they be avoided?*

2 *What is the impact of increasing volume on the vets? How far has the hospital moved from being a 'capability' service towards 'commodity'?*

This illustration is based on material from 'Old Dogs, New Bones', by Anne Musgrave, *The Australian Magazine*, November 30–December 1 1996.

6.5.2 From 'commodity' towards 'capability'

Examples of this type of shift may be found in high-volume consumer services. To avoid the trap of becoming a commodity service, competing on price alone, these organisations may extend the range of services on offer, perhaps providing a degree of customisation for individual customers.

Of course, it may be possible to design a service delivery process that delivers a wide range of commodity services without increasing the complexity of the operations task, thus allowing the organisation to move in the direction of the top right-hand corner of Figure 6.5. This is covered in more depth in later sections on flexibility but may frequently be similar to the manufacturing idea of 'mass customisation' incorporating the following two principles:

1. Develop standard 'modules'

Companies may develop 'menus' of standard services which may then be arranged in appropriate combinations to provide a degree of customisation for individual customers. The customisation therefore lies in the management of the combination rather than in the development of new services. An example of this type of mass customisation is provided by holiday resorts that allow customers to choose a limited number of activities from a predetermined list.

2. Postpone customisation until the latest possible stage in the delivery process

In this approach the delivery process is standardised for all stages until the last. This allows the service operation to gain all the efficiency and consistency benefits of a high-volume/low-variety process. Courier services are adopting this approach by using their basic distribution networks for all customers but using different mechanisms to deliver the package to its final destination.

A major transition occurs when the number of service delivery processes increases significantly. This transition takes the process mix from few runners to several repeaters. Significant changes in the operations task frequently include the following:

- A shift in the focus of the operation from managing back office operations consistently and for maximum efficiency towards building front office flexibility.
- One of the consequences of the increased range of services on offer is that customer-facing staff will be called upon to give informed advice as to the best service for an individual customer. Moreover it has become unacceptable for front-line staff in these organisations to act merely as a 'post box', taking requests from customers for advice but being unable, themselves, to give an immediate response.
- This 'upskilling' of the front line is normally achieved through a combination of greater staff training and the provision of information systems that allow the service provider to act 'as if' an expert.
- Processes, of necessity, become more flexible, often allowing greater discretion on the part of the employee to make choices as to which service commodity will be most appropriate for the customer.

As with the previous case, there are major implications for the service provider and for the role of management. There is far greater onus on front-line staff to possess both technical and interpersonal skills. The service transactions are likely to be longer and more intense in nature. If the customer transaction includes a high degree of diagnosis of customer requirements and the extent to which the various services on offer match these expectations, the front-line employee will require excellent listening and consultative skills.

The second major area for change might be that 'specialist' employees who hitherto had been distanced from the customer, who were able to work in back office functions, now may have direct contact with customers. This is particularly true in call centre or help desk situations where the customer wishes to deal directly with someone who has the expertise and authority to give a decision or advice on complex issues. (This may be less of an issue when more transactions take place electronically through the Internet or through television-based applications.) Of course, not all technical experts have customer-handling skills.

The role of management changes from being the 'enforcer' of the service concept and process owner to ensuring that the service employees are developed and retained. Many jobs in commodity organisations are low paid and need very little training, often a few days or weeks. Commodity organisations that are seeking to become more flexible may find that they need to invest several months' training in front-line staff, meaning that employee retention becomes a major focus for management attention.

6.5.3 Strategies for change

The majority of service operations, of course, do not lie at the extremes of the diagonal. For those in the centre of the spectrum between 'capability' and 'commodity', there are four basic strategies to deal with transition at whichever point they lie. These are illustrated in Figure 6.6. Few organisations are able to manage these changes without some degree of disruption. and the directions for change illustrated in Figure 6.6, therefore, may not be what was planned or desired, but describe what actually occurred.

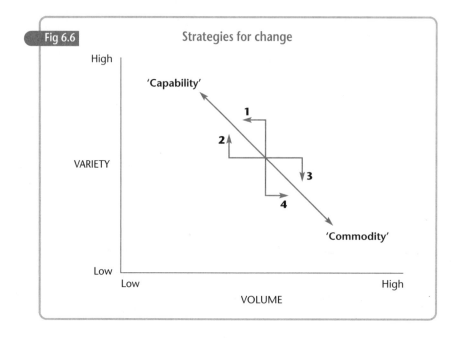

Fig 6.6 Strategies for change

Direction 1: Building capability through systems and training

Here the organisation may be wishing to move towards offering solutions for its customers rather than a relatively narrow range of well-defined services. The mechanism for this (preferred) approach is to invest heavily in more powerful information systems married to an expansion of the role of the front office staff.

The benefit of this approach is that the organisation is then well placed to deal with the new challenge. The downside is that there may be significant 'upfront' investment, which may not give the desired return.

Direction 2: Building capability through incremental development

In this case the organisation may take what appears to be a less risky approach to building capability. It effectively takes on activities or client assignments which are outside its normal sphere of action, but which it believes can be fulfilled by 'learning' from experience.

This process is inherently inefficient and, unless any mistakes are confined to the internal workings of the organisation, potentially damaging to future customer relationships. This is particularly sensitive because 'capability' operations must often work quite closely with customers, in a rather more intimate manner than 'commodity' operations. This clearly means that any deficiencies are not easily hidden.

Direction 3: Moving to a commodity by constraining flexible resources

An example of this would be a gourmet chef being asked to work in a fast-food, limited-menu, restaurant. Although it is possible that the chef would be able to cook burgers and fries, he/she would be over-qualified, too expensive, and after the first meal or two would not be motivated to continue to cook to what will seem a rather repetitive and limiting process.

Moving in this direction poses significant challenges for management, employee morale, and in the development and provision of appropriate cost and quality control systems. If these are not in place, the organisation will rapidly become uncompetitive as other organisations manage mass production more effectively.

Direction 4: Moving to a commodity through investment in process capability

In this case, the organisation will have identified a market need for a high-volume version of an existing service or possibly a completely new service. Rather than try to 'muddle through' with inappropriate processes, systems and people, the organisation will invest in a similar way to Direction 1.

Again, this approach will require initial capital investment, and therefore may appear more risky. However, in some markets there is very clearly a 'first mover' advantage and this approach is becoming more common. In recent years, the investment in a greenfield site for telephone banking has paid significant dividends, not least in allowing these organisations to break away from more traditional (restrictive?) banking practices.

From start-up to starburst

Figure 6.7 illustrates the position that many complex service operations may find themselves in after a period of evolution. The operation at start-up is often very

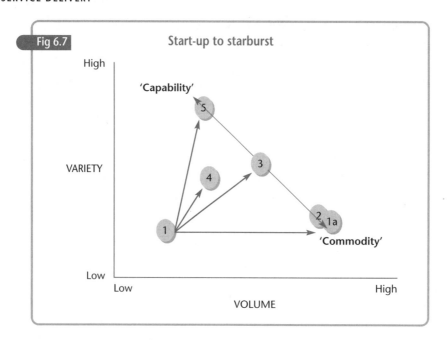

focused around a relatively simple task, e.g. the provision of one 'runner' service. The original intent may have been to grow the volume of this one service, perhaps adding a few similar services through time as the business grew. However, in a way not dissimilar to that described by Wickham Skinner in his paper, 'The Focused Factory' (1974), the service range grows in such a way that operations managers must deliver the full spectrum from 'capability' to 'commodity'.

Computer Service Limited (illustrated in Box 6.2) is an example of the effect described in Figure 6.7. It was originally set up to provide a low-cost repair service for one manufacturer's computers (1). As the business grew, this revenue stream grew with it, to position (1a). The company realised that it could easily provide the same service for customers with a similar make of computer (2). Some of their larger customers asked them if they would consider providing a 'one-stop shop' service for all their computers and peripherals (3). They found that their employees knew quite a lot about the use of computers, as well as service and repair, and moved into the provision of help desks for computer users (4). Finally, the company developed expertise in information systems strategy and offered a consultancy service (5).

The case in Box 6.2 illustrates how a simple task can grow into quite a complex challenge over a period of time. This is not to say that this is wrong – the point for us to consider is the impact on service operations managers. The computer service company was conceived as a low-cost, commodity service handling large numbers of standard transactions (1, 1a and 2). All the management control systems and emphasis continue to be focused on this area. Although the consultancy service (5) is now delivered with separate processes and systems, its performance is judged against that of the high-volume services.

This aspect of company culture can lead to some problems in matching service and process. We have worked with a number of companies who consider themselves as operating towards the 'capability' end of the spectrum, whereas they need

Box 6.2 Computer Service Limited

Computer Service Limited was set up in the 1980s to provide a low-cost repair service for one manufacturer's computers. It was one of the first third-party or independent maintainers competing directly with the original equipment manufacturer's (OEM's) own service function.

Because Computer Service Limited had fewer overheads, it was able to compete effectively on price and drew its workforce from ex-employees of the OEM's service function. At this stage, product life-cycles were relatively long and Computer Service Limited was able to grow and sustain this business for a number of years without a significant increase in complexity. They realised fairly quickly that they would be able to provide the same repair and maintenance service for other makes of computers, though this required the implementation of more sophisticated control systems to manage a growing workforce of service engineers, and more complicated logistics in the purchase and provision of spares for a wider range of computers.

The OEMs realised that they were losing a significant amount of profitable business. Original equipment profit margins were being squeezed and the aftersales service business represented an ever-increasing source of long-term revenue. The OEMs responded to the threat of the independent maintainers by setting up their own service divisions, repairing a much wider range of equipment at lower cost. Computer Service Limited was forced to compete on more than price alone. It was now being asked by some of its customers to provide them with a 'one-stop shop', maintaining all the customer's equipment. This might include computers, peripherals, and other office technology such as photocopiers.

Finally, some of the service engineers employed by Computer Service Limited were skilled not just in the repair and maintenance of the equipment they worked on, but were able to provide support for the applications that their customers used. This enabled Computer Service Limited to extend their service portfolio, providing help desks and eventually outsourced information systems support.

Questions

1 *What are the potential risks and benefits for Computer Service Limited as it grows and extends its portfolio of services?*

2 *Should Computer Service Limited form separate business units to deal with complexity? How might it divide its activities?*

This illustration is based on a real organisation though the names have been changed.

to operate the majority of their activity towards the 'commodity' end in order to reap quality consistency and efficiency benefits. For example:

- A financial services company considers itself a 'professional' service provider. It thinks of itself as moving towards providing tailored solutions for its customers. The problem with this is that while it promises a great deal to its customers and, at first, contact is very friendly, the company fails to deliver a consistent service, continuing to use labour-intensive, inefficient processes.

- A software company values innovation in its products. Most of its senior managers have been software developers at some point in their careers and do not understand the processes required to distribute and service its products to a mass market. As a result, these activities are under-resourced and ineffective, jeopardising the future health of the organisation.

6.5.4 Managing the gap between market position and operations

In the previous section, we indicated that there may often be a divergence between the market position and the operations approach. In selling the benefits of a particular service it is common to find that companies emphasise customer flexibility, providing a personal service whilst continuing to operate on a mass-production basis. Figure 6.8 illustrates this effect. This is often a very effective strategy. The main danger is that customer satisfaction will fall if the 'gap' is too great between what is offered and what is delivered. In order to counteract this, organisations may adopt several strategies to 'manage the gap'.

Customer service departments

Customer service departments fulfil the role of managing the gap in many consumer services, frequently acting as 'sweepers' to deal with customer complaints and to provide a relatively cheap human interface between the customer and the service factory of the back office.

Named personal contact

Named contacts may be used to bridge the gap by providing some personalised attention for the individual. The customer is allocated a specific individual to give confidence that he or she is not solely a number in what may feel like a factory-type process. An unusual but appropriate example is in hospitals where nurses, nursing auxiliaries and volunteers provide the individual care valued by patients

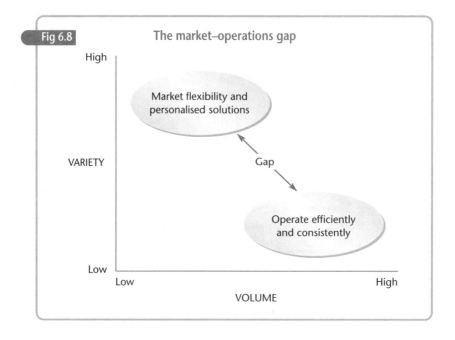

Fig 6.8 The market–operations gap

but not always delivered by a medical system which is focused on maximising utilisation of scarce resource (doctors and consultants).

Account or client managers

Business-to-business services may use account or client managers to provide the point of contact for their customers. In some cases these may operate in a similar manner to the named contact described above. Where there are multiple relationships between individuals or functions/departments in the client and supplier organisations, there is great value in maintaining an overview. Account managers may also play a role in ensuring that the client perceives a level of customisation that is not always as great as it is presented.

Change the nature of the service

The process can be re-positioned from service partnership to DIY or service factory to service project, for example. The provision of Internet-based services, for example, whilst offering the customers the opportunity to request service at their own convenience, may also become a means whereby they 'do-it-themselves' rather than wait for the organisation to respond.

Change customer expectations

Try to align customer expectations with the nature of the service. If it is a high-volume, low-touch process it is important to educate customers not to expect personalised service.

It appears that some service organisations adopt the approach of 'hoping for the best', taking no special action to manage the gap between customer expectation and actual service experience. This is a potentially disastrous strategy, with the organisation running the risk of long-term damage to its reputation and relationship with its customers.

6.5.5 Profiling processes

Figure 6.9 summarises key points from the preceding sections in the form of a chart to assist operations managers to locate their existing processes on the capability–commodity spectrum and to determine whether action needs to be taken to make appropriate adjustments. The figure illustrates the profile for a motor insurance provider, showing the difference between its 'direct' operation providing policies to individual users and its support for insurance brokers.

Use of this profiling approach identifies the potential mismatches to be addressed by service managers. These frequently arise because the service task has changed whereas the delivery processes have not evolved to meet the new requirements adequately.

6.6 'ENGINEERING' SERVICE PROCESSES

Few service organisations, unlike their manufacturing counterparts, employ specialist 'service engineers' or use 'service laboratories' to help them design, test and evaluate their service processes (Shostack 1987). Because of the intangibility of

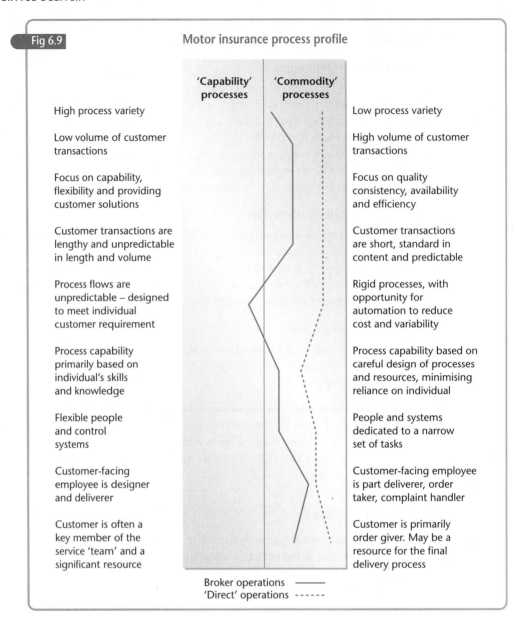

Fig 6.9 Motor insurance process profile

'Capability' processes | 'Commodity' processes

High process variety — Low process variety

Low volume of customer transactions — High volume of customer transactions

Focus on capability, flexibility and providing customer solutions — Focus on quality consistency, availability and efficiency

Customer transactions are lengthy and unpredictable in length and volume — Customer transactions are short, standard in content and predictable

Process flows are unpredictable – designed to meet individual customer requirement — Rigid processes, with opportunity for automation to reduce cost and variability

Process capability primarily based on individual's skills and knowledge — Process capability based on careful design of processes and resources, minimising reliance on individual

Flexible people and control systems — People and systems dedicated to a narrow set of tasks

Customer-facing employee is designer and deliverer — Customer-facing employee is part deliverer, order taker, complaint handler

Customer is often a key member of the service 'team' and a significant resource — Customer is primarily order giver. May be a resource for the final delivery process

Broker operations ———
'Direct' operations - - - - -

service, process design is often an *ad hoc* trial-and-error activity rather than a formal, even proceduralised, management activity. Most faults and problems are effectively 'designed in', albeit inadvertently, and as a result customers experience poor service and the processes are inefficient.

This section introduces the important notion of end-to-end processes and provides three tools to help 'engineer' services.

6.6.1 End-to-end service processes

Managers, including operations managers, have a tendency to draw a boundary around their processes which coincides with the physical or geographic boundary of their responsibility. The problem faced by many customers is at the interfaces between each of these sets of processes. The 'process' from the customer point of view is often quite different from that of the people responsible for delivering a service. A hospital, for example, comprises many departments, each of which may be extremely efficient in its own right, but the results of lack of co-ordination may be experienced by patients, often unknown to the organisation, such as:

- a request to turn up on time for an appointment but insufficient car parking spaces outside
- a desire for prompt treatment but the general practitioner's notes have been delayed or are unavailable
- a request for medicines or equipment held up because of the paperwork.

By assessing and designing service processes from the point of view of the 'thing' being processed, whether it is the customer him/herself, or a file, or information, such as a loan application, we can expose the interface problems to try to provide not only seamless service for the customer but a more efficient and cost-effective process for the organisation. The objective of good service design is to achieve an efficient process from an operations perspective and seamless service for the customer. Mike Shulver from Warwick Business School provided the following 'tests' for seamless service:

Customers should:

- flow smoothly through the service, and
- experience no discontinuity.

Staff should:

- take ownership of processes, and
- take ownership of individual customers.

Managers should:

- take a process not a functional perspective
- understand whole processes
- understand how they fit into the processes
- work in cross-functional teams to assess and improve the design.

The key to good service design therefore is about taking a customer perspective and understanding the whole service process. This may seem obvious yet in many organisations managers and their staff simply get used to seeing – and therefore ignoring – poor processes, or see them from an internal perspective, thus missing the experience from their customers' perspective. Several tools and techniques have been developed to help 'engineer' service, i.e. to design new service processes, or assess and improve existing ones:

- process mapping
- walk-through audits
- service transaction analysis.

6.6.2 Process mapping

Process mapping is the charting of a service process in order to assist in the evaluation, design and development of new or existing processes. There are many types of charting methods in use. However, the essence of mapping is to capture all the activities and their relationships on paper, which normally requires a team of people who understand the various aspects of the process. It is perhaps not surprising that this activity is incredibly time-consuming but it can yield some significant results – the first of which is usually the emergence of a shared view and understanding of a process by all of those involved in it, and thus a realisation of their role in the end-to-end process.

Gaining maximum benefit from process mapping involves two issues, mapping and mapping tools, and turning the map from a descriptive into an analytical tool.

Mapping and mapping tools

The first question to be considered at the start of a mapping activity is the level or degree of detail. Process maps can be used at a macro level depicting major activities and their relationships or at a micro level mapping all the detailed tasks involved in a process or a part of a process, or indeed somewhere in between. The minimum level depends upon the use to which it is to be put but is usually that which exposes the overall process and where the main elements are visible. More detailed individual maps can be created if and when required.

It is also important to agree mapping symbols and structures. The traditional operations symbols are shown in Figure 6.10 (Slack *et al.* 1998).

Different symbols may be appropriate to use in other circumstances and may be more visual and meaningful for the people developing the map, such as a picture of a computer for a computer interface, a queue of people to depict a queue, an in-tray to depict a pile of files in an in-tray. The symbols chosen should be appropriate but should be common and understandable with a single meaning (for more information see, for example, Johnston 1987, Shostack 1987, Kingman-Brundage 1992).

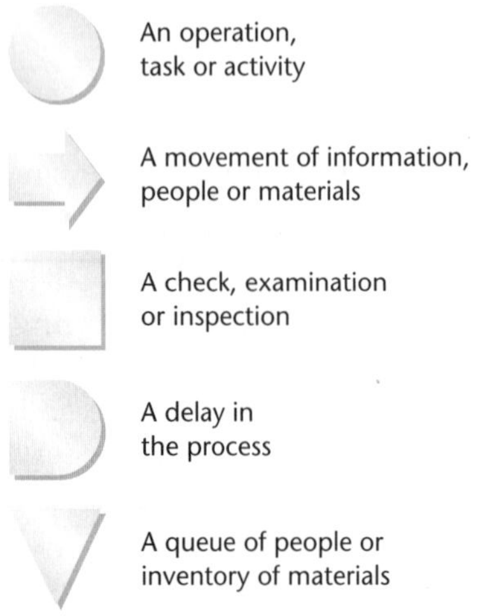

The lines on the chart may be coloured to depict flows of different materials – blue for customers and green for information, for example – or to depict different volumes or routings, such as standard processes versus non-standard processes.

The example in Figure 6.11 shows a simplified process for a loan application depicting customer activities, front office activities (the Customer Service Agent – CSA) and back office activities (the computer). We only identified key information flows in this case to provide an overview of the process. A potential pitfall of process mapping is that too much detail is shown, obscuring the issues and opportunities for improvement.

Fig 6.10 Traditional operations process mapping symbols

- An operation, task or activity
- A movement of information, people or materials
- A check, examination or inspection
- A delay in the process
- A queue of people or inventory of materials

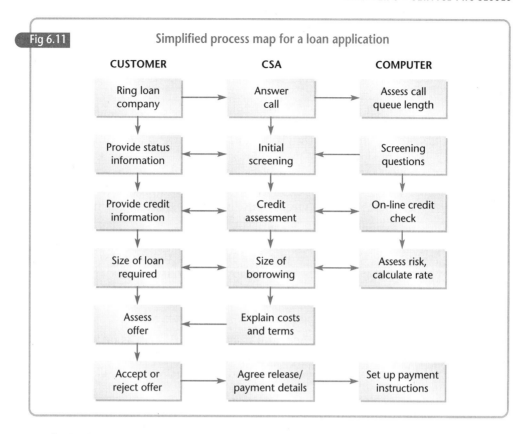

Fig 6.11 Simplified process map for a loan application

CUSTOMER	CSA	COMPUTER
Ring loan company	Answer call	Assess call queue length
Provide status information	Initial screening	Screening questions
Provide credit information	Credit assessment	On-line credit check
Size of loan required	Size of borrowing	Assess risk, calculate rate
Assess offer	Explain costs and terms	
Accept or reject offer	Agree release/ payment details	Set up payment instructions

Analysis of process maps

Process mapping in itself can be a very time-consuming task with little benefit gained. By itself a process map is of only limited benefit and can help communicate the complexity of a process or help individuals agree or realise the steps involved in a process. Process mapping is essentially *descriptive* activity: what is required to derive maximum benefit from a process map is to ask key questions that help turn it into an *analytical* tool.

Does the process support the strategic intentions of the operation?
If the operation is expected to provide, for example, high-quality and speedy service to customers, is the process designed in such a way so that decisions are made speedily, that end-to-end process performance is minimal and that quality controls are in place at all points in the process?

Does each activity provide added value?
Which elements of the process do not add value? Can they be removed or re-designed?

Is the process 'in control'?
For the key elements or maybe every element in the process, what measures and targets are in place to ensure that particular element is performing as expected? Who is responsible for overseeing, controlling and improving that particular element?

Who 'owns' and has responsibility for the process?
How many different individuals and/or departments are responsible for parts of the process? Who in particular, or which group of people, is responsible for the design, delivery and improvement of the whole process?

Is the level of visibility appropriate?
The process map can be used to identify those activities which involve and/or are visible to the customer, thus differentiating between back office and front office tasks. Should or could any of the activities or tasks be re-allocated? Can any of the elements be moved to the back office and away from the customer which might lead to greater efficiencies? Are there elements which could be made more visible to the customer which might lead to a greater sense of involvement and ownership and quality?

How can the process be improved?
Which are the likely or main fail-points in the process? What procedures are in place to deal with these? Does everyone who is involved in the process understand their role in the whole process and the effect of their actions upon it?

How efficient is the process?
By adding times, distances and resources used, such as numbers of staff, to the various tasks in the process map, the efficiencies of the whole process and various parts of the process can be calculated and bottlenecks identified and removed.

6.6.3 Walk-though audits

As most service organisations process customers, a 'walk-through audit' (Fitzsimmons and Fitzsimmons 1997) undertaken by staff, managers or independent advisers, acting as surrogate customers, can help evaluate and improve the service. The audit should be based on a checklist of questions which guide the 'customer's' assessment of the complete service (see, for example, Figure 6.12).

The key requirement for this approach lies in the choice of attributes to assess, and the scales on which the assessment will lie. As the name implies, it should be developed to identify the critical elements of the customer experience from first contact with the service operation through to exit. It is crucial that this audit is not developed solely by people who know the service well as they are prone to miss detail that they think is irrelevant but customers are affected by. The advantage of this type of approach is that it allows the manager to carry out regular service checks on key aspects of delivery, possibly comparing performance at different times of day between service units.

6.6.4 Service transaction analysis

Service transaction analysis (STA) (for more information see Johnston 1999) is a development of the walk-through audit and combines the service concept, the service process, transaction quality assessment and service 'messages' in order to provide a simple but powerful tool to assess and improve the customer's experience of a service process. This tool, an example of which is contained in Figure 6.13, can also be used as the basis of a walk-through audit. STA comprises five key stages:

Fig 6.12   Walk-through audit of an electrical store

1. How easy was it to park the car?

Plenty of spaces				No spaces
1	2	3	4	5

2. How did the store look?

Very clean/tidy				Disgraceful
1	2	3	4	5

3. How attractive were the displays?

Very attractive				Uninviting
1	2	3	4	5

4. How soon were you assisted?

0–5 mins		10–15 mins		15 mins+
1	2	3	4	5

---

1. The service concept needs to be agreed and specified. This alone is often a useful exercise to gain agreement between the employees on the nature of their service offering (see Chapter 2).

2. Mystery shoppers, independent advisers or consultant-customers then walk through the actual process (not the process map) to assess how customers (might) assess each transaction. Each transaction is briefly described in the left-hand column and an assessment of it in terms of delighting (+), satisfactory (0) or unsatisfactory (–) is noted in the middle columns.

3. The interpretation as to why the customer or surrogate customer arrives at this evaluation is entered into the right-hand column which describes the deliberate and the symbolic and subtle messages given off by the service. For example, an open door may provide an 'inviting' message, while a telephone operator unwilling to deviate from a set script may provide an 'unhelpful and unnecessarily bureaucratic' message to the customer.

4. The assessments of +, 0 and – are joined to give a very visible profile of the transaction outcomes and an overall evaluation is entered at the foot of the table.

5. Working from this sheet, service designers, managers and staff can begin firstly to understand how customers might interpret the service process and secondly to discuss the improvements that can be made. The exercise can be repeated with a revised process and the profiles readily compared.

Unlike all other existing service process analysis tools, STA seeks to identify the reason for the outcome of each service transaction so that appropriate improvements can be made.

Its key advantages are:

- It requires managers and employees to think about, and express in words, their service concept. This in itself creates an opportunity for healthy debate, and even disagreement, about what the intentions of the organisation actually are.

Fig 6.13	Example of STA for an estate agent

SERVICE TRANSACTION ANALYSIS SHEET

		Concept
Organisation:	Estate agent	Prestige properties with excellent
Process:	Buy house	service for the discerning purchaser
Customer:	Purchaser	

Transaction	Score +	0	–	Message
High Street location	X			We are accessible and available
Good facilities	X			Expensive but competent
Ignored			X	You are not worth the trouble
Introduction		X		We want to help you
Fill in forms			X	You are just another punter
No pen			X	We don't really care
Nothing available			X	What business are they in?
Go on mailing list			X	Try someone else

Overall evaluation: Poor service design. Little thought for purchasers. Company is not customer orientated. Customer service is a sham.

STA was first published in *Managing Service Quality*, vol. 9, no. 2, 1999, pp. 102–9. This adaptation is reproduced with the permission of MCB University Press.

- It forces managers and employees to see the process from the point of view of the customer, increasing their level of 'customer orientation'.
- It asks directly and explicitly what does each transaction mean to the customer and, importantly, what gives them this impression.
- It assesses the physical, tangible issues as well as the service scripts, but it also asks what messages these give to the customer.
- STA attempts to bring a systematic evaluation of a complete service process. It does not rely upon individual complaints or initiatives but analyses and evaluates a process, step by step, from the customer's point of view.

STA is a simple yet very effective analytical tool that can easily be employed by managers to increase the level of customer orientation of staff and can lead to speedy and easy improvements in service processes.

6.7 CONTROLLING SERVICE PROCESSES

A key operational performance objective is to achieve consistency of outcome for customers. Most service organisations report that reliability is one of the most significant factors in influencing customer satisfaction – in other words, 'saying what you do and doing what you say'. This section considers two aspects of control: assessing the capability of a process, and the role of quality systems, such as ISO 9000.

6.7.1 Capable processes

The concept of building 'capable processes' is helpful here. This is a fundamental principle of quality management and is at the heart of the Deming philosophy, requiring 'evidence that quality is built in' (Deming 1986). Many service operations utilise the statistical process control (SPC) methodology to assess the extent to which a process is in control.

Figure 6.14 shows the distribution of sample means measuring the performance of two hotels (A and B) which deliver breakfast trays to guests' rooms. In each case, the hotel offers guests a choice of times for delivery of their breakfast tray. Both hotels have chosen 10-minute 'windows' in the belief that this is what customers require. Figure 6.14a and b show the distribution of the breakfast tray delivery times for a particular 10-minute window. Hotel A in Figure 6.14a has put in place the systems and capacity to ensure that it consistently keeps its promises, whereas that represented by Hotel B in Figure 6.14b appears unable to do so. The former is an example of a 'capable system' whereas the latter is a process out of control. If the promise of meeting this time window is a key element of the 'contract' between provider and customer, the customer satisfaction ratings for Hotel B will be under threat.

Hotel B has two basic strategies that its management might consider:

1 To invest in the delivery process to ensure that it can meet its process specification consistently, or

2 Relax the process specification, in this case increasing the duration of the 'time window' offered to guests (perhaps 20 minutes instead of the current 10 minutes).

Of course, this can only be implemented once customer research has indicated the importance of this aspect of the service offer.

SPC (see, for example, Oakland 1992) is based on the production of process control charts. It is normal practice to take a series of measurements and then to plot the mean of the sample readings. This is because under the central limit theorem, the distribution of the sample means tends towards a normal distribution even if the underlying distribution is not normal.

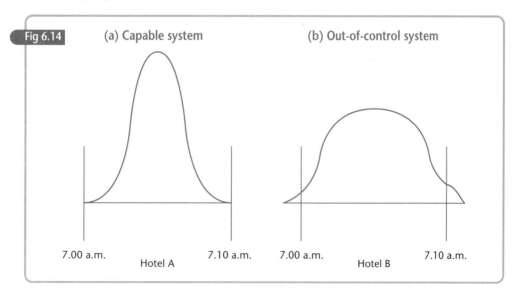

Fig 6.14 (a) Capable system (b) Out-of-control system

7.00 a.m. Hotel A 7.10 a.m.   7.00 a.m. Hotel B 7.10 a.m.

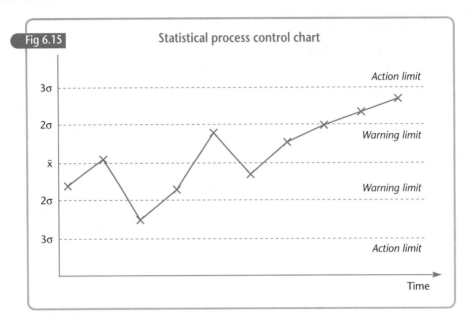

Fig 6.15 — Statistical process control chart

Processes can be plotted onto a control chart, such as Figure 6.15, to give a visual picture of their state of health.

Figure 6.15 shows a plot of sample means taken at random, possibly depicting the times breakfast was delivered in the hotel from the previous example. The chart shows the process mean ($\bar{x}$); warning limits set at ± two standard deviations (2σ); and action limits at ± three standard deviations (3σ). The value of process control charts lies in the removal of a temptation to 'meddle' in the process. A number of readings (5 per cent) will be expected to lie between the warning and action limits. The general advice if a reading is taken in this zone is to take another reading before doing anything. Premature adjustments may take the process out of control.

Figure 6.15 shows a process initially in control (the first six readings are a normal pattern), but then showing signs that the process mean has shifted as a run of points are all moving in the same direction as opposed to the normal scattering of readings. As process managers spend time understanding these processes, it is frequently possible to identify causes of variation. These can be divided into those causes which may be avoided, perhaps through automation or better training, and those which are unavoidable. An example of the latter might be the impact of bad weather on a breakdown service.

SPC has been used extensively to control and improve high-volume, standard processes. Examples include:

● accuracy of cheque transactions in a major retail bank
● computer service response times
● sickness and absenteeism in a call centre
● numbers of customer complaints per thousand transactions.

It would be wrong to give the impression that SPC is easily applied to all service processes. It is clearly applicable to factory-like processes where measures such as response times may be accurately assessed, but it is valuable to apply the technique to attributes such as the number and intensity of customer complaints. As is often the case, the value may come from the discipline of thinking about the process as much as from the monitoring of the control chart.

6.7.2 Quality systems: ISO 9000

Some industries have had a long history of quality assurance, usually for reasons of health, hygiene or safety. Many manufacturing companies have been required to produce evidence of quality plans, schedules of inspection, and records of quality checks being carried out. This activity has frequently been viewed somewhat negatively by operations managers, considering it as something that does not add value to the operations activity, and indeed stifling innovation and change.

It is unfortunate that this quality assurance activity should be viewed as a 'police officer' operating in a somewhat negative way, preventing poor quality but not actively encouraging good quality. The British Quality Standard, BS 5750 (now BSEN-ISO9000), and then the International Standard ISO 9000, and their associated standards, aim to correct this biased view of quality assurance.

High-volume 'commodity'-type services whose processes tend towards runners lend themselves most naturally to the quality systems approach. This is because processes can be mapped and clear, consistent standards can be established and monitored throughout service production and delivery. For example, many hotels have used standard operating procedures (SOPs) for a number of years covering such aspects of service delivery as the way that housekeeping cleans and prepares a room. This activity lends itself to checklists:

- Has the floor been vacuumed?
- Have the complimentary soaps and shampoos been replenished?
- Has the bed been made and turned down?
- Have the waste bins been emptied?

These SOPs translate readily into processes which can be audited for compliance under a quality system. They deal with relatively tangible outcomes rather than less tangible aspects of the customer experience. Call centres attempt to measure these aspects of the customer experience by using checklists which might include statements such as 'Did the agent use the appropriate greeting?' or 'Did the agent thank the customer for the order?'.

The advantages of using quality management systems such as those related to ISO 9000 are as follows:

- Incorporating critical elements of service delivery in a process which has been mapped, described and measured in such a way as can then be audited develops a discipline which may not have existed previously.
- External auditing and recognition of this success in the award of a certificate is good for internal morale and external reputation.
- The better quality management systems include a formal review process which prompts the organisation to consider what needs to be done differently in order to improve.
- The process of preparing for ISO 9000 accreditation requires the organisation to document its processes and should be used as an opportunity for process redesign before application.

There are problems with this approach which have largely arisen because some organisations have applied for the 'badge' of ISO certification for reasons of marketing rather than because it will lead to quality improvement. This 'me too' attitude has given the ISO 9000 initiatives poor publicity. Some of the pitfalls to be avoided include:

- Thinking that if the ISO 9000 processes are in control, then customers will be satisfied. The better companies have recognised this and include customer feedback mechanisms in their procedures. It should be noted that under ISO 9000 organisations are required to operate corrective feedback loops in their quality systems, but these may be largely internal review processes rather than customer driven.

- Trying to write procedures that are too detailed. This is particularly relevant when dealing with 'capability' processes, where individuals require significant levels of discretion. Process descriptions need to be more skeletal, written at a higher level to give appropriate freedom for individual interpretation.

6.8 PREVENTING PROCESS FAILURES

Despite all best efforts to design processes well, things do go wrong and process failures occur. This is not surprising because many services are complex. They are also usually human-based systems involving concurrent provision of services, goods, facilities and environment often with the customer taking part in the process; thus errors, mistakes or failures are inevitable. In the UK banking sector, for example, despite considerable attention having been given to 'zero defects', it is not too surprising that there are errors in view of the volume of transactions handled. In 1996 one of the largest banks in the UK handled approximately 15 million transactions every day for its six million customers, maintaining, for example, over 32.5 million direct debits/standing orders. A MORI survey of 1,879 customers of all banks in the UK (1994) found that nearly half of all customers (48 per cent) had experienced at least one mistake during the previous 12 months. Research by Johnston and Fern (1999) found that 62 per cent of a bank's customers had experienced a failure. The bank did not dispute the findings but added that they thought the percentage was on the decline.

Whilst SPC may help us identify when a failure is about to happen, or has happened, it is appropriate to try to prevent failure happening in the first place. Process mapping is a useful tool in trying to spot where problems lie; however, understanding the types of failures and the technique of failsafing are important ways of preventing failures from occurring.

6.8.1 Types of failure

Problems are not always 'service' problems, i.e. problems with the service process – they could be the result of faults in the goods, equipment or facilities, or often they are faults due to the customers themselves (see Figure 6.16).

Service failures include process problems such as a late-running doctor's surgery or a computer error resulting in an airline 'losing' a passenger. Other problems with a service might include lack of availability of goods and services, unresponsive service, and poor or inappropriate treatment being given to customers.

Equipment failures may also cause problems in the service process. The failure of computers, automatic doors or airbridges in an airport will disable parts of the process and cause problems for staff and customers.

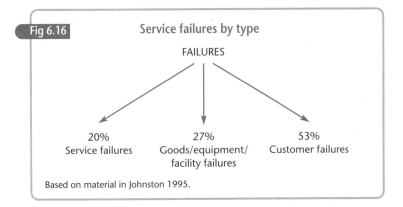

Fig 6.16 Service failures by type

FAILURES

20%
Service failures

27%
Goods/equipment/
facility failures

53%
Customer failures

Based on material in Johnston 1995.

It is interesting to note that the majority of failures are 'customer' failures. Customer failures can be divided into two types: those caused by 'problem customers' and customers who make mistakes (Johnston 1998). Problem customers are those individuals who are involved in serious offences such as staff abuse or drunkenness, for example (Bitner *et al.* 1994, Lovelock 1994). Customers who make mistakes, on the other hand, make simple and often inadvertent errors such as forgetting something or turning up at the wrong time or wrong place (Johnston 1998).

From a customer's point of view, a failure is any situation where something has gone wrong, irrespective of responsibility (Johnston 1995). Even if a customer is late for a plane and the airline may consider it the passenger's fault, the passenger may have been late due to rail strikes or road works, although whatever the reason, s/he will be likely to blame the airline for not holding the plane. Importantly, each failure provides the organisation with an opportunity to turn the potentially dissatisfying situation into a satisfying one.

Chapter 12 focuses on how to recover customers when things go wrong. Earlier in this chapter we explained the use of process mapping which is a useful tool in trying to identify potential and actual fail-points so that corrective action can be taken. The previous section of this chapter has explained how to try and identify when a process is going out of control so that early corrective action can be taken. The remainder of this chapter identifies a simple but highly effective technique used by many service organisations to try to engineer-out failures, particularly those caused by customers, the source of the majority of failures.

6.8.2 Failsafing

'Failsafing' (Chase and Stewart 1994) is one means of trying to reduce the likelihood of failures in service processes. This idea is called *poka yoke* in Japan (from the Japanese *yokeru*, meaning to prevent, and poka, inadvertent errors) and was advocated by Shigeo Shingo (1986). *Poka yoke* are simple failsafe automatic devices that can be designed into a service to prevent many inevitable mistakes becoming failures. *Poka yoke* usually have the dual advantages of cheapness and simplicity, and are used to prevent both staff and customers doing the wrong thing.

Poka yoke can be used to reduce customer failures by 'encouraging' customers to do the right thing. Simple but effective examples include airline lavatory doors which need to be locked to have the light come on. Electronic tags on goods in a store ensure that they are not inadvertently or intentionally taken out of the store.

Computer disks can only be inserted the right way round, thus ensuring there are no (or at least fewer) problems in accessing data.

From an operations perspective *poka yoke* can be used to ensure that staff adhere to procedures in order to reduce or eliminate service failures. Some computerised procedures, for example, will not allow operators to move to the next screen until all the information has been provided on the previous screen. The 'dead-man's handle' on a train will automatically stop the train unless a driver is holding it down.

Equipment failure can be prevented or the consequences minimised by making them literally 'fail-safe': automatic doors that can only fail when open, traffic lights whose fail mode is amber in all directions. Parallel wiring or having back-up components or systems can dramatically reduce the likelihood of equipment failure.

Failsafing – key steps

1 Identify the potential or actual weak points in a process. This can be done using the process mapping tools (process mapping, walk-through audits or STA) or the results of analysis of complaints data.
2 Identify the type or nature of the failure(s) (service, equipment, customer).
3 Focusing on the type of failure, brainstorm various ways of reducing or preventing errors.
4 Select, design and implement the most appropriate *poka yoke*. If the failure is not preventable, ensure good recovery procedures are in place (see Chapter 12).
5 Monitor and evaluate the effect of implementation and repeat the above steps if necessary.

6.9 SUMMARY

Service processes and their importance
- A service process is the set of interrelated tasks or activities which together, in an appropriate sequence, create the service.
- 'Good' service processes not only create satisfied customers but also reduce costs, enhance value added and underpin financial performance.

How to understand service processes
- 'Runners', 'repeaters' and 'strangers' help identify the key issues and tasks for operations managers.
- Value may be added in the front office or back office or both, with varying degrees of customer involvement.

Service processes: tasks and attributes
- The volume–variety matrix helps identify the key attributes of service processes, how processes can be repositioned, and the gap between marketing and operations managed.

Repositioning service processes
- There are pressures on many processes to change their nature.

- There are four main ways in which service processes can be repositioned:
  - ➢ building capability through systems and training
  - ➢ building capability through incremental development
  - ➢ moving to a 'commodity' by constraining flexible resources
  - ➢ moving to a 'commodity' through investment in process capability.
- Process profiling can help identify what needs to be changed to reposition a process.

'Engineering' service processes

- It is important to identify and manage end-to-end processes.
- Three tools that are effective in helping 'engineer' service are process mapping, walk-through audits and service transaction analysis.

Controlling service processes

- Reliability and consistency are important to most service operations and their customers.
- Capable processes can be created through the implementation of statistical process control.

Preventing process failures

- It is in the nature of service processes to fail.
- Failures can be detected, prevented and dealt with through process mapping, statistical process control and service recovery.
- Failsafing is a simple but effective technique to reduce the likelihood of failure and ensure that both staff and customers do the right things.

6.10 DISCUSSION QUESTIONS

1. What examples can you give of 'capability' and 'commodity' service operations? What are the operations management challenges of each type?

2. Undertake a service transaction analysis of a service operation, identifying the critical points for management attention.

3. Identify annoying problems in a process with which you are familiar (e.g. washing clothes and the problem of odd socks) and suggest some *poka yoke* to fix the problem.

6.11 QUESTIONS FOR MANAGERS

1. To what extent are the traditional roles of front office and back office changing? Has your management approach changed in line with the new task? What are the implications of customers potentially penetrating to the heart of the organisation through mechanisms such as Internet-based access?

2. What is the basic culture of your service management approach? Is it 'capability' or 'commodity' based? Are there any people and activities that don't fit with this culture? How well are they managed?

3. Is there a mismatch between the current performance requirements of your service processes and the task for which they were designed? Have you identified future requirements before attempting to redesign your processes?

4. Carry out a walk-through audit of your service processes, looking at them through the 'eyes of the customer'.

5. How many of your customer-critical processes are in control? Do you have statistical evidence of this fact?

6.12 SELECTED FURTHER READING

Fitzsimmons J. and Fitzsimmons M. (eds), *New Service Design*, Sage Publications, 1999, Thousand Oaks, California, 2000.

Gouillart F.J. and Sturdivant F.D., 'Spend a Day in the Life of Your Customers', *Harvard Business Review*, January–February 1994, pp. 116–25.

6.13 REFERENCES

Armistead C.G. and Clark G.R., 'Resource Activity Mapping; the Value Chain in Service Operations Strategy', *The Service Industries Journal*, vol. 13, no. 4, 1993, pp. 221–39.

Bitner M.J., Booms B.H. and Mohr L.A., 'Critical Service Encounters: The employee's viewpoint', *Journal of Marketing*, vol. 58, October 1994, pp. 95–106.

Chase R.B. and Stewart D.M., 'Make your Service Fail-Safe', *Sloan Management Review,* Spring 1994, pp. 35–44.

Clutterbuck D., Clark G. and Armistead C., *Inspired Customer Service*, Kogan Page, London, 1993.

Collier D.A., *The Service/Quality Solution: Using service management to gain competitive advantage,* Irwin and ASQC Quality Press, New York, 1994.

Deming W.E., *Out of the Crisis*, MIT Center for Advanced Engineering Study, Cambridge, Mass., 1986.

Fitzsimmons J.A. and Fitzsimmons M.J., *Service Management for Competitive Advantage* (2nd edition), McGraw-Hill, New York, 1997.

Johnston R., 'A Framework for Developing a Quality Strategy in a Customer Processing Operation', *International Journal of Quality and Reliability Management*, vol. 4, no. 4, 1987, pp. 37–46.

Johnston R., 'Service Failure and Recovery: Impact, attributes and process', *Advances in Services Marketing and Management: Research and practice*, vol. 4, 1995, pp. 211–28.

Johnston R., 'Customer Mistakes: Failure and recovery', in Coughlan P., Dromgoole T, and Peppard J. (eds), *Operations Management: Future issues and competitive responses,* University of Dublin, Dublin, 1998, pp. 243–8.

Johnston R., 'Service Transaction Analysis: Assessing and improving the customer's experience', *Managing Service Quality*, vol. 9, no. 2, 1999, pp. 102–9.

Johnston R. and Fern A., 'Service Recovery Strategies for Single and Double Deviation Scenarios', *The Service Industries Journal*, vol. 19, no. 2, 1999, pp. 69–82.

Kingman-Brundage J., 'The ABCs of Service System Blueprinting', in Lovelock C.H., *Managing Services* (2nd edition), Prentice Hall International, New Jersey, 1992, pp. 96–102.

Larsson R. and Bowen D., 'Organisation and Customer: Managing design and the coordination of services', *Academy of Management Review*, vol. 14, no. 2, 1989, pp. 213–33

Lovelock C.H., *Product Plus*, McGraw-Hill, New York, 1994.

MORI, *Satisfaction with Bank and Building Society Service*, Research conducted for the British Bankers Association, Summer 1994.

Oakland J.S., *Total Quality Management* (2nd edition), Heinemann, Oxford, 1992.

Shingo S., *Zero Quality Control: Source inspection and the poka-yoke system*, Productivity Press, Stamford, Conn., 1986.

Shostack G.L., 'Service Positioning Through Structural Change', *Journal of Marketing*, vol. 51, January 1987, pp. 34–43.

Skinner W., 'The Focused Factory', *Harvard Business Review*, vol. 52, no. 3, May–June 1974, pp. 113–21.

Slack N., Chambers S., Harland C., Harrison A. and Johnston R., *Operations Management* (2nd edition), Pitman, London, 1998.

CASE EXERCISE

Smith and Jones, Solicitors (A)

It was 10.00 a.m. when I approached the office of a reputable firm of solicitors in Stroud. I opened the heavy oak door to be immediately confronted by another door bearing a notice advertising interest rates for a well-known building society. Through this door was a long, well-carpeted corridor with prints of sailing ships on the walls. Turning the corner at the end of the corridor, there was a well-lit room with a desk in the middle. A notice on the desk said 'Reception' and there was a young, well-dressed woman behind it. She had her dictation playback machine running and she was busily typing. Behind her, in and around the doorway to what was presumably the kitchen, were three people chatting over their morning coffee. At the end of the paragraph the receptionist took off her earphones and looked at me.

'My name is Johnston, I have an appointment with Mr Smith at 10 o'clock.' She eyed me suspiciously, maybe my jeans or my jumper spotted with paint offended her. She checked the appointment book.

The telephone rang and she smartly answered it. 'Smith and Jones. ... Who's calling please? ... Mr Thompson, Harris Limited? ... No, I am sorry, Mr Smith is busy at the moment. ... Oh, all right then, 'bye.'

She motioned me towards the black leather suite and I picked up a magazine. A few minutes later, the telephone clicked as a line cleared. She picked it up again and pressed a button.

'Mr Smith, a Mr Johnston for you ... Right-oh.'

'He will see you now, Mr Johnston, upstairs, first on the right.'

I climbed the stairs at 10.07 a.m. and was met on the landing by John Smith.

'Ah, Bob, good to see you. Come along in. I hope you've been looked after. Sorry I'm running a bit late this morning. Would you like another cup of coffee?'

John Smith and David Jones had been employed together in a large firm of solicitors in London. They both felt that London held few attractions for them and that they would prefer their own small country practice. Six years ago they moved to offices just off the High Street in Stroud and set up in competition with four other firms of solicitors. It was a slow start but both partners were now very busy and had a secretarial staff of five, all of whom, apart from the receptionist, shared an office on the second floor. On the first floor were two large rooms for the partners. The ground floor comprised the reception, a filing room with the photocopier, a kitchen and toilets. We had finished our business and our second cup of coffee by 11.00 a.m. John started telling me about the business.

'We have two distinct types of client. There is the personal client who is the local individual with a small legal problem, like a house purchase or a boundary dispute, and there is the commercial client who is a company, a few of which are local but most are based in Bristol, Gloucester, Cheltenham, Bath or Cirencester.

'The personal client comes through the door when he or she has a problem. There used to be a lot of loyalty to the solicitors that the client or his or her family had used in the past, but this is declining. We don't do any advertising – indeed it is only allowed in a very limited form. Most of our clients come either because they want a change from the solicitors they have used before or through recommendations from friends. We have worked hard to build up our local personal clients. I like to try to break down the stuffy image of the law and deal at a simple and straightforward level with the client. This personal approach seems to work very well. You see, many ordinary people in the street are very apprehensive about coming to see a solicitor. To them, I suppose, we are a bit like a dentist – only they extract teeth and we extract money! We always make sure that they are dealt with promptly and pleasantly by a partner, never by a junior clerk. We see ourselves as a small, local, convenient and friendly firm based on a good, personal and caring image.

'When we first came here we obviously had no local work, but we relied upon a few commercial accounts that we brought with us from London. We now work for about ten companies, though no longer for any that are based in London. Some of our commercial work has come about through providing a good service to a personal client. Usually, however, companies have their own favourite firm of solicitors. Sometimes they do give small jobs to other firms just to try them out, so we often get speculative phone calls from potential clients. I reckon sometimes when they ring up they have Yellow Pages in their hands and if you can't help them there and then they will go on to the next firm on the list. Sometimes we get commercial clients through recommendations from other companies or third parties like accountants who have heard that we give a good service. We need to expand our business in this area by giving a good and fast response to our clients.'

Now that the firm was well established, John Smith seemed keen not to stand still. He explained, 'On local, personal business, solicitors tend to think that if you just sit back, business will just come in and you don't need to make any spectacular effort to keep it. As a result clients are frequently abused. Some solicitors think nothing of telling customers who arrive on the doorstep to go away and come back when they have made an appointment. I think that solicitors have a condescending approach to business. I believe that we have a lot of lessons to learn from the modern age and that we can do a lot more thrusting. I am sure there is a lot of scope. I don't believe that everyone is entirely happy with their solicitor. The problem is that although I work tirelessly to build up the practice, we don't seem to be getting any more clients.'

Questions

1 *Evaluate Smith and Jones' service.*

2 *What advice would you give John Smith?*

7

Service Capacity

INTRODUCTION

This chapter addresses one of the central areas of service operations management, the provision and management of capacity. 'Long-term' capacity management is concerned with an operation's structure – its location, facilities and networks – and this is dealt with in Chapter 9. This chapter focuses on 'short-' and 'medium-term' capacity management. This is concerned with ensuring that the service process has sufficient resources to deal with the anticipated levels of customer demand in such a way that quality of service meets pre-set targets in the most cost-effective manner, i.e. making the best use of the operation's fixed assets.

There is no one right way to manage capacity; the capacity management strategy must be aligned with the underlying business model. In some cases, the objective will be to maximise the utilisation of expensive, and/or scarce, resources, whilst in others, the objective will be to provide the highest level of service availability consistent with cost constraints.

The objectives of this chapter are as follows:

- to provide a definition of service capacity
- to describe basic capacity management strategies and their application
- to describe how service organisations might make maximum use of capacity through approaches such as yield management and bottleneck management
- to examine a fourth capacity strategy – 'coping' – and how to manage it
- to provide a framework for understanding short- to medium-term capacity management
- to define operational flexibility and its contribution to capacity management
- to identify the need for organisational support for resource management.

In some organisations, and indeed in some industry sectors, capacity management has been viewed as a low-level task. As a result, this area has received scant attention, is poorly managed within the operations function itself, and does not command sufficient influence to manage key internal relationships essential to effective capacity management. This is particularly noticeable in service sectors where there has been relatively little competition, with organisations able to make sufficient profits without paying attention to operational issues.

The management of capacity is a critical issue for operations managers. Under-utilised resource has the potential to damage the long-term success of the organisation in a variety of ways:

- Expensive resource not earning revenue leads to poor financial results. The airline that fails to achieve a high load factor on its planes will not survive.
- In many services, customers are suspicious of services which appear to be unpopular. Banks and similar financial institutions find that some customers are not happy about using an empty branch, and many diners prefer the 'buzz' of a busy restaurant.
- Service employees may become demotivated if under-utilisation persists. Boredom and concern for their long-term employment may lead to poor service attitudes which again lead to reduced customer satisfaction and lower profitability.

Resources that are overstretched also lead to problems for the success of the organisation:

- Overloaded resources mean that many aspects of service delivery suffer. A sudden surge of customers into a shop means that waiting times increase and staff cannot devote the amount of attention to customers that is desirable.
- Staff that are continually overloaded make more mistakes and, in the longer term, may decide to leave the organisation in search of less stressful employment.
- In order to deal with overload, staff may be drafted into carrying out tasks that they are unfamiliar with or are only partially trained for. The potential for increased error rate is high and, again, stress levels may be intolerable for some members of staff.

The essence of many service capacity problems is simply that the organisation must attempt to deal with highly variable demand levels with relatively inflexible resource. This is fairly easy to manage when the resource that defines capacity is relatively unskilled, poorly paid labour which can be hired and fired very rapidly in response to demand levels. The problem becomes more complex when the organisation must decide when it will commit itself to purchase a major unit of capacity, such as an aeroplane or a new partner in a professional service firm, which will represent significant cost and will not be effective until some time in the future.

7.2 SERVICE CAPACITY

There are several ways of defining capacity, but the basic definition we adopt is that proposed by Slack *et al.* (1998), i.e. *the maximum level of value-added activity over a period of time* that the service process can achieve under normal operating conditions.

We can define and measure capacity relatively easily at the process level. For example:

- the number of calls a customer service agent can consistently handle in the course of a shift
- the number of meals served by a restaurant during the lunch-time period

● the number of repair calls made by a computer service engineer during an eight-hour day.

It is important to note the words 'under normal operating conditions' and 'consistently'. It may be possible, in some cases, for an individual employee to exceed the throughput rate for a short period. If the call centre employee handles 120 calls over 8 hours (15 calls per hour), it may be possible for him/her to achieve as many as 30 calls in one of these hours, but this rate is not sustainable over time.

As we will see later, in section 7.5, overloading resources may appear to increase output. Indeed, if analysed solely in terms of numbers of customer transactions completed, this may seem to be the case. However, there may be an impact on the nature of the service, the service concept, and also the quality of the service provided. Service organisations must take particular care to ensure that the service concept is not changed in the search for greater productivity. For example, the restaurant may decide to encourage customers to leave the table having completed their meal, in order to fit in a second sitting for dinner. On the face of it, the restaurant has doubled its capacity, but customers may feel that the level of service has deteriorated. Of course there are strategies that the restaurant can adopt to manage this sensitively, but the operations manager must be certain that in increasing productivity the desired service concept (outcome and experience) is maintained.

A number of factors make the assessment of service capacity difficult:

● *Service product mix*. If the service product mix is made up of high volumes of 'runners' (see Chapter 6), then the capacity calculation is relatively straightforward. However, once the product mix becomes more complex, incorporating fluctuating volumes of 'repeaters' and 'strangers', the calculation also becomes more complex. The customer service agent may be able to handle 120 'normal' calls in a shift; however, if some of the calls are complex enquiries or serious complaints, for example, the number of calls handled will drop significantly.

● *The impact of location*. At first sight, the measure of capacity for the computer service engineer, above, would seem to be relatively straightforward. However, if you consider the difference between an engineer operating in a major city with another dealing with rural communities, it can be seen that calculating capacity on the basis of calls completed alone would be spurious.

● *The extent of intangibility in the service product*. Service products with low degrees of intangibility are relatively easy to deal with. The numbers of short transactions in a fast-food restaurant are relatively consistent. The moment that customer-facing staff have increased discretion about their task, perhaps spending time with customers in 'building relationships', the individual's capacity becomes more difficult to define. This is, of course, much more complex when dealing with knowledge workers who must combine short-term revenue-generating activities with long-term research and development.

7.3 CAPACITY STRATEGIES

There are three basic capacity strategies, although, as we will discuss, most organisations employ a mixture of all three. These strategies are:

- *The level capacity strategy.* In this case scarce or expensive resources are maintained at a constant level, and the organisation must manage the consequential issues for service quality.

- *The chase strategy.* The service organisation attempts to match supply to demand as much as possible by building flexibility into the operation. The prime objective is to provide high levels of service availability or fast response, in the most efficient manner.

- *The demand management strategy.* Rather than change the capacity of the service operation, the organisation influences the demand profile to 'smooth' the load on the resources.

To these three basic strategies, we will add a fourth, which is termed 'coping'. This is defined as the way that the organisation copes (or doesn't cope) with more demand than the system was designed to deal with routinely. The reason we have termed it a 'strategy' is that because of the 'balancing act' between quality and resource productivity, there will always be surges of demand that take the organisation into overload. It is our contention that service managers need a thought-out strategy to deal with these situations, rather than to just 'suck it and see'.

7.3.1 The level capacity strategy

The prime objective of this strategy is to maximise utilisation of expensive resource. An airline seeks to fly planes that are as full as possible with passengers paying the highest fares. The key operational measure is the 'load factor', with the airline knowing that if it is exceeding a certain figure (about 80 per cent for an international airline), it will be making profit.

In order to achieve this level of utilisation, the service organisation may have to make a number of trade-offs, most notably around quality of service. Figure 7.1 illustrates the situation in a hospital clinic. Here, the task is to make the most of the medical consultant. The clinic has to solve the problem of always having enough patients for the consultant to work on, with the added difficulty of there being a high percentage of 'no-shows'. The clinic has chosen to over-book appointments and believes that it is better to upset a few patients rather than to lose valuable consultant time.

In order to deal with the 'no-shows' problem, the clinic has made four appointments at the start of each 15-minute period, estimating that one in four patients does not arrive and that the consultant will require five minutes per patient. If all goes to plan, the first patient will be seen immediately, the second within five minutes and the third within ten minutes, but it should be noted that they each had the same 2.00 p.m. appointment. In practice, some of the 2.00 p.m. appointments will still be waiting when the next 'batch' arrives for a (supposed) 2.15 appointment.

Some general principles and issues can be drawn from this example about the level capacity strategy:

- Resource utilisation goals are achieved at the expense of service quality.
- Customers may receive inconsistent service levels (those with 2.00 p.m. appointments fare better than those with later appointments).

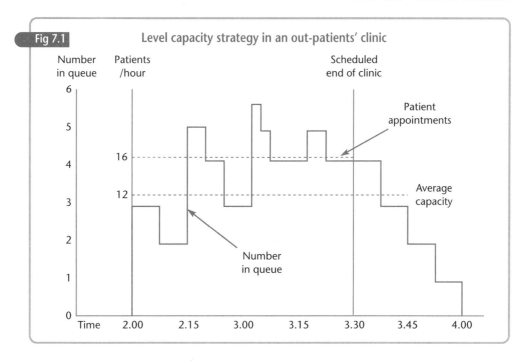

Fig 7.1 Level capacity strategy in an out-patients' clinic

- Customers (patients) accept (or suffer) this poor level of service because it is valuable to them and there may be few or no alternatives.

- There is a danger that the service provider may become complacent and not make attempts to cut the emotional cost of waiting for the customer, making them potentially vulnerable to competition (in this case private healthcare).

In order to overcome this problem of variable service levels, the service provider may use yield management or queue management approaches (described later).

Examples of organisations that use the 'level' strategy as its dominant approach include:

- Airlines who need to maximise the revenue from their most expensive resource (planes).

- Professional services who may have a recognised expert in a specialised field. It is frequently the case that the overall workload will not sustain another professional, leaving clients with a choice as to whether they wait or find an alternative.

- Popular restaurants may intentionally not expand capacity in order to maintain an exclusivity. Having to book days, sometimes months, ahead in order to ensure a table may enhance the service concept.

Examples of approaches adopted under the level strategy include:

- ***Promoting off-peak demand***. This is often combined with a pricing strategy to encourage customers to switch. The organisation must be careful that this does not bring about a change in service concept. A restaurant encouraging customers to move to less popular times may institute a 'happy hour' with cheap drinks which may damage the restaurant's reputation with existing customers.

- *Queue management.* This is dealt with in more depth in section 7.4.3, but it is important to point out here that making an assumption that customers will continue to queue is extremely dangerous. It is, after all, sending the message that their time is relatively worthless, and they are only prepared to wait because they anticipate that the service they receive will be valuable enough to make the wait (lost time) worthwhile.

- *Booking systems.* Making forward bookings is a form of queue management. It allows the organisation to schedule capacity ahead, and for customers to utilise queuing time for themselves. Supermarkets have successfully utilised this system for their delicatessen counters, issuing customers with numbered tickets to ensure that people are served in order, and allowing customers to judge whether they have time to continue shopping before their number is called. As with the physical queue, customers may not want to wait and will go elsewhere. Indeed, if the organisation has the reputation that customers need to book ahead, it may lose potential sales if customers assume that there is no point in trying.

7.3.2 The chase strategy

This strategy is usually adopted by high-volume consumer services, where it is a major part of their competitive strategy to provide ready and rapid access to service. In this case, capital resource utilisation is rarely a prime goal, though cost reduction is. To explain this further, consider the following statements concerning a fast-food restaurant:

- A key objective is to maintain short queue lengths. This is managed by staffing tills and kitchen in line with expected demand.
- If the queues are too long, customers go to another fast-food outlet.
- The premises are not fully utilised because there are only about six hours out of the possible 24 hours when the facilities are 100 per cent utilised.

The challenge of these high-volume standard services is to develop *volume flexibility* (see section 7.7). In other words, the operation must be able to cope with wide ranges of customer demand, providing consistent service standards at minimum cost. Figure 7.2 shows the demand pattern for a fast-food restaurant, with a crew roster to show how the restaurant manager schedules the staff to deal with the variation in demand.

In this restaurant, the staff are organised into three categories: those on one of the core shift teams, those working split shifts, and those working part time. The split shifts allow the manager to schedule staff for the forecast demand peaks. There will probably be a weekly rotation between the core shifts and the split shift personnel. In this example, the early-morning peak load is covered by employing part time labour. In addition, the manager will have a pool of labour to be contacted at short notice to cover absenteeism or an unexpected rise in demand. A common strategy is to extend the length of the split shifts, some organisations operating a 'compulsory overtime' policy as part of their conditions of employment.

General principles and issues for the chase strategy are:

- Most organisations operating the chase strategy must develop a high degree of volume flexibility. In other words, they must be able to respond to changing

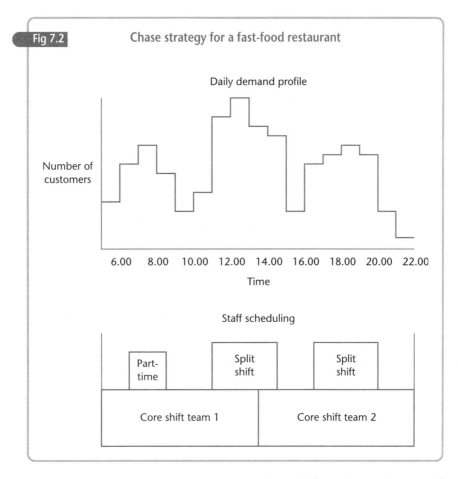

Fig 7.2   Chase strategy for a fast-food restaurant

demand profiles. In most cases this is achieved through employing staff on flexible contracts, allowing the operations manager to decide working hours as required.

- Although a principal objective is to ensure that customer service targets such as availability or response times are achieved, many of these service organisations fall into the 'commodity' category (high-volume/low-process variety). In contrast to the organisations employing the level strategy, they frequently have relatively little means of differentiation and are therefore rather price sensitive. The challenge in adopting the chase strategy, therefore, is to ensure that costs are strictly controlled and that flexibility is not achieved at any price.

Examples of organisations that employ the chase strategy include:

- High Street retailers who need to deal with extremely high demand at weekends and after normal office hours
- direct insurance companies operating extended hours through call centres
- theme parks who may open up more attractions as demand grows.

Typical approaches to the chase strategy include:

- *Flexible staffing levels.* Some organisations use flexible employment contracts, allowing the operations manager to decide when staff will be working. In some cases staff will work a standard core time, but in many retail organisations staff may not know when they will be working beyond the next few shifts. Another approach is to employ part-time staff who must work 'compulsory' overtime as and when needed. Although this gives flexibility, the operations manager must be aware of the possibility of staff resentment at having to work inconvenient hours, and the knock-on effect of poor customer service.

- *The use of subcontractors or temporary staff.* Organisations may use temporary staff or subcontractors to deal with short-term overloads. Although these workers may be readily available, they may not be sufficiently trained or motivated to deliver service in the style of the organisation. That said, some organisations report that their temporary staff may be more responsive and less complacent than long-service staff. Some call centres use organisations who specialise in what is called 'peak lopping'. Excess calls are automatically routed to the organisation and they are answered in such a manner that customers are unaware of the switch.

- *The use of customers.* Many service operations may have the option of changing the service process to utilise customers as temporary employees. In effect this is again changing the service concept. Some regular customers may be very happy to be included in the service process, possibly serving other customers as well as themselves.

7.3.3 Demand management strategies

As has been stated previously, most companies operate a 'mixed' approach to capacity management. Whether 'chase' or 'level', most service organisations operate some degree of demand management. Examples of this approach include:

- *Pricing strategies.* This typically takes the form of offering price incentives to encourage customers to move to off-peak times. The 'happy hour' in the pub or wine bar is a good example.

- *Restricted service at peak times.* The philosophy here is similar, though taking the form of a *dis*incentive. In this case the organisation may provide a limited service at peak times, again encouraging customers to move to less busy times. Some restaurants operate this policy, with a much smaller menu at these times.

- *Specialist service channels.* Rather than provide a general service at all times, the provider may choose to segment the demand and to allocate specific times for special needs. Doctors' surgeries are a good example, with advertised times for services such as immunisations, mother and baby clinics, and counselling provision. This allows the surgery to schedule specialist resources to restricted times, often making better use of scarce resources.

- *Advertising and promotion.* Increasing public awareness of the service and informing customers of special offers will stimulate demand. Bookshops not only advertise, but will also stimulate demand by arranging sessions for authors to autograph their works. A particular problem with advertising is that it tends to increase the inaccuracy of any forecasting model used by the business. Although it is possible to track the effectiveness of advertising in stimulating demand, it is often difficult to pre-judge the likely impact of a new campaign.

Putting the strategies together

Most complex service organisations use both of the major capacity strategies in different parts of their operations, depending on the respective underlying cost models. Some examples are shown in Table 7.1.

Table 7.1 Capacity strategies

	Level capacity strategy	*Chase strategy*	*Demand management*
International airline	Ensure that planes are flying with maximum payload as frequently as possible	Staff reservations department to meet demand to ensure bookings can be made	Promote off-peak demand Try to maximise revenue from each flight (see yield management: section 7.4.1)
Insurance company	Protect back office experts (actuaries and investment specialists) from variations in customer demand	'Direct' sales operation (call centre) scheduled to provide maximum access for customers	Influence selling cycle so as not to coincide with policy renewal peaks
Restaurant chain	Keep manufacturing of basic food materials as close to 'level' as possible. High utilisation of process plant	Staff rosters reflect anticipated demand Use of part-time staff to manage peaks Call in staff for demand surges	Promotional activity to stimulate demand in quiet periods Special offers allow for bulk-purchasing discounts

The prime objective of the airline is to maximise 'load factor' on its flights, the utilisation of its most expensive assets. It employs a number of strategies to ensure that it makes the maximum revenue on each flight, using sophisticated yield management techniques (section 7.4.) to help adopt the optimum pricing strategy to sell unsold seats as departure time approaches. The airline may simply over-sell seats in the belief that there will be a number of 'no-shows'. Passengers who are then not able to obtain the seat they thought they had booked need to be compensated in some way, though unless managed well that can significantly affect customer satisfaction.

In order to maximise the opportunity for customers to book seats, the airline employs a chase strategy in its sales department using relatively cheap resource (as compared with planes), scheduling staff to meet forecast demand patterns. It is better to suffer slightly reduced productivity here rather than lose potential seat revenue.

The insurance company uses a level strategy for its actuarial staff (back office), in part because they are relatively expensive, but more because they are often in short supply. The lead-time to recruit and train an actuary is measured in years rather than weeks and therefore it makes no sense to attempt to chase demand.

Similarly, the restaurant chain will operate a level strategy in its manufacturing function because it has relatively fixed capacity and although it can increase capacity marginally by overtime, significant increases can only be achieved by investing in another factory.

7.4 HOW TO MAKE THE MOST OF CAPACITY

In this section we describe three areas of capacity management used extensively by service operations managers to increase the effective use of existing capacity: yield management, bottleneck management and queue management.

7.4.1 Yield management

Yield management is employed extensively by hotels and airlines to deal with the fact that their capacity is perishable. In other words, if the hotel room is not sold tonight, the contribution from that potential sale is lost for all time (see, for example, Fitzsimmons and Fitzsimmons 1997; Kimes 1989).

Box 7.1 The Kowloon Hotel, Hong Kong

Professor Sheryl E. Kimes, Cornell University

Yield management, the notion of charging higher prices when demand is high and offering discounts at times of low demand, has traditionally been applied in reservations-based industries such as airlines, hotels and car rental agencies. Managers at the Kowloon Hotel in Hong Kong felt that it might offer them the solution to improving their restaurant revenues.

The Kowloon Hotel on Nathan Road in Hong Kong is well known for its sumptuous all-day buffet. The buffet, which includes a selection of sashimi, oysters, salads and desserts, is open from midday to midnight. As is typical with most restaurants, customers only wanted to dine at particular times of day, and the restaurant was often empty in the late afternoon and late evening. To deal with this problem, the Kowloon Hotel's managers decided to move away from a single price for its buffet and charge different prices depending on when customers arrive.

When guests arrive ('check-in') they now receive a 'buffet zone pass'. The cost of the pass varies depending on their arrival time. At noon, the price is 118 HK$, but increases to 128 HK$ at 1 p.m., but then drops back to 118 HK$ at 2 p.m. The 3 p.m. price is even lower (108 HK$), but then progressively increases from 128 HK$ at 4 p.m.; to $168 at 5 p.m.; $208 at 6 p.m.; and $248 at 7 p.m. Following this peak, the price gradually decreases back to $138 at 10 p.m. and only $98 at 11 p.m.

Not only has this new pricing system resulted in a 33 per cent increase in revenue – which was attributed to a fuller utilisation of the restaurant space, hence an increase in revenue per available seat hour (RevPASH) – it has also proved to be a hit with customers with extremely positive customer reaction. As a result the management has decided to continue the time-of-day pricing for an indefinite period.

Yield management is focused on determining the maximum revenue to be obtained from the various segments served by the capacity at hand. Thus the airline estimates how many full-fare paying (business-class) passengers will book for any given flight, and adjusts the remaining capacity for economy-class passengers and other discount, pre-booked customers. As departure time approaches, the airline may release some capacity to discount travel shops and, as a last resort at the very last minute, to stand-by passengers.

Service managers must be aware, however, of the potential damage to the service concept in using this approach. Full-fare paying customers may be unhappy to discover that the person in the seat next to them is flying for a fraction of the price. This may give the impression that the airline is merely after every last dollar of revenue, with customer satisfaction of minor importance. The Kowloon Hotel appears to have overcome this particular objection by creating a completely new concept where the charging policy is clear and unambiguous. Customers can therefore make their choice of eating time, knowing that they will be treated equitably.

7.4.2   Bottleneck management

Bottleneck management, or the theory of constraints, is well understood in manufacturing organisations where it is seen to be important to manage the bottleneck – the stage in the process with the lowest throughput rate which determines the effective capacity of the whole operation (see, for example, Goldratt and Cox 1984).

It is important for service operations managers also to understand where the bottlenecks exist in service processes. For example, a company providing loan finance needed to increase the standard of service provided to its customers whilst also increasing productivity of its risk assessment process. The management was given the task of meeting increasing demand without increasing resources. Initially, it was not clear how this could be achieved, but when the process was mapped it became obvious that a problem lay with the actuaries. Figure 7.3a shows a simplified version of the original process flow, with all proposals passing through an actuary's hands for sign-off.

As can be seen from Figure 7.3a, the original capacity was constrained by the throughput of the actuaries at 15 proposals per hour. It was recognised that many proposals did not require actuarial sign-off because the credit scores indicated a clear accept or reject decision which could be taken by more junior, less expensive

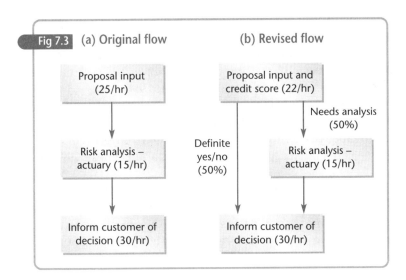

Fig 7.3   (a) Original flow   (b) Revised flow

staff. The initial processing took slightly longer, but in the revised process (Figure 7.3b), only 50 per cent of the proposals needed to be seen by an actuary. The capacity of the process therefore rose by nearly 50 per cent to 22 proposals per hour.

This improvement was achieved simply by monitoring the activity levels within the process and then deciding whether the current resource constraints were really bottlenecks or not. Once the belief that all proposals must be seen by actuaries had been questioned, it became possible to improve response times and productivity simultaneously.

General rules for managing bottlenecks include the following:

- Ensure that only essential work passes through the bottleneck.
- Be ruthless in taking away non-essential activities from the bottleneck.
- Ensure that no sub-standard work passes through the bottleneck.
- Once you have established where the bottleneck is, devote proportionally more management attention to it to ensure maximum throughput and therefore maximum effectiveness for the process.

And finally:

- If you have a complex system, Goldratt and Cox (1984) suggested that you should not attempt to move the bottleneck. It may be difficult to manage but at least you know where it is!

7.4.3 Queue management

Queues seem to be a natural consequence of service activity. Indeed, for any operation using a level capacity strategy queues are 'designed-in'. Furthermore, any capacity strategy is not perfect and queues are usually inevitable. Queues may be lines of people visible to both the customer and employee, or they may be invisible to one and/or the other, for example a queue of callers to a switchboard or a list of customers awaiting a repair engineer.

Whilst queuing theory can be used to calculate the number of servers required to meet forecast demand, resource constraints and forecast inaccuracy invariably mean that operations managers need to look for other ways to minimise the impact of queuing on their customers. It has been shown that not only does dissatisfaction with the wait increase with waiting time (Katz et al. 1991) but also dissatisfaction with the service as a whole (Davis and Vollmann 1990).

Given that perceived waiting time is greater than actual waiting time (Katz et al. 1991), the answer is to try to reduce perceived waiting time, which can also be a great deal cheaper than employing more servers! Ten principles of waiting have been suggested (1–8 by Maister 1985; 9 by Davis and Heineke 1994; and 10 by Jones and Peppiatt 1996).

1. Unoccupied time feels longer than occupied time

It is a good idea to try to provide customers with something to do or forms of distraction so that the time passes more rapidly for them. Some services show promotional videos whilst waiting in a physical queue. Telephone call centres or help desks frequently play music whilst 'on hold', though it would be accurate to say that this is not universally welcomed.

2. Pre-process waits feel longer than in-process waits

Once customers feel that they have made a start inside the service process and that something, however trivial, is happening, they tend to feel happier. A simple acknowledgement by a server that they have been noticed can have a significant impact. Also, both using the time to complete a form or make choices about the service all reduce the perceived waiting time.

3. Anxiety makes the wait seem longer

This relates to customers not knowing whether they have been forgotten or not, which can be allayed by giving them numbered tickets to demonstrate that they are part of the system. Also, the nature of the service will have a significant impact. If the customer is worried about flying or going to the dentist the wait may seem interminable, possibly giving rise to some tense behaviour with service providers. Customer-facing employees should be trained to observe the effects of anxiety and to find ways of giving reassurance.

4. Uncertain waits are longer than known, finite waits

Customers are generally more happy to wait if the expected duration is known, and if there is a good reason for it. If the duration is unknown, research suggests that customers become restless much more quickly. Theme parks frequently position markers at known points in the queue informing customers how long they should expect to wait. Of course, the real wait time is usually a little shorter than this, with customers pleased that they did better than expected!

5. Unexplained waits seem longer than explained waits

Being provided with a plausible explanation of a delay reduces uncertainty for the customer. It also gives the impression that the organisation knows it shouldn't take the customer for granted.

6. Unfair waits are longer than equitable waits

Generally, customers expect that those who arrive first should be seen first. Many organisations have replaced the multiple queue/multiple server system with a single queue/multiple server approach because of the perceived unfairness of being stuck in a slow-moving queue. This approach also eliminates the anxiety as to which queue to join. In some cases, such as a hospital casualty department, there may be good reason why some customers are seen out of turn, but these still need explanation rather than for the provider to assume that other customers will understand.

7. The more valuable the service, the longer customers will wait

The more complex the service, and the more it is customised to the needs of the individual, the more likely it is that customers may be prepared to wait. It should be noted, however, that this should not be assumed.

8. Solo waiting feels longer than group waiting

The realisation that others are also feeling the pain may reduce the customers' anxiety of thinking that they have made the wrong choice. If others think it is worth waiting, it confirms the customers' decision to wait. Also, people tend to talk more to each other, providing a distraction from the length of the wait.

9. Uncomfortable waits feel longer than comfortable waits

By making queuing conditions as comfortable and indeed as distracting as possible, the wait time will be perceived to be much shorter. Uncomfortable conditions sensitise customers to the time and poor service.

10. New or infrequent users feel they wait longer than frequent users

Frequent users of a service may be attuned to a wait and furthermore they may be more relaxed because they know what to expect. New or infrequent users are likely to be more anxious and uncertain, so operations should consider trying to identify them and provide them with information and reassurance.

7.5 STRATEGY 4 – MANAGING THE 'COPING' ZONE

In this section we address a particular issue that all operations managers face. It is impossible to provide sufficient capacity at all times to meet every customer demand, and be profitable at the same time. Operations managers must manage this balancing act between resource productivity and quality. At its simplest, it is very difficult for any operation to deal with a sudden surge of customers who all want to be served before the organisation can add sufficient capacity to cope (Armistead and Clark 1994).

Figure 7.4 shows the profile of customer-perceived quality against resource utilisation and illustrates how quality may suffer through both too many and too few customers.

7.5.1 Managing the 'coping' zone

There are seven steps in building up this profile and managing the 'coping' zone.

Step 1   Identify the service concept

Underpinning the service concept of this gourmet restaurant is the belief that customers may book a table for the whole evening. They will not be rushed to vacate their table so that the restaurant can sell the space twice in an evening. It is intended that the service experience should be relaxed, with staff able to converse with customers and make recommendations about food and wine, where appropriate.

This is a very different concept from a restaurant wishing to create a high-energy situation, often with staff rushing around, and with the customers encouraged to eat up and leave! It is important to be clear as to what the designed or desired service concept is, particularly as the restaurant gets busy.

Step 2   Determine how resource utilisation is to be measured

For the gourmet restaurant, the best measure of resource utilisation is the number of tables, and also chairs, that are occupied during the evening. To some extent,

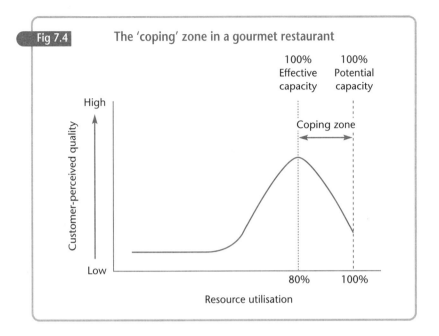

Fig 7.4 The 'coping' zone in a gourmet restaurant

other resources such as serving staff or kitchen capacity can be adjusted to the busy-ness of the restaurant area.

The unit of measure is often best taken at the lowest level at which the business analyses or controls performance. A call centre might look at the average loading of a customer service agent on an hourly basis throughout the day, whereas a profes-sional service firm might look at an individual's case-load.

Step 3 Draw the outline profile

Figure 7.4 shows the relationship between customer-perceived quality and resource utilisation as it exists for the majority of customers on the majority of occasions. This does not represent all customers at all times. Some customers, for example, prefer the empty restaurant and would rank it as high quality at low utilisation. For others, the occasion and their mood will have significant influence on where they would place themselves on the profile. This data can be captured from aggregating customer satis-faction indices and comparing the result to utilisation at the time.

Step 4 Understand the nature and impact of the 'coping' zone

Social aspects are a significant component of this type of service. As a result, low utilisation is potentially as much of a problem for quality of service as is high utili-sation. In some ways it's worse because revenue is also low!

At low utilisation:

● The perception of the overall quality of service experience is low because the restaurant is 'dead'. There is no buzz of conversation, often with prolonged silences.

● Service may be slow, because although there aren't many customers, the kitchen may not be working at maximum effectiveness.

- In the same way, serving staff may be less attentive than might be expected, because again they may not be busy enough to be fully tuned in to customer needs.

At high utilisation – in the 'coping' zone:

- Customers wait longer for food.
- The possibility of 'stock-outs' (items removed from the menu) is increased.
- Customers may feel rushed and under pressure not to ask too much from busy serving staff.
- Staff may feel under pressure and are less likely to give courteous responses or the personalised service expected.

This area where quality of service deteriorates as utilisation increases (the service gets busier) we term the 'coping' zone. It is the area where customers are still served, after a fashion. All the customers are served, but not in the manner which was laid down in the service design.

It is important to recognise that not all services have the same profile as the gourmet restaurant. Figure 7.5 shows the profile for a fast-food restaurant.

There are a number of reasons for the difference between these two profiles. One major reason is the difference in activity type and volume. The gourmet restaurant in Figure 7.4 operates at relatively low volumes of 'repeaters', meaning that small amounts of demand variability may have a significant impact on capacity. This compares with the fast-food restaurant that has high volumes of 'runner' transactions. This results in the flat profile in Figure 7.5 with a steep decline once the coping zone is reached. There is also a small decline at very low utilisation because the restaurant cannot cope with low, intermittent demand.

Another factor which introduces yet more variability in demand for the gourmet restaurant is that a significant part of the service experience for some (but not all) customers lies in the rapport struck up between the customers and the people serv-

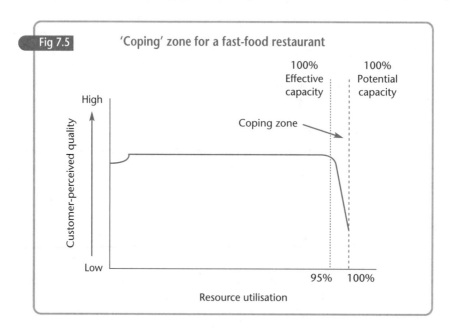

Fig 7.5   'Coping' zone for a fast-food restaurant

ing them. This is particularly important for many of the frequent customers. This means that forecasting demand on resource is particularly difficult, with the potential to enter the coping zone at a much earlier point than the high-volume/low-variety fast-food restaurant.

Step 5 Determine the 'ideal' operating point

In Figure 7.4, we have identified two types of capacity. We have termed the point where all the tables are occupied, 100% potential capacity. Unless we change the basic capacity of the restaurant (or the service concept itself), it is impossible to seat any more customers. For this example there are two broad approaches:

- *Operate at 80 per cent of potential capacity.* This appears that the restaurant could be losing potential revenue. It is true that it might receive lower short-term revenues, but it may also upset longstanding customers by appearing to be greedy, squeezing as many people as possible into every available space. It is critical to understand the difference between customer satisfaction at 80 per cent and at 100 per cent, and to what extent this significantly reduces the customers' likelihood of returning.

- *Operate at 100 per cent of potential capacity.* Generally speaking, this is a short-term cash-generating strategy. It is more appropriate to theme restaurants that are the 'place to be seen' for a period before those customers that are concerned about fashion move on to the next 'in' place. This strategy might also be appropriate for restaurants in holiday resorts which do not expect high levels of customer returns.

Our example restaurant depends on long-term customer retention and word-of-mouth advertising. As a result, it targets its operations at the 80 per cent point. In order to manage this, the owner has removed some of the tables to give a less crowded feel to the area, only replacing them on particularly busy occasions.

As a result, the owner has turned the 80 per cent potential capacity into 100 per cent effective capacity. In other words, at this point the restaurant is making sufficient revenue to meet its short-term financial goals, and is giving a high level of customer satisfaction to safeguard its future business. It is worth noting that because there is a gap between 100 per cent effective capacity and 100 per cent potential capacity, it is possible for the restaurant to be working at greater than 100 per cent utilisation on some occasions. Many managers have told us that this is the norm in their businesses!

Step 6 Understand why 'coping' happens

Clearly, it is impossible to maintain the capacity balance on 80 per cent of potential capacity at all times. Even if the restaurant has a booking policy, there is always the possibility that one of the most valuable customers will book at the last minute and the owner will be reluctant to turn this business away.

In other situations, the launch of a new product or periods of faster than anticipated growth may put parts of the business into 'coping' mode. This has been seen recently in the customer service departments of mobile phone network providers and banks, following product launches. In some cases, some of the coping might have been avoided if the company had carried out some forecasting, or had simply communicated internally.

A key point here is to recognise that all but the extremely resource-rich organisations will be in the 'coping' zone sometimes. If the coping zone is never entered, the inevitable conclusion is that the organisation has too much resource.

Step 7 Develop 'coping' strategies

Most organisations cope after a fashion. In the restaurant, all the diners are given food, but perhaps not with the greatest service experience. Likewise, on the crowded airline flight, all passengers get a meal and a drink, although those that are served last may have limited choice and little time to eat before the aircraft starts its descent.

Left to their own devices, customer-facing staff will find their own ways of coping. Some of these informal coping strategies will be entirely appropriate and innovative, using interpersonal skills and intuition to judge how to handle each customer. Others might be less satisfactory, typified by the following examples:

- the waiter who becomes overly focused on one task, making it impossible for customers to attract his attention to make yet more demands
- the doctor's receptionist, faced with a crowded waiting-room, who becomes extremely efficient in his/her dealings with patients, to the point of rudeness
- the retail assistant who 'forgets' to offer a customer a range of products, knowing that if the customer chooses one of these, his/her work-load will increase.

Operations managers develop coping strategies based on one or more of the following:

- giving more information to customers alerting them to possible difficulties. An example is the electricity company that after a major storm placed a recorded message on its help-line to say 'if you're calling about loss of power in this district, we should be able to restore it within two hours'. This reduces the load on overworked telephone lines and operators
- intentionally reducing the service on offer, perhaps using a limited menu at peak times in the restaurant
- being clear to staff about what really matters most for customers, concentrating on the 'must dos' rather than the 'nice to dos'
- building resource flexibility, bringing staff from a lightly loaded area to assist with the overload. Call centres manage this by switching calls to other centres, whereas Disney brings managers from back office functions to assist with customer-facing operations on busy days. It is important to note that some of this resource may not be as efficient as the normal workforce.

There is a very strong link between prolonged overload and employee stress (see burnout in Chapter 8, section 8.5.1). It is relatively easy for providers to deal with short-term, predictable overloads. If we know we're going to be busy for a week or two, we can prepare for it, and many people get a 'buzz' from working together to cope with a crisis. The real problem with coping comes from protracted periods of overload, without hope of a let-up in the foreseeable future. Management support and appreciation become extremely important at this stage.

If the operation is in the 'coping' zone for prolonged periods, it may be necessary for managers to give their staff 'licence to under-perform'. For example, a nurse in a busy accident and emergency department may not be able to carry out all her/his duties in the way in which s/he was trained. If this persists for any length of time, this will lead to stress and possible burnout. Part of the coping strategy, therefore, is to agree which bits of the service are 'must dos' and which bits can be safely left for the time being.

7.5.2 'Coping': key questions

We have devoted a lot of space to 'coping' because understanding how the organisation deals with this area may give clues as to where capacity management must be strengthened. The key questions to address are:

- What does the customer-perceived quality/resource utilisation profile look like for your service or services?
- How does this vary by service process and by customer group?
- What measures or early warning signals tell you that you are about to enter the 'coping' zone (as opposed to measures like lost customers or increased complaints which tell you that you *were* in the 'coping' zone)?
- What suffers for customers when you enter the 'coping' zone?
- What suffers for employees when you enter the 'coping' zone?
- How could you manage the 'coping' zone better to reduce the impact on customers and employees?
- How could you avoid being in the 'coping' zone for so long?

Of course, coping will affect every part of the organisation, in areas where both chase and level are operating, although coping is perhaps more obvious in operations that are employing a chase strategy. In effect, chase becomes level in the short term because the organisation is not capable of adding another unit of capacity quickly enough to deal with an unexpected surge in demand. Coping is perhaps more sensitive here because, as we have noted, organisations employ this strategy when fast response or high levels of availability to customers are particularly important. These customers are not usually prepared to wait, either because the service is not particularly valuable to them, or because there are alternatives available to them.

7.6 A CAPACITY MANAGEMENT FRAMEWORK

Figure 7.6 illustrates a simple way of marshalling the areas to be addressed in understanding and improving service capacity management. The framework allows the operations manager to identify key issues to understand and manage capacity more effectively.

- *Service output.* This indicates the overall capacity of the service operation, often expressed in units of output over an appropriate period. For example, a call centre may measure calls taken per day or a restaurant number of meals served in an evening.
- *Service resource.* Here we identify the principal resources required to carry out the operation, paying attention to those which are critical or near critical.

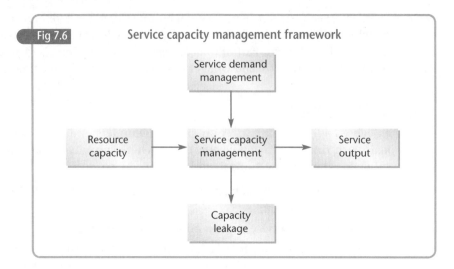

Fig 7.6 Service capacity management framework

- *Service demand.* We analyse the impact on capacity of changes in the demand mix or promotional activity.

- *Service capacity management.* This looks at the effectiveness of various techniques to increase or 'flex' capacity.

- *Capacity leakage.* Here we understand why capacity may be less than anticipated.

7.6.1 Applying the framework

In the following section we will apply the framework to a telephone call centre, indicating what actions could be taken in this case to improve capacity management. Table 7.2 summarises the points and the challenges.

Resource capacity

We need to understand more accurately the capacity of those resources which define the overall capacity of the call centre operation. Typically these would include:

- number of calls processed by each agent per day multiplied by number of agents available to work

- number of lines

- number of workstations.

The key question here is to determine which are the capacity constraints, or bottleneck resources. This might take some analysis, particularly if this needs to be taken to a greater level of detail. The constraint, for example, may not be the total number of telephone service agents but the more experienced people who can deal with more complex issues for customers.

The call centre manager must also be aware of the way that resource constraints may change at different times, with different demand mixes. Immediately after a sales promotion it may be necessary to have more staff simply taking orders, but after these orders have been despatched to be ready to deal with customers wanting to exchange or return goods. This later stage might require more skilled agents than for simple order taking.

Service demand management

Capacity, the ability for the call centre to deal with the demand for its services, clearly depends on the extent to which the demand profile is understood and can be forecast. It also requires understanding as to how a changing mix of demands might affect key resources:

● We need to know how demand profile changes through the day, week, year, and so on.

● Are some services delivered with relatively little resource ('runners' rather than 'repeaters')?

● What is the impact of a changing demand mix on resource constraints?

● What is the impact of promotional activity on activity levels?

It is this last question which causes the most problems. To some extent it may be a technical issue in that it is difficult to forecast the impact of increased advertising spend, or the take-up of a new product (as some financial services have found out to their cost). However, more worrying is the all-too-common situation which arises when promotional activity is only noticed when calls start arriving in the call centre!

Service capacity management

There are some activities that can be undertaken in the call centre, often facilitated by call management software:

● priority management, ensuring that valuable customers receive prompt attention

● work scheduling to pre-set rules such as first in–first out (FIFO), least work in progress first, or a variety of other rules

● management of bottlenecks

● staff scheduling

● peak load management (outsourcing, call switching, compulsory overtime).

Again, the issue here is frequently not the 'simple' calculations which determine day-to-day capacity management, but the extent to which the organisation has invested in the medium- to long-term provision of capacity rather than simply reacting to today's need.

Capacity leakage

This is perhaps the most revealing category. The question posed here is 'Why isn't there as much capacity as we anticipated?' Here are some possible answers:

● *Labour sickness and absenteeism.* Prolonged periods of overload and compulsory overtime usually prove counter-productive, with staff taking time off to recover. Alternatively, the organisation may need to look at its management style, placing more emphasis on team building rather than 'command and control' approaches.

- ***Labour under-performance***, arising from having a 'management by headcount' mentality. It is extremely common to find that call centres may have the right number of 'heads' but they may be ineffective because there has been insufficient investment in training, or employee churn means that experienced staff leave just at the point they are becoming effective.
- ***Scheduling losses***, in the sense that there are times when staff are idle with too much capacity for the demand, whereas at other times there is too much demand for the capacity to deal with. This often arises because demand profiles are not understood or are too volatile or where staff preferences for work patterns do not fit with the business need.
- ***Costs of complexity***. The more the organisation deals with a broad range of services, the greater the possibility that staff deal with a greater percentage of tasks which, if not unknown, may not be part of daily routine. This potential 're-learning' may give rise to inefficiencies and rework.
- ***Quality failures***. The need to deal with quality failures is clearly lost capacity. Of course, part of the role of the call centre may be to deal with poor quality generated elsewhere in the organisation. It is essential that the extent of this rework is understood and charged to the appropriate location.

Table 7.2 Call centre service capacity framework: description and challenges

	Description	Challenges
Service resources	Customer service agents Senior (experienced) agents Telephone lines Seats (workstations) Outsourced capacity (peak load)	Understanding critical resources for different demand mixes
Demand management	Promotional activity, regular and special offers Sales activity – 'runners' Complaint management – 'repeaters' Proactive customer information in busy periods	Obtaining sufficient warning of likely impact of promotions to match staffing levels to forecast load
Capacity management	Staff scheduling Call management (software) Peak load 'lopping' to outsourced capacity Overtime Call switching to other departments Coping strategies	Creation of a master schedule Management of marketing/sales/operations interfaces
Capacity leakage	Staff absenteeism Insufficient training Staff turnover	Management of stress through prolonged overload
Service output	Calls handled per day within target service levels	Reduction of abandoned calls

7.7 RESOURCE FLEXIBILITY

There are four basic forms of operational flexibility. It is critical to define carefully the type and extent of flexibility required in order to develop effective capacity management plans:

- *New product flexibility*. The requirement of the service operation to introduce new services into an existing mix. It will be necessary to define how frequently this might occur and the extent to which the operation will require new capabilities to achieve it. For example, mortgage companies are continually introducing new products with varying interest rates and repayment terms. In this case the frequency of new product introduction is extremely high, but the requirement for new capability is low.

- *Product mix flexibility*. The ability of the operation to deliver more than one service product. An hotel may provide a number of services simultaneously dealing with business people, holiday travellers, conferences, and wedding celebrations.

- *Delivery flexibility*. This is the capability of the operation to change the timing of the activity. Courier organisations are increasing this form of flexibility, offering different speeds of delivery and a range of pick-up and delivery times.

- *Volume flexibility*. This form of flexibility is required by many consumer services operating a chase strategy. It refers to the ability of the organisation to change its level of output to cope with fluctuating demand. Thus the call centre may deal with 6,000 telephone transactions on a normal day, but may have to cope with twice that amount following an advertising campaign or a new product launch. Figure 7.7 shows the concept of 'minimum effective lead times', the time it takes to respond to a change in demand.

Figure 7.7 demonstrates the notion of minimum effective lead times. If an unexpected surge of demand occurs, the call centre manager can increase capacity by

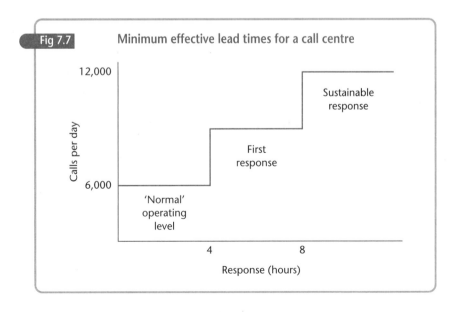

Fig 7.7 Minimum effective lead times for a call centre

50 per cent in four hours. S/he accomplishes this by asking staff to stay on after their normal shift, calling in off-duty staff, and by bringing in other staff from the organisation to man the phones. It should be noted that this is very much a 'first' or emergency response as some of the staff will not be fully trained and productivity levels will probably suffer as a result.

Within eight hours the call centre manager can bring on line more capacity, perhaps from other call centres if the increase in demand is sustained.

This is a valuable tool in assisting operations managers to plan for the foreseeable contingencies. In addition to specifying the type of flexibility required, the service manager must also consider the following:

- *Range*. How much flexibility is required? Does the call centre need to move from 6,000 calls to 12,000 calls or only to 8,000 calls per day? How many new products will be introduced and how frequently?
- *Response*. How quickly must the change be made? Can the call centre change from 6,000 to 12,000 calls in four hours or will eight hours be good enough? Clearly the faster the response, the more expensive it is likely to be.
- *Effectiveness across the range*. Most processes have an optimal range. It is unlikely that they will be equally productive across the potential range, and are likely to strain at the extremes.
- *Cost of providing the flexibility*. What is the premium resulting both from the change in output level itself, and in providing the capability in the first place? For example, providing training such that more staff are multi-skilled represents a significant investment.

7.8 ORGANISATIONAL SUPPORT FOR RESOURCE MANAGEMENT

The challenge for operations managers is to understand resource management in the context of a changing world. Many of the issues need to be resolved by the organisation as a whole, rather than simply confined to the management of service delivery processes. Aspects of this organisational support include:

How is the service concept changing?

To what extent do operations managers have 'visibility' as to the future strategic direction of the organisation? Without this inclusion in the strategic development process it is unlikely that the long-term capacity planning and resource development will be effectively carried out. Often resource managers are left to develop capacity plans which have no relevance because the concept has changed.

For example, many product service companies providing repair and maintenance support for information technology have changed the emphasis of their service concept away from servicing equipment towards supporting customers. The nature and length of customer transactions have changed beyond recognition and require a link between this change in strategic direction and resource planning for it to be implemented.

How well are the internal interfaces managed?

A key role for the operations manager is to manage the internal relationships as well as customer relationships. Co-ordination of marketing promotions and new product introductions are vital, as well as getting to the root of quality failures and long-term quality costs. Successful organisations are often those that manage the internal relationships well. This does not necessarily mean that everyone always agrees, but that there is valuable internal debate. In fact, it could be asserted that an organisation without some degree of conflict will not learn and move forward.

How important is resource management in the culture of the company?

In some sectors, resource management is seen as a low-level task. The 'stars' of the company are often seen as those who deliver the latest deal or solve the latest crisis. Resource management needs a different type of 'hero' who is able to plan longer term and persuade the organisation to think differently about itself.

7.9 SUMMARY

Service capacity

- Service capacity is the amount of value-adding activity sustained over a period of time.
- Service capacity is made more difficult to define, measure and manage by the service product mix, the impact of location and the extent of intangibility in the service product.

Capacity strategies

- The level capacity strategy tries to maintain the use of scarce or expensive resources at a constant level.
- The chase strategy attempts to match supply to demand as much as possible.
- The demand management strategy influences the demand profile to 'smooth' the load on the resources.

How to make the most of capacity

- Use of capacity can be maximised through yield management, bottleneck management and queue management.

Strategy 4 – managing the 'coping' zone

- The 'coping' zone can be managed by:
  - ➢ knowing when quality begins to deteriorate as utilisation increases
  - ➢ developing strategies to manage both customers and employees in the 'coping' zone
  - ➢ understanding how to avoid being in the 'coping' zone too often.

A capacity management framework

- The capacity management framework is a means of bringing the various aspects of capacity management together.
- There is a need to identify the reasons for capacity 'leakage'.

Resource flexibility

- There are four forms of operational flexibility: new product flexibility, product mix flexibility, delivery flexibility and volume flexibility.
- Managers should understand their minimum effective lead times.

Organisational support for resource management

- The key aspects of organisational support for capacity management include:
  - ➤ recognising changes to the service concept
  - ➤ co-ordinating the internal interfaces
  - ➤ recognising the importance of resource management.

7.10 DISCUSSION QUESTIONS

1. Select four service organisations and suggest how they might measure capacity and the problems in so doing.

2. What capacity strategies might be used by a theme park, a dot.com retailer, and cruise ship company? Explain why they are appropriate.

3. Describe the last time you were in a queue. Apply the principles of queuing to assess the waiting experience.

4. What is meant by the 'coping' zone? What are the implications for staff and customers of a supermarket when the operation enters this zone?

7.11 QUESTIONS FOR MANAGERS

1. How important is capacity management to the success of your organisation? What interest do senior managers take in the process?

2. How well is the capacity strategy matched to the financial model of your organisation? Could an increase in customer satisfaction be achieved by an increase in relatively inexpensive resource?

3. Do you know where the bottlenecks or scarce resources are in your processes? How effectively are they managed?

4. What is the impact of the 'coping' zone on your staff and customers? What strategies have you in place to manage this more effectively?

5. What are the main causes of capacity leakage? Are they avoidable?

7.12 SELECTED FURTHER READING

Heskett J.L., Sasser W.E. and Hart C.W.L., *Service Breakthroughs: Changing the rules of the game*, Free Press, New York, 1990.

7.13 REFERENCES

Armistead C.G. and Clark G., 'The "Coping" Capacity Management Strategy in Services and the Influence on Quality Performance', *International Journal of Service Industry Management*, vol. 5, no. 2, 1994, pp 5–22.

Davis M.M. and Heineke J., 'Understanding the Roles of the Customer and the Operation for Better Queue Management', *International Journal of Operations and Production Management*, vol. 14, no. 5, 1994, pp 21–34.

Davis M.M. and Vollmann T.E., 'A Framework for Relating Waiting Time and Customer Satisfaction in a Service Operation', *The Journal of Service Marketing*, vol. 4, no. 1, 1990, pp 61–9.

Fitzsimmons J.A. and Fitzsimmons M.J., *Service Management for Competitive Advantage* (2nd edition), McGraw-Hill, New York, 1997.

Goldratt E.M. and Cox J., *The Goal*, North River Press, New York, 1984.

Heikkilä, J., Vollman, J.E. and Cordon, C., *Nokia Mobile Phones: Supply Line Management*, IMD, Lausanne, 1998.

Jones P. and Peppiatt E., 'Managing Perceptions of Waiting Times in Service Queues', *International Journal of Service Industry Management*, vol. 7, no. 5, 1996, pp 47–61.

Katz K.L., Larson B.M. and Larson R., 'Prescription for the Waiting-in-Line Blues: Entertain, enlighten, and engage', *Sloan Management Review*, Winter 1991, pp 44–53.

Kimes S.E., 'Yield Management: A tool for capacity-constrained service firms', *Journal of Operations Management*, vol. 8, no. 4, 1989, pp 348–63.

Maister D.A., 'The Psychology of Waiting Lines', in Czepiel J.A., Soloman M.R. and Surprenant C.F. (eds), *The Service Encounter*, Lexington, D.C. Heath & Company, 1985, pp 113–23.

Slack N., Chambers S., Harland C., Harrison A. and Johnston R., *Operations Management* (2nd edition), Pitman, London, 1998.

CASE EXERCISE
National Life Assurance

National Life Assurance (NLA) is a company based in Manchester selling life insurance. It has main offices in Manchester, London and Newcastle which maintain about 300 agents who sell the firm's products throughout the UK. NLA is one of the largest independent life assurance companies in the UK with a fund size in excess of one billion pounds.

Madeline Martin was the manager in charge of National Life Assurance's new computer business processing unit (NBPU). All new applications for life assurance are sent to the NBPU, located in Manchester, by the agents in the field. The NBPU employs three insurance underwriters with three support/secretarial staff, a pool of twelve clerks who are responsible for data entry and filing, ten auditors (staff who prepare and issue the policies) and a medical manager (who is a senior member of a nearby hospital employed part time to assess non-standard medical conditions).

Ms Martin had been invited by the chief executive, Peter Greer, to make a presentation to senior colleagues about the reasons for the success of her unit. The reasons for her invitation to the meeting were firstly that the systems used for handling new applications for life assurance were well proven and robust, and secondly that her operation was well known for consistently meeting – and in many cases exceeding – its targets.

Ms Martin set a day aside to collect some information about the activities of the NBPU. She first reviewed her monthly management reports. The computer provided an update of number of applications (by week, month and year), the number and percentage of applications approved, number and percentage of those declined, the number and amount of premium policies allocated, the value of applications processed during the month and the commission payable to the agents. These reports identified that the unit dealt with about 300 applications per week (the unit operated a five-day week) and all the unit's financial targets were being met. In addition, most operational performance criteria were being exceeded. The target for turn-around of an application, from receipt of application to the issue of a policy (excluding time spent waiting for additional information from clients or for medical information) was 40 days. The average time taken by the NBPU was 36 days. Accuracy had never been an issue as all files were thoroughly assessed to ensure that all the relevant and complete data was collected before the applications were processed. Staff productivity was high and there was always plenty of work awaiting processing at each section. A cursory inspection of the sections' in-trays revealed about 30 files in each, with just two exceptions: the 'receipt' clerks' tray had about 400 files in it and the underwriters' tray contained about 120 files.

Processing life assurance applications

The processing of applications is a lengthy procedure requiring careful examination by under-writers trained to make risk assessments. All applications arriving at the unit are placed in an in-tray. The incoming application is then opened by one of the eight 'receipt' clerks who will check that all the necessary forms have been included in the application. This is then placed in an in-tray pending collection by the coding staff. The two clerks with special responsibility for coding allocate a unique identifier to each application and code the information on the application into the computer. The application is then given a front sheet, a pro forma, with the identifier in the top corner. The files are then placed in a tray on the senior underwriting secretary's desk. As an underwriter becomes available, the senior secretary provides the next job in the line to the underwriter. In the case of about half of the applications, the under-writer returns the file to the underwriting secretaries to request the collection of any information that is missing or additional information that is required, such as a medical exam-ination or a blood test. The secretaries then write to the client and return the file to the 'receipt' clerks who place the additional information into the file as it arrives. Once the file is complete, it is returned to the underwriters for a decision on the policy. The file is then taken to auditors who prepare the policy.

The policy itself is then sent, with the rest of the file, to the two 'despatch' clerks who com-plete the documents and mail them to the agent for delivery to the client. Each section – clerical, coding, underwriting, secretarial, auditing and issuing – has trays for incoming work. Files are taken from the bottom of the pile when someone becomes free, to ensure that all documents are dealt with in strict order.

Second thoughts

Ms Martin's confidence in her operation was somewhat eroded when she asked for com-ments from some agents and staff. One agent told her of frequent complaints about the delays over the processing of the applications and he felt there was a danger of losing clients to some of the many other firms offering life assurance. A second agent complained that when he telephoned to ascertain the status of an application, the NBPU staff did not seem to know where it was or how long it might be before it was complete. Furthermore, he felt that this lack of information was eroding his relationship with his clients, some of whom had already taken their business elsewhere. Ms Martin reviewed the levels of business over the last few years which revealed a decline of 5 per cent last year and 2 per cent the year before that on the number of applications made.

Ms Martin then spent about ten minutes with four of the clerks. They said their work was clear and routine, but their life was made difficult by agents who rang in expecting them to be able to tell them the status of an application they had submitted. It could take them hours, sometimes days, to find any individual file. Indeed two of the 'receipt' clerks now worked full time on this activity. They also said that agents frequently complained that the policies seemed to be taking a long time to issue.

She wondered whether she should agree to make the presentation.

Questions

1 *Evaluate the way new applications are processed at the NBPU.*

2 *What recommendations would you make to Ms Martin?*

8

Service People

8.1 INTRODUCTION

This chapter is a central part of this book because service is developed and delivered by people. This remains the case despite the increasing role of information technology, although the part played by both service providers and customers may well change as a result. If we think about service delivery across the span of sectors we discover that people play a variety of roles in the delivery process. For example:

- In most services, the providers form a significant element in the service experience.
- Employees represent a significant part of resource for many service businesses, and are frequently the largest variable cost.
- The essence of professional services lies in the skill, capability and knowledge of the people. Professionals 'are the service', in the sense that it is these people, a blend of their expertise and chemistry with the client, whom the customer is buying rather than the organisation itself.
- Customers are part-time employees and may be considered to be a resource for the business.

The objectives for this chapter are:

- to discuss the complexity of service encounters and the challenges of the various types of encounter
- to describe key aspects of service design and how they impact on service employees
- to outline the role of service leadership and empowerment in operational performance
- to discuss the impact of psychological factors on the service encounter
- to consider the role of the customer as a service employee.

The chapter deals primarily with the leadership and motivation of service people as they relate to service delivery rather than addressing aspects of terms and conditions of employment contracts.

8.2 SERVICE ENCOUNTERS

As we have stated previously, the acid test of many service operations is at the point of delivery. Indeed, it became popular to call any point of contact between the customer and the service operation a 'moment of truth' (Normann 1984). Jan Carlzon, then Chairman of the SAS airline, was widely quoted as estimating that there were 50,000 moments of truth for SAS each day (Carlzon 1987) – in other words, 50,000 activities where the customer would experience a very small part of the total service delivery system, but none the less would judge the whole organisation on the basis of this small service encounter.

The most difficult service encounter to specify and control is clearly that between two people, the customer and a customer-facing employee. Figure 8.1 illustrates the complexity of this type of service encounter.

Many of the influences on the success or otherwise of the service encounter are directly related to the style of management, and the extent to which the service operation has a robust design. The issues for service management are covered in the rest of the chapter. In this section we will examine the nature of the encounter itself.

8.2.1 Types of encounter

There are a number of types of service encounter:

- **Remote encounters.** This refers to the encounter between the customer and the service operation without direct human contact. Traditional examples include

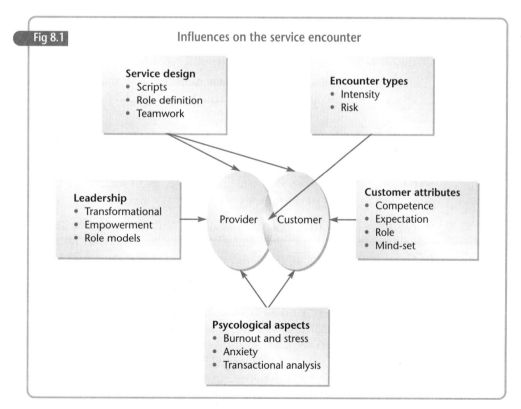

Fig 8.1   Influences on the service encounter

Service design
- Scripts
- Role definition
- Teamwork

Encounter types
- Intensity
- Risk

Leadership
- Transformational
- Empowerment
- Role models

Provider   Customer

Customer attributes
- Competence
- Expectation
- Role
- Mind-set

Psycological aspects
- Burnout and stress
- Anxiety
- Transactional analysis

contact through letters or through automated service processes such as bank ATM systems.

The extension of automated processes to Internet-based services poses some interesting challenges for service designers. Of particular relevance to this chapter is the fact that these services use the customer as a significant part of the service delivery system, depending on customer competence, to a far higher degree than more traditional person-to-person processes.

- *Phone encounters*. These have become extremely common in sectors such as retail and financial services as companies have set up centralised call centres, reducing costs and increasing access to service. This approach has been adopted for many routine, standard transactions such as order taking or handling billing queries.

  The challenge for service providers is that these encounters may have as much potential for customer satisfaction or dissatisfaction as person-to-person encounters, but both parties are at a disadvantage in that they cannot see each other. This means that the potential for misunderstanding is greatly increased. The service provider must be able to judge the mood of the customer by tone of voice without the extra information that might be gained from observing whether the customer is smiling or frowning.

  Again there are implications for the service designer in thinking about the respective roles of service provider and customer alike. Scripting (see section 8.3.1) provides a useful way of reducing uncertainty in this type of encounter.

- *Face-to-face encounters*. Face-to-face encounters are often more complex in nature because there are more elements of variability in these transactions. Some of these encounters are quite personal in nature. The customers' enjoyment of the restaurant meal may be linked directly to the extent to which they 'get on with' the people serving them. This is almost impossible to manage given the almost infinite number of personalities and moods.

  Many 'face-to-face' encounters have more intensity than remote or phone encounters. This is for a variety of reasons, which are described in the following section.

8.2.2 Intensity of service encounters

Figure 8.2 illustrates two dimensions of service encounter intensity. An aspect of variability in the service encounter is the extent to which the customer perceives some degree of risk or uncertainty. This risk may take a number of forms:

- *Financial risk*. In this case, it may be difficult for the customer to assess the extent of risk. The purchaser of a used car does not know how reliable the vehicle will prove to be. In the same way, purchasing a pension plan may feel like an extremely risky activity, particularly for someone who is unfamiliar with financial matters.

- *Physical risk*. Going on an adventure holiday or flying clearly entails some physical risk. In the former, it could be reasonably expected that customers choosing such a holiday have made some assessment of the risks involved and will see them as part of the expected experience. With an airline flight, the physical risk may be expected, but not necessarily enjoyed by passengers!

- *Psychological Risk*. This type of risk may arise from a number of sources. It may come from the customer's lack of confidence or competence. An anxious customer is likely to prove difficult in the service encounter, not because they are intentionally obstructive, but rather because they channel energies into distracting their thoughts from their concerns.

   Nobody likes to feel inferior or incompetent. It is possible that service organisations may make assumptions as to the competence of their customers. If this is combined with a very public display of ignorance, the customer may become very quiet or very noisy.

   Finally, a significant number of people find the presence of large numbers of people in close proximity a trial in itself. For some of these 'private' people, any form of social encounter can be painful. This may be in stark contrast to the customer-facing employee who may have chosen this role in large part because of its high degree of customer contact.

Figure 8.2 illustrates the extent of social interaction in a routine service encounter for a number of service situations. Each of these has an implication for the extent of desired and possible customer relationship as discussed in Chapter 3. For example, in the supermarket visit there are limited opportunities for anything more than superficial conversations, whereas a meal in a restaurant where the customers and staff know each other reasonably well might lead to interaction which goes beyond the baseline of ordering food.

   It should be noted that social interaction is often linked in some way to a mechanism for managing risk. In evaluating the riskiness of the used car purchase, the customer is frequently judging the trustworthiness of the salesperson. The busyness of the cabin crew on a long-distance flight provides a distraction for those who might be tempted to dwell on the risk of flying, and allows the crew to keep an eye on those who might be suffering from extra anxiety.

   There is a wide range of customer variables which will complicate the service encounter. Some of these are listed below:

- *Customer mind-set*. The nature of the service may be reflected in the state of mind of the customer. A customer complaint process will probably not have the customer in the most helpful mind-set! On the other hand, customers who are

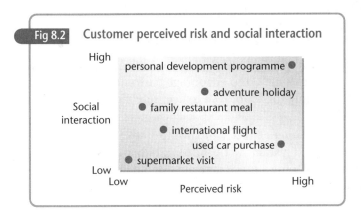

Fig 8.2   Customer perceived risk and social interaction

going to a theme park or to a family celebration in a restaurant are more likely to be predisposed to having a good time.

- **Customer mood**. This is somewhat linked to customer mind-set, in that people who complain might be expected to be angry, whilst people going to a celebration might be expected to be in a happier frame of mind. The message here is that it is extremely dangerous to make assumptions about individual customers. Customers who were in a bad mood because they were under pressure or rushed on a previous occasion may turn out to be model customers the next time.

- **Personality clashes**. Some people simply do not get on. They seem to take an instant dislike to each other, or there is something about the other person that reminds them of another difficult or disliked character. Psychologists call this 'transference', which describes the situation when attributes of a previous relationship are 'transferred' to a current relationship. One of the most common occurrences relates to authority figures.

8.3 SERVICE DESIGN AND THE SERVICE ENCOUNTER

A number of options may be open to the service 'designer' which will assist the service employee in delivering service which is consistent to the expected standards, which might include both attitude and behaviour.

It is in the person-to-person encounters that the skills and personality of the individual matter most. Since this part of the service experience cannot be produced beforehand and can only be delivered at the point of contact, much must be left to the discretion and ability of the individual employee.

This said, it is possible to provide some help for the employee, removing some of the uncertainty surrounding the service encounter.

8.3.1 Scripting

Many mass service companies employ scripting as a technique for providing both consistency and efficiency in service delivery. In addition, as we shall discuss later, scripting may also provide a sense of security for customers and employees alike. A familiar script may allow customers to relax because they understand the 'rules' by which the encounter will be played out.

Tansik and Smith (2000) suggest 11 functions for using scripts in service design:

1 *To assist the service employee to find out what the customer wants or needs*. The script should be designed to encourage customers to describe their needs in such a way as to allow the employee to accurately diagnose them and offer the appropriate service.

2 *To control the customer*. The script should help the employee guide the customer through the system with minimal disruption. This is particularly important where customisation is actively discouraged. 'Can I suggest our special two-course offer?' enables a rapid decision, though there may be a danger of closing off opportunities for selling more profitable services in the cause of an efficient order-taking process.

3 *To establish historical routines that may be relevant to the service encounter*. Frequent customers will often become pre-programmed to carry out the necessary actions in the service process without prompting. An example is provided by airline passengers who have packed their luggage in the most appropriate cases, who anticipate the check-in questions, and who have their documents in order before approaching the check-in desk.

 Tansik and Smith suggest that the service designer should provide the appropriate triggers to what Schank (1980; 1982) termed memory organisation packets (MOPs), which allow the customer to move into what may often be unconscious routines which may lead to early involvement in the service delivery process. There may be a danger of changing scripts in order to make a differentiation between service providers as this may cause confusion rather than build service quality.

4 *To facilitate control of workers*. Scripts may provide the means of increasing consistency across multiple sites and multiple servers. This has the particular benefit of ensuring that the appropriate customer script is activated, and that all the required questions and prompts are given. Scripts have particular value in the process of cross-selling, as for example in a call centre selling direct insurance which encourages the employee to use 'sub-scripts' such as 'Are you sure you have sufficient cover for your house contents?' or 'Can we help you with any other insurance worries?'

5 *To legitimise organisational actions*. Here the script informs the employee as to what behaviours and attitudes the management believes customers expect. TGI Friday encourages staff to display high energy levels in their interactions with customers, whereas gourmet restaurants might prefer staff to encourage a rather more sedate and relaxed form of delivery.

6 *To serve as analogies*. Scripts learned by a worker in a previous employment may be used as the basis for developing new scripts in later, similar situations.

7 *To facilitate organised behaviour*. Scripting may allow for smooth running of a team engaged in interdependent activity. Again, Tansik and Smith provide the example of a surgical team, where the actions of team members are choreographed and rehearsed beforehand. Developing routine medical procedures means that individual team members may change, provided that others can perform their roles. Scripting facilitates this interchangeability.

8 *To provide a guide to behaviour*. Scripts set expectations as to what will happen next in a service encounter. Because customers have experienced this or similar service organisations before, there is no need to provide explanation as to why things are done this way or why certain information is requested before the service may be delivered. It is also suggested that scripts may be used to explain service 'fairness'. Most patients in a casualty clinic will tolerate another patient being seen earlier than their turn if the condition is life threatening.

9 *To buffer or exacerbate role conflict*. A script may deflect difficult questions such as 'Why do I have to give this information?' by the use of scripts such as 'I'm sorry but it's company policy', or 'the financial services regulations require us to gain this information'. Scripts may help when the employee is faced with giving unwelcome or unpopular information to customers.

10 *To provide a basis for evaluating behaviour*. Scripts can be used as a checklist for management to evaluate an employee's behaviour. This is commonly used in telephone call centres where supervisors may routinely monitor large numbers of calls. It is particularly relevant where supervisors may be looking for evidence of specific behaviours such as the generation of sales as well as simple order taking. Scripts such as 'Have you considered...?' may be useful here.

11 *To conserve cognitive capacity*. Scripts allow the employee to work on a number of activities simultaneously because the script may be performed as if on 'automatic pilot'.

As can be seen from the list above, scripts can play a valuable part in service design and delivery. Carefully designed scripts can provide opportunities for early involvement of the customer with the organisation and its employees. Scripts can provide both conscious and unconscious means of support for customers and employees alike. They assist in the management of customer expectations, and may facilitate the smooth passage of the customer through the service delivery system because there exists a good understanding of what will happen and what is required of the customer at each stage to enable this to occur.

There are a number of problems with scripting, however:

1 *They may become too inflexible*. Customers who don't make the appropriate responses to fit the script may provide inexperienced or poorly trained employees with too great a problem to deal with.

2 *They may lead to a customer perception of robot-like behaviour*. The standard restaurant script which prompts the server to ask 'Is everything all right for you?' is frequently greeted with the expected response 'Yes, it's fine, thank you', which is often not a comment about the food, but more likely a way of getting rid of an intrusion as quickly as possible. Because this script is used too often, without the perceived sincerity that would suggest that there is genuine interest in the response, the possible impression is of someone going through the motions of service with none of the personal attributes of warmth or customer responsiveness required.

3 *They may lead to defensive behaviour*. Standard scripts may become a two-edged sword. While they may have a useful role as suggested above in providing employees with a clear form of words to deal with difficult situations, it may be rather too easy to use a scripted response when the situation requires something rather different.

8.3.2 Defining the role of the service provider

Most people work more effectively when they have a clear understanding of their role, what is expected of them, and how they will be assessed.

Research into the effectiveness of service encounters suggests that the following should be minimised if customer-facing employees are to be motivated to provide good service:

● *Role conflict*. In this case, the employee may have a number of responsibilities, it being impossible to carry out each role simultaneously. An example is provided by the call centre employee who is charged with reducing queue lengths and also with trying to persuade customers to purchase more services, a task which requires more time to be spent on each transaction. Role conflict may occur when the basic service design is in error as in the example above or when the demands of the job are in conflict with the individual's personal view of how much status is conferred on the role. In the UK, for example, service jobs are often seen as rather demeaning, with perhaps some feeling that they are similar in nature to the role of servants to the 'lord of the manor'. This feeling of inequality and lack of value may be detected when employees call customers 'sir' or 'madam' in a somewhat sarcastic tone of voice.

- *Role ambiguity*. This occurs when the person is unsure of the requirements of the role (Katz and Kahn 1978). A cause of this for service providers might be that there is a lack of clarity about the guiding philosophy or strategy of the organisation. This is frequently a result of poor leadership both from senior management and from first-line supervisors.

Both role conflict and role ambiguity may occur as the organisation grows and develops. What was carried out by committed individuals in the early stages of the organisation's existence may be taken over by people who have been recruited more recently. In theory this should be an opportunity to formalise roles and responsibilities but this may be resisted as it may be felt to be contrary to the entrepreneurial spirit of the original vision.

Service designers must take into account these issues in order to manage all aspects of service delivery, but must pay particular attention to the roles of customer-facing employees. If these people are experiencing role stress of any nature, their ability to create the required service experience is likely to be significantly diminished.

8.3.3 Teamwork

A critical design decision is the extent to which opportunities for teamwork may be built into the service delivery process.

Many of the total quality management (TQM) programmes of the 1980s and '90s evolved into teamwork programmes as processes were redesigned to reflect the need to become more customer responsive. Several financial services organisations have restructured their customer-facing activities in such a way that a team handles all transactions from sales to service. This has frequently led to increases in both quality of service and productivity as team members develop a greater ownership of customer and delivery process.

Most of the writers on teams (for example Katzenbach and Smith 1998) rightly point out that teams are not appropriate in all situations. For a group of individuals to become a team there must be a real requirement for them to work together because their roles interrelate in some way. In other words, if there is no obvious benefit for the individuals to work together, they remain a group rather than a team. It is important to distinguish here between 'working in a team' and 'working as a team'. Many organisations will foster the latter, but without necessarily requiring everyone to be organised into work groups.

Katzenbach and Smith include the following benefits of what they term 'high-performance teams':

1. Complementary skills and experience exceed those of any one individual. This facilitates a more effective response to demands for innovation and customer service.

2. As teams work together to develop clear goals and to improve the processes they are involved in, they also develop more effective means of communication which allow them to respond more flexibly to changing customer needs.

3. As team members work together and overcome significant challenges, people build trust in others and in others' capabilities. Again, this builds towards a more effective service delivery system.

4. Katzenbach and Smith report the high-performing teams as having more fun than others. This communal sense of humour can be very powerful in dealing with the stress of intensive customer transactions.

A particular point to note for service design is that in some cases the customer is an integral member of the team. This is relevant for professional services where the customer's presence and input are essential for service development and delivery. A firm of management consultants must often work alongside their clients in order to carry out their work. Part of the 'product' might be for the consultants to provide mentoring and development for the client's employees.

While there has been a certain amount of research into the formation of management teams (see, for example, Belbin 1981), there is relatively little comparable work on the formation and management of teams involved in the day-to-day running of manufacturing processes or service delivery. Katzenbach and Smith (1998) again provide some useful principles for developing successful teams:

● Setting a demanding performance challenge is more effective in creating a successful team than the use of team-building exercises or appointing team leaders with 'ideal' profiles.

● Organisations need to pay attention to 'team basics'. These include such things as team size, purpose, goals etc.

● Organisations that emphasise individual performance over team performance erect barriers to team success.

● Teams are a natural unit for integrating performance and learning.

Our work with teams supports these findings. Many team initiatives fail because not enough attention is paid to team design and team processes see the First Mortgage Direct illustration (in Box 8.1). In other words, just saying 'let's be a team' is not sufficient to create one. There must be a genuine requirement for a team to operate together if it is to be a success.

Osburn and Moran (2000) report the results of organisations that have redesigned their operations to move towards 'self-directed work teams'. They give examples of teams that have increased productivity and quality. Shenondoah Life is quoted as processing 50 per cent more applications and customer services requests with 10 per cent fewer people using work teams. A powerful example of the impact of teamwork is provided by the Experian consumer service centre in Texas. In 1994 it had all the typical ailments of call centres: low morale, high employee turnover, fragmented service delivery systems and poor quality compliance. A redesign which included investment in new technology and integrating service functions, combined

Box 8.1 First Mortgage Direct

A call centre within the First Mortgage Group was organised into a number of teams. Team leaders had a range of objectives:

- to organise and co-ordinate the team
- to update training plans
- to produce weekly performance reports
- to monitor and record holidays
- to deal with queries
- to review sickness.

The issue for Mike Walker, the newly appointed manager, was that there was no consistency or co-ordination across teams. In other words, there was no teamwork at team-leader level. Each team operated independently, creating 'mini-call centres' within the unit. This resulted in poor performance, duplication of work and resistance to implementing improvements originating from other teams.

Mike's approach was to clarify the broader vision of the call centre for his team leaders. His objective was to get them to see their role as contributing to the success of the call centre as a whole, rather than simply leading their team. Mike involved his 'team of team leaders' in putting the detail to the vision. This was achieved through brainstorming sessions, benchmarking visits, using advice from the National Society for Quality through Teamwork (NSQT), and focus groups formed from call centre staff.

A number of audits were carried out. A skills audit revealed that there were training and development needs for team leaders to take on more people-focused roles. A task audit showed that team leaders were concentrating on clerical activities to the detriment of less quantifiable tasks such as coaching team members. As a result of this analysis, the team leader role was redefined such that it was expected that 60 per cent of time should be spent in coaching, and only 10 per cent in call handling.

The call centre was re-organised, with an operational support unit dealing with many of the clerical activities previously handled by team leaders. This enabled team leaders to concentrate on performance improvement in line with the vision. Some of the benefits realised by this initiative included:

- more effective team management, despite increases in team size of up to 50 per cent
- 35 per cent increase in productivity
- improved customer service
- increased innovation and proactivity
- fewer ineffective meetings
- a saving in team-leader time of 1.5 days per team leader per week.

Mike Walker reports that the creation of a culture of encouragement and the facilitation of learning has provided a solid platform for future change.

Questions

1 *Do you think that all the team leaders would be happy with the changes made by Mike Walker? How would you deal with this?*

2 *Why do you think this approach has been successful for First Mortgage Direct?*

This illustration is adapted from 'Empowering your Team Leaders' by Mike Walker, First Mortgage Group, *International Journal of Call Centre Management*, vol. 1, no. 2, 1998, Winthrop Publications, London, pp. 91–98.

with a team approach, turned this poor service operation into a benchmark site for call centre operations.

Osburn and Moran agree that not all situations are suitable for teams and provide a helpful checklist for feasibility:

1 Are the work processes compatible with self-directed teams?

2 Are employees willing and able to make self-direction work?

3 Can managers master and apply the hands-off leadership style required by self-directed teams?

4 Is the market healthy or promising enough to support improved productivity without reducing the workforce?

5 Will the organisation's policies and culture support the transition to teams?

6 Will the local community support the transition to teams?

The writers also provide a useful insight into the transition process, pointing out that the organisation is unlikely to be able to move from a situation without teams to the autonomy and employee maturity required for self-directed teams in one step. The change in leadership style and employee discretion is covered in the following section.

8.4 LEADERSHIP AND EMPOWERMENT

There are many aspects of leadership that have a bearing on effective service delivery. We will focus on a few of these in this section:

- transformational or transactional leadership?
- empowerment and discretion
- balancing empowerment and control.

8.4.1 Transformational or transactional leadership?

There is much debate as to the difference between 'transformational' and 'transactional' leadership (see, for example, Kakabadse and Kakabadse 1999). The essential difference between the two is that transformational leaders develop and project a vision of the future, having energy and influence to encourage others to contribute to this new direction. Transactional leadership, often described as the ability to deal with the day-to-day management of operations, is equally important in the effective running of a service organisation.

Transformational leadership, as is implied by its name, is required at times of significant change. Many of the companies with a reputation for increasing the quality of service delivery and customer care have done so with the support and leadership of a chief executive who actively demonstrated their personal commitment. Examples of these include:

- Jan Carlzon of the airline SAS who popularised the notion of service encounters as 'moments of truth' for the service organisation. He is quoted as saying that there were

50,000 'moments of truth' for SAS each day, points of contact between customers and the airline which will either enhance or detract from the service experience.

● Sir Tom Farmer of the tyre and exhaust chain, Kwik Fit, who took every opportunity to preach the importance of customer service for business success and who changed the mission statement of the organisation from 'our aim is 100% customer satisfaction' to 'our aim is 100% customer delight' (see Chapter 12).

What is interesting about these and similar leaders is that they are able to communicate a vision in such a way that it motivates the people in their organisations to performance levels significantly greater than might have been expected.

Bennis (1999) lists four competencies of great leaders:

1 *The management of attention*. The ability of the leader to capture the hearts and minds of people through communicating a focus of commitment and a compelling vision.

2 *The management of meaning*. This relates to the importance of bringing substance to the vision in such a way as to make it clear to those following. This is particularly important when dealing with the type of service that contains a high degree of intangibility. Indeed, it could be argued that the translation of service product-focused delivery into what is achieved in the perception of the customer needs this type of management of meaning. It is very understandable that the person serving in the fast-food restaurant may become overly focused on the number of burgers or pizzas sold per shift, but creating the customer experience requires a rather different focus to be provided by clear leadership.

3 *The management of trust*. One of the key attributes of leaders is consistent reliability. In the same way that customers value reliability of service delivery, employees look to leaders to provide the same degree of security. They don't want messages and programmes that change on what seems like a whim, but to understand what has to be done well. Clearly, lining up actions with words is part of this attribute.

4 *The management of self*. Bennis says that great leaders know their strengths and weaknesses. More specifically, he states that the best leaders do not seem to be easily defeated by mistakes or problems, nor do they start blaming their employees. In a service organisation this is particularly important, enabling employees to listen to customer complaints and institute non-defensive recovery routines.

Each of these attributes has particular application to the leadership of service operations. Of course, not all service organisations are undergoing radical change at all times – although it may frequently feel like it! It is here that transactional leadership is relevant. Some writers have downplayed the importance of this style of leadership, equating it with a mundane form of management which is little more than routine administration of a well-defined concept and its associated processes. This is particularly dangerous in the context of service delivery which depends to a large degree on the example of 'front-line' leaders.

These first-level managers, supervisors or team leaders have the prime responsibility for providing the day-to-day leadership of a service unit which may make the essential difference between a robot-like service delivery and one which has life to it. Larkin and Larkin (1996), in discussing the communication of change, state that their work indicates that most employees prefer to hear it from their immediate supervisor, particularly if senior management is felt to be remote and prone to changing approaches with alarming frequency. There is little doubt that these front-line 'role models' have a major influence on shaping the attitudes and behaviours of those who work with them.

Finally, the individual employee may be capable of a form of service leadership as he or she exercises discretion over the service delivery process, potentially developing new ways of interacting with customers or more productive procedures. This is aligned with developing what psychologists term 'an internal locus of control'. More simply, the aim is to develop a sense of service process ownership in the hearts and minds of the employees. This theme is developed further in the following section on empowerment and employee discretion.

8.4.2 Empowerment and discretion

In order to deal with the impossibility of scripting every possibility within service encounters, many service organisations may give or attempt to give more discretion to customer-facing employees. This lines up with a general trend in organisations to tap into the brainpower and creativity of all employees, not exclusively the senior management team. A move to self-directed or semi-autonomous teams and flatter organisations may build on the need to give more people more autonomy in the workplace.

Figure 8.3 provides a framework for exploring some of the issues around developing or restricting employee discretion. We prefer to talk about discretion because most people are 'empowered' – the critical question is how much discretion they have (see also Bowen and Lawler 1993 and 1995).

The classification of discretion by Kelley (1993) is a useful way of understanding this topic (see also Kelley et al., 1996). He has summarised the work of earlier writers such as March and Simon (1958) to develop three types of employee discretion:

● **Routine discretion**. This means that the employee has discretion regarding 'how' the basic task is performed rather than 'what' task is undertaken. The range of routine discretion may be extended with the complexity of the task. The more complex the task, the less it is possible to describe each step in a rigorously controlled procedure document.

  Kelley uses the example of an investment adviser who draws on a wide range of information sources in order to make the appropriate recommendation to each client. In the same way, customer-facing employees will make changes in the way that they deal with each service encounter.

● **Creative discretion**. Creative discretion is exercised by those who develop both what and how they do things. This may relate to people who don't have a tried and tested formula for doing things, but none the less have some training and experience that allow them to make informed judgements as to what to do. At the extreme end of this spectrum might be those creative people who are involved in the innovative activities of the organisation, as in new product design or in the development of strategies that represent a significant shift from what has been the accepted norm.

- *Deviant discretion*. This type of discretion differs from routine and creative discretion in that it is generally not approved by the organisation, whereas the other two types are recognised and approved by it. In the service context, Kelley gives the example of the retail salesman who gives a customer a refund contrary to company policy. This may gain increased customer satisfaction for this individual, but not be approved by senior management.

  Deviant discretion is potentially disruptive since it usually involves an individual acting on his or her own authority, rather than on behalf of the organisation. Such people may earn the reputation of mavericks or 'just plain awkward'. Indeed, an organisation made up of people who operate in this way would be interesting, but rather chaotic! However, an organisation without such people might easily become rather stagnant without challenge to the status quo.

The compliant organisation (from 'compliant' to 'process ownership')

This type of organisation is frequently found in the high-volume/low-variety service operations discussed in Chapter 6. Compliant organisations have the following characteristics:

- Their focus is on consistent service delivery, often across multiple locations and with many servers.
- Such operations have well-developed process documentation, with training for employees as to how they should behave in each situation.
- High volumes and consistent processes lend themselves to automation and/or the employment of relatively low-cost labour.
- The management style employed is frequently somewhat directive, often because employee turnover is such that they are relatively inexperienced (and with low motivation).
- Performance measurement often relates to short-term indicators such as response times or orders taken.

As Figure 8.3 suggests, the problem for these organisations is that the service delivery process feels as if it is imposed by management. The process has been designed

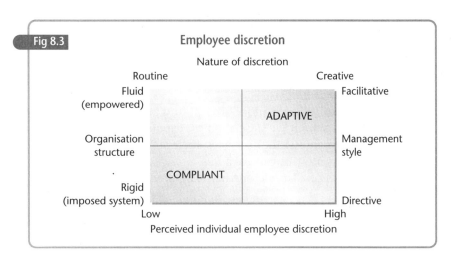

Fig 8.3 — Employee discretion

by headquarters staff, who then carry out periodic audits to ensure compliance to the predetermined design. Local innovations are not desired or encouraged as this might create customer expectations which may not always be fulfilled in every location and will lead to potential increases in unit costs.

The problem therefore for the compliant organisation is that front-line (junior) employees often lack the motivation or ownership of either concept or customer to bring life to a rather mechanistic style of service delivery. The challenge for service managers is to engender both ownership and a spark of creativity in a workforce which might otherwise appear like robots.

In so doing, the aim is to change the emphasis from 'compliant' to 'process ownership'. The objective here is for the employees to take ownership of service delivery, rather than to feel that it is imposed on them. How this may be achieved is covered more fully in the chapters on service culture and continuous improvement (Chapters 14 and 12), but broadly the approaches utilised are as follows:

- *Communication*. Good communication from management as to how well the company is performing and the reason for future strategies. Also, it is useful to open lines of communication from customer-facing staff to senior management in order to facilitate the passage of invaluable customer feedback.

- *Involvement*. Inclusion in process improvement projects as and when possible. The aim here is to foster a sense of ownership of both process and customer, having had a hand in process design.

- *Celebration*. A major problem for the motivation of staff in customer-facing roles is that they are frequently on the receiving end of complaints and abuse and rarely receive praise from customers. Indeed, some customer service functions are set up with the explicit task of dealing exclusively with complaints. Some service organisations counteract both the potential boredom of routine transactions and the deadening effect of dealing with customer complaints by creating rituals of celebration of success.

- *Teamwork*. Organising customer-facing staff into teams may help engender a sense of purpose, and also provide opportunities for job rotation, support and motivation.

All of these approaches have one thing in common: they create a sense that the organisation values the contribution of even the most junior employees. Without this, it is unlikely that service encounters will be anything more than adequate, and will probably not build customer loyalty.

The adaptive organisation

This style of organisation is more often found at the high-variety/low-volume end of the spectrum, which we described as 'capability' organisations in Chapter 6. Many people in professional services such as management consultants or legal advisers might fit into this category.

The characteristics of adaptive organisations are:

- High degrees of creative discretion in developing both product and process.

- Frequent dependence on key individuals' skill and knowledge.

- A resistance to the generation of standard processes, leading to inconsistency in approach.

- An emphasis on innovation.

- Research and development activities are often focused on the professional development of the people in the organisation as opposed to the development of service brands and products found in 'commodity' organisations.

- The management style of these organisations is likely to be 'facilitative', focusing on ensuring that the skilled individuals are able to work to their full potential.

- Performance measures are likely to be rather more long term in nature than is the case for the compliant organisations. Marketing, for example, may have targets which include the development of a number of new service products over a period of months, whilst an academic is required to develop new material for teaching next year's course.

The challenge of these organisations is to ensure that a reasonably consistent approach is adopted to service delivery. In many professional service organisations, client relationships are managed by the individual provider, leading to potential inefficiencies. Another weakness here is that individuals are reluctant to share their knowledge with others because this might weaken their position in the organisation. This may cause major problems when key individuals leave, often taking their portfolio of clients with them.

Management may focus their attention on the following:

- motivation of key individuals by providing opportunities to extend their skill and knowledge

- emphasis on situations that require individuals to collaborate in order to carry out their tasks

- development of multiple links with clients to ensure that these relationships are not severed when individuals leave the organisation.

Managing transitions

Figure 8.4 illustrates two common conditions that describe what may happen when an organisation decides to increase or decrease the nature and amount of discretion given to individual employees.

Compliant to adaptive: the anxious zone

Service organisations may wish to increase the amount of discretion given to customer-facing staff. This is particularly relevant if the strategy is to increase the range of service options available to customers. In this case, individual employees may be asked to take more decisions and to carry out a greater proportion of the service delivery process.

In many cases, of course, the implementation of this change is well planned and executed. Typically, this will involve investment in training and information systems, but no matter how well this is managed, individuals change at different speeds which are dictated by their individual personality and history. Thus, in this case, the individual employee is being moved from what might feel like a reasonably 'safe'

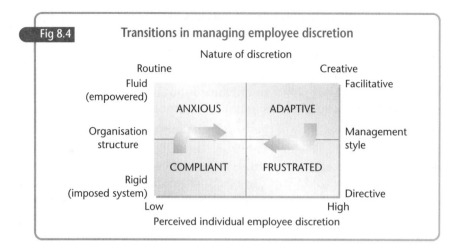

Fig 8.4 Transitions in managing employee discretion

environment where s/he is provided with a clear structure and process to follow, to one where individual decision-making is required.

This may be summed up as 'being empowered but not feeling it'. This zone may be more accurately described as 'Anxious and Excited', when the individuals involved want the challenge but are either unsure of their own ability or are uncertain as to how much real discretion the organisation is willing to give them. In this transition, individuals may well not perform immediately to the level of their capability and, indeed, may be written off by the management as 'not being up to the new task'.

In reality, with support and training, large numbers of staff may be able to deal with the added responsibility of increased discretion. There is often a rich vein of talent for continuous improvement activities and the opportunity to build ownership of the service delivery process. It is important to note, though, that customer-facing employees in the anxious zone will probably not always deliver service to the new (usually more demanding) design standards.

Adaptive to compliant: the frustrated zone
In this case, the organisation is restricting the degree of discretion of some or all of its employees. A common reason for this would be that as a consequence of actual or desired growth, systems and processes are standardised, reducing the opportunity for individuals to develop their own approach to service. This is particularly relevant to professional services seeking to provide consistent services to national or multi-national business clients.

For these 'professional service shops', the implementation of management by process will result in a reduction in autonomy on the part of the individuals in the organisation. A good example is provided by the larger consultancy firms who may seek to develop solutions that may be adapted for a wide range of clients. In this scenario, although consultants may have some discretion to adapt the basic solution to their individual client, the basic design work has been carried out by other people in the firm. This philosophy will clearly change from firm to firm, as will policies regarding brand management and standardisation of approaches to client relationships.

The characteristics of the frustrated zone are as follows:

- Individuals resist the implementation of standard processes (an imposed system), claiming that the system prevents them from operating in the most effective way in delivering solutions to their customers.

- These individuals are frequently extremely vocal about these perceived or real restrictions.

- As can be see from Figure 8.4, employees in the frustrated zone often perceive that they still have high degrees of discretion, despite the standard processes being implemented. The result is that these employees feel that they are 'above' the system, that it doesn't apply to them and that they can circumvent its requirements in order to 'get the job done' in the way that they think best.

The problem here is that individuals who have become used to high levels of perceived discretion find it particularly difficult to work in an environment where they feel that their freedom is restricted. They may 'comply' with the system if the alternative is that they lose pay or status in the organisation, but they find it difficult to accept and are likely to become disaffected as a result.

It is important to recognise the concerns of these individuals because they frequently possess skills which it is essential to retain. This may be achieved in some cases by providing them with opportunities for personal development through involvement in activities which do not conflict with the objectives of the more standardised service delivery processes being implemented.

Box 8.2 Open Door Church, St Neots, UK

The Open Door Church is only a few years old, but is growing rapidly where other, more traditional, groups appear to have reached a plateau, or are actually declining in numbers. There are a number of possible reasons for this success. A fundamental aspect of the Open Door Church is its vision statement of 'Open to God, Open to You', which makes the point that church is not supposed to be the exclusive domain of those who are rich and talented. It is for anyone, including those who may be deemed less acceptable by society at large.

The Open Door Church meets on Sundays in a local school, but in reality the organisation is a cluster of small groups or 'cells'. These meet formally on a weekday evening but are encouraged to build relationships internally and with friends and neighbours. The volume of 'official' meetings is much lower than many churches, to give space for life outside, and for members to be a real part of the community.

Although the basic format of Sunday services for the whole church, with small groups meeting in homes on weeknights, looks similar to other churches, the underlying emphasis is entirely different. Traditionally, the focus is on Sunday services with a small percentage meeting in homes during the week. In the Open Door Church, the focus is on the development of cells with their ongoing relationships. These cell groups come together on Sundays, and attendance at the weeknight meetings is frequently higher than that at the Sunday services.

Tony Thompson, the leader of the church, comments: 'The growth of many churches has been limited by the availability of experienced and talented leaders. We've taken a different approach, encouraging people who are relatively new members to become cell leaders.' This has meant that many more people have the potential to become group leaders, and this in turn has made room for growth.

These new cell leaders are given a great deal of support including training and an 'apprenticeship' as an assistant cell leader. Cell group meetings are quite structured, with a recognised format and detailed notes provided by the church leadership team. John and Janet Lloyd were asked to lead a cell after a short time in the church. 'We were worried that we wouldn't be able to cope with leading the group. We thought we might have to deliver a "second sermon", but the church leaders give us plenty of support and guidance week by week.'

Some people joining the church from more traditional denominations have taken time to adjust to this approach. If they have been group leaders before, it may feel like the role of the cell leader is more defined, possibly lacking freedom. Tony Thompson's response is: 'We have made it easier for people to grow quickly into the cell leader role. It used to be so daunting that few people would volunteer for it. As soon as a cell has a stable membership of about 16 members, we're looking for it to become two cells of eight members. This multiplication may happen as quickly as six months and so we need a lot of leaders to sustain our growth.'

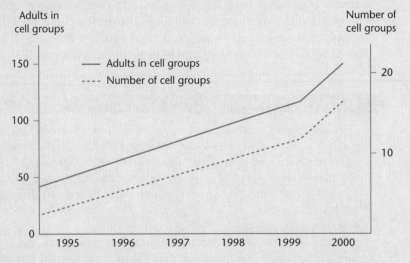

The statistics shown in the chart indicate the speed of growth. From three cells in 1995 to 15 in 2000 has required the identification, training and support of nearly 30 leaders and assistant leaders. This is no mean feat, given that a sizeable proportion of the church's new members are not just new to the church but also new to Christianity.

Questions

1 *How does the Open Door Church's approach to leadership differ from that adopted by more traditional organisations?*

2 *What are the challenges it faces in sustaining the rate of growth experienced so far?*

This illustration has been developed from discussions with Tony Thompson, the leader of the Open Door Church in St Neots, Cambridgeshire, UK.

The illustration provided by the Open Door Church (Box 8.2) demonstrates how organisations in the same service sector may have very different operating philosophies. Individuals who were happy in one organisational culture, may struggle in another. It is important to note that when an organisation wishes to make significant changes, individuals must be treated as such, recognising that some will welcome more empowerment or discretion, others will be happiest in more prescribed roles, whereas others will take time and support to grow into a larger role.

8.4.3 Balancing empowerment and control

As we have seen in the previous section, the dilemma is to know how and by how much individual employees can be 'empowered'. Situational leadership theory (Hersey and Blanchard 1982) suggests that a key issue is the maturity of the 'followers': the extent to which they are both willing and able to take more responsibility.

Simons (1995) suggests there are four control organisational systems which assist the service manager in moving towards employees taking more ownership of their service processes:

- *Diagnostic control systems*. These are the standard performance measures of the organisation and include indicators such as sales per employee, response times and so forth. Managers may watch these indicators and allow employees to decide how they are to be achieved. Simons maintains that the danger here is that there may be pressure to 'massage' the figures in order to demonstrate ability. Thus, these measures are not sufficient in themselves to give management control.

- *Beliefs systems*. These convey the key values of the organisation. We discuss more of these in Chapter 14 on service culture, but Kwik Fit's mission to provide '100% customer delight' would be a good example. At worst, these statements appear to be simply following the latest trend but, at best, they can inspire employees to look for opportunities to contribute and do things better.

- *Boundary systems*. These are best described as systems which state minimum standards or express the rules which govern acceptable behaviour in terms of what is done or not done.

- *Interactive control systems*. Diagnostic control systems detect when the organisation is failing to meet performance standards. Interactive control systems are focused on detecting in what way the environment and therefore the task of the organisation might be changing. Strategic reviews and customer focus groups might form part of an interactive control system.

Simons asserts that managers need to use all four of these 'levers' together in order to provide an environment in which employees may operate more effectively.

8.5 PSYCHOLOGICAL ASPECTS OF SERVICE DELIVERY

Many service activities may be extremely stressful for service employees and customers alike. This is particularly true when the service ethic of the organisation demands that employees display a cheerful attitude, even when this is not what they feel like doing. Hoschild (1983) coined the term 'emotional labour' to describe the aspects of an employee's role that demand communication in non-verbal forms beyond the simply mechanistic.

This section outlines some of the aspects of service delivery that managers and service designers should pay attention to in order to ensure that the desired level of service is maintained.

8.5.1 Employee burnout

Research around the subject of burnout would suggest that for service employees, the simple pressure of being aware of customers and their needs can be sufficient to cause high stress levels for some people. This is not consistent across personality types, some people enjoying the presence of others, whilst some personality profiles may find this a particular strain. Having said this, it would appear that no one is immune from a degree of burnout if pressure is sustained and appears to have no foreseeable end to it. Maslach and Jackson (1981) proposed a 'Burnout Inventory' which links to three categories of impact:

- *Depersonalisation*. The tendency to distance oneself from others and to think of others as things or objects rather than as individual people.
- *Lack of personal accomplishment*. Having no sense of doing well on a task which the individual considers worthwhile.
- *Emotional exhaustion.* Individuals at the 'end of their tether' and unable to cope.

Clearly, each of these categories has significance for managing both internal and external customer relationships. Some strategies for limiting the impact of burnout include:

- *Limiting customer contact time*. A call centre might organise work such that employees are able to carry out back office administrative work to give them a break from the continual demand of customers on the telephone.
- *Investment in training*. One of the causes of stress and burnout for the individual is the feeling that s/he is not confident of her/his ability to meet the demands of the task in hand. This is exacerbated when in the presence of an impatient or otherwise demanding customer because of the possibility of a customer complaint for poor service.
- *Providing support*. Teamwork and the support of colleagues provide an invaluable safety-valve so that difficult service encounters or awkward customers can be talked about and dealt with, rather than leaving employees to 'fester' over what went wrong.

8.5.2 Anxiety at work

James and Clark (1997) describe the relevance of anxiety to service operations and how organisations provide mechanisms to deal with it. They list anxiety as coming from a number of sources:

- individual personality
- personal history
- anxiety inherent in the task itself.

All jobs have some element of anxiety in them. For example:

- The college professor may be concerned that if the marks are incorrect a student may fail, with potential damage to his or her career.
- The investment broker may worry that advice given may lose money for his clients.
- The counter clerk in a bank may be concerned about the possibility of physical abuse or extreme rudeness from customers.
- The chef may worry about food poisoning endangering both customers and business.

Some of these (the food poisoning, for example) are an obvious aspect of the task and some anxiety may be appropriate. In other cases the anxiety may be experienced at an unconscious level. Indeed, too much anxiety would render the individual ineffective or paralysed.

Organisations have developed containment mechanisms to deal with this anxiety:

- Professional services develop industry-wide procedures which, if followed correctly, should reduce the probability of error. Professionals spend many years in training in order to acquire recognised practitioner status.
- Consumer services design detailed procedures and then train employees in them to ensure compliance. Food preparation procedures provide a good example here.

These containment mechanisms generally work effectively, allowing the individual to carry out the required tasks. At times of transition, however, these mechanisms may be disrupted. The professional service which is increasing both the volume and standardisation of its services may be employing more 'semi-professionals', often with much lower levels of training, and concern about falling quality standards may be expressed.

At the other end of the scale, high-volume standard consumer services may be devolving more responsibility to customer-facing staff in an effort to deliver both wider choice and greater personalisation to their customers. In this case these staff no longer have the security of tightly designed procedures to protect them and, again, there will be an anxious reaction expressed in the form of resistance to change.

8.5.3 Transactional analysis (TA)

The work of Eric Berne (see, for example, Berne 1968) provides a useful model for analysing the interaction between people. Berne describes three basic ego states – Parent, Adult and Child. The Parent state contains the messages absorbed from parents or other influential authority figures, whilst the Child contains the ways of acting and thinking we learned in our early years. The Parent can be either critical or nurturing whilst the Child may be rebellious and/or creative. Berne proposes that the Adult has the ability to think and make choices not necessarily governed by either Parent or Child 'scripts'.

It is important to note that healthy individuals will operate from all three ego states. A person who was predominantly Adult might be extremely boring! Indeed, for service delivery, the use of a 'Nurturing Parent' response might be appropriate, as can be seen in Figure 8.5. As the name implies, TA looks at interactions between individuals and divides them into 'complementary' and 'crossed' transactions.

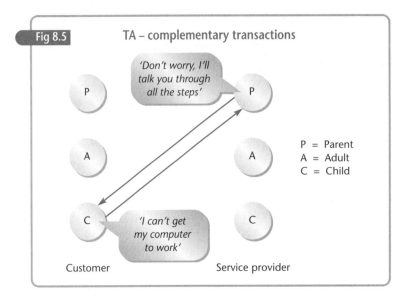

Fig 8.5 — TA – complementary transactions

'Don't worry, I'll talk you through all the steps'

'I can't get my computer to work'

P = Parent
A = Adult
C = Child

Customer   Service provider

Figure 8.5 depicts a complementary transaction. The customer in this case gives an impression of total helplessness in order to gain assistance. In this case we need to look beyond the words, gaining evidence from tone of voice and body language if in a face-to-face encounter. The customer is hoping to 'hook into' the service provider's Nurturing Parent to get more help than perhaps the policies of the organisation might allow for. In this case the first response is promising from the customer's perspective and may form a basis for a satisfactory service encounter.

In Figure 8.6, the same request for help from the customer is met with a different response. In this case the service provider chooses to disregard the 'helpless' plea from the customer and responds in a much more business-like manner. Although this may be technically correct, the response is not what was hoped for. This transaction is

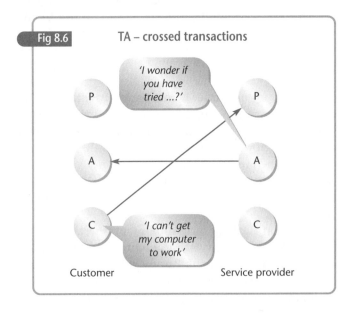

Fig 8.6 — TA – crossed transactions

'I wonder if you have tried ...?'

'I can't get my computer to work'

Customer   Service provider

'crossed' because it is as if these two people are talking in very different ways. It would be possible at a later stage in this interaction for these people to move to Adult-to-Adult transactions, but only when a more secure foundation had been laid.

There is much more theory around TA which can give useful insights into the 'hidden agendas' of person-to-person service encounters. Some companies have invested significant amounts in awareness training which draws on this and related theory.

8.6 THE CUSTOMER AS EMPLOYEE

A key theme of this chapter is the need to recognise that the customer is an integral part of the service delivery system. It follows then that service designers must consider how to manage these temporary 'employees' in similar ways to those who are more permanent members of the organisation (see also Bowen 1986; Johnston 1989; Mills and Morris 1986).

8.6.2 Customer roles

Customers perform a variety of functions in the service delivery system. Their precise role will depend on the nature of the activity and the approach determined by the service designer. These roles include:

- *Service specifier*. In most services the customer must give clear information about requirements before the appropriate service product can be selected and delivered. This may be relatively straightforward in consumer services where the service product is well defined and customers may have wide experience of the scripts (section 8.3.1). It may not be as straightforward, however, in customised service such as many of the professional services, where in many cases the customer has little relevant knowledge or experience. It is particularly important for service providers to elicit all relevant information before deciding how to proceed.

- *Quality inspector*. Many service organisations will use the customer as a quality control inspector. They may provide formal feedback mechanisms such as focus groups or questionnaires, or may encourage a wide range of comments from customers. Some organisations appear to rely on the customers to bring errors to their attention rather than ensure zero defects.

- *Co-producer.* Customers may be an inherent part of the service product. They are part of the 'atmosphere' for other customers in a restaurant or theatre, and form a resource for the organisation in self-service situations.

8.6.2 Benefits of customer involvement

- *Inclusion*. Customers who become actively involved in the service delivery process often develop an increased sense of loyalty. Having started the process, these customers are less likely to stop and find another provider in the short term.

- *Resource productivity*. If the customer is carrying out some of the tasks, the service operation requires fewer resources of its own to run. Self-service restaurants and supermarkets provide a simple example.

● *Customer control.* A major advantage for customers who become part of the service process is that they may feel that they have more personal control over what happens to them. This is one of the attractions for the Internet-based services where customers may access the service at times to suit themselves and also may exit the service at any stage if they so wish.

8.6.3 Customer management issues

Since customers are significant components of service delivery both as recipients and as co-producers of the service experience, it would seem to be sensible to 'manage' customers as if they were employees. This might entail some or all of the following:

● *Defining customer competence.* One of the changes in the service concept which may redefine the way things are done relates to the extent to which the service organisation assumes competent or incompetent customers. For example, telecommunications equipment suppliers formerly dealt exclusively with competent customers in the form of national network operators. The advent of mobile networks and increased competition means that they may now be dealing with entrepreneurs rather than engineers. This opens up possibilities for the development of new services as well as presenting challenges to accepted ways of working.

● *Customer selection.* Most organisations will be clear as to which market segments they are targeting. This has a particular relevance for some services, particularly those where the service experience is made up in part by the other customers. For example, the theatre experience is affected by others in the audience. Some restaurants insist on a strict dress code, sending a clear message as to what types of customer are welcome and what type of behaviour is acceptable.

Center Parcs, the holiday company, will not take bookings from large, single-sex groups (particularly young men), because it doesn't want its reputation as a family-focused holiday to be damaged by too much 'inappropriate' behaviour.

● *Customer training.* In order to develop the customer resource, time must be set aside for training. Although this may incur set-up costs, it may pay dividends in the long run. A security alarm company discovered that many of the service calls it received were avoidable, but tied up expensive resource in answering them. It embarked on a programme of training key personnel in its customers' organisations. The result was significantly fewer 'false alarms', which improved productivity and customer satisfaction.

● *Customer motivation.* Service organisations may devise rewards for 'good' customer employees. Sometimes this can be achieved by customer-facing staff using their discretion to give more than was requested to customers who have been helpful. Many organisations assume that customers will want to be helpful. Moving to the front of a queue in a fast-food restaurant, you are encouraged to present your order in the 'approved' style and are rewarded by prompt service.

● *Customer removal.* As a last resort, service organisations will remove customers. This is particularly important in social situations where one group of customers may damage the experience for the majority.

8.7 SUMMARY

Service encounters

- The success of the encounter depends upon the nature of the encounter, its design, service leadership, customer attributes and psychological aspects of service delivery.
- The main types of encounter are remote, phone and face-to-face.
- Two dimensions of service encounter intensity include risk and social interaction.

Service design

- Scripting helps to provide both consistency and efficiency in service delivery and also provides a sense of security for both customers and employees.
- Motivation is affected by role conflict, role ambiguity and the opportunity to work in teams.

Leadership and empowerment

- Transactional leadership denotes the ability to deal with the day-to-day management of operations, while transformational leadership is required at times of significant change.
- The three main types of discretion are routine, creative and deviant.
- The challenge for compliant organisations is to engender both ownership and creativity in the workforce.
- The challenge for adaptive organisations is to ensure a consistent approach to service delivery and the sharing of knowledge.

Psychological aspects of service delivery

- Many service activities may be extremely stressful for service employees.
- Managers need to pay attention to the problems of employee anxiety and burnout employees.

The customer as employee

- Customers are often an integral part of the service delivery system.
- The key roles taken by customers include service specifier, quality inspector and co-producer.
- The key issues in managing customers include defining customer competence, customer selection, training, motivation and removal.

8.7 DISCUSSION QUESTIONS

1. Identify six service encounters. Assess the level and nature of risk associated with each one.

2. Provide an example of a 'scripted' response. Describe and discuss the advantages and disadvantages in using this script.

3. What are the advantages and disadvantages of using teamwork in student assignments?

4. What do you think were/are the psychological problems of a job you had/have? How well were/are those problems dealt with?

5. Evaluate and assess your role as a customer in a supermarket, Internet-based travel agency, and university/college course.

8.9 QUESTIONS FOR MANAGERS

1. To what extent are service encounters managed or are customer-facing staff left to 'do their best'?

2. Are there opportunities to increase the social interaction in the service experience?

3. What style of leadership is most appropriate? How much discretion do your staff feel you give them?

4. How well are you managing staff in transition? Are they anxious or frustrated?

5. Has your organisation realised the full benefit of teamwork? Are the teams progressing towards being self-directed?

6. What is the incidence of burnout in your staff? Can you manage the stress levels?

8.10 SUGGESTIONS FOR FURTHER READING

Bowen D.E. and Johnston R., 'Internal Service Recovery: Developing a new construct', *International Journal of Service Industry Management*, vol. 10, no. 2, 1999, pp 118–31.
Bowen D.E. and Lawler E.E., 'The Empowerment of Service Workers: What, why, how and when', *Sloan Management Review*, Fall 1992, pp. 73–84.
Tansik D.A. and Smith W.L., 'Scripting the Service Encounter', in Fitzsimmons J. and Fitzsimmons M. (eds), *New Service Design*, Sage Publications, Thousand Oaks, California, 2000, pp 239–63.

8.11 REFERENCES

Belbin R.M., *Management Teams: Why they succeed or fail*, Butterworth-Heinemann, Oxford, 1981.
Bennis W., *Managing People is like Herding Cats*, Executive Excellence Publishing, South Provo, Utah, 1999.
Berne E., *The Games People Play*, Penguin, Harmondsworth, 1968.
Bowen D.E., 'Managing Customers as Human Resources in Service Organisations', *Human Resource Management*, vol. 25, no. 3, Fall 1986, pp. 371–84.
Bowen D.E and Lawler E.E., 'The Empowerment of Service Workers: What, why, how and when', *Sloan Management Review*, Spring 1993, pp. 31–39.
Bowen D.E. and Lawler E.E., 'Empowering Service Employees', *Sloan Management Review*, Summer, 1995, pp. 73–84.
Carlzon J., *Moments of Truth*, Ballinger, Cambridge, Mass., 1987.
Hersey P. and Blanchard K.H., *Management of Organizational Behavior: Utilizing human resources*, Prentice Hall, Englewood Cliffs, NJ, 1982.

Hoschild A., *The Managed Heart: Commercialization of human feeling*, University of California Press, Berkeley, Calif., 1983.

James K. and Clark G., 'Extending a Service Operations Management Taxonomy; the Role of Management as a Container for Anxiety and the Challenges for Service Organisations in Transition', paper to the British Academy of Management Annual Conference, London, 1997.

Johnston R., 'The Customer as Employee', *International Journal of Operations and Production Management*, vol. 9, no. 5, 1989, pp. 15–23.

Kakabadse A. and Kakabadse, N., *Essence of Leadership*, International Thompson Business Press, London, 1999.

Katz D. and Kahn R.L., *The Social Psychology of Organisations* (2nd edition), John Wiley, New York, 1978.

Katzenbach J.R. and Smith D.K., *The Wisdom of Teams*, McGraw-Hill, London, 1998.

Kelley S.W., 'Discretion and the Service Employee', *Journal of Retailing*, vol. 69, Spring, 1993 pp. 104–26.

Kelley S.W., Longfellow T. and Malehorn J., 'Organizational Determinants of Service Employees' Exercise of Routine, Creative, and Deviant Discretion', *Journal of Retailing*, vol. 72, no. 2, 1996, pp. 135–57.

Larkin T.J. and Larkin S., 'Reaching and Changing Frontline Employees', *Harvard Business Review*, May–June 1996.

March J.G. and Simon H.G., *Organizations*, John Wiley, New York, 1958.

Maslach C. and Jackson S., 'The Measurement of Experienced Burnout', *Journal of Occupational Behaviour*, vol. 2, 1981, pp. 99–113.

Mills P.K. and Morris J.H., 'Clients as 'Partial' Employees of Service Organisations: Role development in client participation', *Academy of Management Review*, vol. 11, no. 4, 1986 pp. 726–35.

Normann R., *Service Management*, Wiley, Chichester, 1984.

Osburn J.D. and Moran L., *The New Self-Directed Work Teams*, McGraw-Hill, New York, 2000.

Schank R.C., 'Language and Memory', *Cognitive Science*, vol. 4, 1980, pp. 243–84.

Schank R.C., *Dynamic Memory: A theory of reminding and learning in computers and people*, Cambridge University Press, Cambridge, Mass., 1982.

Simons R., 'Control in an Age of Empowerment', *Harvard Business Review*, March–April 1995, pp. 80–88.

Tansik D.A. and Smith W.L., 'Scripting the Service Encounter', in Fitzsimmons J. and Fitzsimmons M. (eds), New Service Design, Sage Publications, Thousand Oaks, California, 2000, pp. 239–63.

CASE EXERCISE

The Empress Hotel Group

This case was co-written by Bridgette Sullivan-Taylor, Warwick Business School

Davina McColl had just taken over as personnel director at the Empress Hotel Group, a major international five-star hotel chain with its headquarters in Hong Kong. Her tasks in the previous hotels in which she had worked had involved setting up systems and procedures, updating the standard operating procedures, and running customer service training departments which provided and coached scripts, teamwork and allocation of roles and duties. She had personally trained senior hotel managers in leadership and motivation. This hotel chain, she realised, was going to be rather different.

The Empress Hotel Group's Chairman and Chief Executive was Bob Beaver, an evangelical American whose dream was to create 'the most perfect hotel chain in the world'. He felt that the standardised approach to five-star hotels was not appropriate for the discerning international traveller who wanted a taste of local culture and traditions, not a 'McDonalds experience'. He wanted his hotels to be run by the local management teams, not by head office. He felt they should be able to use local furniture and furnishing and decorations, create local menus and use local produce. He thought the uniforms should be different from hotel to hotel and reflect the local culture and climate, and the service should be warm and spontaneous.

Davina, like most of the hotel's management, had come from other mainstream chains which were extremely different. The human resource department's role was to create manuals spelling out exactly what should be done, by whom and how. The role of the operations managers was to implement these procedures and if they were not sure of anything, they always knew they could find the answer in one of the manuals that covered one wall in their office.

It surprised Bob, but did not surprise Davina, that the amount of discretion applied by managers was, in practice, small. Indeed, her predecessor had worked with them to provide systems and procedures, for which he had been sacked. Bob was determined to bring about his vision, and Davina was instrumental in this.

All the staff were paid slightly above the industry average and Empress Hotels were seen as *the* places to work. As Bob ruefully pointed out, 'It is not necessarily seen as *the* place to stay. We need to put my vision into practice.' Davina's job was to persuade both hotel managers and the staff, from front-of-house to pot-washers, to use the discretion they really had to make Empress Hotels the best place in the world to stay.

Davina had to deal with the hotel's facilities, food and service, and she decided to start with the service. On her way to see her mother in Germany she stopped for a night on the way out at the group's highly rated hotel in Dubai and in the Seychelles on the way back.

She realised she had her work cut out. At check-in both hotels 'processed' her very efficiently but there was no warmth or colour. She asked both receptionists, who were not busy, about local attractions and was told 'See the concierge' (Dubai) and 'There are some leaflets in your room' (Seychelles). Davina also asked the difference between the guestroom she had booked and an executive room and was told '350 Dirham' (Dubai) and 'They are on the fifth floor with breakfast included' (Seychelles). At dinner in the hotels' restaurants she was not offered a dessert, although in Dubai she was asked if she would like a coffee.

Back in Hong Kong Davina set herself objectives in three areas:

1 Reception – to try to make the service more spontaneous.

2 Staff training – to encourage the staff to focus on the needs of the guests and not on the procedures.

3 Hotel managers – to help them assess their staff in terms of good service rather than compliance and encourage their staff to do a good job rather than what they have always done.

Davina explained her approach: 'It's about mixing discretion with professionalism. We need to get away from standardisation and focus on the customer and let the local colour and culture come out. Training staff is going to be the key, but it's going to be hard when we can't define or specify what they have to do. They will need to have the right skills, be highly motivated and willing to go the extra mile. We just have to bring it about!'

Question

1 *What would you suggest Davina should do to encourage the staff to exude warmth and spontaneity when their natural instinct is to seek security from procedures and routines?*

9

Structure: Networks, Technology and Information

9.1 INTRODUCTION

All services are delivered within a structure or environment, which utilises technology and information. A dining experience is provided within the restaurant setting, its space, heating, light and style, for example. A call to a telephone call centre is provided within the capabilities of the touch-tone dialling facilities, and the customer relationship management (CRM) technology used by the operator. An Internet service is delivered within a particular informational environment, the layout and colour of the web pages, their interrelationships and ease of use. Such structures, either physical or virtual, together with the technology and information flows, are inextricably part of the service itself.

The objectives of the chapter are:

- to distinguish between structure and infrastructure
- to identify the key issues associated with physical networks
- to identify the key issues associated with virtual networks
- to discuss the impact of technology and information
- to explore the potential of the servicescape
- to provide a framework for integrating structure, technology, and information.

In this chapter we explore the issues associated with the structural elements of an operation – the physical structure of a service organisation, its buildings, facilities and décor, for example, with its technology and informational networks, link in-house and outsourced services. Together these create the physical and virtual networks which, in turn, create the service environment or servicescape for both customers and employees (see Figure 9.1). The servicescape is the structural context in which staff, working in both the back and front offices, support and deliver the service. It is also the place where customers, either inside the operation or at remote service points such as telephones or computers, interact with the organisation and its staff.

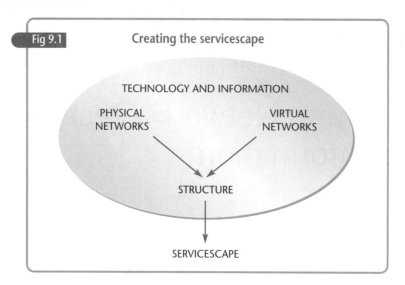

Fig 9.1 Creating the servicescape

TECHNOLOGY AND INFORMATION

PHYSICAL
NETWORKS

VIRTUAL
NETWORKS

STRUCTURE

SERVICESCAPE

9.2 STRUCTURE VERSUS INFRASTRUCTURE

The usual way of describing the two main clusters of operational tasks are those decisions concerned with managing the structure and the infrastructure of the operation (Hayes and Wheelwright 1984). The structure of an operation is akin to a human body – it is the skeleton, organs and muscle structure which create its shape and define its ability. For an operation the structure includes the facilities, buildings and their location, the vista or servicescape created by those facilities visible to customers and staff.

In the age of the Internet the servicescape also refers to the visible aspects of the organisation seen on a computer screen and the speed of interaction, which is determined by the capabilities of the informational highways linking the parts of the structure. These hard or soft structural parts of an organisation define its overall shape and architecture (Slack 1997, p. 121). They impose limits on the operation within which it has to work. A restaurant with only 30 seats, for example, constrains its activities just as the capacity of a telecommunications device, measured in kilobits, may constrain the type and speed of information flows. Structural decisions include the location, capacity (size), capability and the resilience or flexibility of the various physical or virtual parts of the operation.

An organisation's infrastructure, on the other hand, comprises the decisions that affect how the structure is used – the organisation, planning, control and improvement of its processes, staff and customers, for example – and decisions about how performance is measured and improved.

Whilst structural decisions impose limits on the operation, good infrastructural decision-making (discussed in other chapters) attempts to make the best use of the structural resources of the organisation in a reactive way but can also be used to seek proactively to exploit the potential of that structure (see Figure 9.2).

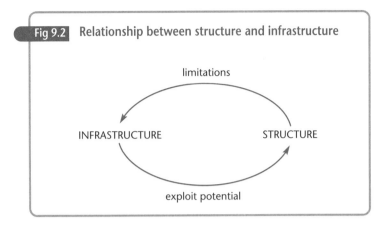

Fig 9.2 Relationship between structure and infrastructure

9.3 PHYSICAL NETWORKS

The key structural decisions associated with an organisation's physical networks include the location, capacity, capability and resilience or flexibility. When making decisions about a new architect's practice, for example, one has to decide where it should go (its physical location in a country, its capacity or size – i.e. how big it should be), its capability (such as ease of access from one level, space for large drawings and models, for example), and its ability to change (the flexibility of its layout, whether walls are load bearing or easily removed, and whether the surrounding space can be converted into car parks etc.).

9.3.1 Location decisions

Location is the geographic positioning of a facility or facilities. Location decisions are often expensive and may have a significant impact not only as an investment cost but also on operations costs, as location may be affected by local wage rates and business rates, for example. Location may also have an impact on revenues, particularly when the operation involves physical contact with customers. For operations which do not require direct physical contact with customers, such as call centres and Internet service providers such as health or benefits advisory services, location decisions can be made to minimise the physical costs of the buildings and the running costs of the operation. For operations which need direct access to customers, expensive High Street locations or out-of-town shopping malls may be essential.

Location decisions are a balancing act between supply-side factors and demand-side factors (Slack *et al.* 1998). Supply-side factors are those that influence the costs and difficulties of a location decision. The demand-side factors are those which influence revenues. Not all the factors below will apply to every location decision but they are an indication of those factors which may need to be taken into account.

Supply-side factors include:

- land costs – the costs of acquiring the land
- labour costs – wage costs, employment taxes, welfare provisions etc.
- energy costs – the cost of energy or the availability or even the consistency of the supply of energy
- transportation costs – the costs of getting resources to the site and of transporting materials to customers
- government factors – local taxes, capital restrictions, financial assistance and political climate, planning restrictions
- social factors – language, local amenities
- working environment – history of labour relations and labour supply.

Demand-side factors include:

- convenience to customers – the site's accessibility for customers, including transport network, parking, distance from markets
- labour skills – the availability of particular talents, skills, accents and cultures
- characteristics of the site – the intrinsic and maybe aesthetic appeal of the site
- image – the reputation of the surrounding area, the extent to which there are complementary services in the vicinity.

9.3.2 Capacity

Another key question is: how big should the facility be? Deciding the size of a supermarket, call centre, airport, surgery or cinema is certainly not an easy task and one has to weigh the costs against forecast demand – not only short-term demand but also long-term demand because the cost of changing facility size can be expensive and sometimes difficult.

The two interrelated issues for operations managers are:

- facilities can usually only be added in large, and expensive, chunks
- capacity needs to match demand.

Adding new facilities usually requires the organisation to commit significant amounts of capital. This can be a risky business because long-term demand can rarely be predicted with any great certainty. If necessary break-even volumes are not met, the facility will not pay for itself. In some cases, such as a theme park where having sufficient customers creates the atmosphere, the service may not be as good as it should be if volume targets are not achieved. If volumes are exceeded, there may be significant localised problems for customers resulting in customer dissatisfaction and lost business. Given that the majority of forecasts will be wrong, operations managers will invariably suffer from the consequences of over- or under-capacity.

Many airports have suffered from the latter problem and owing to the length of time it takes to design a new runway or terminal building, to go through the planning process and build the facility, volumes may again exceed capacity as soon as the new facility is opened. Southwest Airlines (see Box 9.1) owes its success to a careful capacity expansion approach.

Box 9.1 Southwest Airlines

Southwest Airlines has been consistently successful as a service operation because of two aspects of the way it operates. Southwest is often quoted as the 'fun' airline, with cabin crew encouraged to be creative about the way they carry out their duties, sometimes playing games with the passengers during the flight.

Southwest could deliver what became known as its 'luv' strategy because it was founded on sound operational principles, an emphasis on tight cost control, and careful expansion of the network. Each time Southwest acquired a new plane, a decision had to be made as to whether it would be directed to an existing route where demand volumes were predicted to rise or to develop the network by adding a non-stop service between cities previously requiring passengers to take more than one flight.

The airline's pricing strategy has been a key factor in influencing the volume of demand on any given route. Southwest made a policy of pricing against the cost of ground transport, not against other airlines. This could lead to total demand for air transport increasing as much as four or five times the level prior to Southwest's entry. As Southwest grew, so this pattern of market growth was repeated many times over. This allowed the route planners to develop a simple demand growth model to indicate the level of capacity growth required over time.

The graph shows a typical growth pattern from the early 1990s illustrating the impact of Southwest's arrival on total demand and its expected market share:

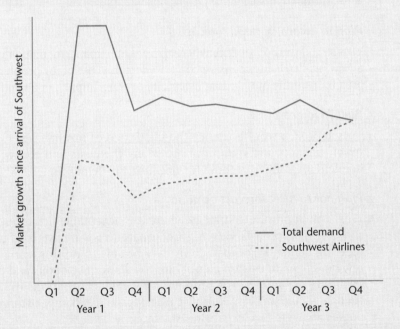

It is interesting to note that the entry of Southwest into a market could be expected to stimulate a significant demand which then drops back to a sustainable level. On many routes, Southwest expected to become the sole carrier after two or three years.

Another factor in making capacity expansion decisions was linked to the number of expected flights per day. Investment in a new destination required investment in departure gates. Although prepared to commence operations with ten departures a day, Southwest wanted to expand rapidly to 20 departures a day to use two gates effectively. The final decision criterion was the availability of people to fit in with Southwest's distinctive culture. Southwest found that this aspect of location decision-making had a significant impact on its success.

Questions

1 *What type of competitive action would have a significant impact on Southwest's forecast market growth curve?*

2 *Which would be the limiting factor in Southwest's growth: availability of routes or availability of people to fit into Southwest's culture?*

This illustration is adapted from material contained in Harvard Business School case Southwest Airlines: 1993 (A) 9-694-023 and from industry sources.

Similar to medium-term capacity (Chapter 7), there are three main strategies for long-term capacity planning:

- plan to exceed demand forecasts
- built to forecast
- plan not to meet forecast demand.

Plan to exceed demand forecasts

This strategy is appropriate where there is an expanding market or the cost of building a new facility is inexpensive compared to the cost of, or problems that would be created by, running out, such as electricity or water supply, or air traffic control facilities.

Built to forecast

This approach would balance the likelihood of not having enough and having too much capacity and is appropriate where the costs and consequences of exceeding demand are similar to those for not meeting demand.

Plan not to meet forecast demand

This is an appropriate strategy where it is acceptable not to meet demand or where the cost of capital is very high compared to the costs and consequences of not meeting demand. Football clubs may be able to do this using price premiums and revenues from television companies to balance the books and even set money aside for future expansion. The problem for some organisations that follow this strategy, such as supermarkets, is that it might give the competition time and income to pursue an aggressive expansionist strategy.

Developing a facility strategy involves a few steps which are easy to describe but difficult to implement:

- establish a measure of capacity
- develop demand forecasts, ideally several forecasts including optimistic and pessimistic, identifying the assumptions on which each is based
- identify alternative means of dealing with the forecasts

- undertake an assessment of the risk involved
- evaluate the alternatives.

9.3.3 Capability

It seems obvious that any new facility should be capable of doing what is required, but this is not as easy as it sounds. There are some airports whose runways are too short to accommodate some of the larger aircraft. A decision taken years ago on the length of a runway when planes were smaller creates constraints on operations now.

Doctors' surgeries have changed significantly over the last few years as doctors form larger practices to share growing administrative costs and ease the burden of 24-hour cover. They also provide many more facilities than previously, such as well-person clinics and routine surgical operations, for example.

We face problems in forecasting not only demand but also the nature of that demand and thus the nature of the services that have to be provided in the future. It is little wonder that many operations management problems stem from the size and nature of the facilities at their disposal.

Although forecasting the size and nature of demand and future services is difficult, if not impossible, the only thing an operations manager can do, besides keeping their finger on the industry's pulse, is to try to ensure that their facilities have some degree of resilience or flexibility.

9.3.4 Resilience or flexibility

Physical network resilience can be created through either structural flexibility or developing the potential of the infrastructure. Building flexibility or resilience into a facility can be done in many ways:

- buying extra land to facilitate any possible future expansion
- having flexible internal structure, open-plan offices and movable walls
- using flexible equipment, such as cordless telephones, or desk-sharing schemes
- adopting different methods of working using more home-based workers
- developing contingencies – railway companies, for example, may plan to use different routes if one route fails.

9.4 VIRTUAL NETWORKS

Virtual networks comprise a combination of physical sites and/or computer sites linked by communication technologies via cable, satellite and fixed lines. They involve the creation of several systems which combined, electronically rather than physically, can provide a particular service or range of services. The electronic parts include computer systems (from stand-alone systems to the World Wide Web), networks such as an organisation's intranets or the Internet, software systems and applications, while end nodes of the networks which are accessed by customers include phones, faxes, televisions and computers.

The organisation may be entirely virtual (see adabra.com in Box 9.2) or primarily a physical structure with some virtual elements.

Box 9.2 adabra.com

adabra is a new Internet company which has created a virtual network to access, supply and service its customers with a wide range of products covering categories including home and garden, sports and leisure, and office and communication. Products sold include cameras, televisions, microwave ovens, telephones, golf clubs and computing equipment. adabra.com specialises in community buying. By linking with interested customer groups, such as over-50s portals, sports and leisure clubs or individuals through its web site, it encourages people to come together and gain discounts from bulk buying. By offering the latest branded products at a range of prices depending upon the number bought within a certain time-frame, its customers can save up to 30 per cent on normal retail prices. Vincent O'Farrell, the company's Consultant Operations Director, summarises their service: 'This is not "auction buying" where consumers compete against each other and drive the price up. adabra is about co-buying, or community buying, which is about consumers working with each other to drive the price down.'

The company is not a 'bricks and mortar' organisation but a value network comprising carefully constructed and managed partnerships to create a new, fun and interesting service for its customers. The network of partners provides products, sales, logistics, customer service, and product servicing and repairs.

Products

The organisation has to make decisions about which are the right products, opting solely for premium brands. By developing partnerships with suppliers, adabra can negotiate not only numbers of products but also the discounts they can offer for a variety of sales volumes, and also have items pre-allocated to speed delivery to customers.

Sales

The company's 'front end' is its web site with information about the products on offer and explanations of how to buy. Access to markets is provided through several channels. Whilst its web site is available direct, most traffic will be driven through other major gateway partner sites such as Egg's site – egg.com – and other specialist community web sites. Such channels not only provide good access to appropriate markets but also provide co-branding which gives customers confidence in the company and its services as well as minimising traditional business-to-consumer marketing costs. 'The key activities for the company,' explains Vincent, 'have included not only the technical development of the web site but also market research to identify what customers want. We have to think about the amount and type of information we provide, for example the number and consistency of product images because this impacts on both quality and download speed, and the provision of a consistent level of information about products made as interesting and interactive as possible.'

Logistics

Distribution is subcontracted to major package-handling companies. adabra uses Securicor as its main delivery partner and a number of other third-party suppliers to deal with large specialised products. Some items such as washing machines are delivered directly by the manufacturers.

Customer service

'Customer service involves dealing with customers' queries or problems and we are currently facing several issues here as we start to ramp up sales,' explains Vincent. 'Should customer service be an internal bricks-and-mortar operation or should it be outsourced? Either way we need to ensure that the right image is created by customer service. What are acceptable turnaround times for responding to emails? How standardised can emails be made without compromising the ability to provide a personalised service? Should there be an answerphone to deal with calls that cannot be taken by customer service agents and, if so, should customers be asked to call back or should they be contacted by outbound agents? Should calls be re-routed to technical specialists? What are the appropriate opening hours? However good our web site and products are, we will not get people coming back, unless we can create the right customer service operation. We need to build a robust structure that can consistently deliver what we need but also has the flexibility to deal with unknown volumes, timings and preferred access routes, for example.'

Product servicing and repairs

Product servicing and repairs are outsourced to companies specialising in this work.

'One key issue we have in managing this network is consistency. Each of our partners has different ways of working, for example delivery lead times and availability. adabra needs to create its own consistent service to shape its brand.'

Question

1 *Identify and assess the problems and benefits of the network that adabra has created.*

The key structural decisions associated with an organisation's virtual networks are the nature of the structure, its capacity, capability and resilience or flexibility, and all of these are closely associated with each other and are difficult to separate out.

9.4.1 Structure

A key decision for virtual networks is the shape of the network. Some networks are star-shaped with several other activities linked to a core process, often a web site. Other networks, such as the Internet, are using structures where access is through connected gateways, or hierarchical structures where activating one service or node can open up other linkages (see Figure 9.3).

Associated decisions include the location of any physical elements of the network (see section 9.3.1) and the nature of the linkages between the elements in the networks. These may include distribution systems involving the flow of goods and materials or information systems allowing access to facilities, systems and information at other points in the network. Ownership is another issue facing virtual structures – what is to be owned and what operations or elements should be outsourced.

Fig 9.3

Virtual structures

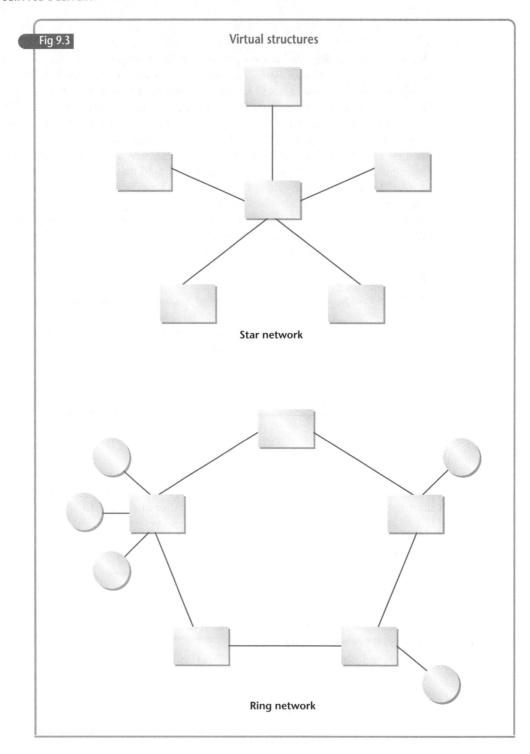

Star network

Ring network

Fig 9.3 Continued

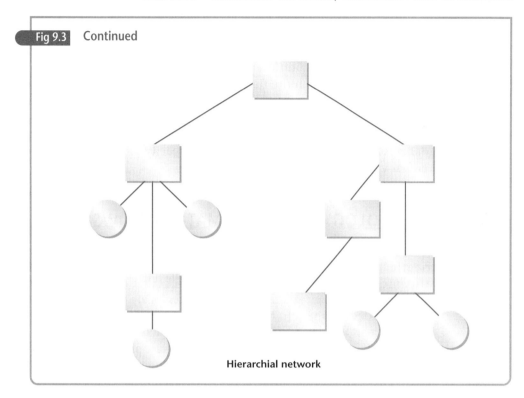

Hierarchial network

9.4.2 Capacity

Capacity in a virtual network refers to both physical and informational transfer capacity between nodes or elements and the size of the nodes themselves. adabra in Box 9.2 uses several types of distribution support: Securicor, other major package-handling companies and the manufacturers for very large items. Information transfer is limited by the capacity of the links between the nodes, usually a digital network. Existing digital phones, for example, can transfer around 10 kilobits per second, while emerging technologies will allow the transfer of over 2,000 kilobits per second. The network capacity is also limited by the capacity of any single node. Often Internet companies find their capacity constraints associated with the more traditional parts of their structures, such as customer service and logistics. In Box 9.2 above adabra's current sales were starting to be limited by its customer service capacity.

9.4.3 Capability

Network capability depends upon the capabilities of the individual elements of the network and also the ability to co-ordinate and control the whole network. As the complexity increases with the number of nodes or the number of interlinkages, the difficulties escalate. adabra's problems were concerned with consistency of service as they linked together more and more organisations with differing service standards.

9.4.4 Resilience or flexibility

Resilience in virtual systems is similar to flexibility in physical systems. Networked structures can provide different routeing for information access or input if one route should fail. The more flexible the network, the greater its resilience should one part fail. The choice of network structure is critical here. The structure chosen will also affect how easy it is to add or remove nodes or other facilities as the demand for service expands or contracts. By linking with very large subcontractors, adabra is able to ensure there is sufficient capacity to cope with the growth that the company hopes will follow.

9.5 TECHNOLOGY AND INFORMATION FLOWS

Technology within operations, either sophisticated or simple, is an intrinsic part of the structure. Information and information flows provide the glue that holds the structure – whether physical or virtual – together and facilitates infrastructural decisions. Technology and information strategies are therefore central requirements for service development in the majority of organisations. The implementation of a new information system or the introduction of a revolutionary new technology can transform the competitive environment. Electronic point of sale systems (EPOS) have revolutionised the retail sector, enabling retailers to track consumer spending and to streamline their supply chains such that high levels of product availability have become the norm.

Investment in information systems is likely to be the major expenditure for many service organisations both at the initial set-up of the operation, and also at frequent intervals as the industry moves forward and adopts similar technologies. Some services are built on the provision of information. In terms of the service concept, the outcome of the service is that the user is provided with information as to where to buy particular goods or obtain service.

Yellow Pages provides a good example of a service built solely on the provision of information for users which has changed its means of operation significantly over the length of its existence. Yellow Pages operations now exist in many countries across the world, providing users with information as to how to contact businesses from abattoirs to zoos. In the UK, this operation was set up by BT (British Telecom) in 1966, with the aim of increasing the use of telephones. For a number of years it was advertised with the slogan, 'Let your fingers do the walking', encouraging users to phone possible suppliers rather than pay them potentially wasted visits.

In 2000, Yellow Pages UK is visited some 46 times a second. There are over 350,000 advertisers who are the paying customers for the service. As the service has grown, so Yellow Pages has adapted its format as new technologies have become available. The original operation was based on the delivery of paper directories to every home in a geographical region. In 1988, the company launched Talking Pages, a telephone-based service, and this was joined in 1996 by yell.com, an Internet site.

In common with many services, changing technologies increasingly mean that the organisation deals with customers in many different ways. Behind all of this lie two customer requirements which are fast defining qualifying levels for service delivery. The first of these is immediate and comprehensive access. Customers now expect to be able to make contact with the service provider in person, by phone or by Internet, 24 hours a day, seven days a week.

The second of these customer imperatives is closely linked to this, and it is the requirement for control. Customers want to feel that they are valued and important, rather than simply another piece of material to be processed. Technologies such as the Internet allow the customer much more perceived control over what happens. They can browse through the on-line retail store, making choices at their own pace. In many cases they feel able to ask more questions than they might have done if they were in a High Street store. Customers are able to compare prices between suppliers before making a purchase. There is no immediate pressure to buy imposed by the presence of a salesperson, or other customers waiting to be served.

9.5.1 The roles for technology in service delivery

The aim of this section is to discuss the role of technology in service delivery, recognising that information systems and the development of facilitating technologies will continue to be areas of key decision-making for the foreseeable future. We will not describe each technological advance in detail, but provide a framework for thinking about implications for the development of the service concept.

Berry (1995) has provided a helpful set of roles to aid the development of a service strategy. These roles are:

- multiplying knowledge
- streamlining service
- customising and personalising service
- increasing reliability
- facilitating communications
- augmenting the service.

To which we would add:

- reducing cost
- increasing customer control.

Reducing cost is often closely linked with the second of Berry's roles, that of streamlining service, but is worthy of separate consideration.

Multiplying knowledge

There are a number of ways that technology can bring both flexibility and an extension to the service concept by multiplying knowledge.

Leveraging knowledge about customers

Information systems that ensure that customer-facing employees have all relevant information about the customer available during the service transaction present a more professional image, and allow the core transaction to be conducted more efficiently. When First Direct, the telephone banking service, was conceived, a fundamental requirement was for an information system that allowed any customer to talk to any service employee at any time.

Some hotels keep comprehensive records of regular guests regarding their likes and dislikes, which room they prefer, and what are their dietary requirements. At a simple but effective level an airport hotel courtesy bus radios ahead as to which customers are on board so that they can be greeted by name when they arrive. This latter example demonstrates that technology does not need to be complex or expensive to achieve a significant impact.

Leveraging knowledge about the service product

Service organisations that are moving away from offering a standard service may need to upskill customer-facing staff. A greater choice for customers may require greater knowledge about the product in order to give appropriate advice. Information systems may allow the customer-facing employees to act 'as if' they were experts. Again, these systems vary from extremely complex to very simple. At one end of the scale, an 'expert system' may harness all the knowledge of recognised experts and specialists. At the other extreme, a simple checklist on a computer screen may deal with many customer enquiries without the need to refer to expensive technical help. Many computer or software help-lines operate on this principle, with on-screen diagnostic routines to aid the customer service agents.

Multiplying knowledge about the customers' use of the product

This is an extension of the previous use of technology, and normally constitutes a change in service concept. Instead of simply selling a product, the service provider seeks to understand how the customer uses it and provides assistance or advice in how to use it more effectively. Truck manufacturers, faced with increased competition, moved the emphasis of their aftermarket operations away from simply selling spares to truck operators. In order to develop customer loyalty they invested in understanding how truck operators might manage their fleets more profitably. This knowledge was then disseminated through the manufacturers' dealer networks by means of an information system, rather than positioning a fleet profitability expert in each location.

Streamlining service

In this case, technology is used to eliminate steps in the service process. It is particularly valuable when applied to activities that have direct bearing on the customer experience. Car rental companies have understood that business customers in particular do not want to spend large amounts of time either filling in paperwork to collect their car or waiting to return it. Smart cards automate the pick-up procedure, and staff with hand-held terminals waiting in the car return lanes speed up the drop-off process. The return process is particularly sensitive as far as the customer experience is concerned because at this stage the customer has effectively obtained all the value he or she required from the service. The processes from this stage on are perceived to be purely for the benefit of the rental firm, not for the customer, and therefore need to be as efficient as possible.

Many telephone-based operations use a customer database to call up addresses sorted by postal code. Rather than ask the customers to give addresses on the telephone – a lengthy process, prone to error – all that is required is a postcode which locates the street name, and then the house number or name within that locality. This relatively simple information system improves service times and reduces error rates.

Customising and personalising service

Supermarket loyalty cards are an example of this use of technology. Tesco, through its loyalty card, has built up a database of customer preferences. As a result it is able to target promotions to particular customer groups.

Increasing reliability

Technology has a major role in automating routine processes, the 'runner' processes described in Chapter 6. Customer information can be made immediately available to all parts of the business without the errors that occur when details are transmitted manually.

The performance of some physical products is now monitored remotely. This is still relatively expensive but is valuable for customer-critical applications. The service provider might monitor the performance of the customer's computer system. Any degradation in performance will trigger a service call to prevent complete failure of the system. In many cases the customer will be unaware that there has been any reduction in performance, or indeed that there has been a service visit.

Facilitating communications

The convergence of voice and data communication systems presents many opportunities for service providers to communicate with customers. A challenge here is to ensure that older technologies are adequately supported. Telephone call centres are being transformed into multi-media customer contact centres, with major opportunities for improvements in communication. However, it is possible that basic operations management principles are not observed in the rush for new technologies. There are many traditional telephone call centres that have insufficient capacity to deal with the increase in demand brought about by greater ease of communication.

Augmenting the service

Technology may facilitate the possibility of the service provider carrying out more for the customer. In the 1990s barcoding and electronic point of sale systems allowed some food manufacturers not simply to supply goods to retailers, but also to manage the customer's shelf space and inventory for them.

Part-time degree courses can be made available globally through the use of electronic conferencing and 'groupware' systems.

Reducing cost

Technology may facilitate the removal of wasteful or repetitive steps in the service process. The resultant reduction in lead time from customer order to fulfilment is in itself likely to yield fewer errors and therefore lower costs.

Financial services, traditionally operating through a network of local branches, are able to reduce the cost of their operations by dealing centrally through telephone or Internet.

Increasing customer control

When there is little or no obvious differentiation between service providers in a given sector, the 'feel good' factor is essential to build customer loyalty. A significant ingredient is the sense that a customer has of being valued by the organisation, and of not being merely another account number or statistic. Information systems allow the organisation to respond in ways that build a perception that the customer is important to the organisation. This is enhanced if the customer feels that he or she can influence the service delivery process in some way, rather than being 'processed' in something akin to an assembly line. As has been described earlier, Internet systems give this sense of customer control.

9.5.2 The Internet and service operations

Many organisations are restructuring their operations to provide electronic-based services for their customers and/or suppliers. Electronic commerce, e-commerce, is challenging traditional business models and is creating new ways of accessing customers and giving customers much more control as information, such as prices, and services offered become much more transparent (Voss 2000). Commerce is also challenging traditional structures and removing intermediaries (Voss 2000) as customers can create and then purchase their own customised products and services via the web, for example holidays, CDs, books and stock trading. e-Commerce is also having a major impact on the cost of doing business, though the costs will vary from organisation to organisation. Thames Water in the UK has identified the costs of various types of transaction for its business (see Table 9.1).

Web-based organisations, either 'brick' (high street businesses with additional web channels) or 'click' (Internet-only organisations), have created, almost overnight, multi-million pound industries in many countries providing instant, innovative, customer-controlled competition for the traditional procedure and service providers. With the rapid availability of the Internet in both business and homes, email and web-based commerce is likely to become a key way of doing business. Already most businesses have email and Internet communications, and during the first few years of 2000 most homes will have access to the web.

9.5.3 e-Service

e-Service is the delivery of service using new media such as PCs but also via other technologies such as digital TV, mobile phones and PDAs (personal digital assistants). Many e-service providers are well established but new start-ups are happening every day, providing competition for traditional service providers and also creating new services (see adabra.com earlier in Box 9.2).

Table 9.1 Comparison of transaction costs for letter, telephone and web

Process	Unit cost	% of telephone cost
Letter	£8.30	451
Telephone	£1.84	100
Web		
query that requires agent response back to customer	£0.92	50
automated billing query with occasional operator intervention	£0.18	10
fully automated billing query	£0.09	5

Source: Thames Water in Voss C., *Trusting the Internet: Developing an eservice strategy*, Institute of Customer Service, Colchester, 2000.

e-Services exist across most of the service sector: banks (e.g. Egg and FirstE), retailers (e.g. Amazon, Nortstar, LastMinute), airlines (e.g. Go and easyJet), information (Scoot, Yahoo!) and utilities (Utilities.com). Job hunting, car purchasing, grocery buying, stock trading, community purchasing, auctioning, can all now be carried out via the web.

For customers this means greater choice, shopping and information gathering from home or office. For business-to-business customers it will mean a more transparent market with transparent pricing, accessibility to more suppliers, the ability to track deliveries and undertake electronic trading such as web-based purchase orders, invoices and payments.

The principal advantages for service providers include:

- *Immediate access for customers*. Customers can visit web sites at any time of day. They don't have to be staffed for 24 hours a day, and 365 days a year, but there is the opportunity for customers to make contact at any time.

- *Local business becomes global*. An advertisement for IBM showed an American couple visiting an Italian shop supplying olive oil. The image was of a poor business, struggling to survive, whilst the couple were running a successful business at home. The couple were amazed to find that, through the Internet, this business was supplying customers in America, and had a wide range of global customers. Small businesses can now compete globally without the investment in physical sales networks.

- *Opportunities for building brands*. Customers form an impression of an organisation from its web site. The messages it conveys, the information it contains, and practical issues such as how easy it is to navigate, present opportunities to support the brand position.

- *Giving perceived control to customers*. Customers can browse web sites at their own discretion. In an on-line retail operation customers can decide at their leisure what goods they wish to purchase, without hassle from sales assistants wanting to boost their commissions, or from other customers in a queue.

- *Making information available to customers*. Web sites allow the organisation to make vast amounts of information available for current and potential customers. Again, the advantage is that the customer can choose what to view and what to leave. The organisation does not need to bombard the customer with 'junk mail' which is frequently seen as both wasteful and intrusive.

- *Linking services*. Opportunities exist to build links between web sites of complementary service providers. This creates the ability to form service alliances to increase the range of choice for customers or to create virtual 'one-stop shops'.

Operations implications

The movement to e-service has many important implications for operations management, including how the web can add value, the changing nature of customer relationships, changing service quality factors, and the importance of web site design.

Value added service

For many organisations e-service will lead to a reappraisal of what adds value in services and indeed what constitutes a service. The support provided by travel agents, for example, may no longer be required by some customers, whereas easy access to operators providing a highly customised service may be of significant value. Music shops providing racks of CDs may be seen to be of less value than in-store or even in-home technology that will allow downloading of preferred tracks to create individualised CDs. Education will need to reassess its teaching role and look at opportunities for web-based learning. From an operations perspective it is likely that there will be a shift to front-line activity becoming a predominantly high value-adding activity focused on the more difficult interactions, with routine and maybe new services provided more cheaply and directly via the web.

The changing nature of customer relationships

The nature of the relationship with customers will change as a result of e-service. Instead of the traditional and often specialist outward-facing customer service role providing the interface between the customer and the organisation, web-based services will allow the customer to infiltrate right inside the organisation. As a result the nature of customer relationships may have to be redefined, as will new ways for more people dealing directly with the customer (see Box 9.3). Operations will need to consider new ways of tracking customer needs and preferences, and of assessing customer satisfaction and retention. Key questions include:

- Which customer segments will use web channels?
- What are the transaction costs?
- What is the nature of the customer relationships?
- How will they be maintained?

Box 9.3 Egg.com

On 11 October 1998 Prudential launched Egg, a new Internet bank, based in a purpose-built communications centre at Pride Park in Derby. Egg's services are available seven days a week, 24 hours a day by Internet, telephone and post, and in due course via digital TV. Sir Peter Davis, Chief Executive of Prudential Corporation, said, 'Egg is part of Prudential's strategy for the UK to provide a broad range of products through a wide range of distribution channels. The launch of Egg anticipates the projected growth in direct distribution and electronic commerce.' The initial services provided by Egg included savings, loans and mortgages. Within its first week of operation Egg's web site had received 1.75 million hits plus around 100,000 telephone enquiries. By 2000 their services had expanded to credit cards, travel insurance, investment services, and web-based shopping. Mike Harris, Egg Chief Executive, said, 'Already Egg has made electronic trading a reality in UK personal finance. The Internet is now set to play an increasingly important role in financial services in this country.'

Egg was the outcome of 12 months of research among 5,000 consumers to determine their financial product and service preferences. 'One of the key points to emerge from our research is that customers want to be recognised as individuals – to be seen as a person, not a number. They want a relationship with someone who can help them to make the choices that affect their lives, rather than being "sold" to,' commented Mike Harris. He added, 'We were talking to people (in one of our pre-launch market research panels) about the digital revolution. One woman said "You know your revolution? It is similar to what Emma Goldman, the early 20th-century American anarchist, said: If I can't dance, I can't come to your revolution." In other words, she was saying that she wanted to deal with an organisation that had a bit of happiness in it, that wasn't austere and dry, but that was an organisation dancing with its customers. We talked to real dancers. And we found they work in three ways. First is interaction when they are dancing – that's what we do on the phone. Second is preparation – so we started to explore just what kind of preparation we could do. Third is sensation – they try to create a response when they dance, so we looked at whether you could have a phone conversation that made people feel good ... If the customer wants to joke, joke; if the customer wants to go quickly, go quickly.'

Customers are provided with a named customer 'relationship' contact, trained in the art of listening rather than selling skills. By developing a close relationship with customers through its customer relationship management (CRM), Egg is able to gain insights into meeting each customer's individual needs. Every conversation and interaction with a customer tries to set up the opportunity for the next – this creates the opportunity for the relationship to develop as the customer's financial and lifestyle needs change, e.g. when moving house, having children or retiring. Egg aims to understand the individual relationships its customers need, and to the degree to which Egg is proactive/reactive in their financial affairs. Egg aims to be head and shoulders above its competitors as a result of its attitude to 'The Customer Experience' and 'Relationship Marketing'.

Questions

1 *Visit Egg's web site and assess how the company provides a value-added service.*

2 *Evaluate the design of Egg's web site.*

This case is developed from material in http://www.egg.com and Voss C., *Trusting the Internet: Developing an eservice strategy*, Institute of Customer Service, Colchester, 2000.

Changing service quality factors

The attributes of service, the service quality factors, may also change. New delivery channels lead to new expectations. Recent research has identified the quality factors for web-based transactions (Voss 2000):

- fast response – both acknowledgement and service provision, from days or weeks in post-based business to hours and indeed minutes in e-service business
- automatic response – instant acknowledgement of emails to reduce anxiety and uncertainty
- customer communication – the provision of information about length of the queue, for example, or how long before a response or delivery is likely
- choice of phone follow-up – the option to communicate person-to-person with the company in case of unresolved queries or concerns
- ability to check status – ability to check location of goods, or the status of an order, the latest estimated time of arrival of an engineer or bank balance
- links to FAQs – the ability to see frequently asked questions (FAQs) to deal with obvious queries.

Web site design

Design of web sites will be crucial in attracting customers and keeping hold of them long enough to interact with the site. Good navigability and speed of downloading will be crucial. Customer's trust of the site is also a key concern that will encourage consumers to use electronic transactions. The entry of big players and major brands will encourage use. Lesser-known brands can also establish themselves by using links through major portals such as Internet service providers (ISPs). Key characteristics of good web sites include (Voss 2000):

- Responsiveness – this includes both speed of downloading information onto the screen and also the response by the organisation to a customer's request.
- Ease of navigation – this was found to be a major determinant of customer satisfaction with a web site. Ease of navigation included limited information on each page, developing a logical and intuitive structure to the pages, and a consistent approach throughout the site.
- Effectiveness – this includes the time required to perform the tasks on the web and speed and satisfaction with the service outcome (the delivery of goods or the provision of service).
- Experience – customer satisfaction with the experience of the site may not simply be limited to the above points but may also include the enjoyment of the experience itself which will encourage them to return to the site. A range of supportive opportunities and features such as games, music, other links, or additional information, may enhance a customer's experience of a site.

Strategies for change

Professor Chris Voss (2000) has identified several key steps in developing an e-service strategy:

- Upgrade the current service interaction – improve existing web-based service by improved response times, automatic acknowledgements, improving navigation of sites etc.
- Understand customer segments – identify likely users and the services that can be best offered to them via the web.
- Understand customer service processes and interactions – this involves identifying service processes, activities, costs and value to help make decisions about the best services or parts of services to make web-based.
- Define the role of live interaction – identify the tasks best suited to live interaction and those best for automation.
- Make the key technology decisions – because technology is moving rapidly, it is too easy to put off purchase decisions rather than investing now, which may improve competitive position but may lead to implementation problems.
- Deal with the tidal wave – be prepared to deal with the significant increase in customer interaction which is associated with web-based services.
- Customer training – develop ways to encourage customers to use the appropriate channels for the appropriate services.
- Channel choice – make decisions about 'brick versus click', a variety of channels of communication or web only, or telephone and web, for example.

● Web relationships – exploit the web experience to build relationships with customers and convert them from browsers into buyers.

As this is written, at the start of the 21st century, Internet businesses are really still in their infancy. One of the pioneers, Amazon.com, the book and gift retailer, has yet to make a profit. Numbers of dot.com businesses have been floated on the stock market to be initially over-subscribed, but then to drop in value as investors begin to worry as to when the promised return will be realised. There is clearly a difference here between businesses that are essentially new services built around the opportunity presented by the Internet, and those which have adapted existing services to capitalise on the Internet channel. Many of the latter continue to operate in more traditional formats, using the Internet to provide greater channel choice for their customers.

Some of the dangers of which Internet services must be wary include:

● **Building high expectations**. The immediacy of Internet access has many benefits. With on-line retail operations, customers may place their order in minutes but then wait weeks for delivery.

● **Creating a limited service offer**. Some Internet services offer limited choice in order to make the customer process less complex. This may result in compromises such as the supermarket offering only one brand of a particular category, then only in one size.

● **Focusing on the web site at the expense of operational structures**. It can be too easy to focus on the more intriguing and interesting front-end systems for interacting with customers. There is still a need to put in place operational structures to deal with logistics and customer service, for example. The complex problems of moving vast numbers of goods to potentially huge numbers of end destinations, or the control and copyright protection of digital information, cannot be ignored. Likewise it is easy to underestimate the high demand for person-to-person interaction to support Internet services as individuals wish to make personal contact with the organisation – whilst new users may need help and reassurance, both old and new users will need to be able to voice and have heard their complaints.

● **Not managing service recovery**. Internet-based services must develop new strategies for managing customer complaints. As a general principle, service recovery is usually seen to be more effective when there is genuine contact between service provider and customer, often with named people involved from the service organisation. Service organisations must work hard to create that personalisation as a feature of their service recovery mechanisms.

9.6 THE SERVICESCAPE

Services are usually delivered in a physical and/or informational environment. The physical environment of a hospital comprises the car parks, the buildings, the décor and the arrangement of seats in a waiting-room, for example. An informational environment may include the accessibility of an organisation's web site, its speed of downloading, its appearance and user-friendliness, for example. In service operations customers often have direct access to an organisation's operation, the physical operation or its systems and processes, and so the part they do see has to represent and reflect the whole organisation, its culture, concept and strategy.

Bitner (1992) coined the term 'servicescapes' to describe the physical surroundings of the service delivery system. We use it here to include both the physical and informational environment in which a service is both created and delivered – the environment for both staff (back office and front office) and customers. The servicescape is the visible physical and/or informational architecture that provides the visible clues and cues to customers, internal and external, about the organisation, its operation and services.

The servicescape is the landscape or backdrop that gives context to a service and is often an integral part of the service. Beside the obvious points of ensuring that the service stage provides an appropriate contact for the service and that it gives appropriate behavioural clues to staff and customers that service designers may easily overlook, the servicescape can:

- help create and support the service concept
- influence the behaviour of customers
- influence employees.

9.6.1 Creating and supporting the concept

When operations managers buy or build their facilities, they need to consider more than the size, type, number and location of those facilities but also their impact on the customer and the service concept. Hard chairs without arms, set out in clinical rows in a waiting-room, provide clues about the nature of the service, whereas clusters of armchairs with coffee tables and magazines imply a quite different style of service. The choice of facilities should therefore be in tune with the service concept. That is not to say that all chairs, for example, should be comfortable. Those in fast-food restaurants may be designed to provide adequate support and comfort for leaning forward and eating but less comfortable for leaning back and relaxing at the end of a meal.

The location of a building, its size, structure and décor will provide very tangible clues about the nature of that service and the reputation and image of the organisation. Customers are adept at decoding the emotional and symbolic importance of environmental clues (Gabriel and Lang 1995). The type of office furniture and the nature of décor in the office of an accountant, engineer, public servant or charity, will give particular clues about their trustworthiness, success, profligacy and the cost of the service.

The hard or soft architecture and other environmental clues, such as dress, furniture and décor, are an important means by which organisations can establish or reinforce their desired image and service concept. The distinctive uniforms of Singapore Airlines, the classic styles of Caesar's Palace or Bellagio's in Las Vegas, the memorabilia of Hard Rock cafés, all seek to create a particular image and in many cases differentiate themselves from the competition.

The Central Samui Hotel, featured in Chapter 4, is a 'new colonial' style hotel, combining space, elegance and individual attention, to create and support its particular concept. The vast Opryland Hotel in Nashville, Tennessee, provides a modern setting with indoor cascades, pools, a canal and themed restaurants to deliver a high-quality American experience. The Holiday Inn Express hotels (Chapter 2), with their no-frills but courteous service, support their 'value for money' concept.

Internet service providers and Internet search engines too have an opportunity through their visual architecture to support their service concepts as major gateways into Internet services or means of finding web pages, email addresses or browsers.

9.6.2 Influencing customer behaviour

Customer behaviour can be, to some extent, determined by the servicescape, its ambience, lighting, décor or indeed the music (see, for example, Milliman 1982). A warm bar may encourage customers to drink more (or leave), the tempo of background music in a shop can influence the pace of shopping and the amount spent by customers. In Box 9.4 we can see how one Austrian food retailer has used the 'aesthetic atmospherics' not only to create a particular service but to encourage shoppers to part with their money.

Box 9.4 M-Preis WarenvertriebsGmbH

Guenther Botschen and David Crowther, Aston Business School, Birmingham, UK

The M-Preis WarenvertriebsGmbH (M-Price Goods Distribution Ltd) is a chain of about 100 food stores operated by several generations of a Tyrolean family in the western part of Austria. Upon taking over the business in 1933, Theresa Moelk, a plump businesswoman from Innsbruck, greeted 'all Tyrolean housewives' and promised to 'try to work for their benefit'. Anton and Hansjoerg Moelk, who run the family-owned company today, also think ahead of their customers' needs. Over the years they have developed a kind of 'Aesthetic Vision and Mission' based on their observations that grocery stores are visited more often than other public places so they should look inviting. At the same time supermarkets are not like churches or museums; they have to be built quickly, be easily adapted to other purposes, and the beauty of exterior design elements and interior decoration must not impair their functionality.

With this picture in mind Anton and Hansjoerg started to individualise the design of existing and new M-Preis supermarkets in collaboration with various architects. The common theme comprised the core elements of freshness, clarity, lightness and modernity. The new buildings created a modern and light feel by combining industrially fabricated elements, such as galvanised steel structures and aluminium glazing systems, juxtaposed with less finely finished, and hence more tactile, timber products and fair-faced concrete. M-Preis's logo, a white M on a deep red background in cubic form, was integrated in multiple facets into every new or renovated site. The freshness theme began at the entrance with the smell of freshly baked bread presented in glass cabinets. Specially shaped fruit and vegetable presentation areas were developed for each new shop and new 'deli-islands' for cheese, fish and meat products were placed around the centre of the shop where specially trained personnel, dressed in Italian designer clothes, serve the customers. In this way each store offers its unique qualities while following a common theme. In an analogy to nature, M-Preis can be compared with a birch tree where the trunk and branches determine the core requirements of a retail outlet and the leaves represent the individual architecture of each site. Each leaf has its unique and somewhat different structure and style in comparison to the others but at the same time each leaf is clearly recognised as belonging to a birch tree. By proceeding along this exterior and interior architectural route the Tyrolean retailer continuously differentiates itself from the highly standardised monotonic presentation of the main competitors in this region. M-Preis's 'aesthetic adventure' recently inspired the owners to further emphasise aesthetics within interior decoration and presentation.

M-Preis's understanding and implementation of aesthetic atmospherics in food retailing has contributed to strong customer attraction and appreciation. The results of a recently published retailing study (A.C. Nielson, *Tiroler Tageszeitung*, 223, 25/26/27 September 1999) found that M-Preis was rated the most sympathetic retailer by 41 per cent of customers, compared with 26 per cent and 16 per cent for its two main competitors. M-Preis supermarkets are visited several times per week by 47 per cent of its customers, and 34 per cent spend more money in these shops, compared to 22 per cent and 10 per cent for its main competitors.

A number of studies have addressed the issue of environmental design effects upon psychological and behavioural responses of consumers in shopping centres, retail outlets and other service encounters (see, for example, Botschen *et al.* 1999; Kaplan 1987; Kotler 1973). Botschen *et al.* (1999), for example, in a study of 600 customers in M-Preis and a similar control store, found that customers perceived M-Preis products to be fresher and their customers purchased significantly more products than at the other store.

The servicescape also influences the nature of the interaction between customers and between customers and employees (Bitner 1992). Seating arrangements or the amount of background noise, for example, may encourage or discourage conversation and/or interaction.

The existence of queues, whether a physical queue or a queue on a telephone, for example, provides physical or informational evidence which influences customers' behaviour. The existence of a queue encourages customers to modify their behaviour: they will wait in turn, physically position themselves relative to others waiting, and, up to a point, be prepared to accommodate a delay in service.

A queue, like other environmental clues such as temperature and lighting, for example, may also generate 'approach' or 'avoidance' behaviour (Mehrabian and Russell 1974). Mehrabian and Russell suggested that individuals react to environments with two general and opposite forms of behaviour – they are either attracted to it or repulsed by it. For some people a queue to enter a restaurant, for example, may signal 'a place to be seen' or a 'popular destination worth trying', whereas to others it may represent 'crowded and trendy' and may act as a de-selection device.

The design of equipment or information interfaces will also have an effect on customers' behaviour, in particular their ability to interact with and obtain service from remote service providers such as organisations using the Internet, remote cash machines or ticketing machines, for example. Fast, easy and user-friendly interfaces will lead to approach behaviour whereas slow and difficult ones may well lead to avoidance.

9.6.3 Influencing staff

Just as the physical and informational aspects of a service environment influence customers, so they also influence employees. It has been suggested that an appropriate environment results in approach rather than avoidance behaviour by employees and as a result they are more committed to the organisation, stay longer, and are more able to carry out their roles effectively (Bitner 1992).

In Box 9.5 we can see how the design of a new headquarters for British Airways created an informal working environment and encouraged communication between staff.

Box 9.5 British Airways, Waterside

In 1998 British Airways opened its new head office, Waterside. The aim of the new building was not only to reduce the high costs of managing 14 offices scattered around Heathrow airport and in the centre of London but also to encourage teamwork and open communication between its employees.

The idea was to create a 'village' atmosphere. A central enclosed 'Street' links all the buildings and makes each feel part a whole. The informal atmosphere is created by trees and fountains, coffee shops and restaurants surrounded by glass-walled offices, walkways and lifts. There are no direct lifts linking the underground car park with offices, forcing employees to use the Street and meet each other. Not only is this a place for managers and administrators but it also brings together cabin crew and customer service staff by combining an office block with training rooms (including a mock-up of a Boeing 747), together with staff facilities such as video dispensers, fitness rooms and hairdressers, for example. To further facilitate communication Waterside's offices are open plan with many small 'club' areas where employees can work informally in lounge areas.

'As a result the atmosphere is informal and transparent,' explained BA's Chief Executive. 'People can see and meet others who work in different departments. In the old building it was different. People worked in their own rooms and had their own space. If you went to visit them it was like going onto someone else's territory. The way we operate here is not only more transparent it is more efficient'.

(*The Times*, Monday 20 July 1998).

The physical or informational architecture, the servicescape, needs to be carefully aligned to the organisation's service concept and can influence not only the behaviour of customers but the behaviour and attitude of employees.

9.7 INTEGRATING STRUCTURE, TECHNOLOGY AND INFORMATION

This section describes an approach to understanding how the various operational resources may be configured or re-configured to deliver service. Armistead and Clark (1993) proposed that the development of a Resource Activity Map of the service organisation provides an opportunity to take an overview of where resources are currently deployed in order to identify opportunities for investment either to reduce cost or to enhance the service offering. We have adapted this approach in order to identify the contribution of structures, technology and information. To these we have added the other operational resources of people and materials. The combination of these resources builds to create the servicescape.

It is important to note that this technique may be used to review a self-contained activity within one service organisation or may look at the key elements of a supply chain. The example below of a domestic appliance retailer includes the design and manufacturing activities of a key supplier.

The process of developing the Resource Activity Map follows these stages:

- Identify the main stages in service delivery.
- Allocate the activities under each major heading to the five resource categories.
- Identify the major cost drivers and places where the organisation 'adds value' for customers. Question whether the cost/value relationship is satisfactory.
- Identify links between resources: those links which are working well, those which could be developed further, and those which currently do not exist.
- Search for opportunities to improve the effectiveness of the total map, recognising that an increase in cost in one area might reduce overall cost.

Figure 9.4 shows an outline Resource Activity Map for the service and support activities of a retailer of domestic appliances. The map identifies the major resources employed by both the retailer and its principal supplier. It identifies the strong links (those which are working well), the missing links which may represent opportunities for improvement, and missing resources which are under consideration for investment.

Inspection of Figure 9.4 identifies a number of issues to be resolved by the company:

- There is a strong link between service history and manufacturing schedules. Good communications and congruence of planning approaches between the service planners and the supplier's production planning activity mean that there is high availability of spare parts, critical to maintaining fast response times and high first-time fix rates.
- There is a missing link between service engineers and product designers. Experience of engineers in the field is not being captured to feed back for design improvements. Investment in handheld terminals for engineers could perform a number of roles including the facility to pass customer feedback to both the retailer's sales staff and the supplier's designers.
- Although customers can use the service telephone call centre, it has been identified that there are a number of potential advantages to creating a company web site. This would facilitate management of customer support requests, it would provide data for customer management, as well as opening another channel for customer feedback for design. Although this retailer does not yet have an on-line sales operation, the possibility is under serious consideration.

We have shown only a few of the possible links within this particular Resource Activity Map. Many more exist, and the map can be used as a brainstorming tool for a service development team to identify possible projects to investigate. It is worth asking two key questions in relation to a Resource Activity Map:

- Is it possible to save cost for the map as a whole by investing in resource in one area? In Figure 9.4, investment in information to track trends in product failure

Fig 9.4

Service and support Resource Activity Map for domestic appliance retailer

	Supplier		Retailer			
	Design	Manufacture	Sales	Service	Logistics	Customer support
People	• Designers	• Production workers	• Sales staff	• Engineers		• Engineers • Support staff
Information		• Schedules • Quality system	• Customer database	• Service history • Call track system	• Schedules	• Support diagnostics
Materials		• Work-in-progress		• Spares	• Product • Spares	
Structure		• Factory	• Stores	• Vans • Call centre	• Warehouse • Lorries	
Technology	• CAD system	• Machines • Computers		• Call monitor • *Terminals*		• *Web site*

Strong links ——   Missing links ----   Missing resource ⟨ ⟩

enabled manufacturing to schedule spares into their master schedule in order to reduce inventory levels and increase service levels.

- Would investment create added value, resulting in increased competitive advantage? Again in Figure 9.4, the web site will not be justified on cost saving, although there are possible savings to be made. It will be justified on the basis of providing better access for the customer to obtain service and support.

Finally, the Resource Activity Map identifies the various contributions to the servicescape. The principal ingredients of the servicescape for the organisation in Figure 9.4 before investment are as follows:

- the competence and appearance of service engineers
- the age and condition of service engineers' vans
- the ease of access to the service call centre
- helpfulness of customer support staff
- the extent to which information systems facilitate service engineer scheduling (can appointments be made 'on-line' with the customer?)
- the extent to which information systems capture the expertise of the organisation in order to deal with customer support requests.

Given the investment suggested above, the servicescape would be enhanced in the following ways:

- the ability for the service engineer to communicate in a professional manner with the organisation through a handheld terminal. This would be particularly useful in dealing with customer complaints
- the ease of access to the organisation through the web site to gain information
- response to customer questions through the web site
- the use of the web site for marketing communication.

This process is, like strategy development, an iterative procedure. It is important to be honest in identifying what is and what is not working well in order to find ways of improving the total Resource Activity Map. This is particularly valuable when considering the contribution of the whole supply chain.

9.8 SUMMARY

Structure versus infrastructure

- Structure comprises the physical and informational aspects of an operation which define its overall shape and architecture and impose limits within which it has to work.
- Infrastructure concerns the way the structure is used, its organisation and decisions about planning control and improvement, for example.

Physical networks

- The key structural decisions associated with an organisation's physical networks include the location, capacity, capability and its resilience or flexibility.

Virtual networks

- The key structural decisions associated with an organisation's virtual networks are the nature of the structure, its capacity, capability and resilience or flexibility.

Technology and information flows

- Electronic commerce is challenging and changing traditional business structures.
- The Internet provides 24-hour access for customers, opens up global opportunities and competition, can help build brands, provides control to customers, improves availability of information and helps form service alliances.
- The implications for operations management include how the web can be used to add value, the changing nature of customer relationships, changing quality factors, and the importance of web site design.

The servicescape

- The servicescape is the physical and informational environment in which a service is both created and delivered; it is the environment for both staff (back office and front office) and customers.
- The servicescape is the visible physical or informational architecture that provides the visible clues and cues to customers, internal and external, about the organisation, its operation and services.
- The servicescape can help create and support the service concept, influence the behaviour of customers, and influence employees.

Integrating structure, technology and information

- The Resource Activity Map can be used to assess the overall configuration of the operation's structure, technology and information together with its people and materials.

9.9 DISCUSSION QUESTIONS

1. Describe the structure and infrastructure of an organisation of your choice and explain the relationships between the two.

2. Assess the physical and virtual networks of the university/college in terms of its location, capacity, capability and flexibility.

3. Select an e-service provider and assess its web site and service.

4. Evaluate the servicescape of a retailer of your own choice.

9.10 QUESTIONS FOR MANAGERS

1. Evaluate how well structural and infrastructural decisions are co-ordinated.

2. What are the key problems you face in managing your networks and how are they managed?

3. What is, or could be, the impact of e-service on your operations?

4. Assess the impact of your servicescape on employees and customers.

5. Apply the Resource Activity Map and identify any missing links and resources.

9.11 SUGGESTIONS FOR FURTHER READING

Bitner M.J., 'Servicescapes: The impact of physical surroundings on customers and employees', *Journal of Marketing*, vol. 56, April 1992, pp. 57–71.

Voss C., *Trusting the Internet: Developing an eservice strategy*, Institute of Customer Service, Colchester, 2000.

9.12 REFERENCES

Armistead C.G. and Clark G.R., 'Resource Activity Mapping: The value chain in service operations strategy', *Service Industries Journal*, vol. 13, no. 4, 1993, pp. 221–239.

Berry L.L., *On Great Service*, The Free Press, New York, 1995.

Bitner M.J., 'Servicescapes: The impact of physical surroundings on customers and employees', *Journal of Marketing*, vol. 56, April 1992, pp. 57–71.

Botschen M., Koll O. and Rigger W., 'The Attraction of Aesthetic Atmospherics', in Hildebrandt L. and Plinke W. (eds), *Marketing and Competition in the Information Age*, Proceedings of the 28th Annual Conference of the European Marketing Academy, Berlin, 1999, CD-ROM.

Gabriel Y. and Lang T., *The Unmanageable Consumer*, Sage Publications, London, 1995.

Hayes R.H. and Wheelwright S.C., *Restoring our Competitive Edge*, Wiley, New York, 1984.

Kaplan S., 'Aesthetics, Affect, and Cognition', Environment and Behavior, vol. 19, January 1987, pp. 3–32.

Kotler P., 'Atmospherics as a Marketing Tool', *Journal of Retailing*, vol. 49, no. 4, 1973, pp. 48–64.

Mehrabian A. and Russell J.A., *An Approach to Environmental Psychology*, Massachusetts Institute of Technology, Cambridge, Mass., 1974.

Milliman R., 'Using Background Music to Affect the Behaviour of Supermarket Shoppers', *Journal of Marketing*, vol. 46, Summer 1982, pp. 86–91.

Slack N., 'Operations Activities', in Slack N. (ed.), *Encyclopedic Dictionary of Operations Management*, Blackwell, Oxford, 1997, pp. 121–2.

Slack N., Chambers S., Harland C., Harrison A. and Johnston R., *Operations Management*, 2nd edition, Pitman, London, 1998.

Voss C., *Trusting the Internet: Developing an eservice strategy*, Institute of Customer Service, Colchester, 2000.

CASE EXERCISE

The North Island Hospital

This case was co-written by Dr Elaine Palmer, University of Auckland, Auckland, New Zealand

Rod Dowling is the Chief Executive of the North Island Hospital (NIH) in New Zealand. His clinical directors had just submitted a report for some new laser technology which treats kidney stones. This would require a capital outlay of NZ$1,500,000, which would only be needed two and a half hours per week. Whilst this seemed to make little financial sense, the medical case was compelling.

Lithotripsy

Lithotripsy is the diagnosis and treatment of kidney stones. The traditional treatment involves radiography to locate precisely the stone or stones in the patient's kidney and then surgical removal under a full anaesthetic. Both of these treatments are not without risk and require four to eight days' post-operative recovery. However, these operations can be carried out routinely using the existing theatres, urologists, nursing staff and equipment.

The new laser treatment represents a significant advance on previous treatment. It is non-invasive and in essence 'explodes' the kidney stones through precisely directed laser beams. The resultant particles are then small enough for the patient to pass with their urine. The procedure does not require any anaesthetic. After treatment patients need to be observed for an hour or so in a pre-operative area and then spend three hours in a day unit where they are encouraged to drink quantities of water. Patients can go home the same day. The specialist laser equipment needs to be operated by a technician.

The financial case

Current numbers of patients requiring treatment for kidney stones at the NIH are running at just less than 100 per year. The hospital charges its patients for treatment as per Table 1, with the average costs for removal of kidney stones being around NZ$8,500 (£2,600). (The theatre charge is a standard charge which covers the use of the facilities and equipment depreciated over three years.)

Table 1 Charges to patients for traditional treatment

Treatment:	
radiography services	15 mins @ $500/hr
use of operating theatre	60 mins @ $1000/hr
anaesthetist	60 mins @ $900/hr
urologist	60 mins @ $1100/hr
theatre nursing	90 mins @ $100/hr
Post-op care	6 days @ $900/day

Table 2 Charges to patients for laser treatment

Treatment:	
laser technician	60 mins @ $500/hr
use of operating theatre	60 mins @ $1000/hr
theatre nursing	90 mins @ $100/hr
Post-op care	4 hours @ $900/day

Although the new laser equipment is compact, theatre space is at a premium at NIH and Rod is already under pressure to build a new theatre (at an estimated cost of NZ$500,000). Rod is aware that the four other hospitals on the Island are using the traditional treatment for kidney stones. (The five hospitals lie around the perimeter of the Island at about 200-mile intervals.) Rod starts to wonder if he could provide laser treatment to all patients on the North Island – maybe he could zap patients by Internet or use 'star wars' technology?

Questions

1 *Assess the advantages and disadvantages of investing in the new technology for the hospital and its patients.*

2 *What advice would you give Rod?*

Part 4

PERFORMANCE MANAGEMENT

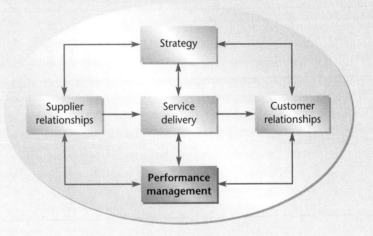

10

Performance Measurement

INTRODUCTION

Some organisations have turned performance measurement into a cottage industry. They have created measures and systems that require extensive management time and effort but provide little benefit in terms of controlling or improving their performance. This chapter provides some simple but powerful tools and frameworks, that have been used to great effect in many service organisations, to assess and develop performance measures and systems that help create action and drive organisational improvement.

The objectives of the chapter are:

- to identify the purpose of performance measurement and ensure it is being met
- to encourage the use of a balance, or mix, of measures in measuring performance
- to investigate the relationships between the various types of measures
- to identify different types of targets and their link to improvement and rewards
- to discuss benchmarking and how it can be undertaken.

The art of performance measurement has moved apace recently. Indeed, we would suggest that it is becoming more of a science as managers – in particular operations managers – try to understand the effect of their decisions. For example, before pulling one lever they need to know, with some degree of certainty, how it will affect not only their operation, but also their customers, their staff and indeed the financial state of the organisation. Although we still have a long way to go, some organisations are starting to get to grips with these linkages and also ensuring that the information they have on performance measurement is not just collected for its own sake but leads to appropriate action.

10.2 PURPOSE OF PERFORMANCE MEASUREMENT

Performance measurement is costly. Few organisations have calculated just how much time and energy they spend on measuring their performance. Even fewer have calculated if all their systems, procedures and person-hours spent on performance measurement provide them with value for money.

Two useful tests of a performance measure are, firstly, what is its purpose and, secondly, what systems are in place to support or achieve that purpose.

10.2.1 Purpose

There are four main purposes or reasons to take measurement: communication, motivation, control and improvement.

Communication

By measuring something the organisation is saying that it is important; conversely, by measuring everything they are implying that nothing is important! A measure therefore informs employees as to what the organisation requires them to strive for and indeed what they as an individual or a department may be accountable for. It is also an important means of communicating and implementing strategy (see Chapter 11). By measuring speed of response in answering telephone calls, for example, an organisation is saying this is important and it is implied that employees are expected to strive to meet targets or improve the speed of answering.

Motivation

As such the measure, or set of measures, used by an organisation creates a particular mind-set which influences employees' behaviour. If speed of response is measured but not the quality of the interaction, employees may find themselves, albeit subconsciously, compromising quality for speed. It is important therefore to have the right mix or balance of measures (see section 10.3 below) and also a set that supports the strategic intentions of the organisation (see Chapter 11).

Control

One key purpose of performance measurement is to provide feedback so that action can be taken to keep a process in control. This requires a complete control loop, with measures, targets, a means of checking deviation against, feedback mechanisms and means to take appropriate action if the process is not meeting the target. This may be used to ensure consistent performance not only within an organisation but also across organisations, such as government health and safety regulations or discrimination legislation.

Improvement

Performance measures can provide a powerful means of driving improvement. Often simply by communicating a measure, improvements can be obtained. By linking them with rewards (such as bonuses) and/or punishments (such as no job), measurement can motivate individuals to improve performance – assuming they have control over that which is being measured! Information about what pushes the process on or off target can also help individuals and organisations learn how to manage better the process involved.

Systems to achieve the purpose

Having established the purpose for any measure, the acid test then is to check that there are systems or procedures in place to support the achievement of that purpose. We often find that although a manager purports that a certain measure is there to help improve the performance of the organisation, for example, there is only a flimsy and indeed sometimes non-existent process in place to drive improvements. Similarly for the purposes of control, the vital part of the control loop that is frequently missing is action to put the process back on target.

Box 10.1 Motor Finance Company

Motor Finance Company (MFC) is a subsidiary of a major bank that provides car loans. MFC deals directly with car dealers rather than the public so that when a dealer is faced with a customer buying a car, they are able to arrange a loan. The dealer will take down the purchaser's details and then ring MFC direct who will give them an immediate decision on a loan. The dealer is paid a commission by MFC.

Sean Williams is the senior manager leading their performance measurement evaluation team. 'The team is currently evaluating seven key performance measures that form part of our quality index,' he explained. 'We have two key measures for controlling the operation, Same Day Funding (whether the loan is agreed on the day it was requested) and Proposal Turnaround Time (how long it takes us to generate the paperwork for an agreed proposal). The volumes of loan requests we receive on a daily basis, all of which are by telephone, are very variable and so we plot Turnaround Time on an hourly basis. We then use statistical process control (SPC) to help identify trends and the effect of any process changes. This helps us avoid any unnecessary reaction to normal variation within the process. Same Day Funding is essential to help us ascertain if targets are being met. The measures are known for each team and area and collated into a departmental measure. Feedback is provided on a daily basis to team leaders and team members. Meeting targets is linked to the bonus scheme.

'We have five measures that are used to try to improve our performance: Telephone Response Times, Calls Not Answered, Commission Amendments, Monies Collected and Recruitment Lag Time. Telephone Response Times are collected daily by the department though not broken down by area or teams. This helps us identify the speed of service. There are no targets used for this measure, as it is simply needed to raise awareness. Two managers have access to this data. The same is true for Calls Not Answered though we are thinking about linking it to bonus payments.

'Commission Amendments can exist for many different reasons, so at a high level this gives us a useful overview of the whole commission process, though in fairness there is little we can do to change things. We have been measuring Monies Collected recently and it has certainly raised awareness in the Collections Department. In the past we just measured how many cases each person was dealing with. Monies Collected seems to be much more useful. Whilst there is no systematic use of Recruitment Lag Time to improve the process, just the communication of this measure has helped people understand how we are doing. I reckon this has resulted in vast improvements.

'Although this is early stages, we have put considerable effort into the development of the individual measures that are believed to be robust and informative. On reflection it seems that some are used systematically whereas others are merely reported; maybe we need to give more attention to the purposes of measures and the systems to support them.'

Question

1 *How well do you think the measures used by MFC meet their desired purposes?*

This illustration is based on a real organisation, although all names and places have been changed.

Displaying performance measures

One important way of using measures to achieve their purpose is to have a means of displaying the measure. Whilst most managers recognise that displaying only a small number of measures is helpful, the way in which data is provided can be a key means of helping achieve its purpose.

Figure 10.1 (developed by Carole Driver, Plymouth Business School, and based on material by Neely 1998) shows a display for a single (important) performance measure which includes four quadrants. Rather than simply showing the figure (in this case percentage errors) for this month (February), the chart (top left) provides a clear view of the trend and the associated target, thus allowing changes over time to be seen. The top right quadrant provides an analysis of February's data to identify the most frequent source of errors. As a result of the analysis, the bottom left quadrant reports on the actions to be taken to try to deal with the most common errors, who will be responsible for taking the action and by when they should report. The final quadrant provides an implementation record which checks the impact of previous action plans: who was supposed to do what, by when, and the effect that it had.

We would suggest that performance measurement reports should include only a small number of key measures and that for each measure there should be a display of:

- trends over time
- performance against target
- supporting data and analysis
- identification of causes/problems
- action to be taken, by whom and by when
- an assessment of action taken.

10.3 A BALANCE OF MEASURES

Just as companies compete on a wide range of dimensions, so organisations need to evaluate their performance on a range of measures, not purely financial or indeed operational. Section 10.4 deals with how organisations can understand the links between these various measures; this section considers the mix of measures available and the need to strike a balance.

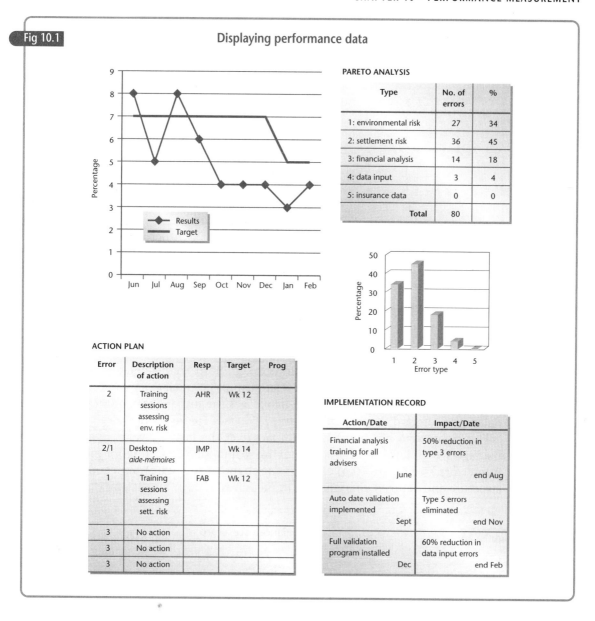

Fig 10.1 Displaying performance data

The 'traditional' concerns for performance measures are represented in Figure 10.2. Senior managers tend to be most concerned about financial (F) performance measures – share price, return on capital employed, costs and profits. At an operations level the concern is perhaps for operational issues and measures (O) such as speed, productivity, equipment utilisation and staff absenteeism. The activities and indeed language of these two groups, supported by the measures they use, create a chasm of understanding that middle managers have traditionally tried to bridge (Johnston and Fitzgerald 1999). In the middle of the organisation these managers

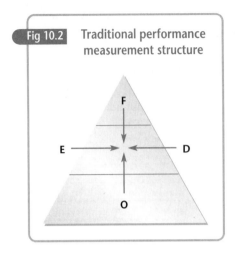

Fig 10.2 Traditional performance measurement structure

try to reconcile operations measures from below with financial needs from above – for example, the requirement to 'increase revenue' or 'decrease costs' is parried by the statement 'but we are already at full capacity'. Additional pressures arise from external data and measures (E) such as market share figures, customers lost, and customer satisfaction data, and from the development (D) needs of an organisation to learn, change and develop through, for example, training, research, communication, and problem identification and problem solving.

These often conflicting pressures and performance measures have been recognised and frameworks developed to help managers cope. The results–determinants framework (Fitzgerald *et al.* 1991) identifies that these pressures are of two different types, the determinants and the results. There is little use in driving an organisation only by knowing what the results (Financial and External data) are because there is no means of knowing what is determining those results. Conversely, driving an organisation by determinants alone (Operational and Development data) gives no understanding of the results of actions taken. Both are needed at all levels in an organisation to help understand the relationships between action and results.

The best-known framework that encourages the use of a mix of measures is the Balanced Scorecard (Kaplan and Norton 1992) (see Figure 10.3).

This framework has had a huge impact over the last few years in encouraging managers at all levels to invest in moving to a more balanced set of measures. The framework (see Figure 10.4) changes the shape of the performance measurement structure and exposes all managers to measures of both results and determinants.

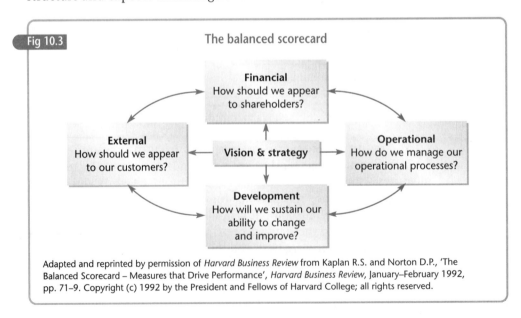

Fig 10.3 The balanced scorecard

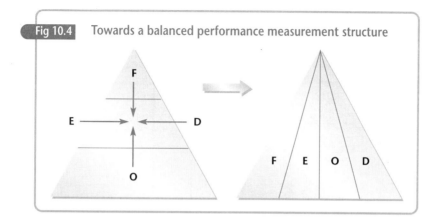

Fig 10.4   Towards a balanced performance measurement structure

This is the first stage in starting to understand the links between them (see section 10.4) and helps create a structure of performance measurement that links strategy with operations.

Recent research (by Brignall *et al.* 1999) into the performance measures used in service operations in the UK found that there was a reasonable balance, overall, in the mix of measures used (see Figure 10.5).

The key measures used by operations managers to control and assess their service processes were primarily internal operational measures, such as productivity, through-put times and volumes. Many financial measures were also used, for example costs and revenues. Customer-based measures such as satisfaction and market share were also in evidence. However. there was only limited evidence of the use of the fourth Balanced Scorecard measurement 'perspective', development, learning and growth.

This overall picture, however, disguises the true state of affairs, as can be seen in Figure 10.6. Most operations managers were using only two types of measures (pre-dominantly financial and internal measures). Only 15 per cent used three measures and 7 per cent used all four types.

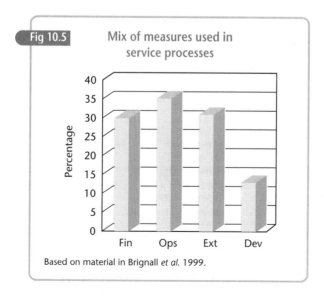

Fig 10.5   Mix of measures used in service processes

Based on material in Brignall *et al.* 1999.

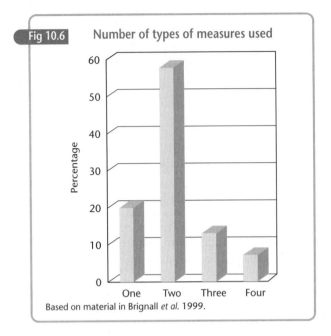

Fig 10.6 Number of types of measures used

60
50
40
30
20
10
0
Percentage
One
Two
Three
Four

Based on material in Brignall *et al.* 1999.

10.3.1 Performance measures for service operations managers

Operations managers need to ensure that they have a mix or balance of measures to communicate their intentions, motivate their workforce, control and improve their processes. Figure 10.7 provides a selection of measures that might be used, or developed for use, by service operations managers.

Fig 10.7 Measures for service operations managers

Financial
total costs
cost per customer
labour costs
processing costs
total revenue
revenue per customer
operating profit
profit per customer
External
market share
customer satisfaction
customer loyalty
repurchase intentions
retention rates
new customers
no. of complaints
type of complaints
Operational
equipment or staff availablility
waiting times
throughput times
no. of customers by type
no. of staff by process
on-time delivery
facility utilisation
no. of faults
Development
no. of suggestions
no. of improvements
employees involved in improvement teams
staff satisfaction
staff turnover
no. of service innovations

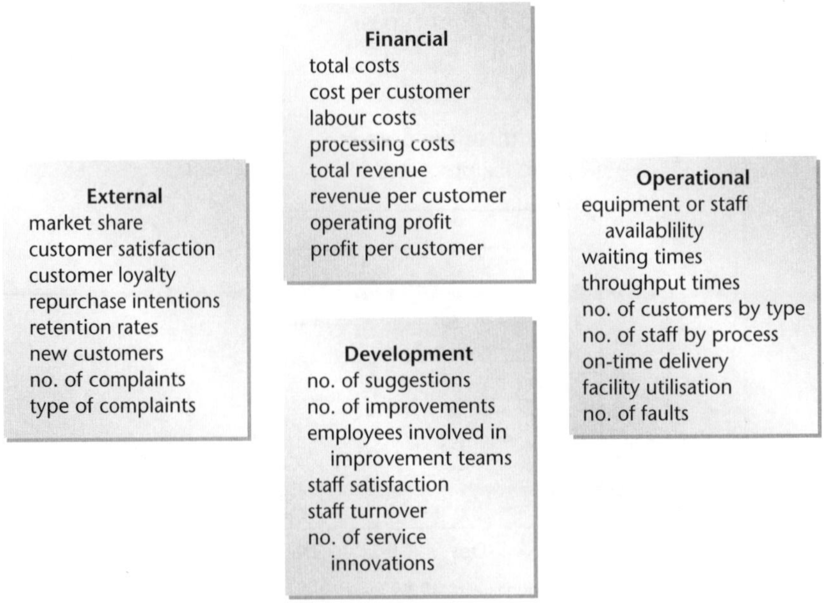

Customer-based measures

External data are important to allow operations managers to know how effective their actions are, yet often the measures they use to assess their processes miss out on a customer perspective. An interesting question to ask is: looking at the set of measures used by an operation, would its customers measure its performance in the same way? Measuring what is important to customers can easily be overlooked by organisations. Whereas they may well measure customer satisfaction, they may ignore, or overlook, measures of performance that are important to their customers and thus concentrate on the more comfortable and familiar operations measure of performance. Jan Carlzon, for example, when he was chief executive of SAS, noted that their cargo operations were measuring the wrong things. 'We had caught ourselves in one of the most basic mistakes a service-oriented business can make [their cargo customers wanted prompt and precise cargo delivery]… yet we were measuring volume and whether the paperwork and packages got separated en route. In fact, a shipment could arrive four days later than promised *without* being recorded as delayed' (Carlzon 1987).

Several tools that can be used to help identify, and then measure, what is important to customers were provided in Chapter 3.

10.4 INTERLINKING

Having got a mix of measures in place, some organisations are now starting to try to understand the relationship between the various measures (see Figure 10.8) so that they can improve their decision-making. This has been called 'interlinking' (Collier 1994).

By using knowledge about the relationships between operational, financial, external and development performance measures, organisations can become systematically smarter. Managers will begin to understand, with greater certainty, the likely effect of making resource decisions, which helps them set appropriate targets and better support the strategic intentions of the organisation. Indeed, we believe that tomorrow's leading-edge organisations will be those that understand and exploit these relationships.

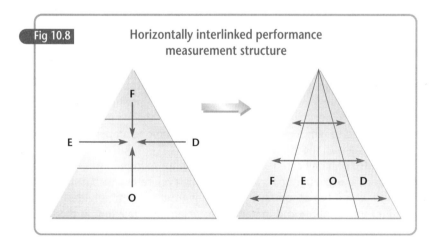

Fig 10.8 Horizontally interlinked performance measurement structure

In Box 10.2, Sean Guilliam, the head of Lombard Direct's call centre, explains how his operation is taking the first steps towards understanding the relationships between operational, external, developmental and financial measures.

Box 10.2 Lombard Direct

Lombard Direct must have one of the best-known telephone numbers in the UK, 0800 2 15000, which is based on their slogan 'loans from 800 to 15,000 pounds'. Lombard Direct is a subsidiary of Lombard Bank, part of the National Westminster Bank group. Unsecured loans over the telephone constitute about 90 per cent of the company's business, other products including insurance on loans, house, contents and motor insurance, savings and a credit card.

The main call centre, in Rotherham, South Yorkshire, is a 24-hour operation that operates every day of the year. The centre handles over two million calls a year. Monday is a typically busy day and around six to seven thousand would be received. The call centre has around 200 seats (desks for the customer advisers, CAs) and employs around 250 full-time equivalent staff, with a large contingent of part-timers. Callers are asked a number of questions to rate their creditworthiness and are allocated into a band. This risk assessment together with the size of the borrowing requested determines the rate of interest to be charged.

Sean Guilliam is the head of the call centre and he judges the performance of its CAs on six key performance measures. 'The measures we use are the following:

- Telephone availability – the time an individual is available to take calls.
- Insurance sales – because we want to encourage the people who take out loans with us to take out our insurance cover on the loans.
- Media and product code accuracy – this is very important for our marketing people to know where the customers heard of us. However, our systems are a bit lacking in this area and sometimes the CAs have difficulty finding the right code, there are so many!
- Call conversion – where we calculate the number of successful loans sold compared to the number of calls taken.
- CATS, which is procedural accuracy, such as giving the right advice and adhering to data protection requirements.
- Call analysis – an assessment of the interactions with a customer and compliance with the correct procedure.

'We have four "spot" levels and CAs are reviewed every three months. Each level has a set of criteria based on the six key measures. If someone attains a higher level for two assessments they go up one spot level; if they perform less well over three periods they will go down. Each level is worth about an extra £1 per hour so it is quite significant. Also they need to get to Level 2 before we will offer them a permanent contract, though I think we need to remove this barrier and put everyone on permanent from the start to bring us in line with the industry.'

Sean adds, 'At a call centre level I also monitor loan volumes, utilisation, talk time, service levels and abandon rates. Service level refers to the percentage of calls answered within ten seconds. Utilisation is total talk time divided by total pay time (including training time and maternity, for example). Talk time is the time each operator spends talking to customers. When you compare this to telephone availability you have to be careful. Yes, you want high productivity, i.e. lots of talk time when available, but too much talk time could indicate either we need more staff because operators could be busy and we could be losing calls, or an individual spends too much time talking to customers. Similarly, when I compare loan conversions and insurance sales, although we want a good ratio of insurance sales to loans, too high a ratio might mean that staff could be doing too hard a sell. We don't want customers put off from using us again. The problem is in balancing flexibility with control! Especially when a 1 per cent increase in insurance sales can contribute a quarter of a million to the bottom line.

'One of the big problems in manpower scheduling is that call volumes are partly dependent upon marketing spend. And, just to make things interesting, volumes are also affected, as you might expect, by weather, holidays and sporting events, for example. We use the volume expectations from marketing spend to create a volume forecast, we then pro-rata this to forecast the volumes of calls we expect individuals to be dealing with: this determines the number of CAs I need and therefore the costs of the operation. I also monitor "people measures" such as attrition, absenteeism and staff morale. It can be all too easy to trade off volumes for morale. We have a great atmosphere here and morale is very high.

'To help my planning we have created a correlation model which has looked at the relationships between volumes, utilisation, service levels, abandon rates, costs and "people measures". I can see the effect of a change in volume on all my key statistics. I want to get high utilisation, high service levels, low abandon rates, low costs and high morale. When we look at our performance data we are now trying to look across the rows and not up and down. It's a new development but it's about how things link together. It helps us understand the relationships between the key variables and also helps us ask the right questions.'

Questions

1 *Categorise the measures used by Sean. How 'balanced' are they?*

2 *What are the advantages and disadvantages of the correlation model he has developed?*

10.4.1 Linking measurement to strategy

A key objective of performance measurement systems and the control systems in which they are embedded is that they should link strategic planning and day-by-day operations (Brignall *et al.* 1999). By having a balanced portfolio of measures throughout the organisation it is easier for managers, especially operations managers, not only to start to understand the link between the different types of measures (interlinking) but also to see the link between measures at an operational level, measures higher up the organisation and corporate strategy.

As the triangle in Figure 10.8 implies, the number of measures may well be reduced as they move up the hierarchy to a relatively small number at the apex of the organisation which should reflect the organisation's strategic intentions. However, if these are linked both up and down the organisation (see Figure 10.9), it

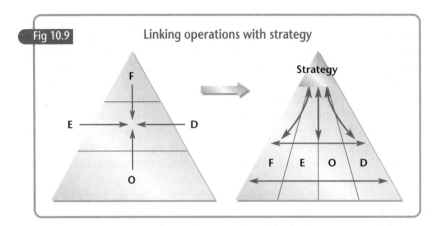

Fig 10.9 Linking operations with strategy

will allow managers to 'drill down' the organisation to understand the relationship between operational actions and organisational outcomes. If this structure is not in place, 'drilling down' is simply a myth and an expression used by misguided senior managers who are misleading themselves and their colleagues.

Organisations which can translate their strategy into their measurement system are far better to be able to execute their strategy because:

- they can communicate their objectives and their targets (Kaplan and Norton 1996)
- it creates a shared understanding of the organisation's strategic intentions
- it helps managers and employees focus on the critical drivers (Kaplan and Norton 1996)
- it enables the organisation to align investment, initiatives and actions with accomplishing strategic goals (Kaplan and Norton 1996)
- it provides a means for operations to communicate with and influence strategic decision-makers.

In Chapter 11 we will investigate the relationships between measures in more detail and look at how to create models to investigate and understand the relationships between the operational decisions and business performance.

10.5 TARGETS AND REWARDS

Whilst not all measures will have targets associated with them, targets can be a useful means to control performance, judge improvements, motivate employees and communicate the speed and size of the change required. Indeed, target-setting is a key element of driving performance improvement. There is evidence to suggest that performance improves when clear, defined, quantitative targets are provided (Berry *et al.* 1995). Operations managers need to decide how targets will be set for their measures to support process improvement, control communication and stimulate motivation. This section considers types of targets, the use of stretch targets, the impact of involving employees in target-setting and the effect of linking targets to rewards.

Types of targets

There are essentially three types of targets, or benchmarks, against which performance can be compared: internal, external and absolute (see Figure 10.10).

Internal targets

Internal targets are the basis of internal benchmarking. Such targets may be based upon the past performance of the process under consideration (process-based). The target is usually similar to the previous period's target, or slightly greater or lower in order to drive gradual improvements in the process. The key disadvantage of using the process itself as the base for comparison, whilst undoubtedly encouraging improvements in performance, is that it only provides information as to whether the operation is getting better over time rather than whether performance is satisfactory (Slack *et al.* 1998).

The targets may be based upon the performance of other similar internal processes (other process-based). This encourages comparisons across processes and the sharing of practices between them to try to meet the performance of the best. Comparison with other internal processes has the additional advantage that it provides a relative position for each process within the organisation.

External targets

External benchmarking uses targets based upon comparison with other organisations, using either competitor-based targets and/or 'best-in-field' benchmarks. Competitor-based targets are based on the performance of similar operations in other similar, competing organisations. Best-in-field benchmarks are based upon the performance achieved by organisations which may or may not be in the same industry but where the performance is considered to be outstanding.

An important, though often overlooked, external target base for service operations is customer-based targets (just as customer-based measures too are easily overlooked), i.e. for a particular activity what level of service do customers consider to be appropriate?

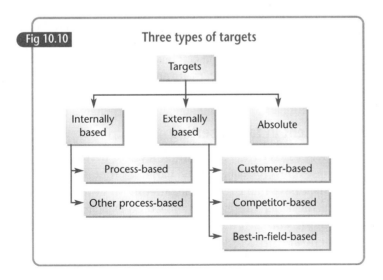

Fig 10.10 Three types of targets

Absolute targets

Some processes need to be operated with absolutely no defects or 100 per cent adherence to standard. It is unacceptable for life-support machines or stock-market computers or national defence systems to fail; although they do occasionally fail, with serious consequences, their operational targets are absolute.

10.5.2 Stretch targets

One critical question is: by how much should the target be above the current level of performance? Essentially, this depends upon the size of the change in performance required, on the assumption that it is feasible and desirable that such a change can be made.

Internally based targets are appropriate for operations wishing to improve their performance continually and incrementally (Johnston *et al.* 1999). This would target performance improvements relative to their historical achievements. Often organisations using a continuous improvement strategy, or *kaizen* (see Chapter 13), tend to be both successful and competitive: they may have already outperformed competitors or be the best-practice leader focusing on building upon their existing strengths (Ruchala 1995).

Organisations undertaking radical change of a process should set stretch targets. These are likely to be based on external benchmarks because of the need to improve performance dramatically in relation to that of competitors (Johnston *et al.* 1999). Reference to external sources for targets, such as competitors, brings both legitimacy and a sense of urgency to those faced with the need for radical change.

Recent research (Johnston *et al.* 1999) has shown that few operations are actually using externally based targets to drive changes. In a study of about 40 operations in the service sector undergoing improvement, out of the 141 measures in place to help drive those improvements less than 20 per cent used externally based targets (see Figure 10.11).

In the study the researchers expected that those organisations seeking radical changes in process improvement would be predominantly using external benchmarks whereas those seeking gradual and continuous change would be using internally based targets. Although they found that most gradual changers did indeed use predominantly internally based targets, the radical changers still used external targets less than anticipated (see Figure 10.12). Perhaps many organisations, especially those seeking significant improvements, are not using externally based targets as much as they might.

10.5.3 Employee involvement in target setting

To motivate employees to try to reach a target level of performance it is essential that the operator has some control over the variables that affect the performance, and also it helps if they have had a role in negotiating what that target would be, i.e. what they think is achievable. This is what one would expect to find for all processes undergoing continuous, *kaizen*-type, improvement as employee involvement and participation are central to the philosophy of *kaizen*. This approach encourages employees to address questions such as: how can they improve what they are doing,

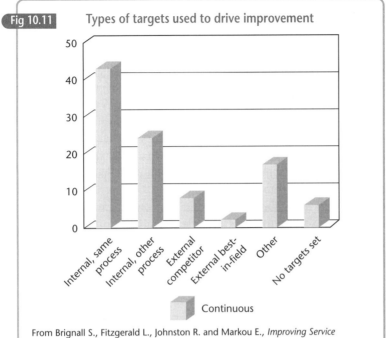

Fig 10.11 Types of targets used to drive improvement

From Brignall S., Fitzgerald L., Johnston R. and Markou E., *Improving Service Performance: A study of step-change versus continuous improvement*, CIMA, London, 1999, reprinted with permission of the Chartered Institute of Management Accountants.

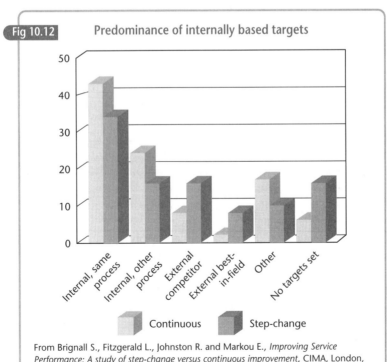

Fig 10.12 Predominance of internally based targets

From Brignall S., Fitzgerald L., Johnston R. and Markou E., *Improving Service Performance: A study of step-change versus continuous improvement*, CIMA, London, 1999, reprinted with permission of the Chartered Institute of Management Accountants.

how can they improve the process by which they are doing it and how can they improve the way in which they interact with other people? This in turn requires the encouragement, support and authority (empowerment) to propose and implement these improvements, backed by a supportive organisational culture and a 'team' approach to problem-solving and improvement (Imai 1986). Because of this philosophy of empowerment, participation and involvement, where the responsibility for process improvement rests with employees rather than quality specialists for example, targets should be set through a process involving employees. The employees would decide what might be achievable over a period of time, as it is they who have the responsibility for change and the authority to carry it out.

For organisations undergoing more radical change one might expect targets to be imposed by the senior managers overseeing the change programmes on a command-and-control basis. One would therefore expect radical change programmes to have targets imposed by managers, with overall responsibility resting with senior management champions who devote a substantial amount of their time and effort to both the design and implementation of process change.

10.5.4 Linking targets to rewards

Organisations need to decide what rewards/penalties will be associated with the achievement of their chosen targets (Fitzgerald and Moon 1996). For rewards linked to targets to work as intended, they must be clearly perceived as sufficient to justify the additional effort to obtain them, directly related to the required performance, perceived as equitable, and must take into account the complexities of individual versus team-based effort (Berry *et al.* 1995). In addition, the reward structure must also be accompanied by appropriate feedback mechanisms (Mullins 1989).

Rewards take a variety of forms from purely financial to a mixture of financial and non-financial, such as achievement awards and other forms of recognition (Ezzamel and Willmott 1998). Again we would suggest that in order to be effective the rewards need to be tailored to the specific requirements of the performance improvement programmes in use within an organisation. Whilst we would expect to find financially based rewards applied in all forms of change programmes, we would suggest that non-financial, and therefore less threatening and more encouraging, forms of rewards would be used to promote continuous change. Ittner and Larcker (1995), for example, contended that continuous improvement strategies require 'reward systems that place greater emphasis on quality and team-based performance' since they are specifically concerned with the motivation of employees (Juran 1989) and the elimination of the fear of job losses (Deming 1986). We would therefore expect that processes undergoing continuous change will base their rewards on a mix of financial and non-financial rewards targeted at encouraging improvements in team-based performance.

In contrast, radical change strategies emphasise individual performance, so the performance measurement system 'should measure the location of specific results and individual employee performance' (Hall *et al.* 1993). Given the higher costs and risks associated with step-change improvements, we would expect rewards associated with such changes to be primarily financial in nature.

10.6 BENCHMARKING

A benchmark is a reference point, originally a surveying term for a mark cut in a building used as a base point for measuring altitude (*Concise Oxford Dictionary*). As implied in section 10.5.1, benchmarks are targets against which performance can be measured. Benchmarking is therefore the measuring of a process or an organisation against some target, whether an internal target (internal benchmarking) or an external target (external benchmarking).

However, many people use the term 'benchmarking' to mean external, best-in-field, benchmarking. Because the purpose of benchmarking is to search for the best practices that will lead to the superior performance of the organisation (Camp 1989) this usually implies seeking out best possible practices whether they are within or outside the industry.

The advantage that 'benchmarking' provides over 'target-setting' is that by benchmarking practices against other organisations managers can gain an insight as to how the desired level of performance has been achieved by other organisations, thus providing an insight as to how it can be achieved in their own organisation.

Benchmarking can help organisations:

1 assess how well they are performing

2 set realistic performance targets

3 search out new ideas and practices

4 stimulate creativity and performance innovation

5 drive improvement through an organisation.

The critical purpose – driving improvement (point 5) – can easily be overlooked in an organisation's desire to undertake 'benchmarking'. Indeed often the benefits attained get no further than 1 and sometimes 2 above. The real benefits obtained through 3, 4 and 5 are often not achieved. The reason for this is that many benchmarking activities become concerned and then bogged down with metrics, the establishment of good comparators of performance between operational processes so that an organisation can (as in 1 above) assess how well a process is performing. This tends to be a very difficult task because organisations measure things in different ways, collect different data etc., and so a great deal of time and effort can be spent on trying to establish a base by which performance can be compared. Once this is achieved, it is possible to evaluate the targets used and set realistic and indeed possibly stretch targets. This hopefully will lead to improvements in performance (point 5 above). This process of 'metric benchmarking' is shown in Figure 10.13.

Whilst this fulfils the desire to know whether performance is relatively good or bad, it does not necessarily help managers understand *how* they might go about improving their own processes. This activity of 'practice benchmarking' can indeed be carried out without knowing how good or bad the respective processes are, but is an attempt to search out new ideas and practices and stimulate creativity and performance innovation (points 3 and 4 above). This involves seeking out ideas and practices that might be adapted for the benefit of the organisation (see Figure 10.14). It is important to recognise that this approach is further removed from the strict definition of benchmarks (creating a reference point) and much more concerned with the *purpose* of benchmarking, trying to achieve superior performance.

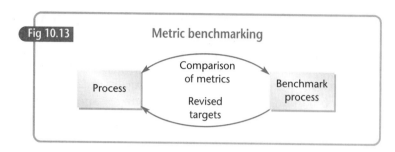

Fig 10.13 Metric benchmarking

Whilst metric benchmarking is essential for establishing whether the performance of a particular process is relatively better or worse and therefore by how much a process can be improved, practice benchmarking is important in understanding how the process can be improved. There are dangers with each approach. Whilst the metric approach can get bogged down in discussions about 'apples' and 'pears', practice benchmarking can easily fall into the trap of 'industrial tourism', where managers enjoy looking at other processes and operations although those experiences may not lead to improvements. The acid test for benchmarking is whether it leads to improvement. We would recommend that organisations undertake practice benchmarking in order to obtain an understanding of other processes and to benefit from quick gains, and then follow this with metric benchmarking once a relationship and mutual benefits have been obtained. It is essential to keep an eye to the continuous improvements that need to be obtained from such an activity.

Benchmarking has developed into a structured and proactive process to improve operations processes (see, for example, Camp 1989). From our experiences we would suggest that there are six key steps to benchmarking.

1. Define the objectives and select type of benchmarking

It is essential to undertake benchmarking with clear objectives, to bring about not only improvements in a process, but clarity about the nature of changes required and the speed of change.

The nature of change required is a function of the organisation's strategy. Does the organisation wish to pursue a strategy of lowest price, or highest quality, or speediest delivery, or most able to customise? Whilst all of these might be desirable

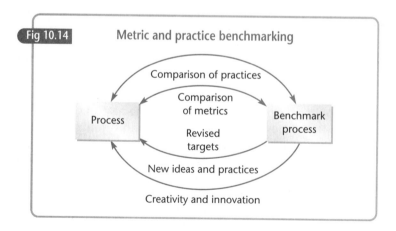

Fig 10.14 Metric and practice benchmarking

at once, there is a need to concentrate and focus on which performance criteria need to be improved and this then limits the type of organisations that might be chosen for benchmarking.

The rate of change required might also affect the benchmarking activity. The desire for continuous and incremental improvements might only require internal benchmarking. For radical step-changes in performance one might expect to use external benchmarks (see section 10.5.2).

2. Focus on a process and assess the process

Whilst benchmarking can take place at an organisational level – i.e. a comparison of key performance measures such as profit, share price, turnover – benchmarking is usually applied at a process level. The process chosen should therefore be one that will have an impact on the desired objectives (see above). Key activities at this stage include:

- Select an appropriate process.
- Define the process and its objectives.
- Map the process.
- Assess the process.
- Identify and define all the measures and targets used.
- Assess the measures and targets.
- Determine current performance and practices.

3. Select method of benchmarking

There are several ways of going about benchmarking. This may involve a one-to-one relationship between two organisations and indeed two particular departments. Alternatively, benchmarking data and round-table discussions may be facilitated by a third party, such as a benchmarking club or an industry body. Or thirdly, benchmarking may be part of a large-scale assessment activity such as the European Foundation for Quality (EFQM) (see Chapter 11), where one organisation's performance is compared to many other organisations and questions raised that may lead to changes in practice. Other benchmarking mechanisms specifically designed for service organisations have been developed recently including Service Probe, National Customer Satisfaction Barometers/Indices and one dealing specifically with complaints, the Complaints Management Excellence Programme.

- Service Probe – This is a well-developed, refined and tested instrument which benchmarks service organisations against a database on many aspects of the drivers and results of business performance. With over 100 questions it provides organisations with a detailed understanding as to how they stack up against other service organisations, in total and by sector, on a wide range of criteria, such as management style, service culture, employee management, service quality, service design and development, delivery system and processes, service effectiveness, service recovery and business performance. The questionnaire is administered by the Confederation of British Industry (CBI) in London, England.
- National Customer Satisfaction Barometers/Indices – The first national customer satisfaction index for domestically purchased and consumed products and services was established in 1989, the Swedish Customer Satisfaction Barometer

(SCSB) with an original database of 130 companies from Sweden's largest industries (Fornell 1992). The American Customer Satisfaction Index (ACSI) was introduced in 1994, and other barometers have been introduced more recently in Europe, New Zealand, Austria, Taiwan, and Korea. These instruments all use multiple survey items to operationalise quality, satisfaction, loyalty and other constructs as latent variables within a drivers–results model.

- The Complaints Management Excellence Programme is a detailed benchmarking instrument with over 200 questions assessing many different aspects of complaint management. It is based on a drivers–results model and provides detailed feedback positioning participating companies against a database in terms of their employee practices and attitudes, complaint processes, customer satisfaction and financial benefits, for example. The programme is administered by the Customer Service Network, in Cheddar, UK.

4. Select partner(s) (for one-to-one benchmarking)

The type of organisations will in part be determined by the level of benchmarking selected and the performance objectives for that particular process. For best-in-field benchmarking it is important to 'think outside the box' and to move away from traditional sources of comparison to seek out truly different and challenging good performance.

5. Dealing with the partner(s) (for one-to-one benchmarking)

It should be remembered that benchmarking is not a one-way activity, and that both partners can and should gain a great deal from it. Indeed it is through benefits going both ways that a benchmarking activity will stay alive and purposeful. Some key points for dealing with benchmarking partners are the following:

- Look for win-win outcomes.
- Start with practice benchmarking.
- Discuss step 1 above with partners to ensure there is comparability of objectives.
- Help partner undertake step 2.
- Set up regular meetings to discuss practice and methods of improvement.
- Evaluate relative performance through joint definition and agreement of measures and performance levels.
- Focus on improvement.

6. Improving performance

Given the intricate and often difficult tasks outlined above, it is understandable why the improvement objective can be missed – so much time and effort is involved in the process of benchmarking. This sixth stage is the most critical, and indeed there should be performance measures in place to assess the benchmarking activity and these should be about improvements created. The UK school performance or 'league' tables described in Box 10.3 highlight some of the problems of providing comparative performance data and question the benefits of this activity. Some key activities that can help realise improvements as a result of benchmarking include:

- Assess differences.
- Focus on improvement – the 'how'.
- Focus on the rate of improvement.
- Focus on action.
- Develop stretch targets coupled with action plans to achieve the targets.
- Draw up improvement plans.
- Adapt not adopt.
- Assess results against objectives (step 1 above).

Box 10.3 School Performance Tables

Since 1996, the UK Government's Department for Education and Employment has published performance tables for schools. The tables for secondary schools present statistics on such things as examination performance and the extent of unauthorised absence. These tables appear to be very useful for parents wishing to find out which school to send their child to, rather than having to rely on a school's reputation in the area or trying to make a judgement based on meeting the head teacher.

One of the prime measures for a school teaching 16-year-olds, the school leaving age, is the percentage of students achieving good grades in nationally recognised qualifications. These are the General Certificate of Secondary Education (GCSE), and General National Vocational Qualification (GNVQ). Performance statistics are produced for each school showing the trend in its achievement for recent years, its position against other schools in the same local education authority, and comparison with national statistics.

These statistics have great appeal for government ministers, not least because the current tables at national level show a continuing rise in the percentage of students achieving good GCSE/GNVQ grades. It is clear, however, that not everyone is happy with these tables. In an article published on BBC News Online in 1998, Dr Keith Devlin of St Mary's College of California said that it was very dangerous to take numbers developed to deal with the inanimate world and apply them to the world of people with all of their imprecision and unpredictability.

The need to be aware of the impact of chance is confirmed by others. Professor Ted Wragg of Exeter University, also reported by BBC News, suggested that there were not enough children in the individual schools to make the figures statistically significant, though clearly the national statistics are not a problem. A senior teacher commented that schools that are in prosperous catchment areas perform relatively consistently, but those in poorer areas seem to oscillate, having alternate good and bad years. He said that this 'yo-yo' effect can be very demoralising to staff who feel that they are judged on statistics which, to some extent, may be outside their control.

Teachers feel that the statistics may be positively dangerous. This may be in part due to the reluctance of professionals to be measured by an external agency, but they are concerned that reducing the performance of a school to a limited set of statistics may mislead parents. The figures, for example, do not demonstrate how well the school has developed the gifted student, the one who would perform well in almost any circumstance, nor do they indicate whether genuine learning has taken place as opposed to good preparation for examinations.

There is also concern that the statistics may be used to remove underperforming teachers using information which could be flawed. As a result, some teachers spend time ensuring that their figures are presented in the best possible light, knowing that unhelpful conclusions may be drawn if the school is seen to be failing using this set of statistics. There is frustration that so much emphasis is placed upon school performance tables, particularly since they do not appear to present a fair and rounded picture of the school.

There is growing interest in the concept of 'value added', which would measure the progress of the child from entry to exit. This would undoubtedly put some of the schools in poorer areas in a higher position in the league table than they currently occupy. Professor Ted Wragg suggested that the adoption of the 'value added' concept would send shock waves through the education system, not least because some schools, traditionally seen as excellent performers, might slip down the rankings because they were working with good 'material' (students) in the first place. There are signs that this approach is gaining support, with education authorities placing more emphasis on the process of learning rather than simply examination success.

Questions

1 Is it better for the Government to compile no statistics rather than performance tables that appear to be unhelpful, if not dangerous?

2 What pressures are there on teachers and head teachers to present their school's performance in the best possible light? Is this an appropriate use of their time and energy?

3 Do you think the performance tables lead to improvements in performance?

This illustration was compiled from information gained from http://www.news.bbc.co.uk, http://www.dfee.gov.uk, and from interviews with teachers.

By undertaking benchmarking, success is not guaranteed. Indeed benchmarking can be a very slow and costly activity. It requires a culture that supports learning and improvement together with the necessary investment and allocation of staff to undertake the work.

10.7 SUMMARY

Purpose of performance measurement

- Performance measurement is a costly activity and should provide value for money.
- Performance measures can be assessed in terms of their ability to facilitate communication, motivation, control and improvement.

A balance of measures

- A balanced set of measures would include operational, financial, external and developmental measures.
- Having a balanced set of measures is the first step towards understanding the relationships between them and corporate strategy.

Interlinking

- Interlinking is about using knowledge about the relationships between operational, financial, external and development performance measures.
- Tomorrow's leading-edge organisations will be those that understand and exploit these relationships.

Targets and rewards

- Target-setting is a key element of driving performance improvement.
- There are three main types of targets, or benchmarks, against which performance can be compared: internal, external and absolute.
- To link rewards to targets requires the rewards to be seen as sufficient to justify the additional effort required, be directly related to the required performance, be perceived as equitable, and be accompanied by appropriate feedback mechanisms.

Benchmarking

- Benchmarking is the measuring of a process or an organisation against some target, an internal target (internal benchmarking) or an external target (external benchmarking).
- Benchmarking can help managers:
  - ➤ assess how well they are performing
  - ➤ set realistic performance targets
  - ➤ search out new ideas and practices
  - ➤ stimulate creativity and performance innovation
  - ➤ drive improvement through an organisation.

10.8 DISCUSSION QUESTIONS

1. Key measures used by some call centres are speed of response and call abandonment rate. Assess these measures as drivers of improvement.

2. A tour operator specialising in holidays for young people is concerned about the quality of service provided. Each month the marketing manager reports on the number of complaints received. How could this be better reported to help the firm improve its service?

3. Select a process you are involved in, such as being taught, cooking, cleaning etc. What might be the benefits of benchmarking this process and with whom could you compare your performance? How would this lead to the benefits identified?

10.9 QUESTIONS FOR MANAGERS

1. Assess the purposes, and systems to deliver the purposes, for your key measures.

2. Evaluate the mix of measures used at various levels in your organisation. What are the implications of this?

3. Evaluate some of your operational targets. How could benchmarking help?

10.10 SUGGESTIONS FOR FURTHER READING

Holloway J., Lewis J. and Mallory G. (eds), *Performance Measurement and Evaluation*, Sage Publications, London, 1995.

Neely A., *Measuring Business Performance,* The Economist Books, London, 1998.

10.11 REFERENCES

Berry A.J., Broadbent J. and Otley D. (eds), *Management Control: Theories, issues and practice*, Macmillan Press, Basingstoke, 1995.

Brignall S., Fitzgerald L., Johnston R. and Markou E., *Improving Service Performance: A study of step-change versus continuous improvement*, CIMA, London, 1999.

Camp R.C., *Benchmarking: The search for industry best practices that lead to superior performance*, ASQC Quality Press, Milwaukee, Wisc., 1989.

Carlzon J., *Moments of Truth*, Ballinger, Cambridge, Mass., 1987.

Collier D.A., *The Service/Quality Solution: Using service management to gain competitive advantage*, Irwin and ASQC Quality Press, New York, 1994.

Deming W.E., *Out of the Crisis*, MIT Center for Advanced Engineering Study, Cambridge, Mass., 1986.

Ezzamel M. and Willmott H., 'Accounting, Remuneration and Employee Motivation in the New Organisation', *Accounting and Business Research*, vol. 28, no. 2, 1998, pp. 97–110.

Fitzgerald L. and Moon P., *Performance Measurement in Service Industries: Making it work*, CIMA, London, 1996.

Fitzgerald L., Johnston R., Brignall T.J., Silvestro R. and Voss C., *Performance Measurement in Service Businesses*, CIMA, London, 1991.

Fornell, C. 'A National Customer Satisfaction Barometer: The Swedish experience', *Journal of Marketing*, 56, 1992, pp. 6–21.

Hall G., Rosenthal J. and Wade J., 'How to Make Re-engineering Really Work', *Harvard Business Review*, vol. 71, no. 6, 1993, pp. 119–31.

Imai M., *Kaizen: The key to Japan's competitive success*, McGraw-Hill, New York, 1986.

Ittner C. and Larcker D., 'Total Quality Management and the Choice of Information and Reward Systems', *Journal of Accounting Research*, vol. 33, Supplement, 1995 pp. 1–34.

Johnston R. and Fitzgerald L., 'Performance Measurement: Flying in the face of fashion', working paper, University of Warwick, 1999.

Johnston R., Fitzgerald L., Markou E. and Brignall S., 'Target Setting for Evolutionary and Revolutionary Process Change', working paper, University of Warwick, 1999.

Juran J.M., *Juran on Leadership for Quality, an Executive Handbook*, Free Press, Homewood, Ill., 1989.

Kaplan R.S. and Norton D.P., 'The Balanced Scorecard – Measures that Drive Performance', *Harvard Business Review*, January–February 1992, pp. 71–9.

Kaplan R.S. and Norton D.P., *The Balanced Scorecard,* Harvard Business School Press, Boston, Mass., 1996.

Mullins L.J., *Management and Organisational Behaviour* (2nd ed), Pitman, London, 1989.

Neely A., *Measuring Business Performance*, The Economist Books, London, 1998.

Ruchala, L., 'New, Improved or Re-engineered?', *Management Accounting*, December 1995, pp. 37–41.

Slack N., Chambers S., Harland C., Harrison A. and Johnston R., *Operations Management* (2nd edition), Pitman, London, 1998.

The Squire Hotel Group

The Squire Hotel Group (SHG) runs a chain of 20 hotels, with between 40 and 120 bedrooms, in locations which include Oxford, Warwick and Southport. SHG sees itself in the three-star market with hotels that have their own personality and style, providing high-quality food and service at an affordable price. The majority of mid-week guests are commercial clients. The normal mid-week occupancy rate is about 80 per cent. Weekend occupancy is about 30 per cent, comprising mainly weekend break packages. The company does not have any major expansion plans but is trying to strengthen its existing market position.

Squire's Managing Director, Justin Palmer, believes that they have a high degree of customer loyalty in the commercial sector. He explains: 'The hotel managers are expected to integrate with their local community through Chambers of Commerce and Round Tables, primarily to gain visibility but also to demonstrate a local and caring attitude. The image they try to create is a good-quality, small and friendly hotel that local business can rely upon for their visitors. The hotel managers are expected to work hard to develop personal relationships with local firms and may also try to promote other hotels in the chain for any "away" visits. We get most of our repeat bookings because of the reputation we have developed for the quality of our food and attentive and courteous service.'

The Squire Hotel Oxford

The Squire Hotel Oxford has 41 bedrooms and is situated close to Magdalen College. The entrance lobby is small but pleasantly decorated. The room is dominated by a grandfather clock and an elegant mahogany desk. 'I do not like the traditional counter arrangement,' explained Charles Harper, the hotel's manager. 'I like a simple, open and friendly situation with a clear desk to demonstrate our uncluttered and caring attitude. Even our computers are kept in a small room just off the lobby, out of sight. I want my guests to feel that they are important and not just one of the 70 that we are going to deal with that evening.'

SHG's hotel managers are totally responsible for their own operations. They set staff levels and wages within clear guidelines set by head office. Though pricing policy is determined centrally, there is scope for adjustment and they can negotiate with local firms or groups in consultation with head office. Mr Harper added: 'Every year, each hotel manager agrees the financial targets for his own operation with head office, and if the manager does not reach his target without good reason, he may well find himself out of a job. I believe that it is my job to be constantly improving and developing this business. This is naturally reflected in the yearly profit expectations.' The hotel managers report performance to the group monthly on four criteria: occupancy, profit, staff costs and food costs. The information provided allows senior managers to drill down to the costs of individual people and meals.

Mr Harper explained: 'My job is to try to get and maintain 100 per cent occupancy rates and keep costs within budget. During the tourist season Oxford has more tourists looking for beds than it has beds, so in the peak season, which is only two months long, we expect to achieve 100 per cent utilisation of rooms. Indeed, I am budgeted for it. This has been a bad year so far. The high value of the pound has kept many American tourists away and our occupancy has sometimes been as low as 90 per cent. In the off-season our occupancy drops to 60 per cent – this is still very good and is due to our excellent location. In the peak season we charge a premium on our rooms. This does not cause any problems but our guests do expect a high standard of food and service.

'We get very few complaints. Usually these are about the food, things like the temperature of the vegetables, though recently we had a complaint from two elderly ladies about the juke-box in the bar. We don't have any formal means of collecting information about quality. Head office may come and check the hotel once or twice a year. We always know when they are coming and try to look after them. We don't use complaints or suggestion forms in the bedrooms because I think it tends to get people to complain or question the service. However, I do try to collect some information myself in order to get an indication from guests about how they feel about the quality or the price. I don't document the results but we know what is going on. Our aim is to prevent complaints by asking and acting during the service.

'I have 40 staff, most of whom are full-time,' added Mr Harper. 'Ten work mainly on the liquor side, twenty on food and ten on apartments. There is a restaurant manager and a bar manager. Staff turnover is 70 per cent which compares very well with most hotels where turnover can be as high as 300 per cent. In general the staff are very good and seem to enjoy working here.'

The Restaurant

The restaurant at the Squire Hotel in Oxford has 20 tables with a total seating capacity of 100. The restaurant is well used at lunchtime by tourists and visitors to the local colleges and by local business people. There are several excellent and famous restaurants that tend to draw potential customers and even hotel guests away from the hotel restaurant in the evenings.

The restaurant managers have considerable discretion in menu planning, purchasing and staffing, providing they keep to the budgets set by head office. These budgets specify, for example, the food and staff costs for an individual breakfast, lunch and dinner. Overall food costs and staff costs are reported weekly to the hotel manager. The style of restaurants in the hotels varies considerably from carvery to à la carte, with the decisions made on the basis of the type of hotel and the requirements of the local community.

'My job is concerned with keeping to food and staff budgets,' explained Elizabeth Dickens, the restaurant manager, 'and so most of my time is taken up with staffing, purchasing and menu planning. At lunchtime, for example, I provide four items, three traditional and one vegetarian, and these change weekly. We aim to serve a main course within fifteen minutes of taking an order. I am constantly looking for new ideas for our menus and better ways of serving but I am constrained by continually tightening budgets from head office. I think we have now reached the point where we are starting to lose many of our established customers. We really do need to respond to the changing demands of our customers in terms of speed of service, particularly at lunchtimes, and changes in diet together with the desire for a greater and more interesting range of meals. I think head office is out of touch with reality.'

Questions

1 *Evaluate the performance measures in place at the Squire Group.*

2 *What improvements would you suggest?*

11

Linking Operations Decisions to Business Performance

11.1 INTRODUCTION

It is important that operations managers understand the impact of any changes they make to their delivery system. Although we can usually calculate or estimate the costs associated with any particular change or initiative, we are often much less certain of their impact on the organisation's wider business performance, for example an increase in customer satisfaction, retention, revenues, market share and profit.

The objectives of this chapter are:

● to discuss the need to understand cause–effect relationships between operational decisions and business performance

● to develop a framework, the Service Performance Network, to try to capture these relationships

● to identify the key stages in developing a network

● to define world-class service and its key characteristics.

One might argue that many management decisions are simply an act of faith, based upon a well-intentioned belief that one's actions and decisions will be to the benefit of the business. We believe that most managers have little evidence to support their actions. This chapter, therefore, sets out to identify the relationships between operations actions and business performance, and demonstrates that world-class performance is achieved through understanding and exploiting these relationships.

11.2 UNDERSTANDING THE RELATIONSHIP BETWEEN OPERATIONAL DECISIONS AND BUSINESS PERFORMANCE

The problem is that the cause–effect relationships between operational decisions and business performance in most organisations are extremely complex, involving many factors with inherent lags and delays in their relationships. This complexity is enough to put off many managers who retrench into 'seat-of-the-pants' management. We believe that leading-edge organisations are moving beyond intu-

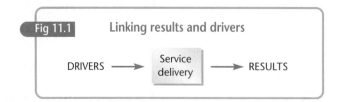

Fig 11.1   Linking results and drivers

ition-based management and are working at understanding the links between their operational drivers and business results (Figure 11.1).

As a result of data collection and analysis some organisations understand the relationships between their operational drivers of service delivery performance, such as employee involvement, or improved complaint management systems, or customer management, and the resulting impact on customer satisfaction, retention and profit, for example.

The Sears company, for example, has made great strides in understanding these relationships in an initiative driven by its Chief Executive, Arthur Martinez. In Box 11.1 two Sears Vice-Presidents, Anthony Rucci and Steven Kirn, and a past Vice-President, Richard Quinn, explain the organisation's understanding of the relationship between some of the key variables.

Box 11.1 Sears, Roebuck and Co.

R.W. Sears Watch Company, founded in Minneapolis in 1886 by Richard Sears, has developed into one of the largest stores and mail order businesses in the USA – Sears, Roebuck and Co. Although the company was one of the early pioneers of mail order shopping, in 1925 it branched out into retail stores. By 1997 Sears operated 833 department stores and 1,325 furniture, hardware and car parts stores. In addition, Sears sells appliances, hardware and car parts through 1,384 independently owned stores. Sears continues to provide home shopping and other home services. The company's turnover in 1998 was over $41 billion.

The company is known for its innovation and creativity. Back in 1906 Sears was facing significant operational difficulties following the opening of its new three million square feet mail order plant (the largest business building in the world at the time). After a deal of experimentation the mail order executives introduced a system that involved scheduling of individual orders through the plant to the shipping of goods. This was facilitated by an intricate system of belts and chutes. This method of controlling and transporting items around the plant system led to a ten-fold increase in volumes handled. The operation became a sort of 'seventh wonder' of the business world and Henry Ford is reported to have visited the Chicago plant to study the assembly-line technique used in the system.

More recently, creativity has been applied to understanding the linkages between its employee policies and profit. Rucci, Kirn and Quinn (1998) explained: 'The basic elements of an employee–customer–profit model are not difficult to grasp. Any person with even a little appreciation in retailing understands intuitively that there is a chain of cause and effect running from employee behaviour to customer behaviour to profits.' Many companies do not have a grasp of these relationships but Sears claims that it does, as a result of data collection, analysis and modelling. 'We understand the several layers of factors that drive employee attitudes, and we know how attitudes affect employee reten-tion, how employee retention affects the drivers of customer satisfaction, how customer satisfaction affects financials and a great deal more. We have also calculated the lag time in any of those metrics and a corresponding change in financial performance, so that when we see a shift in, say, employee attitudes, we know not only *how* but also *when* it will affect our results.'

Questions

1 *What are the benefits of understanding the links between the variables mentioned above?*

2 *What do you think the problems are in trying to understand the links between the drivers and results?*

This illustration has been developed from material from www.sears.com and Rucci A.J., Kirn S.P. and Quinn R.T., 'The Employee–Customer–Profit Chain at Sears', *Harvard Business Review*, January–February 1998, pp. 83–97.

11.2.1 Chains of cause and effect

We believe managers need to try to understand the chains of cause and effect between their operational drivers and business performance so that they know how to get the right response and the most effective one from their limited resources. What is needed is a method or framework to help managers do this. Over the last few years several tools have developed to try to give managers a better understanding of these relationships, such as the Balanced Business Scorecard (Kaplan and Norton 1996), the Service Profit Chain (Heskett *et al.* 1997), the Results Determinants Framework (Fitzgerald *et al.* 1991), the Performance Pyramid (Lynch and Cross 1991), Return on Quality (Rust *et al.* 1995) and the Business Excellence Model (European Foundation for Quality Management (EFQM) 1999).

11.2.2 Awards for excellence

The use of such tools and frameworks has been spurred on by the interest in, and proliferation of, quality awards, so much so that many organisations are incorpo-rating such cause – effect frameworks into their decision-making structures.

There are awards for quality in many countries in the world, supported by local quality foundations or governments that recognise outstanding organisations: the European Quality Award and the Malcolm Baldridge Award (in the USA), for exam-ple. The European Foundation for Quality Management (EFQM) was founded in 1988 by the presidents of 14 major European companies, with the endorsement of the European Commission. The European Quality Awards are presented to organi-sations that 'demonstrate excellence in the management of quality as their fundamental process for continuous improvement' (EFQM 1999).

The quality awards are usually based on a cause – effect model. Figure 11.2 provides the model that underpins the EFQM award. This model depicts how customer satis-faction, people (employee) satisfaction and impact on society are achieved through leadership which drives policy and strategy, people management, resources and processes, and which ultimately leads to excellence in business results. The enablers,

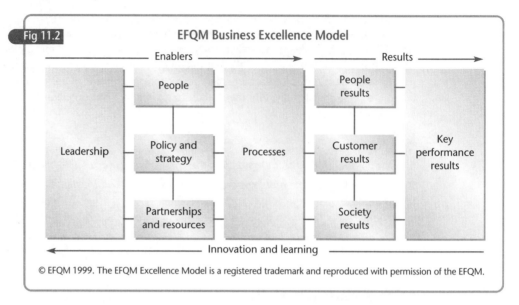

Fig 11.2   EFQM Business Excellence Model

© EFQM 1999. The EFQM Excellence Model is a registered trademark and reproduced with permission of the EFQM.

or drivers, are concerned with *how* the results are achieved and the results are concerned with *what* the organisation has achieved. Innovation and learning feedback to the other parts to enable a continuous cycle of improvement and development.

11.3   THE SERVICE PERFORMANCE NETWORK

Simply stated, cause–effect thinking maintains that there are direct and strong relationships between service delivery (as a result of service design, employee management, customer management and infrastructure management), an organisation's financial performance (such as reduced costs and/or increased revenues) and broader aspects of business performance (such as improved customer satisfaction, retention and attraction).

What managers need to know is how these variables are related to one another so that they can have greater confidence, certain that by spending £X on making decision Y there will be a return of £Z. (A 'return' is defined as what is financially important to the organisation – for a charity this might mean greater donations, for a public-sector organisation it might mean a reduction in costs, in a for-profit organisation it might mean profit or return on capital employed.) These relationships may not be linear and so by simply spending more and more on certain aspects of service delivery, there may actually be diminishing returns: we need to be able to find the optimum points.

This section develops a network that sets out the possible relationships and then the following section goes on to explain how we can start to understand the relationships between the variables in any given organisation.

11.3.1   The Service Performance Network

The Service Performance Network is the combination of two networks, the interrelated set of results (the results network)and the interrelated drivers (the drivers network), and the relationships between them. At the centre is service delivery, which concerns the value of the service (experience and outcomes) as perceived by customers and/or the organisation. This Service Performance Network can be used by both for-profit and not-for-profit organisations to help understand the relationships between operational drivers and business results.

11.3.2 The results network

Interest in the impact of service delivery on financial and broader business performance, particularly between service quality and profit, started with the PIMS study (Profit Impact of Market Strategy) (Buzzell and Gale 1987). Many ensuing studies have explored and confirmed the relationships between various elements in the network (see, for example, Georgiades and Macdonell 1998; Loveman 1998; Reichheld and Sasser 1990; Reichheld 1996; Rust *et al.* 1995; Heskett *et al.* 1997; Schneider and Bowen 1995; Schneider 1980; Anderson *et al.* 1994; Rust and Zahorik 1993; Voss *et al.* 1997; Voss and Johnston 1995; Anderson *et al.* 1997; Jones and Sasser 1995).

Drawing on all of these studies, we have tried to identify all the main results of service delivery and the relationships between these aspects of business performance (see Figure 11.3).

Service delivery → Financial performance

A change in service delivery, resulting in an improved service experience and/or service outcome for the customer, may well represent a cost to the organisation and therefore have a negative impact on financial performance. Improving processes, increasing staff, redesigning jobs, increasing capacity, improving quality, for example, are all likely to incur costs. On the other hand, improvements may reduce costs in the longer term. For example, an investment in an improved process, although requiring initial investment, may allow for reduced staffing levels, or improved quality may reduce the need for resources committed to dealing with problems.

Operations managers need to understand not only the balance between short-term costs and longer-term financial benefit, but also the wider-scale impact of changes to the delivery system that can have significant beneficial impacts on financial performance. Knowing these relationships moves service operations management from an act of faith to a co-ordinated and controlled activity.

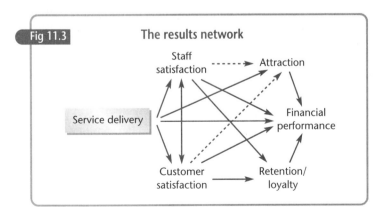

Fig 11.3 The results network

Service delivery → Customer satisfaction

Improvement in service delivery should result in improved perceptions of performance leading to increased customer satisfaction (this part of the chain was covered in Chapter 4). It should be noted that what satisfies customers is not just quality of the service but the perceived value of that service, including, for example, its quality, reliability, dependability, flexibility and cost.

Customer satisfaction → Financial performance

Improved customer satisfaction can have a direct and positive impact on financial performance. A charity that raises its profile by increasing its impact through improved use of its resources may lead to existing donors being more satisfied with its work and willing to give more than they might have done previously. In for-profit organisations happier customers may also be willing to spend more, as Lord Marshall, Chairman of BA, points out: 'many service companies (even at the lower end of the scale) ignore the fact that there are plenty of customers ... who are willing to pay a little more for superior service' (Prokesch 1995).

Also, more satisfied customers means less dissatisfied customers and therefore less money needs to be committed to dealing with dissatisfied customers.

Customer satisfaction → Retention and loyalty

There is no shortage of evidence that customer satisfaction, both transaction-specific and overall satisfaction, has a measurable and positive impact on customer retention (see, for example, Anderson *et al.* 1994; Loveman 1998; Rust and Zahorik 1993; Rust *et al.* 1995). If existing customers are more satisfied because they have experienced a better service than before and/or better than that provided by alternative or similar suppliers, they are more likely to become repeat buyers and be more loyal. This is sometimes referred to as 'defensive marketing' (see, for example, Rust *et al.* 1995).

The nature of the relationship between satisfaction and loyalty depends upon the nature of the organisation. Jones and Sasser (1995) conducted research between customer satisfaction and customer loyalty in 30 different organisations in five service industries and found clear but differing relationships between satisfaction and loyalty. These relationships varied from a very low propensity to switch whatever the customer's level of dissatisfaction, to an increasing propensity to switch as satisfaction with the service declined (see Figure 11.4). In some organisations where the customers had, for example, no choice over supplier, their loyalty and repurchase intentions were high whatever the level of satisfaction or dissatisfaction with the organisations' services. In the more competitive organisations highly dissatisfied customers switched and delighted customers stayed. Interestingly, those customers who were just 'satisfied' were significantly less loyal than completely delighted customers. Xerox's 'totally satisfied' customers were six times more likely to repurchase Xerox products over the next 18 months than its satisfied customers. Merely satisfying customers who have the freedom to make choices is not enough to keep them loyal. The only truly loyal customers are totally satisfied customers (Jones and Sasser 1995).

The degree to which the customer is free to choose or is 'locked-in' to the service primarily depends on the nature of the organisation, switching costs and substitutability. The freedom to choose will vary considerably between monopolistic

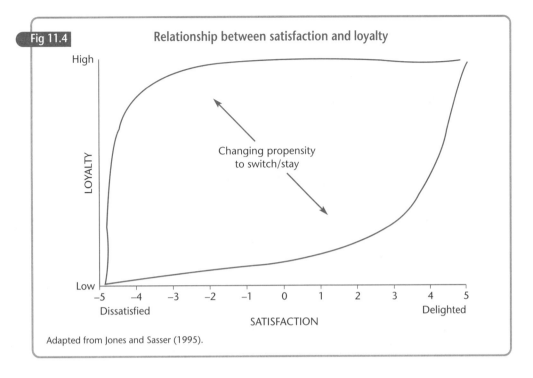

Fig 11.4 — Relationship between satisfaction and loyalty

Adapted from Jones and Sasser (1995).

organisations or institutions, where the customer has absolutely no choice, and organisations operating in highly competitive environments. Switching costs include not only the financial costs or penalties involved in moving from one service provider to another but also the time and effort required. Some financial institutions, for example, sell multiple products, such as current banking, loans, house loans and insurance, and so the customer may feel it is too much trouble or too difficult either to untie an individual service or to transfer all of them. Other switching costs might include an emotional tie, such as a legal firm that one's family has used for years, or where the partner is a friend of the family. Services that are easily substituted can be more easily changed. More 'commodity-like' services, such as food, clothes, mobile telephone providers for example, may be more easily exchanged than diagnostic, professional-type services that are based on an understanding of the customer or his/her business and where services have been customised to meet their needs.

Retention and loyalty → Financial performance

Customer retention and loyalty have a direct impact on revenue and profitability (see, for example, Anderson *et al.* 1994; Loveman 1998; Rust and Zahorik 1993; Rust *et al.* 1995). Loyal customers continue to purchase the service, generate long-term revenue streams, tend to buy more, and may be willing to pay premium prices, all of which increase revenue and profitability. Furthermore, it has been shown that customer loyalty is a more important predictor of profitability than market share (Reichheld and Sasser 1990; Reichheld 1996). Loyal customers may also lower marketing costs since retaining customers is usually significantly cheaper than attracting new ones. A study by the US Department of Consumer Affairs found that the cost of winning new customers is five times more expensive than keeping old ones (Peters 1987).

Retention and loyalty can also be applied to employees. Higher staff retention and loyalty will reduce recruitment costs and training costs, for example.

Customer satisfaction → Attraction

Organisations may also attract new customers through increased word-of-mouth recommendation as a result of delivering good service to its existing customers (Rust *et al.* 1995).

Service delivery → Attraction

Organisations are likely to be able to attract new customers as a result of improved or superior service delivery and its ability to advertise these improvements. This is often referred to as 'offensive marketing' (Rust *et al.* 1995). Charities known for their effective delivery systems, that have minimal overhead costs or who are fast at moving into conflict areas, for example, may find it easier to attract new donors. Similarly, public-sector organisations may find it easier to attract funds if they have a reputation for good service delivery.

Attraction → Financial performance

Attracting new customers may mean increased revenues and an increased market share, and, providing the services sold are profitable, this will lead to increased profit.

Service delivery → Staff satisfaction

If employees perceive that service delivery is effective and/or improving, they may become more satisfied with the organisation. Fewer failures and problems and fewer complaining customers should result in a feeling of greater control over the work situation and thus less stress (see, for example, Matteson and Ivancevich 1982). In turn, less stress tends to be associated with greater job satisfaction and organisational commitment, better job performance and health (Fox *et al.* 1993; Motowidlio, *et al.* 1986).

Customer satisfaction ↔ Staff satisfaction

Greater staff satisfaction leads to greater customer satisfaction as the positive and supportive behaviour of staff leads to more satisfied customers, just as greater customer satisfaction leads to greater staff satisfaction, i.e. happy staff results in happy customers which results in happy staff. This virtuous cause–effect relationship between customer and staff satisfaction has been called the 'satisfaction mirror' (Heskett *et al.* 1997). Several studies have shown a high correlation between these two variables (see, for example, Schneider 1980; Heskett *et al.* 1997; Schneider and Bowen 1995).

Staff satisfaction → Retention and loyalty

Higher levels of staff satisfaction result in less stress, attrition and absenteeism and greater staff loyalty and retention.

Staff satisfaction → Financial performance

High levels of staff satisfaction should have a direct impact on financial performance, through reduced absenteeism and the costs associated with this. Happier staff tend to be more productive, again reducing costs.

Staff satisfaction → Attraction

Positive word-of-mouth by staff about their organisation and its services and success at improving those services may well lead to the attraction of new customers and indeed new high-quality staff.

Not all of the linkages will apply to every situation and to every organisation but by trying to unravel these linkages, managers can start to understand the direct impact of changes they make to the service delivery on the organisation's financial and broader business performance.

11.3.3 The drivers network

The drivers are the levers operations managers can apply to gain an anticipated result (see Figure 11.5). The key operational drivers are:

● process (Chapter 6)
● capacity (Chapter 7)
● people, both staff and customers (Chapter 8)
● structure, networks, technology and information (Chapter 9).

Several organisational variables have a significant bearing on the operational drivers of performance. Much of this can be summarised under the popular description of 'the way we do things around here' – what is expected, what things are rewarded and so forth. Leadership is generally recognised as a key driver of sustainable success, being the ability to command attention and influence people in such a way that challenging performance objectives are achieved (see, for example, Deming 1982 and 1986; Feigenbaum 1986; Bennis 1999).

In order to accomplish this, leaders develop, own and communicate a clear vision for the organisation. This sets the context and provides meaning for all the other activities of the organisation, its people and functions. The overarching vision of what type of organisation the leadership envisages, can then be matched against the current and potential service concepts, recognising that leadership may be required to change people's perceptions as to what it is that customers are really buying. Leadership, too, is required to take an organisation into uncharted waters where a strategy cannot be formulated by rational analysis of undisputed facts alone. It is here that the vision and character of leadership are tested, as the dream is translated into tangible commitments in terms of resources and actions.

Finally, to return to the influence of culture on organisational decisions, and thence to service delivery, organisational culture has a dynamic quality to it. It shifts and changes with successes and failures, and as people in the organisation interpret key decisions. They observe what is valued by leadership and then make

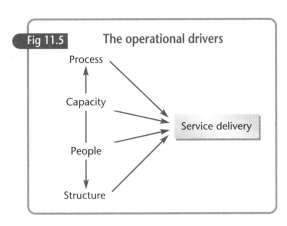

Fig 11.5   **The operational drivers**

Process

Capacity

People

Structure

Service delivery

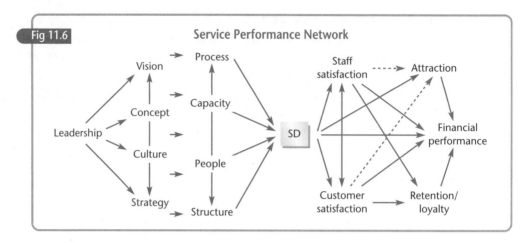

Fig 11.6 — Service Performance Network

choices as to their own actions and decisions. It is important to recognise therefore that organisational culture can and should be influenced in order to develop the required attitudes and actions. An extremely powerful means of influencing is for leaders, be they senior or junior managers, to act as role models for the desired behaviour. Including these variables completes the Service Performance Network (see Figure 11.6).

Leading-edge research by Georgiades and Macdonell (1998) has demonstrated significant relationships between all of the main variables in the network. They found high correlations between leadership, vision and culture with management practices – what we have referred to here as the operational drivers – that are correlated with staff satisfaction, customer satisfaction and profit.

11.4 KEY STAGES IN DEVELOPING A NETWORK

Whilst high positive correlations have been demonstrated between the variables in the network for particular organisations or types of organisations, the strength of the individual relationships may vary considerably from organisation to organisation. For those organisations wishing to know the relative power or strength of any particular operational driver compared to another, or to create a particular effect, such as increasing the number of new customers/supporters/donors or increasing spend of existing customers or having a major impact on cost reduction, they need to understand the nature and strength of the relationships for themselves. This, at a simple level, involves three main stages: create a model, collect data, analyse the data.

11.4.1 Create a model

It is unlikely that organisations in the early stages of understanding relationships within the network will be able or willing to investigate all the possible relationships. It would seem sensible therefore to start with what are considered to be the key variables and, over time, expand it to a more complete model of the business.

The existing models, such as Service Profit Chain (Heskett *et al.* 1997), Service Organisation Profile model (Georgiades and Macdonell 1998), EFQM Business

Excellence Model etc., all use particular features and can be used directly or adapted for a particular situation. Each model takes a particular thread or threads through the Service Performance Network. An organisation wishing to focus on the effects of teamwork on staff satisfaction, customer satisfaction, retention and profit, for example, could take that particular thread through the network (see Figure 11.7). The limitations are clearly that only part of the variance will be explained or captured by the relationships.

11.4.2 Collect data

For many larger organisations the problem will not be data collection but finding the data within the organisation. The information on culture change, staff satisfaction, levels of empowerment, process changes, customer satisfaction, costs reductions and profit, for example, may all be collected but may be held in different parts of the business. This activity should therefore be undertaken as an organisation-wide initiative requiring top-level commitment and widespread organisational support.

Other organisations may have to start collecting data. We would recommend that considerable time be put into the planning stages of this because the longitudinal strength of the model created can be undermined by frequently changing the collection instruments.

11.4.3 Data analysis

Simple regression analysis and graphical representations are powerful enough to permit a basic understanding of the relationships. Other, more complex methods such as structural equation modelling (see Hoyle 1995 and Maruyama 1997, for example) and data envelopment analysis (see Norman 1991, for example) may be considered.

The critical point is that data must be collected over time and regression analyses undertaken at intervals because relationships may not be linear. It may be important to identify optimum points in the relationships between variables so that effort can be moved from one driver whose power is waning, to one that might have an increasing effect.

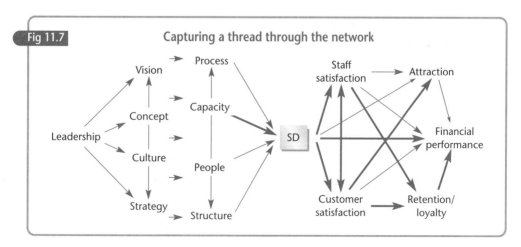

Fig 11.7   Capturing a thread through the network

Box 11.2 shows how one organisation, BUPA, has gone about understanding the relationships between some of its drivers and profit.

Box 11.2 BUPA

In 1947 seventeen British provident associations joined together in order to provide high-quality private healthcare for the general public. The result was The British United Provident Association, or BUPA. Fifty years later, BUPA is still the UK's leading independent health and care organisation and is a major international organisation. It has nearly four million members in 180 countries world-wide, and has offices in Hong Kong, Ireland, Saudi Arabia, Spain, Thailand and the UK.

As a provident association, BUPA has no shareholders to pay. This means that any money it makes is invested back into the business. BUPA is best known for its private medical insurance; however, it now owns and operates many associated facilities. BUPA has 36 hospitals in the UK and one in Dublin, owns and runs 34 health screening centres, operates 221 care homes and 54 retirement home developments, and runs home care and nursing services. BUPA also owns Sanitas, the leading private healthcare organisation in Spain. BUPA's services also include travel, dental, disability and critical illness cover.

Catrin Weston is a senior manager in the Organisation Development Department at BUPA. She has worked closely with Dr Nicholas Georgiades of consultants TLC Ltd in attempting to validate aspects of the Service Value Cycle which is based upon the Harvard Business School Service Profit Chain (see Georgiades and Macdonell 1998).

'What we've done so far is to establish significant correlations between the results we get from our annual staff survey with our customer surveys and the profit for each of our 36 hospitals in the UK. We have been tracking the staff satisfaction score, the customer loyalty indicator and the profit for each hospital. We have calculated these correlations twice now and we will be repeating it again this autumn.

'Our staff opinion survey, the Service Organisation Profile (SOP), was developed by Dr Georgiades and TLC Ltd. They run this for us each year, which is quite a big job because around 12,000 employees and 1,000 managers are currently involved in the survey. The SOP is an empirically developed staff opinion survey based upon the Burke Litwin Model of Organisation Performance. The SOP provides us with a valuable way of mapping the performance of business units, departments and individual managers in the organisation. It is easy to understand and communicate and not only provides a measure of current performance but also helps managers put together action plans to work on critical issues in their work groups. The questionnaire covers ten key factors: leadership, customer service mission, adaptive culture, management practices, group climate, group tension, job satisfaction, role overload, role ambiguity and career development.

'Each year we ask our staff to complete the questionnaire confidentially, and return it to TLC Ltd. TLC undertakes the analysis at an aggregate and individual manager level so every manager gets their own feedback about how their team sees them as a manager. It also provides information about staff perceptions about BUPA as a whole, its leadership, the organisation's commitment to customer service and its prevailing culture.

'When the managers receive their feedback they are charged with sitting down with their team to have an open discussion in order to explore the key issues. They then agree an action plan to deal with these issues. These plans are then reviewed to check progress at subsequent meetings. Some managers are good at this, others less so!

'Some of the issues can't be dealt with at team level because they relate to organisation-level concerns so every manager sends me a copy of their action plan and I go through them to identify what needs to be done at an organisational level. As a result you get a good idea what influences staff opinions.

'Dr Georgiades and I have been working to test the validity of the Service Value Cycle in the 36 BUPA hospitals. The model suggests that employee motivation, loyalty and commitment drive customer loyalty and satisfaction and that in turn customer loyalty and satisfaction drive profitability.

'We took the total score on the SOP (averaged for each hospital) as the measure of motivation, loyalty and commitment, and related that score to each hospital's customer loyalty score (taken from consumer opinion surveys) and the profitability measured against target. The evidence was sufficiently strong to suggest that pursuing the goal of improving staff satisfaction, loyalty and commitment was not just a liberal "good employer – nice thing to do" but had real, tangible results for our customers and for BUPA's profitability.

'We are at an early stage in our research at the moment but it is very exciting and has already provided us with some invaluable information.'

Questions

1 *Identify the threads through the Service Performance Network captured by BUPA.*

2 *Evaluate Catrin Weston's attempts to understand the relationship between staff satisfaction and profit.*

11.5 WORLD-CLASS SERVICE

World-class service organisations have superior business performance that is the result of best-practice service management, i.e. superior process management, customer management, staff management and structure management. In turn these behaviours result from a clear vision, a clearly articulated service concept and strategy, and an appropriate culture driven by good leadership. World-class organisations tend to have gone beyond the intuition stage and not only understand the relationships between their operations decisions and business performance but also use this understanding to tremendous effect.

11.5.1 Relationship between results and drivers

Figure 11.8 shows the relationship between an aggregated drivers score against an aggregated results score for over 100 UK service organisations. The strong positive correlation demonstrates that, overall, the better an organisation manages its drivers – such as process, capacity, employees, customers and structure – the better will be its results, including market share, customer and staff satisfaction and profit.

Those organisations at the top right are considered to be world-class organisations, closely followed by contenders for world-class status and some promising organisations (see Figure 11.9).

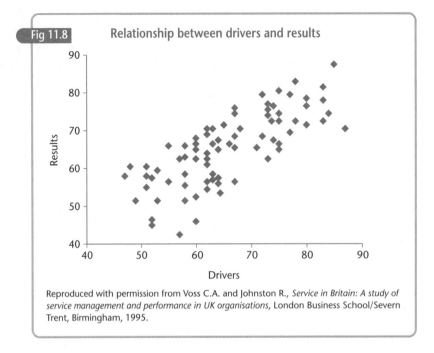

Reproduced with permission from Voss C.A. and Johnston R., *Service in Britain: A study of service management and performance in UK organisations*, London Business School/Severn Trent, Birmingham, 1995.

Figure 11.10 shows the percentage of organisations in each of the above categories based on two studies undertaken in the UK and the USA (Voss and Johnston 1995 and Voss *et al.* 1997). Although UK service organisations have fewer world-class organisations than the USA, the USA appears to have a longer tail of poor performers (additional information can be obtained from http://www.severn-trent.com/usdocs).

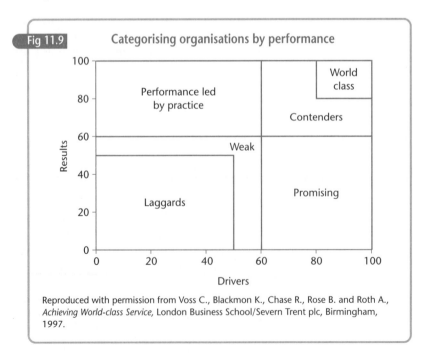

Reproduced with permission from Voss C., Blackmon K., Chase R., Rose B. and Roth A., *Achieving World-class Service,* London Business School/Severn Trent plc, Birmingham, 1997.

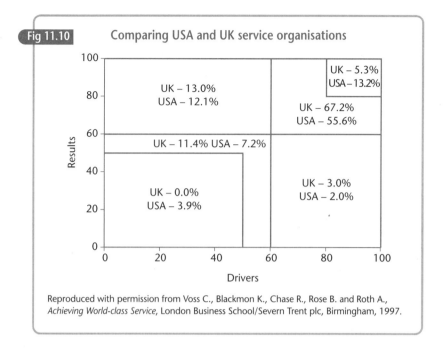

Fig 11.10   Comparing USA and UK service organisations

Reproduced with permission from Voss C., Blackmon K., Chase R., Rose B. and Roth A., *Achieving World-class Service*, London Business School/Severn Trent plc, Birmingham, 1997.

11.5.2 Characteristics of world-class service organisations

World-class service organisations tend to have impressive business results, both financial and non-financial. The non-financial measures include employee satisfaction, customer satisfaction and market share. These organisations are generally recognised by customers, industry organisations and business commentators. They are often quoted as benchmark organisations, their approaches imitated by others, and they accumulate a range of accolades and service and quality awards. So what are the key characteristics that drive this success? We suggest that there are two types of drivers, at corporate level and operational level.

The characteristics of world-class organisations at a corporate level usually include:

- great leadership
- clear vision
- clarity of concept
- supportive culture
- a well-developed strategy.

At an operations level world-class organisations are set apart by their:

- willingness to listen to customers
- continuous process development
- consistency of service
- responsiveness
- 'can do' attitude

- big and little thinking
- supportive and committed staff
- excellent performance management
- lack of complacency.

Great leadership

The key to great service 'is genuine service leadership at all levels in an organisation' (Berry 1995, p. 7). Clear and purposeful leadership right from the top of the organisation is needed to develop and sustain a world-class organisation. Furthermore, that purpose and the organisation concept must be continually emphasised and enacted. A willingness to listen encourages communication up and down the organisation. Good leadership is also characterised by a belief in and investment in people, systems, training and the delivery of outstanding service (see, for example, Georgiades and Macdonell 1998; Roberts 1989).

Clear vision

Service vision is more than simply having clarity about where the organisation is going but also an ability to enthusiastically communicate to others. Vision, created by great leaders, provides employees with something to believe in, something that challenges them, provides the emotional energy required to deliver outstanding service and generates commitment to the provision of service (Berry 1995).

Clarity of concept

'Excellent service companies define their business in strikingly clear terms' (Berry 1999, p. 238). In world-class organisations the service concept is well defined, communicated and well understood by employees and customers. This brand image is well known in the marketplace and the organisation is known to be a market leader. Other organisations may try to emulate and reproduce the concept but are continually outrun by the organisation that invests in continuous process development.

Supportive culture

Great service is delivered by employees who don't need to be defensive in their dealings with customers. A positive attitude is generated by an organisational culture consistent with the declared competitive strategy, and that values the contributions of all members. A supportive culture is self-renewing, not looking back to the 'good old days' but encouraging the development of new ways of thinking and acting. For a good overview of cultural effects on service provision, see Georgiades and Macdonell (1998).

Well-developed strategy

World-class organisations have clear plans in place that set out how they will achieve their goals and their vision. The vision is not pie-in-the-sky but something concrete that employees feel is both achievable and desirable. The strategy communicates how this will be achieved and defines their part in the activity. An essential attribute of a well-developed strategy is that it has been formulated with the ownership and buy-in of all levels in the organisation.

Willingness to listen to customers

World-class organisations take great efforts to listen to their customers. They use many methods of listening (see Chapter 4) and take all comments very seriously. Customers' views are used to drive developments, although the need to be financially and commercially viable is never forgotten. The nirvana that world-class service companies seem to have found is in meeting, without compromise, both customer needs and their own criteria for financial success. For world-class service organisations, these two requirements, so often at odds, seem to go hand in hand.

Continuous process development

World-class organisations try to continually develop their service. This is not just redesign but requires more fundamental questioning that leads to 'reinvention' of their services (see Chapters 2 and 12). This vigorous search for distinctive service can only be undertaken in an organisation that is confident in its ability to ask and deal with difficult questions. World-class service organisations firmly reject 'me-too-service'. Any changes they make are usually based on detailed research but they also take risks and sometimes 'take a flyer' when it feels right. They are equally willing to drop an idea, despite the investment cost, if an innovation is not seen to be working. They also see service delivery boundaries as flexible and carefully manage overlaps with other service providers.

Consistency of service

David Good, the General Manager of the Central Samui Beach Resort Hotel we described in Chapter 4, made the point that 'high-quality service is about consistency'. World-class service organisations don't just deliver outstanding service – they do it routinely and consistently. World-class service providers may surprise their customers with their level of service, their willingness to deal with an issue, their ability to recover the customer after a problem and the speed of their service. World-class service organisations, however, go beyond making the customers say 'wow' about the service by getting customers to say 'wow' the next time because it was like that again. 'Great service companies … couple the basics of service with the art of surprise' (Berry 1995, p. 78).

Responsiveness

Customers of world-class service organisations find that not only are they listened to, but the organisation is happy and able to respond to reasonable requests for service. Customers are not greeted with a mechanistic response such as 'I'm sorry, we don't do that', but staff are encouraged to try, within reasonable limits, to satisfy customers. A cliché in hotel receptions is the standard response, 'No problem'. For world-class service organisations, this is reality. Another test of a world-class service organisation is to ask yourself after having made a request, 'Do I feel that I have been heard and that the organisation will deal with my request, or do I feel that my request has disappeared into a black hole?'

'Can do' attitude

World-class service organisations are concerned with the longer-term relationships between customer and provider and try to find ways to please the customer. Berry and Parasuraman (1991) summed this up as 'purposely treating customers personally'.

Big and little thinking

Lord Marshall, Chairman of British Airways, referred to this as 'Nothing too big. Nothing too small' (Prokesch 1995). World-class service organisations never lose sight of the 'big picture', keeping strategy, concept and vision at the forefront, while at the same time, however, they pay close attention to the detail. David Good, the General Manager at the Central Samui Beach Resort Hotel, said, '… it's about the little things, personal touches, such as taking time with guests; a few minutes here and there to acknowledge people, or spend a few minutes talking with them'. Getting the detail right makes outstanding service providers stand head and shoulders above the rest. It is through the detail that the customer confronts excellence.

Supportive and committed staff

Excellent service is delivered either directly or indirectly by employees. World-class service organisations use approaches such as empowerment or self-directed work teams appropriately rather than implement these ideas because they've seen them work elsewhere. Staff are committed to the organisation and to the service concept because they are involved in the process of service development, they are encouraged to own the service delivery process, to look for ways of improving it, and they are motivated by the right mix of recognition and reward.

Excellent performance management

Performance measurement is an important driver of world-class success. Key drivers are measured, service is carefully quantified and targets set in key areas of the business. Results, both financial and operational, are shared throughout the business. Targets are based not only on what was achieved in the past but also on the activities of competitors and other excellent organisations, perhaps not even in the same field. World-class organisations have a good understanding of the rest of the industry and regularly, and systematically, check out their competitors' services, not just for the sake of comparison but to promote learning and development and growth. Furthermore, world-class organisations 'celebrate excellence' (Berry 1995, p. 244). Measuring performance and knowing what is excellent is only one step – recognising the people who have achieved excellence and then regarding it through a mixture of financial and non-financial ways validates those achievements, motivates others and sustains excellence.

Lack of complacency

One key trait that seems to separate the outstanding from the very good is a lack of complacency. World-class organisations never accept they have reached their goals, they always need to stretch the organisation and its staff. Indeed it is this continual questioning of boundaries and encouragement of talent that keeps such organisations forging ahead. In the study of UK and US service organisations mentioned earlier (Voss and Johnston 1995 and Voss et al. 1997) a clear link was found between the performance of organisations and their assessment about how well the organisation's managers believed it was able to compete with the best of its competitors. The resulting 'complacency index' shows that managers who viewed their organisations as strong compared to their competitors had below-average performance, whereas those who viewed themselves as 'having a good deal to learn and not as good as their competitors' turned in the best performances (see Figure 11.11).

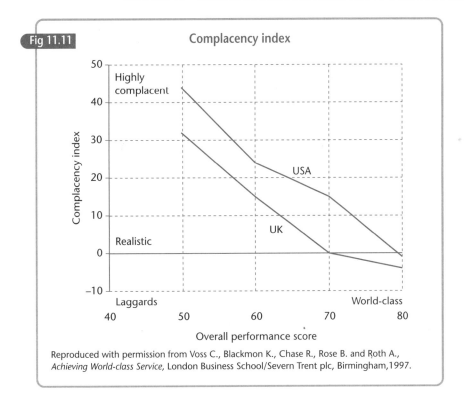

Fig 11.11

Reproduced with permission from Voss C., Blackmon K., Chase R., Rose B. and Roth A., *Achieving World-class Service*, London Business School/Severn Trent plc, Birmingham, 1997.

In Box 11.3 we can see many of those world-class characteristics in Singapore Airlines.

Box 11.3 Singapore Airlines (SIA)

How does SIA, an airline from a small country-state, earn a reputation for being 'the most consistently profitable airline in the world, despite various world-wide recessions'? How does SIA get voted, year after year, 'the best airline', 'the best for business travel', 'the best air cargo carrier', and even 'Asia's most admired company'? In what must be one of the most ruthless and competitive of all international trades, what puts this airline head and shoulders above the big players like British Airways, KLM, United Airlines, North West Airlines, JAL and Qantas?

There are many reasons and a lack of complacency is one. SIA's Managing Director, Dr Cheong Choong Kong, is resolute that SIA cannot afford to be complacent. He explained: 'It's going to be much harder because ... the worthy competition is getting better every year.'

Dr Cheong Choong Kong also attributed the company's consistent success to recognising the importance of the passengers. He explained: 'Our passengers .... are our *raison d'être*, they are what this whole bewildering [airline] business is about. If SIA is successful, it is largely because we have never allowed ourselves to forget that important fact.'

SIA is well known for its innovation in the industry. It has an ongoing research programme and is involved in a number of overseas ventures. Mr B.K. Ong, the Senior Manager for Customer Service Affairs, explained: 'We aim to stay ahead of the competitors in everything we do …. When we have a big idea and see potential and big benefits, we put money into it.' Recent innovations have included personalised in-flight entertainment systems, gourmet cuisine, larger seats and increased seat pitch in Raffles class, footrests and winged headrests in economy. Away from the airport SIA provide the SIA Hop-On, an air-conditioned tourist bus that takes in the main shopping area, hotels and some of the cultural and entertainment areas. SIA's passengers are entitled to free and unlimited rides any time during their stay in Singapore.

In the pursuit of excellent service, SIA never underestimates the importance of attention to detail. The company knows that this makes the difference between 'good' service and 'excellent' service; something even as simple as installing double castor wheels on the cabin carts which eases and speeds the service of meals. It has also developed a wide choice of menus including lighter or healthier options. There are also special food events held to coincide with major festivals and celebrations.

SIA's people-centred approach starts at the top. Mr Ong said, 'The commitment of top managers is the driving force behind our success. At all levels we recruit the best people available. We like to inject new blood where and when we can to bring in fresh ideas. We also want to recruit people who can make an impression. We are also serious about training. We recently spent S$80m on our own training centre: training is a big business for us. At our centre we undertake three major types of training: functional, related to the job such as ticketing reservations; skills improvement, such as supervisory skills; and management development where we run a range of management programmes.'

Mr Ong explained the company's approach to managing its staff and outlined one of its most recent initiatives in customer service. 'We believe in empowering our staff because it involves them more in their work, makes them more motivated, eases decision-making and, of course, improves customer service. Our most recent initiative is called OSG – Outstanding Service on the Ground. We know cabin service is vital and we have put a lot of time and effort into it, but there is only so much you can do during a flight. The problems are not usually in the air where we have direct control over many of the factors but are away from the flight, such as service on the ground where we might be only one of many players. Outstanding service here is noticed by our customers, as is poor service, but it is more difficult to achieve because it often involves dealing with many other bodies, like handling agents for example. This is not a programme, it is a movement, led by the Managing Director. We are putting all of our ground staff through OSG courses now. We want people to (1) show they care, (2) dare to care, that is to go and make decisions, and (3) be a service entrepreneur, look for opportunities to impress. We are also running "take the lead" programmes for supervisors to carry through and support OSG.'

Mr Ong added, 'We try hard to quantify levels of service to help establish what is expected of staff, but they also have to be realistic. We have standards about how each task should be carried out, for example time taken to serve a meal, telephone pick-up times, check-in times, times for bags to be delivered, punctuality targets, mishandling rates, complaint/compliment ratios, and deadlines to reply to complaints.'

'We constantly monitor passenger feedback, re-examine service procedures and study new technologies to discover ways in which to further improve the service we provide,' said Dr Cheong Choong Kong. Mr Ong explained the details. 'We employ varied and systematic methods to obtain information from our passengers. We carry out quarterly passenger surveys and undertake focused group work with our frequent flyers. We do get some complaints and pride ourselves in being able to resolve them quickly. We analyse them and try to improve what we do and feed the information back to the people who can make it happen. We really value complaints and see them as opportunities to improve what we do and how we do it. We put a strong emphasis on service recovery, not damage control. We do have many contingency plans in place for when things go wrong and we have a philosophy of "making good": trying to provide on-the-spot recovery and fair compensation for anything adverse that has happened.

'We also check out the service for ourselves. We conduct on-site audits with test calls to reservations, for example, to see how service is being delivered. When any member of staff flies in our aircraft we ask them to submit reports of their travel experiences. Senior staff members must submit a comment sheet on each flight with their expense account. We even monitor our competitors and often go and check out their service. We monitor and assess their levels of service and their amenities.'

Question

1 *What makes SIA a world-class service provider?*

This illustration is abridged from 'Singapore Airlines' by Robert Johnston, published in Johnston R., Chambers S., Harland C., Harrison A. and Slack N., *Cases in Operations Management* (2nd edition), Pitman, London, 1997, pp. 509–18.

11.6 SUMMARY

Understanding the relationships between operational decisions and business performance

- Understanding the chains of cause and effect between their operational drivers and business performance helps managers make efficient and effective decisions.
- Leading-edge organisations are working at understanding the links between their operational drivers and business results.
- There are several frameworks that help us understand the chains of cause and effect.

The Service Performance Network

- The Service Performance Network documents many of the cause–effect linkages between operational drivers and business results.

Key stages in developing a network

- The key stages in developing a network are: create a model by capturing several threads through the Network, collect data, and analyse the data to understand the relationships between the variables.

World-class service

- World-class service organisations have superior business performance and understand relationships between their operations decisions and business performance.
- The characteristics of world-class organisations at a corporate level include:
  - ➢ knowing who is the customer
  - ➢ great leadership
  - ➢ clear vision

➤ clarity of concept
➤ supportive culture
➤ a well-developed strategy.

● The characteristics of world-class service at an operations level include:
➤ willingness to listen to customers
➤ responsiveness
➤ continuous process development
➤ consistency of service
➤ 'can do' attitude
➤ big and little thinking
➤ supportive and committed staff
➤ excellent performance management
➤ lack of complacency.

11.7 DISCUSSION QUESTIONS

1. Compare and contrast the EFQM Business Excellence Model and the Service Performance Network.

2. Apply the characteristics of world-class service to an organisation of your choice.

3. Can a world-class operation exist within a run-of-the-mill organisation and vice versa? Explain your answer and provide some examples.

11.8 QUESTIONS FOR MANAGERS

1. How well does your organisation understand the links between drivers and results?

2. Evaluate the relationships between some of your key drivers and results.

3. How does your organisation stack up against the characteristics of world-class organisations and operations?

11.9 SELECTED READING

Berry L.L., *Discovering the Soul of Service*, Free Press, New York, 1999.
Georgiades N. and Macdonell R., *Leadership for Competitive Advantage*, Wiley, Chichester, 1998.
Heskett J.L., Sasser W.E. and Schlesinger L.A., *The Service Profit Chain*, Free Press, New York, 1997.

11.10 REFERENCES

Anderson E.W., Fornell C. and Lehmann D.R., 'Customer Satisfaction, Market Share, and Profitability', *Journal of Marketing*, vol. 58, July 1994, pp. 53–66.
Anderson E.W., Fornell C. and Rust R.T., 'Customer Satisfaction, Productivity, and Profitability: Differences between goods and services', *Marketing Science*, vol. 16, no 2, 1997, pp. 129–45.

Bennis W., *Managing People is like Herding Cats*, Executive Excellence Publishing, South Provo, Utah, 1999.

Berry L.L., *On Great Service: A framework for action*, Free Press, New York, 1995.

Berry L.L., *Discovering the Soul of Service*, Free Press, New York, 1999.

Berry L.L. and Parasuraman A., *Marketing Services: Competing through quality*, Free Press, New York, 1991.

Buzzell R. and Gale B., *The PIMS Principles: Linking strategy to performance*, Free Press, New York, 1987.

Deming W.E., *Quality, Productivity and Competitive Position*, MIT Center for Advanced Engineering Study, Cambridge, Mass., 1982.

Deming W.E., *Out of the Crisis*, MIT Center for Advanced Engineering Study, Cambridge, Mass., 1986.

European Foundation for Quality Management (EFQM), http://www.efqm.organisation, 1999.

Feigenbaum A.V., *Total Quality Control*, McGraw-Hill, New York, 1986.

Fitzgerald L., Johnston R., Brignall T.J., Silvestro R. and Voss C., *Performance Measurement in Service Businesses*, CIMA, London, 1991.

Fox M.L., Dwyer D.J. and Ganster D.C., 'Effects of Stressful Job Demands on Physiological and Attitudinal Outcomes in a Hospital Setting', *Academy of Management Journal*, vol. 36, 1993, pp. 289–318.

Georgiades N. and Macdonell R., *Leadership for Competitive Advantage*, Wiley, Chichester, 1998.

Heskett J.L., Sasser W.E. and Schlesinger L.A., *The Service Profit Chain*, Free Press, New York, 1997.

Hoyle R.H. (ed.), *Structural Equation Modeling*, Sage, Thousand Oaks, Calif., 1995.

Jones T.O. and Sasser W.E., 'Why Satisfied Customers Defect', *Harvard Business Review*, November–December 1995, pp. 88–99.

Kaplan R.S. and Norton D.P., *The Balanced Scorecard*, Harvard Business School Press, Boston, Mass., 1996.

Loveman G.W., 'Employee Satisfaction, Customer Loyalty, and Financial Performance: An empirical examination of the Service Profit Chain in retail banking', *Journal of Service Research*, vol. 1, no. 1, 1998, pp. 18–31.

Lynch R.L and Cross K.F., *Measure Up! Yardsticks for Continuous Improvement*, Blackwell, Oxford, 1991.

Maruyama G.M., *Basics of Structural Equation Modeling*, Sage, Thousand Oaks, Calif., 1997.

Matteson M.T. and Ivancevich J.M., *Managing Job Stress and Health*, Free Press, New York, 1982.

Motowidlio S.J., Manning M.R. and Packard J.S., 'Occupational Stress: Its causes and consequences for job performance', *Journal of Applied Psychology*, vol. 71, 1986, pp. 618–29.

Norman M., *Data Envelopment Analysis: The assessment of performance*, Wiley, Chichester, 1991.

Peters T.J., *Thriving on Chaos: Handbook for a management revolution*, Harper and Rowe, New York, 1987.

Prokesch S.E., 'Competing on Customer Service: An interview with British Airways' Sir Colin Marshall', *Harvard Business Review*, November–December 1995, pp. 101–12.

Reichheld, F. *The Loyalty Effect*, Harvard Business School Press, Cambridge, Mass., 1996.

Reichheld F.F. and Sasser W.E., 'Zero Defections: Quality comes to services', *Harvard Business Review*, September–October 1990, pp. 105–11.

Roberts W., *Leadership Secrets of Attila The Hun*, Bantam Press, London, 1989.

Rucci A.J., Kirn S.P. and Quinn R.T., 'The Employee–Customer–Profit Chain at Sears', *Harvard Business Review*, January–February 1998, pp. 83–97.

Rust R.T. and Zahorik A.J. 'Customer Satisfaction, Customer Retention, and Market Share', *Journal of Retailing*, vol. 69, no. 2, Summer 1993, pp. 193–215.

Rust R.T., Zahorik A.J. and Keiningham T.L., 'Return on Quality (ROQ): Making service quality financially accountable', *Journal of Marketing*, vol. 59 (April), 1995, pp. 58–70.

Schneider B., 'The Service Organisation: Climate is crucial', *Organisational Dynamics*, Autumn 1980, pp. 52–65.

Schneider B. and Bowen D.E., *Winning the Service Game*, Harvard Business School Press, Boston, Mass., 1995.

Voss C.A. and Johnston R., *Service in Britain: A study of service management and performance in UK organisations*, Severn Trent plc, Birmingham, 1995.

Voss C., Blackmon K., Chase R., Rose B. and Roth A., *Achieving World-class Service*, London Business School/Severn Trent plc, Birmingham, 1997.

CASE EXERCISE

Superstore Plc

This case was written by Dr Rhian Silvestro, Warwick Business School, and Stuart Cross whilst undertaking postgraduate studies at Warwick. Stuart Cross is now Head of Strategy Development, Boots the Chemist.

The UK supermarket industry is dominated by four leading chains, with all others competing in the second tier. The four main players have all diversified into the non-food sector and at the end of the economic recession, with a slow-down in price-based competition, the emphasis has shifted to competition based on customer loyalty and quality.

Superstore is one of the big four supermarket chains in the UK and operates a chain of hundreds of stores which retail in excess of 40,000 product lines, including food products and non-food items like music, personal care products, clothing and pharmaceutical products. It has positioned itself as a family store offering good value and, like many of the large superstores, the company has introduced loyalty card technology and a self-scanning service with a view to improving customer loyalty.

In a recent Annual Report the company's chief executive stated that customer satisfaction and loyalty were the real drivers of the company's profit and growth, and that these were influenced by how its people felt about their work, their rewards and their manager. This was also a central theme in the company's management training programme.

To test out this contention Julie Carroll, a senior officer in the Personnel Department, collected together some existing performance data. The data was a mixture of internal measures, based on the performance of 15 stores, and a survey of customer and employee perceptions based on six stores (see Table 1).

Table 1 Performance data

Internal data:
    profit margin
    sales per square foot
    employee turnover
    employee absence
    operating ratio

Customer/employee survey data:
    service delivery value – customers' perceptions of the value of the service delivered by the store
    share of grocery budget spent at the store
    average basket size (i.e. value of the average basket)
    customer referral – customers' willingness to refer the store as a good place to shop
    customer satisfaction with the store
    employee referral – employees' willingness to refer the store as a good place to work
    overall employee satisfaction
    employee satisfaction with the style of supervision

Table 2 Correlations coefficients between the various data sets

	Sales per square foot	Employee turnover	Employee absence	Operating ratio	Service delivery value	Share of grocery budget	Average basket size	Customer referral	Customer satisfaction	Employee referral	Employee satisfaction	Satisfaction with supervision
Profit margin	0.77	0.18	–0.35	–0.75	0.88	0.91	0.88	0.86	0.70	–0.25	–0.87	–0.63
Sales per square foot		–0.10	–0.04	–0.65	0.92	0.95	0.60	0.91	0.59	0.03	–0.61	–0.36
Employee turnover			–0.36	–0.27	–0.09	0.02	0.30	0.06	–0.35	0.34	0.10	0.73
Employee absence				0.25	–0.60	–0.51	–0.58	–0.57	0.24	–0.44	0.13	–0.22
Operating ratio					–0.97	–0.96	–0.80	–0.93	–0.86	0.36	0.76	0.46
Service delivery value						0.98	0.94	0.98	0.86	–0.21	–0.64	–0.26
Share of grocery budget							0.91	0.99	0.78	–0.24	–0.69	–0.33
Average basket size								0.89	0.72	0.05	–0.60	–0.34
Customer referral									0.82	–0.22	–0.62	–0.18
Customer satisfaction										–0.53	–0.83	–0.19
Employee referral											0.61	0.42
Employee satisfaction												0.82

One particular measure calls for some explanation: store operating ratio is a ratio of actual to planned working hours. This was considered by the company's management to be an indicator of the quality of working life at a store because, as the ratio of planned to actual working hours increases, it was believed that the workplace became more stressful and that therefore the quality of working life diminished.

Julie calculated the correlation coefficients between the various data sets and her results are shown in Table 2. The correlations entered in bold indicate a significance at the 95 per cent level or higher. (The minimum value of the calculated correlation coefficient necessary for 95 per cent confidence was 0.51 when the sample size was 15 stores, and 0.81 when the sample size was six stores.) Julie was not sure what to do next.

Questions

1 *What conclusions could Julie draw from the data?*

2 *What are the issues and implications for the store?*

12

Driving Operational Improvement

12.1 INTRODUCTION

One important aspect of performance management is performance improvement. This chapter considers some ways in which improvements to operations are not simply encouraged but are used to drive change through organisations.

The objectives are:

- to assess service recovery and how it can be used to drive improvements
- to consider how service guarantees can drive improvement.

Whilst processes, capacity, people, technology and culture (Chapters 6–9 and 14) can promote and indeed inhibit operational improvements, there are three ways in which operations managers can identify ways in which they can make significant improvements to their operations. Performance measurement, with its focus on improvement, was dealt with in the previous two chapters. This chapter focuses on two service management tools that have also been used to great effect in the drive for operational improvement: service recovery and service guarantees.

12.2 SERVICE RECOVERY

The key purpose of service recovery is not to satisfy the customer *per se*, but to use the information gleaned from the failure and its consequences to continuously drive improvements through an organisation by focusing managerial attention on specific problem areas (Van Ossel and Stremersch 1998; Slack *et al.* 1998). If the focus of service recovery is solely to satisfy the complaining customer, its potential to prevent the problem recurring and thus more dissatisfied and lost customers and reduced financial performance is lost. Research shows that this is too often the case. 'Customers are often fobbed off with money or promises that the system has been changed for the future, but they are often left with the feeling that they, the customers, have basically expected too much, and any action is a goodwill gesture on the part of the service provider' (Armistead and Clark 1994).

One of the first definitions of service recovery, used in British Airways' 'Putting the Customer First Campaign' back in the 1980s, was 'to offset the negative impact of a screw-up' (Zemke and Schaaf 1989). Whilst dealing with the customer after something has gone wrong is without doubt an essential ingredient of recovery, we would argue that an additional and indeed critical benefit of service recovery is that of driving improvements in business performance. Sadly, many organisations don't obtain these benefits and view service recovery simply as a means of trying to pacify and mollify a dissatisfied customer.

We therefore define service recovery as the action of seeking out and dealing with failures in the delivery of service in order to improve delivery performance. Recovery is part of a continuous learning and improvement cycle, using feedback from customers and employees about actual and potential failure and problems to bring about process improvement (see Figure 12.1).

This definition expands service recovery away from complaint management by another name to the activity of finding failures and potential failures – preferably before the impact of which has been felt by the customer – and putting them right, i.e. driving improvements to operational processes. The act of recovering from a failure should also lead to satisfied, even delighted, customers. This should lead to higher retention rates and therefore all the financial benefits this provides (long-term income streams and reduced costs etc.) as well as positive word-of-mouth recommendations. Reduced costs may also be an outcome of improved processes, just as improved processes may attract more customers and themselves lead to increased revenue. Improved processes should lead to greater staff satisfaction, retention and possibly easier attraction (see Figure 12.2 and also Chapter 11).

Without doubt the numbers of customers who are complaining are on the increase. Complaints about local government services have increased from about 12,500 a month in 1992 to over 15,500 a month in 1995, and complaints about the family health service increased from 1,700 in 1988 to 2,500 in 1994 (Williams 1996): 'Retailers, education establishments, hotels, banks ... all report that complaints are on the increase.' There are several possible reasons for this growth. Maybe the quality of service has declined, or more likely the perceived quality of service has declined, as customers become increasingly service aware and more intolerant of poor service. This might have been brought about by greater pressures on time and/or on available money, making consumers – and indeed businesses – much more concerned about value for money. Secondly, there has been recent growth in consumer movements and government initiatives which have not only alerted people to their rights and the obligations of organisations but have also made customers more aware that organisations are trying to satisfy them! Whatever the reasons, service recovery is becoming an increasingly important task for service organisations.

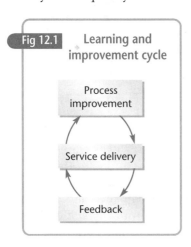

Fig 12.1 Learning and improvement cycle

Process improvement

Service delivery

Feedback

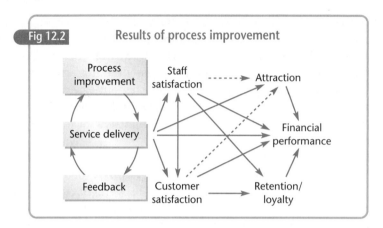

Fig 12.2   Results of process improvement

12.2.1   The four acid tests of service recovery

We suggest that four acid tests (Johnston 2000) can be applied to an organisation's service recovery process to assess its success in driving improvements in business performance:

1. Does it lead to increased customer satisfaction (at least for those customers that the organisation wishes to retain)?
2. Does it improve retention rates?
3. Does it drive process improvements?
4. And, as a result of the above, does it improve financial performance?

Customer satisfaction

When things go wrong, organisations have a chance to demonstrate what they can do for their customers. Indeed for some organisations, such as utilities, the occurrence of a failure or a problem is one of the few times that the organisation's staff may come into direct contact with customers! Whilst employee unwillingness to recognise and deal with problems is known to be a driver of dissatisfaction (Bitner *et al.* 1990), it is known that good service recovery is a key source of delighted customers (Johnston 1995). In a study of critical incidents (Johnston 1995) it was found that over half of delighted customers felt so because of something having gone wrong and the organisation dealing well with them and the problem.

Customer retention

Satisfied customers may not be enough – some customers who are satisfied still switch organisations! For the financial benefits to be gained customers need not only to be satisfied but also to be retained through recovery. Recovery can lead to retention for two reasons: first of all, good service recovery can generate high levels of satisfaction (see above), which increase the likelihood of the customer staying, but furthermore, the principle of reciprocity applies. Because the organisation has been seen to go out of its way to sort out a difficult situation for a customer, customers may feel obliged to reciprocate this by not only staying but becoming a champion for the organisation (see section 3.4.2) and so not only being more supportive of the organisation during service delivery but also acting as an advocate of its staff and services. In their book on breakthrough service, Heskett, Sasser and Hart (1990) stated: 'Mistakes are a critical part of every service ... errors are inevitable. But dissatisfied customers are not. A good recovery can turn angry, frustrated customers into loyal ones.'

The potential of failures and service recovery to retain customers has not been lost on British Airways. Chairman Lord Marshall explained how BA changed the nature of its complaint department: 'We have transformed customer relations from a defensive complaint department into a department for customer champions whose mission is to retain customers' (Prokesch 1995).

Process improvement

What seems to make customers annoyed, even angry, after a failed service recovery, is not so much that they were not satisfied but that they feel the system has not been changed to prevent the problem from arising again. They often feel fobbed off with excuses or empty promises. We believe one acid test, failed by many organisations, is their ability to take problem data, from customers or even staff, and turn it into real improvements. Little time or effort is put into creating systems or procedures to facilitate this – indeed some organisations make it particularly difficult by setting up remote and disconnected 'customer service centres' whose role is to pacify customers whilst not disturbing the rest of the organisation and letting it get on with its 'real' task. Some organisations just let their staff soak up the pressure resulting from their inadequate service systems, leading not only to dissatisfied and disillusioned customers but also to stressed and negatively disposed staff who feel powerless to help or sort out the problems. This helpless feeling (known as 'learned helplessness' – see, for example, Martinko and Gardner 1982) 'encourages' or rather induces employees to display passive, maladaptive behaviours, such as being unhelpful, withdrawing or acting uncreatively (Bowen and Johnston 1999). The employee alienation associated with this helplessness will be compounded when employees feel that management does not make efforts to recover them (the employees) from this helpless state.

Information from customer complaints and from other failure or problem situations can provide organisations with the means (and motivation!) to improve what they do and make things better for the future, not only for their customers but also for their staff who may experience on a regular basis what might seem one-off failures to customers. TNT, the international distribution and logistics company, has achieved some astonishing advances after they used the results of their complaint information (see Box 12.1).

Financial performance

Exploiting the above benefits would therefore lead directly to enhanced business performance for the organisation. There should be increased revenues from higher levels of retention, from positive word-of-mouth from delighted customers, reduced costs through higher retention levels, and from continuous process improvements making the process more effective and reducing the costs (financial and emotional) in dealing with dissatisfied customers.

Indeed, defined in this way, service recovery and complaint management could be viewed as profit centres; sadly, for many organisations they are seen as a

---

Box 12.1 TNT

TNT is a leading global express distribution, logistics and international mail company which moves documents, consignments and business mail. TNT serves 200 countries and carries over two million consignments per week passing through its 969 depots and 85 international mail distribution centres. It has 50,000 employees and a 17,000-strong vehicle fleet plus 40 aircraft dedicated to its operations. TNT is a subsidiary of TNT Post Group (TPG), a publicly listed company, with its headquarters in Amsterdam.

TNT's philosophy focuses on the customer and aims 'to be your business partner devising solutions for all our customers' distribution needs by combining our core capabilities to create new products and services'. The organisation is serious about complaints and works hard to derive improvements from problems and complaints. It uses a world-wide reporting system to identify all failures in detail, without exception, and then weekly in-depth root-cause analysis is used to identify and solve problems. Indeed, by focusing on complaint data, TNT has improved its performance dramatically, including a 96 per cent improvement in on-time delivery and missed pick-ups down by 78 per cent. This has resulted in less problems and hassle for staff which has reversed the company's employee turnover figures and led to significant reductions in absenteeism. The impact on financial performance has also been evident, with profit before tax up by 81 per cent over two years.

Question

1. *Visit TNT's web site, http://www.tnt.com/, and evaluate the organisation's methods of collecting feedback from customers.*

This illustration was developed from material in http://www.tnt.com/ and Barlow J. and Møller C., *A Complaint is a Gift*, Berrett-Koehler, San Francisco, 1996.

---

necessary evil and a sunk cost. To understand better these relationships and to understand the relationships between complaints/recovery and financial performance, organisations need to collect and analyse the data to help them exploit the value of service recovery for the organisation.

12.2.2 Consumer behaviour

Before identifying what makes a good recovery system, it is important to understand how customers react to service failures. How they react will be a function of the type of person they are and their attitude to complaining, the perceived likelihood of successful redress, and age and sex (see, for example, Blodgett *et al.* 1993; Day 1984; Landon 1977; Oliver 1997). We believe one key driver of consumer reaction is their level or intensity of dissatisfaction (see Johnston 1998 and Prakash 1991).

By scaling consumer dissatisfaction (see the satisfaction continuum in Chapter 4) from 0 to –5, where 0 is not dissatisfied (i.e. satisfied) through extremely dissatisfied to customers who feel absolutely furious, we can obtain a picture of their likely responses to failures given their level of dissatisfaction (see Figure 12.3). (It should be noted, however, that many other connections are possible – an extremely dissatisfied customer, for example, may exhibit only a mild reaction and vice versa – but in most cases the outward display of reaction may be the only means of assessing a customer's level of dissatisfaction.)

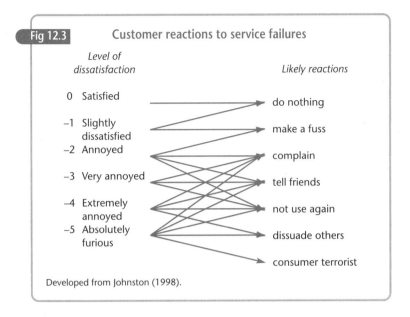

Fig 12.3 Customer reactions to service failures

Level of dissatisfaction   *Likely reactions*

0 Satisfied   do nothing

−1 Slightly dissatisfied   make a fuss

−2 Annoyed   complain

−3 Very annoyed   tell friends

−4 Extremely annoyed   not use again

−5 Absolutely furious   dissuade others

                                          consumer terrorist

Developed from Johnston (1998).

The more dissatisfied customers are, the more extreme and more types of complaint behaviour they will exhibit (Johnston 1998).

For some people a problem or failure may have little effect – they may be tolerant or expect poor service. Others, level −2, may just store up a black mark for future recall when something else goes wrong. Others may make a fuss – not quite a complaint, more of a verbal warning: 'I'm not complaining but ...'. Complaining formally, verbally or in writing, is the next level which, like all of the others, will not necessarily be mutually exclusive. Some customers may exhibit several behaviours! Dissatisfied customers may tell friends and colleagues, indeed may go further and actively dissuade them from using the service again. Others may go to the extreme of becoming a terrorist and campaigning against the organisation by putting up signs, taking out newspaper advertisements, seeking legal redress and sometimes illegal acts!

Whilst figures abound about how many people a dissatisfied customer will tell, again it has been shown (Johnston 1998) that the number they tell will depend upon their level of dissatisfaction. Slightly dissatisfied customers told on average three other people, whereas extremely annoyed customers told over 15 each, and absolutely furious customers usually exceeded 25.

Why this is important in the design or assessment of service recovery and complaint systems is that the type of response to a customer may need to take into account the level of dissatisfaction of the customer. There is little sense – indeed it could be counterproductive – to offer a furious customer a small token gesture.

12.2.3 Recovering customers

Service recovery as defined at the start of this chapter implies more than just dealing with customers who have experienced a failure; likewise service recovery as an activity must do more than this. Service recovery has three essential ingredients:

1. designing-out failures to prevent them happening in the first place
2. excellent complaint handling
3. proactive service recovery, seeking out problems and potential problems.

Designing-out failures

The best way of preventing complaints and eliminating the need for service recovery is to prevent problems happening in the first place. Chapter 6 dealt with service design and section 6.8 specifically dealt with preventing failures.

Excellent complaint handling

A good deal has been written over the last ten years or so on the 'ingredients' of recovery (see, for example, Armistead and Clark 1994; Bell and Zemke 1987; Bitner *et al.*, 1990; Hart, Heskett and Sasser 1990; Johnston 1995; Johnston and Fern 1999).

Essentially excellent complaint handling consists of three key operational activities: dealing with the customer, solving the problem for the customer, and dealing with the problem within the organisation.

Dealing with the customer

This involves five key activities:

1. *Acknowledgement* – acknowledge the problem has occurred. For some customers, if staff are dismissive of the problem it can create a good deal of dissatisfaction and bad will.
2. *Empathy* – following from acknowledgement, try to understand the problem from a customer's point of view.
3. *Apology* – for many people, certainly at levels 1, 2 or 3, an apology may certainly satisfy the customer and is all that might be required. Some organisations may have difficulty in saying sorry because they may be concerned that it implies fault, opening the way for litigation. In such circumstances, words similar to 'I am sorry this has happened to you' may do the trick! A written apology or a verbal follow-up call from management may delight customers at the lower end of the dissatisfaction scale but may be expected by customers at the top end.
4. *Own the problem* – if a member of staff gives the customer some confidence in the system and the outcome by getting hold of the problem and assuming clear ownership, and reinforcing this to the customer, the sense of relief felt by a customer may become an outpouring of support that creates a positive cycle and bond between customer and employee.
5. *Involve management* – for more severe cases (customer dissatisfaction levels above annoyed), customers often expect that a more senior person will deal with their problem. This should be part of the system, even if the employee is perfectly competent to deal with it!

Solving the problem for the customer

This involves two key activities:

1. *Fix the problem for the customer* – or at least (appear to) try to fix it. For customers who are above 3 on the scale staff may need to be seen to be putting themselves out to fix it and 'jumping through hoops'. At the higher end of the scale the fixing may need to be seen to be done or at least overseen by someone in higher authority.

2. *Provide compensation* – some organisations seem overly keen to dispense compensation or tokens, assuming that this alone will appease customers. Often customers simply want the problem fixed and dealt with so that it does not happen again (see below). Token compensation may be unnecessary for level 1 and appreciated by level 2, while levels 3 and 4 may require equivalent compensation – refund and making a token gesture – whereas level 5 customers may need 'big gesture' compensation – either monetary, goods or services, or acts of contrition by management!

Dealing with the problem within the organisation
Within the organisation there are three essential steps:

1. *Find the root cause* – there should be clear operational responsibility to deal with the opportunities identified by customers. Root-cause analysis should identify the real causes, being careful to put aside blame which can destroy such processes.

2. *Solve the problem* – if it is felt to be appropriate to solve the problem, this needs to be done. If it is deemed too expensive or inappropriate for other reasons, a procedure needs to be put in place to ensure staff know how to deal with the situation should it occur again.

3. *Provide assurance* – for customers at level 3 or beyond, it may be appropriate to provide them with assurance that the problem has been/will be sorted and should not occur again. For level 4 and 5 customers written explanation as to the investigation that was carried out, its outcome and the steps being taken may be expected.

Proactive service recovery

Unfortunately the majority of customers do not complain. The proportions vary significantly between organisations and also depend on the nature of the person involved and indeed the seriousness of the complaint and intensity of dissatisfaction felt. Williams (1996) suggested that 49 per cent of dissatisfied customers in a restaurant will not complain. In stores this is about 44 per cent, whereas for a council with monopoly control over local services only 30 per cent of customers complained when dissatisfied.

The alternatives to complaining were identified in section 12.2.2. But why don't these people complain? Not only will this have the benefit of (hopefully) fixing the problem for the future but also of recovering the customer. Research suggests that customers feel it is just not worth the effort (OFT 1990; Johnston and Fern 1999) – see Table 12.1.

Table 12.1 Reasons for not complaining

Reasons for not complaining	Percentage citing those reasons
Did not think anything would change	50
Too much effort	17
Did not want to cause trouble	17
Too busy	8
Too stressful	8

Johnston and Fern (1999).

In order to encourage feedback, complaints and helpful suggestions from customers, organisations need to deal with the root causes of this problem. This involves making it easy for customers to provide feedback and ensuring that – and assuring them that – things will change and that the organisation takes the feedback seriously and acts on it (see process improvement in section 12.2.1). The MTR in Hong Kong goes to great lengths to solicit customer feedback (Box 12.2).

Box 12.2 Mass Transit Railway Corporation (Hong Kong)

The MTR's four lines – Kwun Tong, Tsuen Wan, Island and Tung Chung Lines – cover over 40 kilometres connecting 38 stations in Hong Kong. The trains move around 2.5 million people every weekday, making it one of the most heavily used mass transit systems in the world. Besides running a mass transit system the Corporation is also actively involved in the development of key residential and commercial projects above existing stations and along new line extensions. In 1998 its turnover was close to HK$7 billion with a profit of nearly HK$3 billion.

'The MTR Corporation's key mission is to be the best mass transport company in the world for customer service, and recent benchmarking studies have confirmed that the MTR is one of the world's finest railways for reliability, customer service and state-of-the-art technology,' explains Jack C.K. So, Chairman. To meet this aim the interval between peak-time trains is less than 2 minutes, with dwell time at stations around 30 seconds. All the trains and underground stations are air-conditioned and are kept scrupulously clean. The Corporation has recently embarked on an HK$8 billion five-year capital works programme to continue improving its stations and trains. Improvements to stations include better entrances, more lifts and escalators, new concourses, and platform screen doors to improve platform management and make it easier to maintain comfortable environmental conditions on the platforms.

Customer service is one of the Corporation's three core values and it strives to provide the highest standards of service and reliability. To help it understand how it can better meet the changing needs of passengers, the Corporation makes enormous efforts to listen to its customers' concerns and needs. Its staff undertake annual passenger surveys, home interview surveys, biannual customer service surveys, and focus group discussions. They also run a customer telephone hotline, have station suggestion boxes and even hold station coffee evenings and the occasional radio phone-in. The MTR is obsessed with how customers feel and with developing its services and facilities to meet their needs. 'We listen, we act,' said Nancy Pang, Marketing and Communications Manager.

Questions

1 What are the benefits of using several different methods of listening to customers?

2 What do you think are the effects of the MTR's efforts to obtain customer feedback on its customers, staff and financial performance?

This illustration was developed from material in http://www.mtrcorp.com, and Tocquer G.A. and Cudennec C., *Service Asia*, Prentice Hall, Singapore, 1998.

Methods for encouraging feedback

Comment cards

The feedback sought should allow customers the chance to air their views (What did you like? What went wrong?), ask how the customer thinks the service could be improved and ascertain information about whether they will return (Will you use us again?) as well as provide other ways of dealing with their complaint if comment cards are not felt to be appropriate (e.g. freephone customer service numbers). Some organisations also use incentives, such as prizes, to encourage positive and negative feedback.

Notices

Notices are useful in explaining to customers the process for making a comment or complaint. Freephone numbers may help encourage those who would otherwise not provide feedback. A small number of organisations are trying to demonstrate how seriously they take feedback and involve senior managers or sometimes even the Chief Executive (see Kwik-Fit illustration in Box 12.3).

Box 12.3 Kwik Fit Encourages Customer Feedback

'What differentiates us from the competition,' explained Kwik Fit's Customer Services Manager, Kenny King, 'is that we actually entice people to call us or write to us.' Indeed Sir Tom Farmer, Chairman and Chief Executive, has his picture all over KwikFit's corporate literature exhorting customers to do just that.

From the opening of the first Kwik Fit Centre in Edinburgh in 1971, the Kwik- Fit Group is now one of the world's largest automotive parts repair and replacement specialists, providing and fitting tyres, exhausts, brakes, shock absorbers, batteries, oil filters, wiper blades and child seats. It operates around 2,000 centres across Europe, with plans to open further centres in other countries. Over 9,500 repair centres (which include recent acquisitions of Speedy and Pit-Stop) in England, Scotland, Wales, Ireland, Holland, France, Belgium, Germany, Spain and Switzerland now service the needs of almost 7.5 million motorists a year.

Sir Tom Farmer believes that the growth of this company, now with a turnover of over £500 million, has been due to their aim to deliver 100 per cent customer delight. Alongside his image can be found Kwik Fit's freephone number and customers are encouraged to ring it. An operator will take down details of the problem and pass the information on to the area manager with responsibility for the centre involved. After talking to the centre the area manager will call the customer to discuss the problem and also what needs to be done. On occasion, if it is necessary, the area manager will also visit the customer in person. The area manager then takes the appropriate action and prepares a report for the centre involved. Kwik Fit aims to have all complaints resolved within three days.

Not only does Kwik Fit encourage customers to call them with comments, it also actively solicits them. Kwik Fit's customer survey unit calls several thousand people each evening and solicits information that may not have been serious enough to warrant a complaint but still made the customer unhappy or concerned.

Sir Tom Farmer is well aware that as well as making customers happy, this philosophy makes sound financial sense. Kenny King explained: 'If a customer is in the position where he or she thinks, "Well, I wasn't satisfied earlier, but I am now", they're more likely to blow Kwik Fit's trumpet.' Car servicing is just the sort of conversation that crops up in the pub and Kwik Fit's approach to customer service provides them with service champions and converts.

Sir Tom Farmer added, 'At Kwik Fit, the most important person is the customer and it must be the aim of us all to give 100 per cent customer satisfaction 100 per cent of the time. Our continued success depends on the loyalty of our customers. We are committed to offering them the best value for money with a fast, courteous and professional service.'

Questions

1 *What are the disadvantages of encouraging customer comments?*

2 *Evaluate the impact of the Chief Executive's involvement in soliciting feedback.*

This illustration is based on material from http://www.kwik-fit.com/ and 'Satisfaction Guaranteed', *Management Today*, British Institute of Management, April 1998, p 92.

Web sites

Whilst the number of 'unofficial' web sites is increasing where terrorist customers are providing others with an opportunity to voice their opinions about organisations, other organisations are taking the proactive step of capturing feedback via the web. TNT Express Worldwide is one company that has done this (http://www.tntew.com).

Staff feedback

Front-line staff are often the people who pick up the small comments or grumbles and are usually in a position to provide feedback to managers. Sadly, few organisations seem to harness this information stream by having formal or informal feedback and improvement mechanisms, whether unit meetings or paper-based systems.

Preventing issues becoming failures

Front-line staff have a critical role to play not only in complaint management and staff feedback, but also in spotting something before it goes wrong or before dissatisfaction escalates. Employees, who are 'tuned-in' to customers and observant, caring and thoughtful, can have a significant impact on preventing issues becoming failures. There are several ways in which employees might do this:

- be sensitised to customers' body language, mood, looks, sighs, expressions
- look for potential fail-points and deal with them

- check if everything is OK and mean it
- catch problems early as grumbles to prevent escalation
- if something goes wrong, tell the customer before they find out
- take action in response to failures, not just complaints.

12.3 SERVICE GUARANTEES

Like service recovery, service guarantees are an important means of driving change through a service organisation and improving its service processes. Indeed, service guarantees are an extension of service recovery. A service guarantee – a promise to recompense a customer for service that fails to meet a defined level – makes clear for customers what they should expect to receive should the service fail. And for some organisations (see Radisson in Box 12.4), service guarantees are a key part of a customer-focused strategy.

Box 12.4 Radisson Hotels Guarantee 100% Satisfaction

Radisson Hotels Worldwide is a world leader in the hotel industry and operates, manages and franchises hotels and resorts. It has over 385 hotels, providing around 92,000 guest rooms throughout the United States and around the world, including North America, Europe, the Middle East, Latin America and Asia/Pacific.

The company pursues a strategy of combining global brand strength with local market expertise and service delivery provided by its partners and franchisees. At all levels the company is committed to providing personalised, professional guest service and genuine hospitality at every point of guest contact. The company's vision is centred on quality of facilities and services, 'beginning with the guest in mind'. The company's chief mission is to create loyal, satisfied customers who will return to Radisson.

Radisson has many initiatives in place to try to provide total guest satisfaction, including training programmes in marketing, operations, training and public relations, computerised reservations, sales and service, and a sophisticated global reservations system.

Radisson also highlights its hotel employees' 'genuine hospitality' with an advertising campaign – 'The difference is genuine'. The campaign focuses on Radisson hotel employees' proactive efforts to provide high-quality service to the guests, not because of training or operating procedures, but because of the spirit of hospitality which puts the guest first. This philosophy is underpinned by a guest relations training programme called 'Yes, I Can!'. This programme tries to instil in staff the need to act positively in all customer interactions, and the company believes that this makes its service distinctive.

Furthermore, in 1998, Radisson implemented a 100% Guest Satisfaction Guarantee as part of the brand's world-wide initiative to achieve total guest satisfaction with every guest stay at each hotel, and build long-term guest loyalty. The guarantee found in every room and on all guest keycard holders states:

'100% Guest Satisfaction Guarantee.

Our goal at Radisson is 100% Guest Satisfaction.

If you aren't satisfied with something, please let us know and we'll make it right or you won't pay.'

Questions

1 *What are the benefits of offering this guarantee?*

2 *What are the disadvantages?*

This illustration is based on material from http://www.radisson.com/.

Guarantees require an organisation to formalise the service recovery process and cycle of improvement (see Figure 12.1). A service guarantee includes the setting up of a clear and inviting mechanism for customers to trigger the guarantee, as well as training and empowering employees to deal with invoked guarantees (Hart 1993a, pp. 117–33) and it should specify the compensation for the failure (Wirtz 1998). The guarantee can also be used proactively: for example, a pizza restaurant developed explicit recovery procedures, which included front-line staff invoking the guarantee on behalf of the customer if the pizza was late, apologising and immediately presenting the guest with a voucher for a free pizza (as promised in the guarantee) (Wirtz 1998).

12.3.1 The four acid tests of service guarantees

The same four acid tests of service recovery can therefore also be applied to a service guarantee:

1. Does it lead to increased customer satisfaction?
2. Does it improve retention rates?
3. Does it drive process improvements?
4. And, as a result of the above, does it improve financial performance?

Customer satisfaction

A restaurant that promises to serve a lunch to customers within ten minutes of order not only focuses the organisation on what is important to customers, reduces the risk for them and provides them with a positive attitude towards the service, but also provides a mechanism for dealing with any dissatisfaction.

Focus on satisfying the customer

A guarantee helps to focus an organisation and its employees on satisfying the needs of a customer. It sharpens them and acts as a constant reminder of the need to satisfy customers.

Reduces perceived risk

For the customer it may reduce any risk in the purchase, which is important since many services cannot be assessed until experienced. A service guarantee can reduce risk by clarifying the standards of performance the customer can expect, promising high-quality performance in those service elements which are perceived as important by the consumer, and by the promise of a pay-out and/or rework should the service fail.

Creates a positive attitude

According to the theory of reasoned action, an increased strength of the belief that buying the service will lead to a favourable outcome induces the customer to form a more favourable attitude towards buying, which in turn leads to a stronger behavioural intention towards buying (Wirtz 1998). This strengthening of behavioural intention has a positive impact on customer beliefs, attitude, purchasing intentions and number of customers actually buying.

Dealing with dissatisfaction

A well-designed guarantee provides customers with clear standards against which to assess a service performance (Wirtz 1998). The guarantee also promises the customer a meaningful compensation if guaranteed standards are not met. This therefore encourages complaining, indicates that it is acceptable – indeed encouraged – and provides staff with mechanisms to deal with dissatisfaction. This in turn increases the chance of recovery and therefore customer satisfaction.

Customer retention

Not only customer satisfaction but also customer retention is increased when complaints are resolved (Gilly *et al.* 1991) and/or guarantee pay-outs are made (Berry 1995, p. 117; Hart 1988).

Also by providing a guarantee organisations may retain customers who might otherwise switch because of a perceived increased risk of purchasing elsewhere.

Furthermore, well-designed service guarantees have a high communications quality in themselves and may induce customers to talk about them (Heskett, Sasser and Hart 1990).

Process improvement

Service guarantees, just like service recovery, help identify fail-points in an organisation. As Hart (1993a, p. 28) expressed it, service guarantees turn up the pressure, and like turning up the pressure on a garden hose, leaks become more apparent. Often in the design stage of a guarantee, the organisation is forced to confront its delivery systems and support systems to try to ensure that it will meet the required standards (Hart 1993b). Indeed Hart (1993a, p. 85) found that many companies actually re-engineer their processes from top to bottom in order to bring quality up to the requirements of their guarantees.

When invoked, service guarantees provide data on poor performance, track errors and thereby help organisations identify and remove fail-points. By their existence, they also reinforce the need for employees to provide error-free service.

Financial performance

Service guarantees, well designed and well applied, should therefore lead to customer satisfaction, which drives retention and long-term revenue streams. Reduced perceived risk in the purchase of the service not only helps satisfy existing customers but will help attract new customers to the organisation. Improved process performance should also help retain existing customers as well as attract new ones. Improved performance may also help reduce both the costs of the process and the costs of losing customers or rework. Significant cost savings can emerge, even though they were not the initial motivation for the introduction of the guarantee (Firnstahl 1989; Hart 1993a, p. 32).

An additional cost, however, is the cost of the compensation specified in the guarantee. This may not be insignificant if the guarantee is to have any meaning for customers, although at least this puts a clear internal cost on failure which the organisation can seek to reduce.

Also, since the perceived probability of a favourable outcome is increased and the potential negative consequences are reduced, the expected value of a service is enhanced, and therefore consumers are likely to be willing to pay a price premium for the service (Hart *et al.* 1992).

Furthermore, services are real-time performances and cannot be executed 100 per cent failure-free all of the time, i.e. occasional service failures are unavoidable. Given the more positive attitude of dissatisfied consumers towards complaining and invoking the guarantee, pay-out costs will be incurred (Maher 1991) and over-all expenses increased.

Guarantees may also reduce employee costs. Hampton Inns introduced a service guarantee, and subsequent employee surveys showed that the guarantee increased employee morale. This was also reflected in a drop of employee turnover from 117 per cent to 50 per cent within three years (Greising 1994).

Downsides

Service guarantees do, however, have their downsides. They imply that the service may well fail – thus the existence of a guarantee will sensitise customers to the per-formance of the service and maybe even make them look for poor service.

The standards set in the guarantee may be higher than customers need or even expect, thus unnecessarily increasing the costs of the service.

A frequently quoted concern is that customers may cheat. It has been known for students to order a pizza with a guaranteed delivery and then to barricade doors and corridors to ensure it is late and therefore free!

Design of a guarantee

There are two key aspects to the design of a service guarantee: the design of the promise and the design of the procedure to invoke the guarantee and the pay-out.

Design of the promise

There are five key elements in the design of the promise (Hart 1988):

- *Meaningful* – the promise needs to be based on customers' expectations and to cover what they regard as being the critical determinants of success or failure. If an organisation guarantees something that is of little consequence, the guaran-tee will have little value. Before embarking on guarantees organisations should conduct market research to better understand customer needs.

- *Easy to understand* – a guarantee should be simple to understand and commu-nicated in a clear way. Guarantees that involve pages of fine print will be regarded with scepticism. Indeed guarantees that include constricting condi-tions which are only revealed on close inspection might be regarded as misleading and lead to dissatisfaction with the service in particular and the organisation in general.

- *Explicit* – the most powerful form of guarantee is one that is explicit – it is quite clear about what is being guaranteed and what the pay-out will be for failure.

Some organisations, particularly professional service organisations, may use implicit guarantees, where it is implicit that any problems will be dealt with (in an unspecified way). Federal Express was the first express company to offer a money-back guarantee – their guarantee states 'on time delivery or your money back' (http://www.fedex.com).

- *Unconditional* – the most powerful promise is one that guarantees satisfaction without conditions. The GTE Management Education and Training Center in Connecticut, USA, guarantees that its participants will be satisfied with all of GTE's training courses. Radisson's 100% Guest Satisfaction Guarantee promises: 'If you aren't satisfied with something, please let us know and we'll make it right or you won't pay.' Less powerful, though sometimes expedient, are guarantees that offer pay-outs with conditions attached. Airlines providing guarantees of punctuality may not cover instances when the delays are not their fault. The aircraft may be late due to typhoons or air traffic control problems.

- *The pay-out* – the service promise needs to have an appropriate level of pay-out. Too high a level – for example £1,000 for a late delivery of a pizza – may encourage cheating or may even put customers off claiming their rights! Inappropriately small payouts (£0.01 for a late pizza) may be deemed to be insulting and not worth informing the organisation of the problem (which was part of the intention in the first place!).

Design of the procedures

Easy to invoke

If the customer is expected to fill a set of forms in triplicate and get signatures from all parties involved as well as a written statement from a third party, the guarantee loses all of its credibility and all of its potential. The system should be easy, non-threatening, clear and known. The GTE Management Training Center explains its procedure:

- Contact the programme manager.
- Inform him/her you want to invoke the guarantee.
- Give the reason the programme did not meet your expectations.
- Provide some suggestions for improving or correcting the problem.

This organisation makes the procedure not only clear, but also non-threatening and clearly linked to trying to improve the process. Participants are thus encouraged to give constructive feedback – indeed, few to date have invoked the guarantee though many suggestions for improvement have been gained.

Improve systems and procedures

A final and critical test often lost in the marketing hype of service guarantees is that one of their key purposes, and in our opinion the most important, is to help drive improvement through the organisation. If the guarantee simply proceduralises a system of pay-outs without providing information to the organisation about failures and encouraging improvement, we believe it is of limited value.

Box 12.5 Holiday Inn's Hospitality Promise

'We promise that throughout your stay with us we will endeavour to meet the high standards you expect from Holiday Inn hotels. However, should anything not be to your satisfaction, please do not hesitate to tell us. Just call the duty manager who will make every effort to put things right, as you are not expected to pay for unsatisfactory service. If, for any reason, the hotel staff are unable to resolve the problem to your satisfaction, please write to the managing director. We call this the Holiday Inn Hospitality Promise – a promise made by no other major hotel chain.

A promise of hospitality from the people of Holiday Inn Hotels.'

Question

1. *Evaluate the Holiday Inn's Hospitality Promise.*

The Holiday Inn Promise is found in all of Holiday Inn's hotels.

Box 12.6 Service Guarantee – Datapro Singapore

Professor Jochen Wirtz, National University of Singapore

Datapro Information Services provided IT and telecommunications information and consulting services around the world. It employed over 400 analysts and consultants. Although having sold its pre-packaged information services in Asia for many years, Datapro only started offering consulting services throughout South-east Asia in 1993 via its Singapore office. Being confident about the high quality of its work, but at the same time somewhat lacking the brand equity other providers of similar services enjoyed, Datapro decided to become Asia's first IT consulting firm that explicitly guaranteed its services. Every proposal contained the following guarantee in the last section just before the acceptance form:

Datapro guarantees to deliver the report on time, to high quality standards, and to the contents outlined in this proposal. Should we fail to deliver according to this guarantee, or should you be dissatisfied with any aspect of our work, you can deduct any amount from the final payment which it deems as fair, subject to a maximum of 30%.

In the event Datapro should fail to deliver the commissioned report in its entirety at the end of the period, you will have the option to deduct 10% off the price of the study for each week the said study is overdue subject to a maximum of 20%.

We are able to offer this guarantee as we are confident about the good quality and professionalism of our work. We have secured a large number of blue-chip clients who have been completely satisfied with our services. Our clients in the last twelve months have included: British Telecom, Fujitsu, Sony, Hewlett-Packard, Philips, Intel, etc.

In 1994, Datapro developed and introduced the guarantee above in collaboration with the author of this case. Datapro had ideally wanted to provide a 100 per cent money-back guarantee, but at the same time wanted to limit the potential financial risks inherent in the introduction of such guarantees. These risks were considerable, with typical projects exceeding a value of well over US$100,000. The guarantee contained a full-satisfaction clause, as well as concrete promises like on-time delivery. This mixed design has been shown to be considerably more effective than either full-satisfaction guarantees or other specific guarantees alone (see Wirtz 1997).

The marketing impact was dramatic. Clients were delighted that Datapro was willing to stand by its word and guarantee deadlines as well as content quality – especially as deadlines were a thorny issue in Asia's rapidly growing IT markets, and clients were often promised the sky during the proposal stage only to be confronted with late deliveries subsequently. The guarantee allowed Datapro credibly to promise delivery dates, which otherwise might have been discounted by its clients. Datapro's management felt that the guarantee was an effective marketing tool that helped to sell a number of projects, and Datapro's consulting unit was extremely successful, with a revenue and profit growth of around 100 per cent per annum for a number of successive years.

On the operations side, the guarantee pushed Datapro to keep up its quality. For example, it did not have a single late delivery after the introduction of the guarantee, mainly for two reasons. Firstly, case leaders were cautious not to promise delivery dates they knew they could not keep. Secondly, in the case of unforeseen problems or delays, case leaders would move heaven and earth to bring the case back on track. A similar pressure was on the case teams to keep their clients happy, as a dissatisfied client could mean a significant reduction in revenue and profit for that case, resulting in a steep reduction in staff bonuses.

Datapro was very successful, especially in breaking into the high-growth telecommunications consulting market, and was taken over at the end of 1997 by the Gartner Group, the world's largest IT consulting firm.

Question

1. *Evaluate the guarantee provided by Datapro.*

12.4 SUMMARY

Service recovery

- Service recovery is the action of seeking out and dealing with failures in the delivery of service.
- Service recovery should lead to increased customer satisfaction and retention, process improvements and improved financial performance.
- Service recovery has three essential ingredients:
  - ➤ designing-out failures to prevent them happening in the first place
  - ➤ excellent complaint handling
  - ➤ proactive service recovery, seeking out problems and potential problems.

Service guarantees

- A service guarantee is a promise to recompense a customer for service that fails to meet a specification.
- Service guarantees should lead to increased customer satisfaction and retention, process improvements and improved financial performance.

● There are two key aspects to the design of a service guarantee: the design of the promise and the design of the procedure to invoke the guarantee and the pay-out.

12.5 DISCUSSION QUESTIONS

1. What is the difference between a service guarantee and service recovery?

2. Explain why some organisations' service recovery procedures, though intent on satisfying customers, tend to lead to dissatisfaction.

3. Select a guarantee provided by a service organisation. Discuss its strengths and weaknesses.

4. Design a guarantee for a particular service. Explain how it would work, its benefits and any difficulties in its implementation or use.

12.6 QUESTIONS FOR MANAGERS

1. Evaluate your recovery processes. How could they be improved?

2. What would be the impact of offering a guarantee on the service that *you personally* provide?

12.7 SELECTED FURTHER READING

Barlow J. and Møller C., *A Complaint is a Gift*, Berrett-Koehler, San Francisco, 1996.

12.8 REFERENCES

Armistead C.G. and Clark G., 'Service Quality and Service Recovery: The role of capacity management', in Armistead C.G. (ed.), *The Future of Services Management*, Kogan Page, London, 1994, pp. 81–97.

Barlow J. and Møller C., *A Complaint is a Gift*, Berrett-Koehler, San Francisco, 1996.

Bell C.R. and Zemke R.E., 'Service Breakdown: The road to recovery', *Management Review*, October 1987, pp. 32–5.

Berry L.L., *On Great Service – A Framework for Action*, Free Press, New York, 1995.

Bitner M.J., Booms B.H. and Tetreault M.S., 'The Service Encounter: Diagnosing favorable and unfavorable incidents', *Journal of Marketing*, vol. 54, January 1990, pp. 71–84.

Blodgett J.G., Granbois D.H. and Walters R.G., 'The Effects of Perceived Justice on Complainants' Negative Word-of-Mouth Behavior and Repatronage Intentions', *Journal of Retailing*, vol. 69, Winter 1993, pp. 399–428.

Bowen D.E. and Johnston R., 'Internal Service Recovery: Developing a new construct', *International Journal of Service Industry Management*, vol. 10, no. 2, 1999, pp. 118–31.

British Institute of Management, 'Satisfaction Guaranteed', *Management Today*, April 1998, p. 92.

Day R., 'Modelling Choices Among Alternative Responses to Dissatisfaction', in Kinnear T. (ed.), *Advances in Consumer Research*, vol. 11, 1984, pp. 496–9.

Firnstahl T.W., 'My Employees are My Service Guarantee', *Harvard Business Review*, July–August 1989, pp. 28–32.

Gilly M.C., Stevenson W.B. and Yale L.J., 'Dynamics of Complaint Management in the Service Organization', *Journal of Consumer Affairs*, vol. 25, no. 2, 1991, pp. 295–322.

Greising, D., 'Quality: How to make it pay', *Business Week*, August 8, 1994.

Hart C.W.L., 'The Power of Unconditional Service Guarantees', *Harvard Business Review*, July–August, 1988, pp. 54–62.

Hart C.W.L., *Extraordinary Guarantees – A New Way to Build Quality Throughout Your Company & Ensure Satisfaction for Your Customers*, Amacom, New York, 1993a.

Hart C.W.L., 'The Power of Guarantees as a Quality Tool', *CMA Magazine*, July–August 1993b, p 28.

Hart C.W.L., Heskett J.L. and Sasser W.E., 'The Profitable Art of Service Recovery', *Harvard Business Review*, July–August 1990, pp. 148–56.

Hart C.W.L., Schlesinger L.A. and Maher D., 'Guarantees Come to Professional Service Firms', *Sloan Management Review*, vol. 33, no. 3, 1992, pp. 19–29.

Heskett J.L., Sasser W.E. and Hart C.W.L., *Service Breakthroughs: Changing the rules of the game*, Free Press, New York, 1990.

Johnston R., 'Service Failure and Recovery: Impact, attributes and process', *Advances in Services Marketing and Management: Research and practice*, vol. 4, 1995, pp. 211–28.

Johnston R., 'The Effect of Intensity of Dissatisfaction on Complaining Behaviour', *Journal of Consumer Satisfaction, Dissatisfaction and Complaining Behavior*, vol. 11, 1998, pp. 69–77.

Johnston R., 'Complaint Management: The acid tests', in Edvardsson B., Brown S.W., Johnston R. and Scheuing E.E. (eds), *Service Quality in the New Economy: Interdisciplinary and international dimensions*, ISQA, New York, 2000, pp. 13–21.

Johnston R. and Fern A., 'Service Recovery Strategies for Single and Double Deviation Scenarios', *The Service Industries Journal*, vol. 19, no. 2, 1999, pp. 69–82.

Landon E.L., 'A Model of Consumer Complaint Behavior', in Day R. (ed.), *Consumer Satisfaction, Dissatisfaction and Complaining Behavior*, Indiana University Press, Bloomington Ind., 1977, pp. 31–5.

Maher D., 'Service Guarantees: Double-barrelled standards', *Training (TBI)*, vol. 28. no. 6, 1991, pp. 27–30.

Martinko M. and Gardner W., 'Learned Helplessness: An alternative explanation for performance deficits', *Academy of Management Review*, vol. 7, no. 2, 1982, pp. 195–204.

OFT, *Consumer Loyalty*, Office of Fair Trading, 1990.

Oliver R.L., *Satisfaction: A behavioral perspective on the consumer*, McGraw-Hill, New York, 1997.

Prakash V., 'Intensity of Dissatisfaction and Consumer Complaint Behaviors', *Journal of Consumer Satisfaction, Dissatisfaction and Complaining Behavior*, vol. 4, 1991, pp. 110–22.

Prokesch S.E., 'Competing on Customer Service: An interview with British Airways' Sir Colin Marshall', *Harvard Business Review*, November–December 1995, pp. 101–12.

Slack N., Chambers S., Harland C., Harrison A. and Johnston R., *Operations Management* (2nd edition), Pitman, London, 1998.

Tocquer G.A. and Cudennec C., *Service Asia*, Prentice Hall, Singapore, 1998.

Van Ossel G. and Stremersch S., 'Complaint Management', in Van Looey B., Van Dierdonck R. and Gemmel P., *Services Management: An integrated approach*, Financial Times Pitman Publishing, London, 1998, pp. 171–96.

Williams T., *Dealing with Customer Complaints*, Gower, Aldershot, 1996.

Wirtz J., 'Is Full Satisfaction the Best You Can Guarantee – An Empirical Investigation', in the *Proceedings of the Eighth Biennial World Marketing Congress 1997, Kuala Lumpur, Malaysia: Academy of Marketing Science*, vol. 8, 1997, pp. 416–18.

Wirtz J., 'Development of a Service Guarantee Model', *Asia Pacific Journal of Management*, vol. 15, 1998, pp. 51–75.

Zemke R. and Schaaf R., *The Service Edge: 101 companies that profit from customer care*, NAL Books, Beltsville, Maryland, 1989.

Gold Card Protection Service

Executive Bank plc is a bank that attracts premium customers, usually international travellers. As part of its exclusive, and expensive, gold charge card service it offers its customers the opportunity to join, for a small additional annual fee, its card protection scheme, the Gold Card Protection Service.

The card protection scheme simply provides insurance against the theft and misuse of its customers' charge and credit cards (the cards may be issued by any bank, credit company or store). In addition, this service also provides a wide range of benefits which are not dissimilar to the card protection schemes run by other companies. These include:

- a 24-hour world-wide freephone number
- a single call to cancel all cards and order replacements
- £1,000 insurance against misuse prior to notification
- unlimited cover after notification
- £1,250 interest-free emergency cash if the customer is stranded abroad
- a lost key and luggage retrieval service
- help in the emergency replacement of driving licence and passport
- payment of emergency hotel bills up to £500
- emergency airline or ferry tickets up to £1,000
- emergency car-hire assistance.

The Card Protection Service boasts that it provides a 'friendly, efficient and thorough service to all its customers' and that it will 'answer calls within an average of ten seconds, generate loss reports to the card issuers, by fax or telex, within 20 seconds after the call and always send prompt confirmation of action taken'.

The following is a letter sent by a customer after having experienced the service.

6 February

Mr Daniel Payne
Customer Services Manager
Gold Card Customer Services
Executive Bank plc
London

Dear Mr Payne

I am writing to express my profound dissatisfaction with the service provided by your organisation.

At 9.30 a.m. on 17 January I was robbed whilst entering a bus near Warsaw railway station on the way to Warsaw airport. My wallet, containing all my credit and charge cards and a number of personal items, was stolen. I reported this loss to your Card Protection Service at 11.00 a.m. on my arrival at Warsaw airport. I greatly appreciated the opportunity to make a reverse charge call.

I was told that all my cards would be stopped immediately and replacements requested. The operator asked if there was any cash in the wallet. I told her that there was about £20 in the wallet. She asked me if I had cash with me and I confirmed that I had. The operator asked for a number where I could be contacted that evening. This was provided.

I was impressed by the arrival of my replacement Executive Gold Card on January 19.

By Wednesday 24 January all the replacement cards had arrived with the exception of my Standard Bank Cashline card. This was an important card as it was my main means of obtaining cash. Having been without the card for a week, this was becoming a problem!

On returning home from work at 8.00 p.m. on 25 January I found that the card had still not arrived. I rang the Standard Bank's telephone banking service to ask when I should expect to receive my card. I was told that the card had been stopped but no replacement ordered. I was told they would notify my branch but I should ring the branch the following day. I then rang your organisation to try to discover why the replacement card had not been ordered. I spoke to James Creek who informed me that the Standard Bank did not accept orders for replacement cards from anyone but the customer and that I should contact my bank directly. I complained that I had not been told this – indeed one week had gone during which I had assumed it was on its way. James apologised and said the operator should have told me. I then asked James if the small amount of cash that I had in my wallet was also covered. James told me it was and he offered to send me a claim form. I asked why the operator had not checked this with me at the time. James said she should have done so and again apologised and promised to send me a claim form immediately. I felt very dissatisfied with your service at this point. One of my card issuers had sent me, with their replacement card, information about their card protection scheme which I noticed provided free cover for family members. I pointed this out to James and asked him to send me information about your card protection scheme so I could make a comparison. He agreed to do this and also offered me free cover for my spouse for one year to make up for the inconvenience I had suffered. James told me that he would contact my bank to try to sort out the replacement. He sincerely apologised for all the errors.

On 26 January, I rang my bank to check that a card had been ordered. My branch confirmed that a replacement had been ordered by your organisation and it would arrive about the 30th. I would then have to return the confirmation slip and when they received it the card would be operative (over two weeks after it had been stolen). I complained that it was my only means of getting cash. I was told there was nothing that could be done though I could speed the process by taking the confirmation slip to my branch as soon as I received it. I suggested that might be difficult as I had a full-time job.

On 30 January, my Cashline card arrived and I returned the confirmation slip by post. There was no material from your organisation. I rang and spoke to you and you apologised for the incidents. You agreed that the material should have arrived by now as stationery orders are processed overnight. I agreed to wait a few more days.

Today is February 6th. I have just received the PIN number for my Cashline card and have managed to use it – nearly three weeks after the robbery. I am still without the promised material from your organisation.

I would be grateful if you could answer the following questions:

1. Why did the operator not tell me that my Cashline card would not be replaced unless I contacted my bank?

2. Why did the operator not tell me that the cash in my wallet was also covered by your scheme and volunteer to send me a claim form?

3. Why did the operator not ring me in the evening to tell me about the problem with the Cashline card or to confirm that all the instructions had been carried out? I would have very much appreciated this reassurance.

4. Why could James order a replacement on the 25th but the initial operator could not do so on the 17th? Did I need to contact the bank or not?

5. Why did James not ring me a few days later, on the 27th for example, to check that I had received the material he promised and that everything was now all right?

6. Why did I not receive the material?

7. Why do you wait till the customer is so fed up and has to ask you to sort something out? I have now made five telephone calls and written this one letter. I have not yet received any call or correspondence from yourselves. I can only conclude that you just don't care.

8. Why do you only do what appears to be the minimum possible to deal with an aggrieved customer?

9. Please would you tell me why I should continue to pay the large annual fee for the Executive Gold Card and the additional cost for the Card Protection Service for this appalling lack of service?

Yours sincerely
David Smith

Question

1. *How would you respond to this letter?*

Part 5

MANAGING STRATEGIC CHANGE

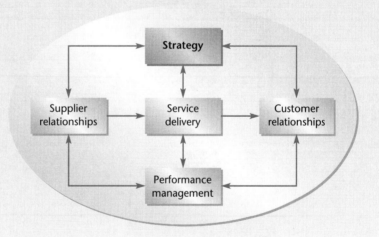

13

Service Strategy

INTRODUCTION

'All great service companies have a clear, compelling service strategy. They have a "reason for being" which energises the organisation and defines the word "service"' (Berry 1995, p. 62). In having a clear strategy managers know what initiatives to approve and those to reject, customers know what to expect, employees know what to provide and operations knows how it has to deliver the service. If employees don't know what the organisation's strategy is, or each person has their own view, success is going to be hard to achieve.

A service strategy (or a manufacturing strategy come to that) provides the intellectual frameworks and conceptual models that allow managers to identify opportunities for bringing value to customers (Normann and Ramirez 1993) and for delivering that value at a profit or within budget. The role for service operations managers is to help create and deliver that value by contributing to the strategy debate and by developing the operation, its resources, people and processes, to provide for the future success of the organisation.

The objectives of this chapter are:

- to define what is meant by a strategy and identify its key components
- to discuss the use of 'service' as competitive weapon
- to explain how competitive criteria are turned into operations priorities
- to describe strategy formulation and development
- to distinguish between evolutionary versus revolutionary change
- to explore the issues involved in sustaining a strategy.

A strategy is only as good as its implementation. The organisation needs to call on a wide range of abilities in order to create an effective strategy, from the visionary thinker at director level, through the interpretation of this strategy into policies and plans by senior and middle management, to the involvement in and ownership of service delivery by front-line staff. It is not the purpose of this book to describe the strategic process in detail. We are concerned with the creation and implementation of strategy insofar as it has direct relevance to service delivery. In this sense, the three major components of strategy – market and competitive analysis, strategic choice, and implementation – are very real issues for the service operations manager.

13.2 SERVICE STRATEGY

Research into strategy development asserts that effective strategies generally are evolutionary rather than revolutionary (Quinn 1978; Bailey and Johnson 1992). Quinn suggests that although there is often refined strategic analysis embedded in strategic formulation, the real strategy evolves as internal decisions and external events combine to form a widely shared consensus for action among key members of the management team. Today, we would suggest that key contributors to strategy development must include those in constant contact with market requirements: the customer-facing staff.

These employees, often rather junior and poorly paid in many consumer services, have a key role in strategy development. They often have advance information as to customer likes and dislikes, and about the way that customers' tastes are changing. Crucially, these staff have the task of 'living the strategy'. If they are not committed to the goals and objectives of the organisation, it will be plain for all to see. The old adage that strategy should be 'top down and bottom up' has much to commend it.

3.2.1 Defining service strategy

Service organisations, like all businesses, need to have overarching strategies in place to try to prevent non-aligned and disjointed activities and decisions (Lovelock 1994; Senge 1993). A strategy is usually seen in market terms as an organisation's plan to achieve an advantage over its competitors. Some organisations, however, may not wish to achieve advantage but see their role as maintaining their position in the marketplace. Others operate in non-competitive situations and wish to ensure that they are able to adapt to their own changing environments. Service strategy is therefore defined as the set of plans and policies by which a service organisation aims to meet its objectives.

3.2.2 Strategy: harnessing five elements

A strategic plan will harness the various aspects of an organisation and ensure that they support each other and are consistent with the direction indicated by the drivers of change. Five critical elements of strategy are: the creation of corporate objectives, an understanding of the environment, the development of an appropriate service concept, the identification of appropriate operations performance objectives, and the development of an appropriate operation – see Figure 13.1 (see also Johnston 1988 and 1989; Heskett 1986; Heskett, Sasser and Hart 1990).

Corporate objectives

Corporate objectives provide the targets or goals for the strategy. If a strategy is a set of plans or policies to meet objectives, there needs to be a statement of those objec-

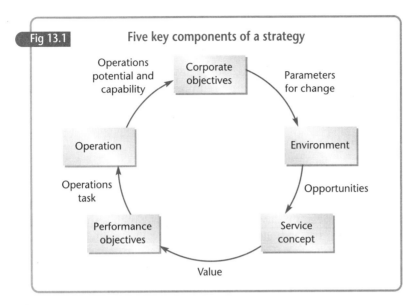

Fig 13.1 — Five key components of a strategy

tives. In part they provide the motivation for change but also set out the size and speed of change. Such a statement is an important step in making the change 'public' so that employees are made aware of what is expected of them. In essence the objectives set out the parameters for change.

Environment

All organisations operate in a context and that environment needs to be understood to assess not only the opportunities that it might afford but also the likely response of other organisations and the reaction of customers to change.

Concept

The service concept identifies the proposed nature of the business, the service in the mind that the organisation wishes to create. This helps the organisation focus on the value that it can provide to customers.

Performance objectives

Performance objectives provide the means by which a strategy is translated into operations language, setting out the priorities for the operation. Together with the service concept they specify the task for operations.

Operation

The operation – its people, processes, structure, performance measurement systems, supply chains etc. – may have to be developed and changed to implement the strategy. Also the operation may provide the impetus for change through its current, or potential, capability.

13.2.3 An iterative and continuous process

Strategy is an iterative process. The key components, objectives, environment, service concept, performance criteria and operations, all need to be aligned in the delivery of service and the achievement of the strategic objectives. This requires a constant checking of all the elements to ensure that objectives can be met.

Strategy formulation is also not a one-off activity. Organisations need to respond to the two main forces of change that operate upon them, the external and internal environments. As a result, a strategy requires continuous assessment and, if necessary, amendment.

13.2.4 Planned or emergent strategies

Strategies may be intended, formal and planned; alternatively, they may either emerge from an intended strategy which was not realised or emerge not having been part of a formal planning process (see, for example, Mintzberg 1998). The creation of intended strategies tends to be a top-down approach, starting with either a statement of corporate objectives or an evaluation of the environment and market opportunities. Emergent strategies tend to be a bottom-up process, often starting with an idea for a new service concept or the emergence of new operational capabilities. Both types of approaches may be at work in successful organisations (Burgelman and Grove 1996).

13.3 SERVICE AS COMPETITIVE ADVANTAGE

Many organisations, both manufacturing and service, are recognising that by improving the service provided they can make significant and sustainable gains in the marketplace. Service and service delivery can be, and increasingly are, a competitive weapon.

For manufacturing and product-oriented organisations, service may be an important means of differentiation, particularly if they are operating in markets where there is little product differentiation or where product development is slow, difficult, expensive or short-lived. The nature of the services available and the way in which services are delivered may provide a means to competitive success.

Service-oriented companies are also recognising that there may be a need to provide high levels of customer service. Increasing competition, declining sales and more service-aware customers are putting pressure on service organisations to rethink and improve the levels of service that they offer. The effect of good service on customer retention and loyalty and on attracting other customers, as well as on the financial position of an organisation is important (see Chapter 11).

13.3.1 Competing on outcome and/or experience

Some service organisations compete on their service outcomes and others on the experience, while some manage to compete on both (see Figure 13.2).

As Figure 13.2 suggests, there are a number of positions that the service organisation may take up when compared with the competition. It is worth pointing out at this stage that public-sector and not-for-profit organisations can apply this type of analysis in a similar way as they too are in a form of competition for resources. Civil service departments compete for a larger slice of the country's budget, and charities compete for donor funds.

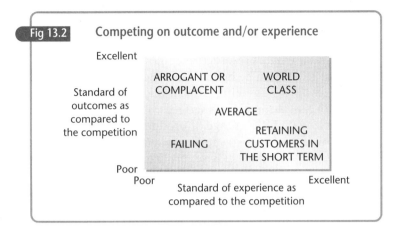

Fig 13.2 Competing on outcome and/or experience

The five positions suggested by Figure 13.2 are as follows:

- *Failing*. The organisation's outcomes are below industry specification, and its customer service is poor. Traditional services that have failed to move with market trends find themselves in this position. Some years ago in the fast-food market, Wimpy found that it was left behind by McDonald's in terms of higher food standards and faster service.

- *Complacent*. In these organisations, the service outcome is excellent, but the way that customers are treated is poor. Professional services sometimes fall into this category, being experienced as arrogant by their clients. They may well know better than their clients but this does not excuse service which can often be offensive. The medical profession often comes in for criticism in this area, failing to deal with patients as human beings, but rather as another condition to be treated.

- *Retaining customers in the short term*. It is possible to develop customer loyalty through good customer service. However, if the total service outcome falls below standard, customers will tolerate this for a relatively short period. If the service experience is excellent, the emotional switching costs are quite high for customers, but eventually they will leave. Some computer companies have used this strategy to retain customers in the period between phasing out an old product and launching a new one.

- *Average*. This is the position that many high-volume, business-to-consumer services believe they occupy. In many of these traditional service sectors there are frequently a number of reasonably established competitors, all conducting business in a similar fashion. The consumer financial service sector in the UK was a good example, with several players and little to choose between them. As the competition has become more fierce, many have chosen to try to differentiate themselves through the way that they deal with their customers.

- *World class*. These organisations are universally recognised as being the best in all that they do. There are few of these in existence.

Most large organisations will find that they can position their range of services at different points. Some may be world class, while others are failing. It is important to distinguish between them because each will require a different strategic approach.

3.3.2 Understanding perceived user value

To understand how service or services can be used to create a competitive edge it is essential to understand what is regarded as important by customers. The notion of perceived user value (PUV) can be helpful here (Bowman, 1998). PUVs are the criteria regarded by customers as being important, on which they will base their assessment of the organisation and its services. The PUVs for a supermarket chain might include stock availability, range of products, store location etc. Figure 13.3 shows a comparison of PUV for two supermarket chains.

The scores in brackets on Figure 13.3 denote the relative weighting that customers ascribe to each criterion. Therefore stock availability is weighted at 9/10 whereas check-out speed scores 5/10. This analysis allows the operations manager to determine priorities for action (see also section 13.4.3) and also to know in what way operations contribute to the overall competitiveness of the organisation. Operations contribute directly to some aspects of PUV (stock availability, check-out speed and customer service advice). Operations may contribute indirectly to other aspects of PUV. For example, how the service is delivered may have an impact on brand image and the relationship formed with customers, which may facilitate feedback to revise product range.

By separating out price from the other PUVs we have a useful framework for identifying and assessing current and future strategies (Bowman, 1998). This allows exploration of the possibility of competing by more than simply being cheaper or differentiated, i.e. competing in both ways (see Figure 13.4).

The analysis from Figure 13.4 shows that Supermarket A is of similar size (depicted by the size of the circle) and strategic positioning (weighted average PUV)

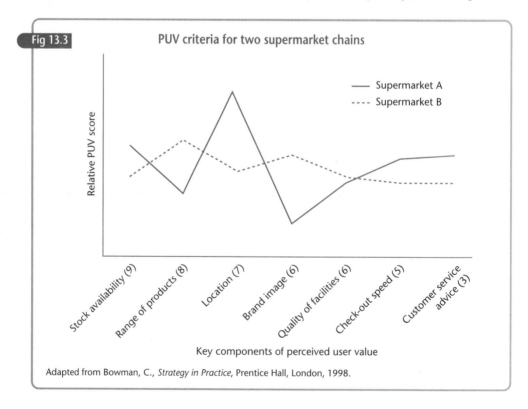

Fig 13.3 PUV criteria for two supermarket chains

— Supermarket A
- - - Supermarket B

Relative PUV score

Stock availability (9) Range of products (8) Location (7) Brand image (6) Quality of facilities (6) Check-out speed (5) Customer service advice (3)

Key components of perceived user value

Adapted from Bowman, C., *Strategy in Practice*, Prentice Hall, London, 1998.

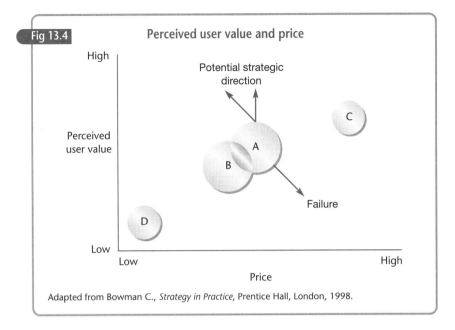

Fig 13.4 Perceived user value and price

Adapted from Bowman C., *Strategy in Practice*, Prentice Hall, London, 1998.

to Supermarket B. There is a smaller rival, C, which is perceived to be of higher quality but is very expensive. Likewise, D is the low-cost provider in this market-place and is only slightly smaller than A and B.

The question to be addressed here is to understand which strategic direction to adopt. If A wishes to maintain the price position but wants to increase perceived user value, inspection of the analysis from Figure 13.3 will be a good starting-point. Clearly, high stock availability and product range provide opportunities for enhancing PUV. If this strategy is adopted, operations can determine its contribution in terms of improving service standards without increasing operations cost. If the preferred strategy is to increase PUV and decrease price, then operations have a major task if the reduction in price is not simply to be achieved by reducing margins.

Box 13.1 Telecorp

Telecorp is one of the major global suppliers of telecommunications equipment, its competitors including Ericsson, Motorola and Nortel. The traditional business of these suppliers has been in the development and production of fixed network equipment, the switches that form the heart of a country's telecommunications structure.

In recent years, the traditional business of these telecommunications suppliers has been under threat. Existing stable customer relationships have been broken up. For example, Ericsson, being a Swedish company, has been the preferred supplier to Swedish Telecom, in the same way that Alcatel would relate to France Telecom. In many countries the national telecommunications provider (for example, BT in the UK) has been privatised with the objective of injecting competitive forces into the industry. Alongside this has been the advent of mobile phone networks. These are often owned by companies that do not have a long history and technical expertise in the telecommunications market, and operated for profit rather than public service.

These forces have combined to threaten Telecorp's profitability in its traditional business. Manufactured product margins have declined significantly, and in some cases have become non-existent. A possible strategy is to remain as a manufacturer in the 'Commodity' box, and to become very lean in its operations, but Telecorp has chosen instead to develop services to be sold with its manufactured products and systems to help its new, relatively inexperienced, network customers operate more effectively.

Whilst this general approach is agreed and seen as necessary by the senior management group, the interpretation of the vision to develop significant revenues has caused some discussion. In essence there are two points of view. The first view, largely held by those managers brought up in the 'fixed network' environment, is that Telecorp should continue to be seen as an innovator of telecommunications (physical) products and systems, who also helps customers use Telecorp's products more effectively. The opposing viewpoint is that Telecorp should become a service provider, generating solutions for its customers. In this case, Telecorp should act as systems integrator utilising its own or competitors' products in the most appropriate combination. This second view is largely held by managers from the mobile network side, who have often been recruited from other industry sectors.

Questions

1. *What are the differences in implications for the service operations manager in implementing the two approaches outlined above?*

2. *How would you demonstrate the strategic options using the tools described in this section?*

This illustration is based on a real organisation although all names and places have been changed.

The next section develops the strategic positioning analysis from section 13.3, using additional performance objectives and more detailed scales, to identify operations priorities.

13.4 TURNING PERFORMANCE OBJECTIVES INTO OPERATIONS PRIORITIES

Whilst the service concept defines the nature of the service to be provided, the performance objectives define the competitive or strategic priorities for the operations. 'Identifying a service strategy boils down to searching for a match between what needs doing and what the firm can do exceedingly well' (Berry 1995, p. 71). The operations performance objectives will (or rather should!) include, or incorporate, customer-based PUVs together with the organisation's view as to how it does or should compete as a whole. Performance objectives are also the basis for the development of performance measurement systems and a key way of linking operations performance measures to strategy. Organisations have to do well, and competitive organisations have to compete, on many different criteria. These might include:

- price
- quality
- availability

- reliability
- speed of service
- flexibility
- range of services
- new service development
- uniqueness.

Two dimensions – importance and performance – can be used to help operations managers prioritise these objectives so that they know where it is appropriate to spend time, effort and money.

13.4.1 Importance

The importance of a factor can be assessed in terms of its importance to customers (internal or external). Three categories of importance are order winners, qualifiers, and less important factors (see Hill 1993; Slack 1991; Slack *et al.* 1998).

Qualifiers are those factors that may not win business but play an important part in retaining business, by which we mean customers or sources of funding for example, and if performance falls below a certain point compared to other organisations, business may be lost. An Internet service provider (ISP), for example, may lose customers if access to its network is slower or more difficult than through its competitors. A university that does not perform well in research league tables may lose out on government funds.

Order winners are those factors that both maintain and win new business, funds or customers for the organisation. These are special qualifiers which the organisation has chosen as part of its strategy to use as a means of securing an advantage, or a point of differentiation, over other organisations. An ISP may choose price as its order winner, for example. By making its service free to its customers or even providing free phone access to its network, an ISP may gain a significant advantage over its competitors and increase its customer base. A university may attract executive courses by having outstanding facilities even though its staff may be no better or worse than those in other institutions.

Less important factors are those which are relatively unimportant but should not be ignored because they may become a source of advantage at some future point in time. In the case of a bank the comfort of the banking hall may be a less important factor, or the speed of the search routines provided by an Internet service provider.

Using the results network from Chapter 11, the order winners are all those factors which contribute to both attraction and retention of business. The qualifiers are those that contribute to retention of business only (see Figure 13.5). Attraction, as before, can be defined as attracting new customers in a competitive environment, attracting new donors for a charity or attracting new funds for a public-sector organisation, and also attracting good staff. Retention refers to retaining customers, staff and funding.

To help judge the relative importance of individual factors and help identify priorities for improvement, a more discriminating nine-point scale can be used with three points per category (see Table 13.1).

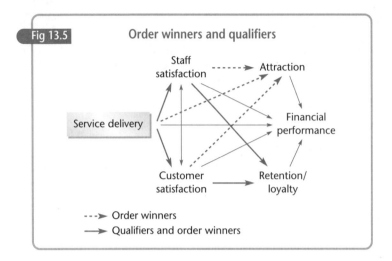

Fig 13.5 Order winners and qualifiers

- - - > Order winners

——> Qualifiers and order winners

Table 13.1 Judging importance

Order winners	Strong	1	Crucially important to attract business
(attractors)	Medium	2	Important to attract business
	Weak	3	Useful for attracting new business
Order qualifiers	Strong	1	Vital for retention
(retainers)	Medium	2	Important for retention
	Weak	3	Useful for retention
Less important	Strong	1	Not usually important
	Medium	2	Rarely considered important
	Weak	3	Not at all important

Developed from Slack *et al.* (1998).

13.4.2 Performance

Performance, the second dimension for assessing performance objectives, is concerned with the performance of each objective against other or competing organisations, whether they are competing in the traditional sense or competing for funds, staff or even kudos! A nine-point scale can again be used to assess relative performance of any of the factors (see Table 13.2).

13.4.3 The importance–performance matrix

By taking its importance score and the performance score, each performance objective can then be plotted on an importance–performance matrix (Slack 1991; Slack *et al.* 1998). Figure 13.6 shows the matrix, which is divided into four zones.

The 'appropriate' zone

The 'appropriate' zone is where performance is better than other organisations for the order winners and at least the same as others for qualifiers and less important

Table 13.2 Judging performance

Better than others	Strong	1	Considerably better than others
	Medium	2	Clearly better than others
	Weak	3	Somewhat better than others
The same as others	Strong	1	Marginally better than others
	Medium	2	The same as others
	Weak	3	Marginally worse than others
Worse than others	Strong	1	Somewhat worse than others
	Medium	2	Usually worse than others
	Weak	3	Considerably worse than others

Developed from Slack *et al.* (1998)

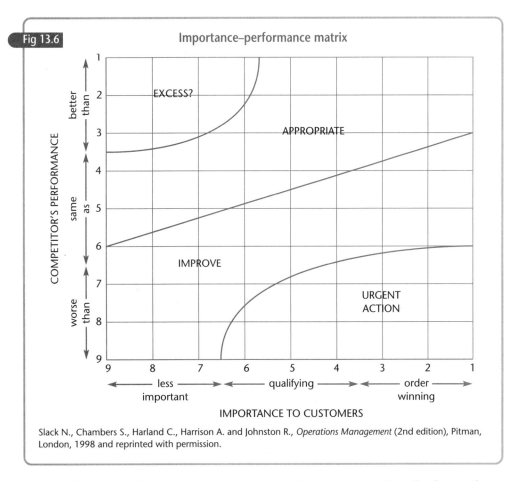

Fig 13.6 Importance–performance matrix

Slack N., Chambers S., Harland C., Harrison A. and Johnston R., *Operations Management* (2nd edition), Pitman, London, 1998 and reprinted with permission.

criteria. Factors in this area may not require action to improve but the focus of performance measurement systems may be to keep the factor in control. To maintain an edge over other organisations it may be worth considering trying to develop performance in some factors in this zone.

The 'improve' zone

The 'improve' zone identifies factors which need some attention, such as order winners where performance is similar to others and qualifiers where performance is slightly worse. The focus for performance measurement should be improvement rather than control and strategies developed to improve performance (see Chapter 12).

The 'urgent action' zone

The 'urgent action' zone identifies factors where urgent attention is required to improve performance on that factor (see Chapter 12). It is likely to be an immediate priority to move factors in this area up to at least the 'improve' zone and into the 'appropriate' zone in the medium term.

The 'excess?' zone

Factors lying in the 'excess?' zone may have higher performance than is necessary. Performance that is significantly better than others in terms of qualifiers and certainly the less important factors may be a waste of resources. On the other hand, if these factors are considered to be emerging qualifiers or winners, such expenditure may well be warranted.

By applying the importance–performance matrix operations managers can translate strategic intentions into clear priorities for the operation, identifying where limited resources may best be spent to support the organisation's strategic intentions.

13.5 STRATEGY FORMULATION AND DEVELOPMENT

13.5.1 Strategy drivers

Whether a strategy is planned or emergent, it is usually driven by some force which may be external or internal. The internal forces or strategy drivers might be existing operational capabilities, or new skills or technologies that have become available or been developed. The changing needs of stakeholders may also act as a force for change – pressure from shareholders, political masters, management or employees for an increased share value, change in direction, reduced costs or improved services, for example. External forces or strategy drivers might include the activities of competitors or changing needs of customers, for example (see Figure 13.7).

Operations-led strategy

Opportunities for change may arise from new developments from within the organisation such as new services, skills, technologies or processes. The availability of eCommerce technology provides opportunities for new delivery channels for many organisations requiring a rethinking of strategy, including how to manage, market and finance such developments.

Externally driven strategy

Modifications to strategy may be driven by changes in the organisation's external environment, either actual or anticipated. Such changes might include new

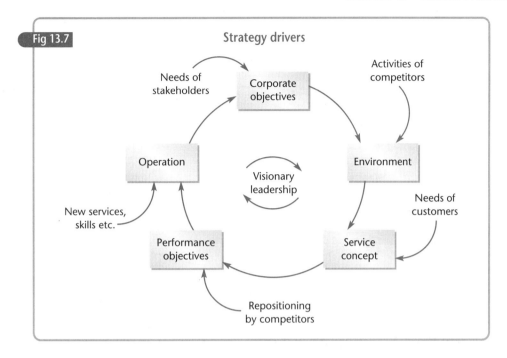

Fig 13.7 — Strategy drivers

competitors entering the marketplace or the strategic developments of competitors through different positioning or service developments, or the changing needs of customers who require a different service concept which may be the result of the activities of the competition, or the loss of customers because their needs are not being met.

Corporate-led strategy

The impetus for change may come from the organisation's executive, driven by a desire or need by its stakeholders for a greater return on assets, expansion, retrenchment, diversification, for example.

Visionary leadership

Any one of the above drivers may be sufficient to begin the cycle of strategy formulation and development, though clearly the more drivers that are in evidence, the more pressure there is on the strategy cycle to move. One condition that we believe has a major impact on the strategy formulation process is visionary leadership. This is usually provided by an individual, usually at corporate level though possibly a senior figure within operations, marketing or finance, who takes responsibility for strategy development and acts as the linchpin in the wheel, pulling all the forces together and helping them move in the right direction.

Visionary leaders understand the current organisation and its service, its processes, people and culture, for example, and are able to create an attractive vision for the future. They are also able to communicate that vision and enthuse others, and thus galvanise the whole organisation to bring about the realisation of that vision (see Figure 13.8).

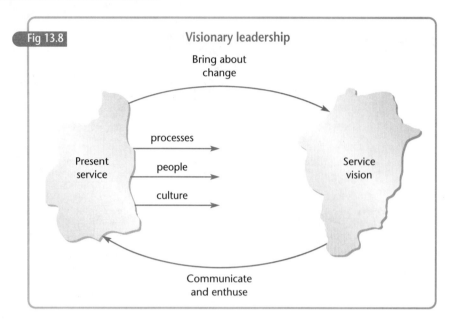

Fig 13.8

Visionary leadership

Bring about change

processes

people

culture

Present service

Service vision

Communicate and enthuse

13.5.2 Key issues in strategy development

Objectives

The development of clear corporate objectives is based on the strategy drivers – the internal or external pressures or opportunities for change. The objectives may well be expressed in financial or competitive terms over a set period of time, for example return on investment, profit, number of new customers or market share. These objectives need to be clearly stated and will provide the means of measuring and monitoring the success or otherwise of the strategy. The key questions that need to be asked are:

- What are the objectives?
- Are they achievable?
- What investment is required?
- What is the time-frame?
- What methods for review are in place?
- What are the contingencies?

Environment

In order to ensure that those objectives can be achieved, there is a need to develop a clear understanding of the market and the environment in which the organisation currently operates, or plans to be operating. This will include an understanding of the size and nature of the competition, the nature and size of the market or potential market, existing competing and complementary products and services, the ways the market is currently segmented, and the likely reaction of the competition. One key outcome of this activity is the identification of a potential target market and an assessment of the perceived needs and expectations of the target customers.

The key questions include:

- What are the characteristics of the market or market segment?
- Is the strategy appropriate for them?
- What are the needs and expectations of customers in this market?
- How well are these needs being served, by this organisation, by other organisations?
- What are the weaknesses, strengths, opportunities and threats?
- What might be the reaction of other providers to a change in strategy?

Service concept

The service concept is a clear statement about the nature of the service:

- the service experience – the customer's direct experience of the service process including the way the customer is dealt with by the service provider
- the service outcome – the result for the customer of the service
- the service operation – the way in which the service will be delivered
- the value of the service – the benefit that customers perceive to be inherent in the service weighed against the cost of that service.

This identifies not only what customers and providers would have in their mind but also what operations have to provide and marketers market. It also identifies the degree of focus, the extent to which the service attempts to do 'everything for everybody' or focus on meeting particular needs of a particular customer segment. The key questions to be asked are:

- What is the concept?
- Is it aimed at a particular market?
- Is it appropriate for that market?
- Can it be understood by customers and providers?
- How will it be communicated to customers and providers?
- Can it be delivered by the operation?

Performance objectives

Having identified a target market and developed a service concept, the operation needs guidance as to how it should manage its resources and activities. This will ensure that the service it provides will meet the corporate objectives, the needs of the target market and will establish how it will differentiate itself from the competition. A clear understanding of the performance objectives and their relative priorities is required (see importance–performance model earlier). The key questions include:

- What are the order winners and qualifiers?
- What are the priorities for change?
- What are the measures of performance associated with each objective?
- What are the targets?
- Are they achievable?
- By when have the targets to be achieved?
- What investment is required?

Operation

The design or development of an appropriate operation may be a complex activity requiring a large number of interrelated decisions connecting processes, employees, customers and infrastructure. New investment may be required or a redeployment of existing resources. The operation plan then needs to be checked against the objectives to ensure that the total strategy is consistent and will achieve the objectives that have been set. Thus the process may have to go through several iterations before a consistent and cohesive strategy is created. The key questions include:

- What changes are required to processes, employees, customer management and infrastructure?
- How will the changes be brought about?
- What resources are required?
- Can the new concept be delivered?
- Will it meet the perceived needs of the target market?
- Can the performance objectives be achieved?
- Can the objectives be met?

Box 13.2 Anglian Water Services Limited

In the early 1990s Anglian Water Services, in common with the other water companies in the UK, was facing a new challenge. It had been newly privatised and was struggling to understand the new environment it was operating in.

A new challenge for the water industry was that water users were now to be thought of as customers, not least because in the not-too-distant future the utilities were to become open to competition. Indeed, today, the old demarcations between water, gas and electricity companies have disappeared, with a number providing all three traditional services and offering telecommunications as well.

John Green, then Operations Director of Anglian Water Services, met with his team of senior managers, including a newly appointed marketing manager, in order to formulate a customer service strategy. The first requirement was to understand the relevance of customers to the success of the company. The water companies had previously operated more as custodians of water hygiene than as customer-focused organisations. This did not mean that they did not have a service ethic but rather that it was not customer-focused.

The key question to be addressed was 'Did customer service matter?' After all, water users had no choice as to where to go. However, the water companies were subject to close inspection by the industry regulator, OFWAT. This body regularly published statistics which included customer service performance, comparing the various companies. These statistics were felt to be a significant factor in influencing the stock market rating of the company, essential in competing for investment funds.

Perhaps more importantly, deregulation was seen not as a threat, but as an opportunity for the company to grow into new areas not directly controlled by OFWAT. The development of a customer service strategy was therefore to be seen as a vehicle for bringing about a culture within the organisation as a whole.

John Green's team set about defining a new service vision. In order to do this they carried out an audit of current performance, recognising that there were a number of customer segments with different requirements including domestic users, industrial users, and property developers. The points of contact with customers were reviewed, and the supporting processes mapped. A number of workshops were held with key staff from all parts of the operation, resulting in a draft customer strategy document to be discussed at board level.

This was the start of many initiatives in the development of service strategy. Early debates as to what perceived quality might mean were an important stage in the process. It was important to consider the possibility that consumers might want water that looked and tasted nice even though it might not be as hygienic in scientific terms. Anglian Water has developed this strategy considerably since the initial workshops. A major systems review was carried out, creating a new organisational structure including the appointment of a Director of Customer Service. Today, Anglian Water has an international business, and a reputation for a commitment to learning.

Questions

1. *What were the main drivers for the development of a customer service strategy for Anglian Water Services?*

2. *How well do you think the strategy development process was carried out? What could have been done differently?*

13.6 EVOLUTIONARY VERSUS REVOLUTIONARY CHANGE

The previous sections have been concerned with the nature and direction of strategic change. One further question to be considered in the development of a strategy is the speed of change. Change strategies are traditionally split into two types which represent different and, to some extent, opposing philosophies (see, for example, Imai 1986; Slack *et al.* 1998; Tapscott and Caston 1993; Venkatraman 1994). These two philosophies are continuous, incremental change and radical, step-change.

Continuous improvement, often referred to as *kaizen*, is an evolutionary approach to operational change and is synonymous with the concept of Total Quality Management. Radical change, in contrast, is a revolutionary approach concerned not with amending processes but totally reinventing them. Table 13.3 summarises the key differences between these approaches.

Continuous change involves modest but continual changes to an existing process, whereas step-change seeks radical changes – indeed the total redesign of existing processes coupled with a significant improvement in performance. The benefits from small, successive continuous improvements are expected to be attained over a long period of time, unlike radical change which aims to create major improvements in the short to medium term. Continuous incremental improvement involves everyone in an organisation and the changes are driven by them, thus requiring little senior management time and effort, unlike radical change which is usually driven by a senior management champion requiring substantial senior management time and effort. Senior management involvement is required because the risk involved in the total redesign of cross-functional processes is often high and capital expenditure, often involving the use of IT, can be substantial (see, for example, Hammer 1990;

Table 13.3 Summary of the key differences between continuous and step-change strategies

	Continuous change	Step-change
Existing process	Little change	Redesigned
Improvement expected	Modest	Substantial
Benefits attained	Long term	Short term
Change driven by	Employees	Senior management
Senior management time/effort	Small	Substantial
Business risk	Small	High
Capital expenditure	Small	Substantial
Use of information technology	Little	Significant

Brignall *et al.* (1999).

Imai 1986; Brignall *et al.* 1999; Slack *et al.* 1998; Tapscott and Caston 1993; Venkatraman 1994).

The two most well-known forms of continuous and radical operational change are Total Quality Management and Business Process Re-engineering.

13.6.1 Total quality management (TQM)

Total Quality Management is one of the best-known approaches to continuous improvement and has had a major impact on organisations by putting the customer at the heart of quality decisions and improvements. TQM was developed in the 1950s by Armand Feigenbaum although it has lost some of its cachet over the last few years as employees and managers have become unhappy about what some people see to be a 'flavour of the month' approach to management.

It should be made clear, however, that TQM is not a 'programme' or an activity with a definitive start and end, but simply good management practice; however, it does require a thought revolution in management (Ishikawa 1985). The main sources of inspiration for the TQM approaches are the quality gurus, such as Deming, Juran, Ishikawa and Crosby. The two foundation stones of TQM are customer focus and total involvement.

Customer focus

The TQM philosophy is centred on customers, meeting their expectations in order to retain those customers and capture others so as to enhance profitability and meet the strategic needs of the organisation. This necessitates identifying which customers the organisation wishes to serve, understanding their expectations and ensuring that all systems, procedures, activities and culture are focused on meeting those needs.

Total involvement

The main difference between the more traditional approaches to quality and TQM is the word 'total' (Slack 1991). TQM is based on a culture of continuous improvement, shared and enacted by everyone in an organisation working with a single purpose of improving what they do.

TQM as a continuous improvement activity has a great deal to offer service organisations and many of its elements are now traditional activities of many

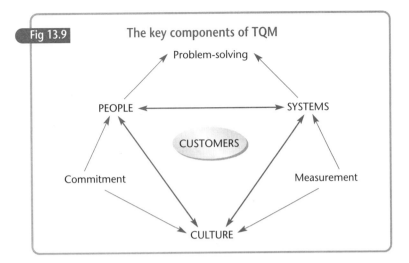

Fig 13.9 The key components of TQM

organisations, though not necessarily parading under the banner of TQM. The key elements are expressed diagrammatically in Figure 13.9.

The three corner-stones of TQM concern people, systems and culture (covered in more detail in Chapters 6, 7, 8, 9 and 14). People, i.e. employees, are responsible for and capable of driving change in the systems and this is encouraged by an appropriate people-centred, supportive and improvement-based culture. Employees are given the responsibility for improvement supported by training in the use of quality tools and techniques, with an understanding of the systems and processes to which they contribute.

To support this there is training in the use of quality tools, for example process mapping and fail-point analysis (see Chapter 6). Measurement systems provide feedback on actions taken and information is provided at the level of the operator (see Chapter 10). Top-management commitment is essential to the successful implementation of TQM because it requires changes organisation-wide and a supportive and appropriate culture (see Chapter 14).

13.6.2 Business Process Re-engineering (BPR)

A well-known radical approach to improvement and change is Business Process Re-engineering (BPR), a concept introduced into the literature in 1990 (Hammer 1990). BPR is about 'the fundamental rethinking and radical redesign of business processes to achieve dramatic improvements in performance'.

The main principles of BPR involve the following:

A cross-functional approach

BPR recognises the need to take a cross-functional approach to improvement and that most processes cut across traditional functional boundaries. It is therefore only through the creation of cross-functional teams working together on their processes that these processes can be radically redesigned.

Out-of-the-box thinking

BPR is meant to be radical and so requires radical thinking. To do this traditional beliefs and views need to be challenged – indeed put aside – to allow total redesign starting with a clean sheet of paper. BPR is about rejecting the conventional wisdom and received assumptions of the past to create something new and very different.

Simplification

BPR attempts to discard wasteful activities and focuses on simplicity and logical ordering. However, the often significant use of IT to enable radical changes can create a source of complexity that can undermine improvements.

Implementing BPR (see, for example, Harrington 1991) requires the formation of a high-level team with a champion to co-ordinate action. It requires a clear understanding of current processes, facilitated by process mapping (see Chapter 6). Redesign is then a key activity for the team, involving both visioning and detailed concern for measurements and control to ensure not only the efficacy of the new process but also its improvement.

BPR is clearly a risky activity, both because current processes are rejected and also because of the high capital expenditure required and frequent reliance on IT. It is not surprising therefore that many BPR activities – as many as 70 per cent (see, for example, Hammer and Champy 1993 and Macdonald 1995) – fail to meet their original objectives. Another key factor in their failure is that, because of their emphasis on business processes, systems and structure, the 'people factor' tends to be overlooked, ignored or under-estimated (Clark 1995). Indeed, because of the job losses incurred in such radical change, BPR has become synonymous with downsizing.

13.6.3 Benchmarking and improvement

In Chapter 10, in the section on stretch targets (10.5.2), we argued that one would expect that processes undergoing continuous improvement are likely to employ internal benchmarks based on their past performance or the performance of similar processes within the same organisation (Brignall *et al.* 1999). Conversely, one would also expect that organisations undertaking radical change of a process are more likely to adopt external benchmarks for setting performance targets because of the need to improve performance dramatically in relation to that of competitors.

13.7 SUSTAINING A STRATEGY

Without constant appraisal of the changes to the internal and external environments and consequent adjustments to strategy, organisations may decay. Lovelock (1994) refers to this process as 'institutional rusting'. Strategy therefore involves the process of continually checking the organisation's plans for direction, progress and cohesion in terms of the continually changing environment.

The main operational difficulties faced by organisations in sustaining a strategy are:

- conflicting objectives such as the need to provide a customised product using existing processes capable only of delivering a commodity-type service
- inappropriate and inflexible operations processes and resources, such as inappropriate equipment and untrained employees
- inappropriate investment – inadequate investment to provide the resources required or develop the existing ones

- undetected changes to the service concept as delivered by the operation as opposed to what was originally intended – failure to detect how managers and employees may be reinterpreting the concept in the way that they are comfortable with, as opposed to what is required by customers (concept contamination)

- the addition of multiple (similar) service products to a service process originally designed for one product – resulting in potential compromise of service standards across all products.

13.8 SUMMARY

Service strategy

- Service strategy is the set of plans and policies by which a service organisation aims to meet its objectives.

- A strategy involves the creation of corporate objectives, an understanding of the environment, the development of an appropriate service concept, the identification of appropriate operations performance objectives and the development of an appropriate operation.

Service as competitive advantage

- Organisations may compete on the excellence of their outcomes, experiences or both.

- Perceived user value provides a means of identifying current and future strategies.

Turning performance objectives into operations priorities

- The importance–performance matrix helps identify operational priorities.

Strategy formulation and development

- Strategy drivers include existing operational capabilities, or new skills or technologies that have become available or been developed, the changing needs of stakeholders, the activities of competitors and changing needs of customers.

- Strategy development is an iterative process which should result in a consistent and cohesive strategy.

Evolutionary versus revolutionary change

- Continuous change, often referred to as *kaizen*, is an evolutionary approach to improvement and is synonymous with the concept of Total Quality Management.

- Radical change is a revolutionary approach concerned not with amending processes but totally reinventing and re-engineering them.

Sustaining a strategy

- It is necessary to continually check the organisation's plans for direction, progress and cohesion in terms of the changing environment.

13.9 DISCUSSION QUESTIONS

1. Select four organisations in the same sector, such as four food outlets, pubs or libraries, and assess their relative positions in terms of their outcomes and experiences.

2. Identify the PUV criteria for two competing organisations. Score them on each criterion and assess their strategies. What options would they have if they wanted to differentiate themselves from the competition?

3. Which change strategy do you think is more successful, TQM or BPR, and why?

13.10 QUESTIONS FOR MANAGERS

1. Define and evaluate your service strategy.

2. Do you compete in terms of outcome and/or experience? In what ways could you change?

3. Identify your PUV criteria. How do you score against your key competitors? What are the options for change?

4. Identify all your performance criteria and undertake an importance–performance analysis. Do the priorities identified reflect the organisation's priorities?

5. Evaluate your process for strategy formulation and development.

13.11 SUGGESTIONS FOR FURTHER READING

Berry L.L., *On Great Service: A framework for action*, Free Press, New York, 1995.
Normann R. and Ramirez R., 'From Value Chain to Value Constellation: Designing interactive strategy', *Harvard Business Review*, July–August 1993, pp. 65–77.

13.12 REFERENCES

Bailey A. and Johnson G., 'How Strategies Develop in Organisations', in Faulkner D. and Johnson G. (eds), *The Challenge of Strategic Management*, The Cranfield Management Series, Kogan Page, London, 1992, pp. 147-178.
Berry L.L., *On Great Service: A framework for action*, Free Press, New York, 1995.
Bowman, C., *Strategy in Practice*, Prentice Hall, London, 1998.
Brignall S., Fitzgerald L., Johnston R. and Markou E., *Improving Service Performance: A study of step-change versus continuous improvement*, CIMA, London, 1999.
Burgelman R.A. and Grove A.S., 'Strategic Dissonance', *California Management Review*, Winter 1996, pp. 8–28.
Clark J., *Managing Innovation and Change: People, technology and strategy*, Sage Publications, Thousand Oaks, California, 1995.
Hammer M., 'Re-engineering Work: Don't automate, obliterate', *Harvard Business Review*, July–August, 1990, pp. 104–112.
Hammer, M. and Champy J., *Re-engineering the Corporation: A manifesto for business revolution*, HarperCollins, New York, 1993.
Harrington H.J., *Business Process Improvement – The Breakthrough Strategy for Total Quality, Productivity and Competitiveness*, McGraw-Hill, New York, 1991.

Heskett J.L., *Managing in the Service Economy*, Harvard Business School Press, Boston, 1986.

Heskett J.L., Sasser W.E. and Hart C.W.L., *Service Breakthroughs: Changing the rules of the game*, Free Press, New York, 1990.

Hill T., Manufacturing Strategy – Text and Cases, Irwin, Homewood, Ill., 1993.

Imai M., *Kaizen: The key to Japan's competitive success*, McGraw-Hill, New York, 1986.

Ishikawa K., *What is Total Quality Control? – The Japanese Way*, Prentice Hall, New Jersey, 1985.

Johnston R., 'Service Industries – Improving Competitive Performance', *The Service Industries Journal*, vol. 8, no. 2, April 1988, pp. 202–11.

Johnston R., 'Developing Competitive Strategies in Service Industries', in Jones P., (ed.), *Management in Service Industries*, Pitman, London, 1989.

Lovelock C.H., *Product Plus*, McGraw Hill, New York, 1994.

Macdonald J., 'Together TQM and BPR are Winners', *The TQM Magazine*, vol. 7, no. 3, 1995, pp. 21–5.

Mintzberg, H., *The Strategy Process*, European Edition, Prentice Hall, London, 1998.

Normann R. and Ramirez R., 'From Value Chain to Value Constellation: Designing interactive strategy', *Harvard Business Review*, July–August 1993, pp. 65–77.

Quinn J.B., 'Strategic Change: Logical incrementalism', *Sloan Management Review*, vol. 1, no. 20, Autumn 1978, pp. 7–21.

Senge P.M., *The Fifth Discipline*, Century Business, London, 1993.

Slack N., *The Manufacturing Advantage*, Mercury, London, 1991.

Slack N., Chambers S., Harland C., Harrison A. and Johnston R., *Operations Management* (2nd edition), Pitman, London, 1998.

Tapscott D. and Caston A., 'The Demise of the IT Strategic Plan', *Information Technology Magazine*, January 1993.

Venkatraman N., 'IT-Enabled Business Transformation: From automation to business scope redefinition', *Sloan Management Review*, Winter 1994.

CASE EXERCISE

Smith and Jones, Solicitors (B)

At the end of our discussions (see Smith and Jones (A) in Chapter 6) John Smith told me that he felt that the time was right for his firm to expand, although these views were less than enthusiastically shared by his partner, David Jones. John, however, was determined.

'It's time the business grew,' he explained. 'We are as established as all the other firms in the area, and although we hold on to a share of clients, it never seems to increase, despite a fair growth in the town's population over the last few years. During that time our costs have been increasing. Our overheads on the property and what we have to pay to keep good staff and lease the equipment is considerably greater than what it was even two years ago. It is not easy to just put up our fees to cover these increases. I know you think we pluck figures out of the air, but most of our clients use us several times and they remember how much we charged them last time. As a result our margins have been getting tighter. However, to expand the business we need another solicitor, but it's going to be difficult to attract someone into the office when they see what their share of the spoils might be. Both David and I would also have to take a cut in our slice of the rapidly declining cake. If we are going to expand and bring someone else in, we will need to put a lot of time and effort into generating more work.'

John added, 'I'm also concerned about the role the building societies and banks may play in the future. The Government seems determined to give away our bread-and-butter business. If we lost conveyancing there wouldn't be enough work for even the two of us.'

John explained his ideas for getting more business. 'With personal work, I think we need to become more visible. We don't make any efforts to sell our services. We are currently thinking about putting a brochure together listing our services, like one of our competitors has done. We could distribute these to potential clients and also to our current clients to maintain our name in their minds and inform them of our other services.

'More personal and commercial work can be brought in by making more contacts. It's surprising what work you can get out of meeting people on trains or at croquet matches. All you have to do is mention that you are a solicitor and you find that they have a problem. We have recently had some business cards printed for occasions like this.

'You might think that joining Rotary or a golf club would be a good idea, but I have not joined them for two reasons. Firstly because they are full of solicitors touting for trade. And, secondly, I can't play golf. You see, you can't afford to run the risk of being a "bad egg": unless you are a "good" Rotarian or golf player you may tend to lose credibility. I prefer to play croquet and there is only one other solicitor in the club. I'm also not too bad at it! David Jones has some good ideas for getting business clients. He is making contacts with trade organisations and associations like local chambers of commerce. This could provide a lot of good contacts and also give us a feel for local needs.'

I asked John to explain which type of work was the more profitable.

'Some of the jobs for personal clients are not very profitable,' he said. 'Indeed, margins in this type of work generally are small. But it is an important part of our business: it accounts for about 85 per cent of our income. The rest of our income comes from a handful of commercial clients. This may at first seem small scale but this work does command high margins. The jobs are sometimes relatively simple, like arranging insurances. Our fees are based on a percentage. It only takes one or two large transactions to generate a substantial amount of income.

'Because the commercial jobs command higher margins I want to see us make substantial increases in this area. I think that unless we improve our income from commercial work to around 50 per cent of our total turnover in the next two or three years, we will have done badly. I don't think our location is a bad one. We have some big cities quite close by and we have good connections in Bristol and London.

'We have a good location with good staff and the latest equipment – photocopiers, fax, word processors, laptops, email, and we even have our own web site, thanks to David. I must admit that, although I think there are lots of good possibilities, I am not really sure what more I can do.'

Question

1. *Develop a new service strategy for Smith and Jones.*

14

Service Culture

INTRODUCTION

It is tempting to see organisational culture as some sort of 'magic dust' that may or may not exist but which somehow makes the difference between success and failure. However, it is useful to reflect on the reasons why some service organisations have been more successful than their competitors despite having similar technologies, processes and skills.

The objectives of this chapter are:

- To understand organisational culture and how to influence it
- To identify types of culture and the implications for service delivery systems
- To provide four dimensions of national cultures
- To describe how organisations might manage the change and the pitfalls to avoid.

This chapter explores the nature of organisational culture and its impact on the task of the service operations manager. We outline some ways of describing and diagnosing organisational culture and propose some ways that organisational culture can be influenced to assist the operations manager in the task of providing high levels of service outcome and experience, cost effectively.

UNDERSTANDING ORGANISATIONAL CULTURE

There are two broad schools of thought around organisational culture. The first proposes that culture is something tangible, almost to the point where it can be written down in much the same way that an organisation chart can be included in the company's operating manual. In this sense, culture is something that the organisation possesses in much the same way as it might possess a set of resources or products.

The opposing view is that culture is much less tangible, and only really exists when people in the organisation talk to each other and by their words and behaviours act out the 'culture' of the organisation. Writers on organisational culture refer to this view as 'culture as personality' (Morgan 1986; Oswick *et al.* 1996). Described in this way, the culture of the organisation is often hidden below the surface of organisational life, requiring a degree of awareness to understand what might be going on.

It is this latter view of culture that informs the major part of this chapter.

14.2.1 Schein's model of organisational culture, basic assumptions and service operations

Schein (1985) is one of the leading thinkers on organisational culture. His model, shown in Figure 14.1, suggests that organisational culture has a number of levels or layers to it. It is dangerous to assume that what we might observe on the surface is all that there is to the organisation. There is much to organisational life that is 'beneath the surface', often exerting powerful influences on the decision-making process. This is one of the reasons why seemingly irrational decisions are frequently made by senior managers who are influenced by unspoken (and often undiscussable) aspects of the way that the organisation thinks about itself, what it is good at, how it assesses success, and what it values.

Schein proposed the following three levels of organisational culture.

Artefacts

These are the visible aspects of the organisation, its structure and processes, and other physical evidence that can be observed or felt. Although these artefacts may be observed, it is very often not clear what they really mean for the organisation, though they might give some clues.

For the service operation, there may be some understanding to be gained by the celebrations of success of good customer service, or in the position of the champion of service within the organisation (at board level or not). Other visible signs of culture of particular relevance to the service operations manager include the measurement and control systems employed. Control systems that emphasise the importance of customer satisfaction ratings alongside the financial metrics may be evidence of a customer-focused culture.

Fig 14.1 Levels of organisational culture

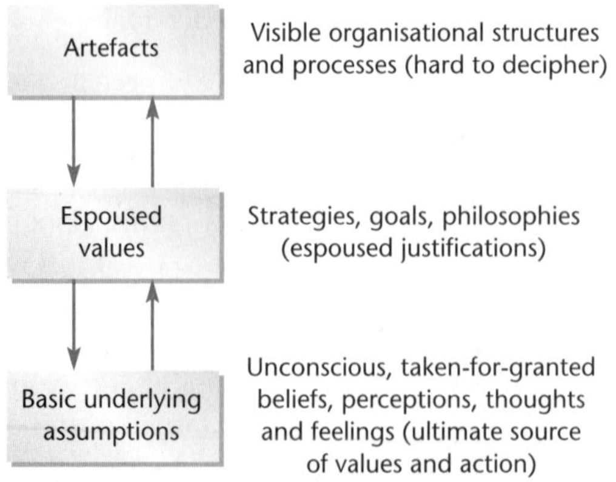
Artefacts
Visible organisational structures and processes (hard to decipher)
Espoused values
Strategies, goals, philosophies (espoused justifications)
Basic underlying assumptions
Unconscious, taken-for-granted beliefs, perceptions, thoughts and feelings (ultimate source of values and action)

From Schein E.H., *Organizational Culture and Leadership*, Jossey-Bass, San Francisco, 1985.

Even at this level there may be significant differences between operations within the same broad service sector. The hotel that aspires to be a four- or five-star operation but which doesn't invest in replacing tired or broken chairs in the lounge is probably not taking the task seriously. Schein makes the important point that it is very dangerous to draw conclusions from the evidence of the artefacts alone, without knowing the deeper levels of culture which may explain them. However, it is necessary to point out that customers will do just this. Customers will look at the physical evidence and draw their own conclusions.

Most organisations provide instructions to employees as to what to do in the event of fire. The emphasis is normally to leave what you are doing immediately and evacuate the building. A financial services company has a slightly different policy, instructing employees to 'secure company valuables' before leaving. It was interesting in developing service recovery procedures with operations managers that a key concern was that the company's money should not be risked in any way, in any event.

Espoused values

This next level of culture operates at the cognitive level. It describes the *stated* strategies and beliefs of the organisation. Thus, this level may include aspects of the company's mission statement – the general strategy as declared and set down by the leadership team – and statements as to the general values or guiding principles of the organisation. Kwik Fit's statement that 'our aim is 100% customer delight' would certainly fall into this category, as would lists of company values that include some of the following:

- We develop teamwork.
- We respect the individual.
- We are committed to outstanding customer service.
- We aim to be the benchmark for the industry.
- We operate with integrity.
- We encourage initiative.

The issue here is that this aspect of culture still refers to a conscious level of human interaction and thought, and there is frequently a sense that these espoused values and beliefs are what the organisation might like itself to be, rather than what it is in reality. It is relatively common for organisations to prepare statements which might contain phrases such as 'we work together as a team' or 'we value individuals' which do not necessarily reflect the experience of the members of the organisation.

In the same way, the organisation might have stated ambitions in terms of its basic service strategies which are also not borne out in practice. Again, of relevance to service operations managers might be the stated belief of the organisation that delivering 'service excellence' is the key to success. At one level (espoused values) this might be a genuine desire on the part of the organisation's management and employees, while at another, deeper level this may not be as strongly held as one might think at first sight. It is the final level of organisational culture, the basic underlying assumptions, that holds the key to our understanding of why there might be observable differences between what is aspired to and what takes place in practice.

Basic underlying assumptions

Basic underlying assumptions refer to those unconsciously held views that are undiscussed and generally unchallenged. Basic assumptions are those beliefs and ways of working that have worked well for the organisation in the past, and are, indeed, its secret of success in the past. It is our view that these basic assumptions are expressed in rather more simple, even primitive, terms than many competitive strategies. It is this 'primitive' aspect to the basic assumption that means that it is often deeply held and fiercely defended if anyone (often a newcomer to the organisation) challenges it or suggests it should be changed.

An example of a basic assumption, at an individual level, might be the belief that all workers are lazy. This might lead to some unhelpful behaviour on the part of the management, but also from their subordinates as they 'live down' to expectations. Again applying this idea to a service organisation, it would be extremely difficult to implement long-term customer retention strategies in an organisation that has been extremely successful over a significant period of time by managing short-term revenues.

Almost by definition, it is difficult to identify basic assumptions. The individuals in the organisation may only recognise them when deeply held principles are challenged. To make it harder still, the individual may, at a rational level, agree with the challenge, but still resist it unconsciously. An example is provided by the medical doctor who agrees to a change in surgery procedures such that a patient is seen by the next available doctor. At the rational level s/he may see the efficiency benefits and agree to the change, but unconsciously s/he hasn't changed her/his basic assumption that the doctor/patient relationship is central to good practice and s/he will resist the change to the point of ensuring that any pilot scheme is a failure.

We have worked with companies that have a strong track record in producing innovative manufactured products, but who realise that they have to develop revenue-earning services to replace declining manufacturing margins, and then find it is much harder to achieve than they thought. Clearly, this can be explained in part by the need to develop new competencies, but a significant issue is the resistance to change brought about by a reluctance to give up the old, tried-and-tested basic assumption that good manufactured product innovation is the way to success. This is often reinforced by the fact that most, if not all, of the senior management come from the 'good old days' and are also reluctant to move away from areas that they feel competent to deal with. This is why significant change is often only brought about by a change of chief executive.

It is important to grasp the notion that organisational culture is only really understood when the 'unconscious' part of the organisation's personality is revealed. One of the most powerful ways of uncovering the key elements of culture is to provide a framework for members of the organisation to discuss these aspects of their world and to begin to understand the various impacts on their behaviour and, therefore, eventually on the service they may provide to customers. The next section describes the cultural web (Johnson and Scholes 1988 and 1993), which is an instrument that provides a helpful framework for discussion and dialogue.

14.2.2 The cultural web

Figure 14.2 depicts the components of an organisation's cultural web. In this section we first describe the elements of the web and then provide examples of aspects

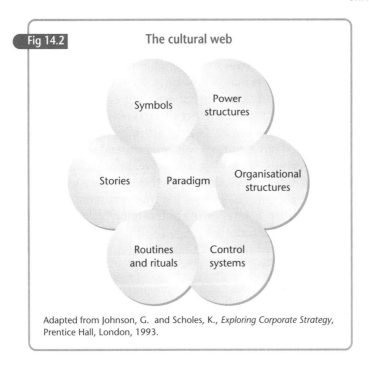

Fig 14.2   The cultural web

Symbols

Power structures

Stories

Paradigm

Organisational structures

Routines and rituals

Control systems

Adapted from Johnson, G. and Scholes, K., *Exploring Corporate Strategy*, Prentice Hall, London, 1993.

of culture which might help or hinder the generation of a customer-focused organisation or an organisation committed to service excellence.

The paradigm

This word has unfortunately been somewhat overworked in recent years, which is a great pity since it is particularly important in understanding organisational culture. It basically means the way that we view the world, the sets of values, principles and possibly prejudices that inform our judgements. Another word used for this is 'worldview', which can be likened to the set of spectacles that we view the world through. A simple illustration is given by a person's reaction to being offered a sum of money. A person whose belief is that the world is a good place might take the money without suspicion, whereas a person whose belief is that the world is a dangerous place would first ask, 'What's the catch?'

The organisation's paradigm may have a number of facets:

- A description of the sector of which the organisation is a part, for example hotels, computer service or financial services.

- The principal customer segments that it seeks to serve: global organisations, small businesses or individual consumers.

- In some cases the organisation may express what it does in terms of what the customers are buying rather than what the organisation is providing. For example, the theme park may express its mission as providing magical experiences rather than selling rides; the financial service as providing hope rather than pensions.

- The paradigm may contain some beliefs about what the organisation thinks is good about itself, such as being a risk-taker, innovative, or responsive to customers.

- Finally, it may contain some aspects of the way people think about the organisation which are less positive: it is ruthless, risk averse or arrogant.

There is some commonality between the paradigm as described here and Schein's basic assumptions. Certainly, it may not be obvious to long-serving members of the organisation that it is viewed as somewhat arrogant or ruthless by the world outside. However, if this is the case, the organisation will find it hard to become customer-responsive, having a 'we know best' attitude. A group of managers from a retail service chain carried out a cultural web analysis and were shocked to find that they had not used the words 'service' or 'customer' at any point in their paradigm. They had spoken a great deal about what they thought they were good at, but very little about the need to give the customer what they wanted.

It is important to identify aspects of the paradigm which are helpful for service delivery as well as those which hinder. Organisations that believe that long-term customer satisfaction is more important than short-term profit will generally find a supportive environment for service delivery.

Organisational structures

This aspect of the cultural web deals with the organisation's structure as it works, at least on paper. It is the structure that may be published in the form of organisational charts showing who reports to whom. Some of the dimensions of organisational culture are:

- Is the structure hierarchical or flat?
- Is it organised geographically or by product area?
- Is it function or process driven?
- Is it bureaucratic or flexible?
- Is it based on teams or individuals?

The form of the organisation will determine to a large extent how responsive to customers it will be. For customer-facing activities it is helpful if the unit serving the customer is virtually autonomous, able to satisfy most customer requests from its own resources. This of course may be seen as rather inefficient, and the management may prefer to centralise many activities in order to reduce costs.

Much of the value in recent business process re-engineering (BPR) projects has been a greater emphasis on linking together processes and activities which contribute to customer value rather than functional expertise. This may result in the generation of customer focus rather than operational focus. Examples of this may be found in the creation of teams to handle the entirety of a group of customer transactions. This was the case at Cigma in Greenock in Scotland, a company which handles employee benefits for corporate clients. Cigma reorganised its function-based groups, handling sales, service and credit control, into client-focused teams, and discovered that there were quality and productivity improvements as a result.

Some companies have customer service organisations which, in fact, are set up to protect the company and its workings from the customer. Customer complaints are handled efficiently by this group, but the downside is that fewer people meet and deal with customers or hear what really upsets them. Birmingham Midshires

Building Society made a practice of handing complaints to the process owners for these people also to own the process of customer complaint resolution.

It is clear that organisational design often contains compromise. Ericsson, the telecommunications company, rightly states that it is a global company. Until recent reorganisations, it was true that Ericsson had global presence, but did not act globally in any co-ordinated fashion. The view was that each Ericsson country president should have local autonomy. What was very flexible and responsive to local needs was less appropriate when dealing with multi-national customers wanting consistency of approach across the world.

Power structures

This aspect of the organisation's culture is particularly important when it comes to changing the way things are done. Power structures may have nothing to do with the way the organisation chart is drawn. Some individuals appear to have far more power than their status would suggest, either because of the force of their personality or because they exert some power based on expertise.

The importance of power structures as they relate to service delivery might be the negative power sometimes wielded by front-line employees. It would appear to delight some employees to withhold information from customers because this gives them perverse satisfaction. If this is the case, it is quite possible that these employees feel that they are so powerless and undervalued in the organisation that they will employ this negative power tactic as a means of asserting their importance. Managers must be alert to this, partly because customer satisfaction will suffer as a result, but mainly because it may be that there are issues of leadership and motivation to be addressed.

Leaders use a combination of personal charisma, expertise and positional power to bring about change. In bringing about change it is critical to know where the powerful 'pro-change' people are in order to build alliances to see the change through. It is equally important to identify those who are able to block change. It is often necessary to look beyond the ranks of senior management to find individuals who, by reason of their character or past experience, are extremely influential.

In working with a water company it became clear that a major factor in the delivery of a customer service strategy was the extent to which a group of relatively junior employees would buy into a new customer-focused approach. Rather like non-commissioned officers in the armed forces, this group had the ability to prevent anything occurring which didn't fit with their views. The implementation of the service strategy therefore had to include time for getting understanding and commitment from this group.

Of course, power can be used very positively to engender customer focus. No one can dispute the influence of Lord Marshall at British Airways or Jack Welch at GE in driving through improvements in customer service.

Control systems

Control systems are the guiding infrastructure of the organisation. What is of interest here is the identification of the control systems that have significant impact on the way things are done. For some organisations, everything must follow well-defined company procedures which, as we have seen in Chapter 8, may deliver consistent results but leave little room for flexibility. Others have very little in the way of formal controls apart from the need to deliver certain long-term goals. The means by which these are achieved are left to the discretion of the individual.

Performance measurement is at the heart of most control systems. Tony Hughes, Managing Director of Bass Leisure Retail, frequently uses the quote 'What gets measured gets managed, but what gets rewarded gets done'. A good illustration of the effect this produces is provided by the UK's National Health Service (NHS) waiting lists. Waiting-list statistics are used by opposing political parties to demonstrate or attack the effectiveness of current government pollicies. As a result, waiting lists receive a high degree of attention and there is a view that the statistics are manipulated to ensure that they don't become bad enough to attract attention. There is no great reward attached to removing waiting lists, with the result that the basic question of how to reduce lists often goes unanswered. More significantly, the NHS does not publish regular statistics on waiting *times*, a figure which is of far greater relevance to patients.

More positive examples may be provided by those companies which have made it a point to reward people for customer satisfaction performance above profit. A company that has made it a point to reward managers for customer satisfaction performance is Rank Xerox. The company has consistently measured its performance against four key performance criteria: customer satisfaction, employee satisfaction, market share, and return on assets (ROA). Until recently, the company has made it clear that the priority has been very much in the order given above, with the firm belief that satisfying customers and employees leads to enhanced market share and therefore ROA.

Kwik Fit has clearly focused the efforts of branch managers and staff on customer service by managing inventory and other administrative processes centrally. To avoid losing a business focus, each group of branches has its own 'profit and loss' account to understand how the mission of achieving '100% customer delight' links with business success.

A key point here is that organisational control systems often lag behind that which is desired to reinforce new behaviours. The manager of a unit responsible for the development of new revenue-earning services for a computer hardware company was frustrated because the regional sales managers were bonused solely on hardware sales. He was on the brink of signing the first major services deal but it was threatened because the hardware content was so small that it would damage the sales manager's bonus. He decided that in order to establish the fact that services were essential for the long-term survival of the company, he would carry the loss-making component on his own budget to maintain the sales manager's support and interest.

Routines and rituals

These are the activities which are not necessarily in the company procedure manual but nevertheless have special significance for the organisation. They might range from the 'informal system', such as ways of getting round bureaucratic or inflexible procedures, through to celebrations of success such as pub nights or parties.

The Managing Director of Credit Card Sentinel sent thank-you cards to people that had done well, a relatively inexpensive exercise which brought about tremendous returns in employee satisfaction. Avis and other companies practise 'visible management', where head office managers spend time each year in the front-line units. Avis finds that this is invaluable for head office staff to understand the issues of the front line, and they frequently discover that renting cars is not as easy as it looks on paper.

Other routines and rituals may be less helpful. The ritual hunt for a scapegoat after each disaster does not contribute greatly to team spirit! Other rituals may become a way of dealing with the difficulties of the job. This is particularly true where staff have to deal with emotionally difficult situations such as in a hospital or at an accident site. Hospitals develop an almost mechanistic approach to their patients to guard against becoming too emotionally involved. This may have an unfortunate impact on patients, who feel treated as another statistic rather than as human beings with feelings.

The analysis of the routines is extremely rich as it betrays much of the 'under the surface' life of the organisation. It gives clues as to how things really happen as opposed to the sanitised version in the official handbook. When people are able to discuss them honestly, it may uncover such things as how important decisions are made (corridor conversations and inner cabinets), and how people are promoted (not on merit but on whom they know). Recognising this aspect of organisational life is important in order to influence it to support service delivery.

Symbols

Symbols are the physical evidence of who or what is important in the culture. Twenty years ago or more it was relatively easy to see who was important in a large organisation because the manager's status was linked to which floor his office was on, with directors at the top and junior staff at the bottom. Today, with a move towards flatter organisations and a reduction in overt differences between management and staff, the organisational status symbols have become more subtle.

Who has a parking space or a fitted carpet in their office (or who has an office at all) become major talking points. In open-plan offices, the size of a person's desk, or who has a special chair, suddenly become all-important. It is as if these symbols take on a life of their own, as anyone who has been involved with a company car scheme will testify. It may seem on the surface that people have accepted quite major shifts in role during organisational change programmes, but their reaction to the loss of a valued symbol may demonstrate that they are far from happy.

Symbols may also be the human role models of the organisation. Certain charismatic leaders may become symbols of change, as, for example, Richard Branson of Virgin, Herb Kelleher at Southwest Airlines, or Tom Farmer of Kwik Fit.

The relevance for customer focus may lie in how symbols become linked to service. In a security alarm company, sales staff had cars, service engineers had vans. This might make rational sense, but sent a clear message that service was very much the poor relation. A compromise was reached by providing service engineers with estate cars which could, of course, be used for private as well as company use.

Stories

The final aspect of the cultural web is the stories that circulate in the organisation. These are sometimes called the 'war stories' and are generally told to new starters early in their stay in an organisation. In some companies, these stories are generally positive ('we're ahead of the competition, this is a good place to work'), whilst in others they tend to be negative ('welcome to the mad house, don't take any risks, keep your head down'). In large organisations which have been in existence for several years, and have been through major change, stories relating to the 'good old days' abound.

Part of a process of influencing culture might lie in creating a new set of stories linking heroic acts of customer service to success. The famous stories such as Federal Express taking initiative to hire a helicopter to get an essential package through, or of Nordstrom refunding a customer for a faulty tyre even though Nordstrom had never sold tyres, do build a culture of customer ownership. On the other hand, stories of staff who have been disciplined for giving relatively small refunds for poor service because they didn't follow company red tape are extremely damaging.

Using the cultural web

Table 14.1 shows the cultural web analysis for a financial service company. A typical process for developing this analysis is as follows:

1. Develop a common understanding of the key elements of current culture, possibly through the use of facilitated focus groups.
2. Examine the current paradigm and decide what aspects would be desirable to change to fit with future strategic direction.
3. Identify mismatches between desired paradigm and current elements of the cultural web.
4. Develop action plans to influence or change where possible.

Managers may feel that there is little that they can do to change the organisation's culture. Certainly, to make a major shift in culture is not something that can be accomplished by one individual overnight. However, most managers are part of the power structure, and are able to influence in their areas of operation. The value of cultural web analysis as shown in Table 14.1 is that it is possible to identify means of changing aspects of the culture. For example, new reward systems change the emphasis of the control systems relatively quickly. Likewise, it is easy to develop new stories, or to at least ensure that the positive stories are communicated effectively.

14.3 TYPES OF CULTURE

14.3.1 The 'gods' of management

It is important to know the difference between cultures, recognising too that different cultural environments exist within the same organisation. The culture of the boardroom will be rather different from that in the call centre. Likewise, the culture of the accounts department will be very different from that of the sales team. There are a number of factors which influence this diversity, which include individual personalities, the nature of the role undertaken, and the extent to which people have direct customer contact.

Writers on leadership and culture identify various types of culture (see, for example, Kakabadse and Kakabadse 1999; Handy 1991). Handy and Kakabadse both

Table 14.1 Cultural web analysis for a financial service company

	Existing cultural web	Desired cultural web
Paradigm	• Provider of general insurance and pensions • We deal through brokers, not the general public • We are profitable because of good investment management • We are generally risk averse • We are a 'nice' company	• To be seen as providing freedom from worry for our customers • To be profitable through acting with integrity, providing innovative financial products to meet the changing needs of our customers, and delivering them through excellent service
Organisational structures	• Regionally organised with branches and sub-branches • Hierarchical, with several management grades • Insurance and pensions are separate organisations	• Organised in teams around customer delivery processes • Providing total solutions for our customers in 'one-stop shops' • Service delivered direct to consumers
Power structures	• Executive Management Committee • Managers who came from Company 'A' prior to the recent merger • Actuaries	• Executive Management Committee • More influence for those in customer-facing roles
Control systems	• Company procedures manual • Financial services legislation • Risk analysis • Sales incentives	• Long-term customer retention and profitability • Emphasis on developing competence of employees • Team incentives
Routines and rituals	• Management dinners • Senior management visits to branches • Promotion on seniority • Poor performers 'promoted' to 'special projects'	• Recognition of excellent performance in both sales and service • Promotion on merit
Stories	• Amount spent on directors' dining room • How good Christmas parties were years ago • Senior manager fired for fraud	• Celebrations of actions 'beyond the call of duty' • Generation of new business through customer referrals
Symbols	• Who has a personal assistant • Quality of company car • Latest laptop/organiser/IT	• Certificates for achievement

identify power, role and task cultures. Handy, however, uses the term 'club culture' for power culture, and introduces a fourth category, the existential culture.

Handy aligns each of these cultures to a Greek god, giving a useful insight into the various characteristics of these cultures:

- *Zeus – the club culture.* Zeus was the king of the gods, ruling by patronage combined with fear. This culture is found in entrepreneurial organisations and frequently at the very summit of large organisations. It is excellent for speed of decision-making, where key people are chosen because they think and act like the (central) leader. Such organisations can be very effective when they are based on trust, but can be terrible places when an evil Zeus abuses his power.

- *Apollo – the role culture.* This culture is one of rules and order. It is stable and predictable, excellent when the market is not changing rapidly. The individual's role in the organisation is clear, and little initiative is required. The traditional role culture is safe, because nothing changes and someone else (or the system) takes care of things.

- *Athena – the task culture.* Athena is a warrior-goddess, a problem-solver. The basis of this culture is expertise, not experience, age or position. Handy states that this culture works well when the product of the organisation is the solution to a problem. They are expensive cultures, because they are staffed by experts and the outcomes are not predictable, often requiring development time and resource. Athena cultures when they get large require Apollonian cultures to manage the routine activities.

- *Dionysus – the existential culture.* Here the emphasis is that the individual is in charge of his or her own destiny. Handy suggests that in the other three cultures, the individual is there to help the organisation achieve its purpose, but that in this culture the organisation exists to help the individual. Professionals may be grouped together in one building because someone can then organise support systems such as telephones and catering, but there is no interdependence between them.

Table 14.2 provides a summary of some of the ways that these different cultures operate.

The shape of organisational life is changing. The large Apollonian cultures are fast disappearing as they need to adapt more rapidly to changing market demands. More organisations are taking on the form of Athena, the task culture, though frequently with Apollo-like support structures, and with a Zeus at the top.

Recently there has been the emergence of 'virtual' organisations or 'hollow' corporations. These are somewhat Athena-like in concept in that the organisation exists for a particular task and then disbands. Film and television programme-makers operate in this fashion, with a producer being commissioned to gather together a team for the one project. Networks of experts, part Athena, part Dionysus, form loose associations constantly changing shape to meet the current need. It would be wrong to believe that Apollo does not exist any more. There are plenty of Apollo-like organisations in existence still, able to operate consistently and efficiently.

Table 14.2 Summary of different cultures

	Thinking and learning	Influencing and changing	Motivating and rewarding
Zeus **(Club culture)**	● Trial and error ● Watching other Zeuses ● Learning by sitting with the 'master' ● Admission of need to learn is a sign of weakness	● Change by replacing people, not development ● Judged by whom, not what you know ● Credibility is the key	● Money is highly valued ● Reward is to be given responsibility and resource by Zeus ● Winning is crucial
Apollo **(Role culture)**	● Logical and analytical ● Acquisition of more knowledge and skills through training courses ● Appraisals and job rotation	● Power from position, role or title ● Rules and procedures ● Managers implement directors' decisions	● Pensions schemes and career planning ● Increase in formal authority ● Status symbols
Athena **(Task culture)**	● Problem-solving ● Brainstorming ● Learning as a team ● Opportunities for development	● Persuasion through expertise ● Debate and consensus ● Problem definition	● Need a new problem to solve ● Objectives, not role definitions ● Variety
Dionysus **(Existential culture)**	● Learn by total immersion ● Give-up, having mastered a new skill	● Difficult to influence ● Unpredictable, need to negotiate	● Opportunity to make a difference in their terms ● Freedom

14.3.2 The 'gods' and service delivery

Inspection of Table 14.2 suggests a number of ways that these different cultures might impact service delivery:

- **Zeus.** Zeus cultures are very responsive to customers. They are able to react quickly and harness resources to meet the current need. They are good when a personal relationship between the two chief executives is fundamental to the success of the deal. This relationship, if founded on mutual respect and trust, can be very fruitful in developing long-term business. Service delivery to these valued customers is likely to be of high quality as Zeus will ensure it. Service delivery to other customers might be less consistent.

  In terms of the Runners, Repeaters and Strangers, categories described in Chapter 6, Zeus cultures may create Repeaters and Strangers, when some attention to planning might turn them into Runners.

- **Apollo.** These organisations are extremely consistent. Most of the high-volume services such as retailers, utilities, insurance companies and so forth have much of this culture. The problem is that they may be experienced as rather inflexible by their customers. The attitude of 'that's more than my job's worth' or 'I can't do that' is the downside of the reliability and efficiency that they deliver.

This culture thrives on Runners, tolerates Repeaters, and resists Strangers.

- *Athena.* As discussed in the previous section, this culture is appropriate when the output is a solution for customers, rather than a packaged commodity which an Apollo organisation might deliver. This organisation is flexible, and is good at involving its customers in the development process. Specialist software developers and consultants may fall into this category. The problem with these organisations is that although they are innovative, they get bored with the continual delivery of the same solution. At this stage, an Apollo-like organisation form is more appropriate for consistency and cost.

  This culture seeks for Strangers, the opportunity to develop new capability; it tolerates Repeaters in order to generate sufficient revenue; and resists Runners.

- *Dionysus.* This culture is a nightmare as far as service delivery is concerned. These individuals will only operate if the task is of interest, and no amount of pleading or bribery will change their mind. Customers are liable to be made to feel that they are somewhat inferior to the service provider, only taken on because they are an 'interesting case'.

  This culture is only interested in Strangers, and will not even consider Runners.

Finally, it is worth noting that an understanding of the difference in organisational culture is particularly relevant in a business-to-business relationship. Apollo cultures are likely to be confused and frustrated by Athena cultures and vice versa.

Box 14.1 First Direct

Visitors to First Direct's web site are bombarded with words that this bank uses to describe itself. These include: foremost, visionary, responsive, futuristic, warm, revolutionary, friendly, safe, invigorated, and quixotic.

First Direct, the first 'branchless' telephone bank in the UK, commenced operations in 1989. Its concept was simple: to provide 24-hour banking for 365 days a year. At the heart of the operation was an information system that allowed the customer to handle any traditional branch transaction in a single telephone call. It would have been tempting to recruit staff for this new operation from First Direct's parent, the then Midland Bank (now HSBC).

The management team took a significant decision to look for people who were fast and efficient, able to work under pressure, but, critically, people with warm personalities. Much of this is due to the vision of its first CEO, Kevin Newman, who is quoted as saying:

> I believe that in going forward three things need to be developed. We have to be utterly low cost. We must be able to individualise the manufacturing process and recognise that all our customers are individuals. Thirdly, we must build a strong brand as people need to identify with institutions they can trust.

First Direct identified five core values as central to the way it was to operate and these were incorporated in the training programme for staff, who were to be known as

Banking Representatives (BRs). These were responsiveness, openness, right first time, respect, and contribution. These values were reinforced by Newman and his management team who spent a significant amount of their time talking to BRs. Right from Day 1, Newman wanted First Direct to have a different culture from traditional banks. Everyone ate in the same cafeteria, and managers were on first-name terms with BRs. The only perk that Newman enjoyed was a company car. There was no 'headquarters' – managers and directors sat at desks in the same area as the BRs. There was minimal hierarchy, with managers encouraged to concentrate on leadership and guidance rather than interference and instruction.

BRs undertook a seven-week training course before dealing with customers. The first four weeks were dedicated to understanding the bank's products, whilst the latter three weeks concentrated on telephone role-playing and building techniques. First Direct made limited use of scripting techniques, and BRs were encouraged to build rapport, using language appropriate to the individual customer. BRs worked in teams with a team leader acting as a coach. The teams were encouraged to develop their own identities, and to create team names. First Direct invested in facilities for the 24-hour workforce. A security firm guarded car parks and reception areas, and hot food was available from 7 a.m. until 9 p.m. Staff are encouraged to attend lifestyle classes covering subjects as diverse as foreign languages and yoga.

Much of the continued success of First Direct has been attributed to its friendly, responsive culture. First Direct's web site proclaims that it 'actively promotes a positive working environment'. This has been achieved without the loss of efficiency or consistency. Clearly, this is due in no small part to the culture created by Newman, his management team, and those who followed them.

Questions

1 *What do you think are the significant elements in the success of First Direct? What contribution does First Direct's culture make to this success?*

2 *What actions should First Direct take to maintain the enthusiasm of the initial launch of its branchless banking service?*

This illustration is based on personal experience, from information in First Direct's web site (http://www.firstdirect.co.uk), and Insead case study: First Direct: Branchless Banking 597-028-1.

14.4 NATIONAL CULTURES

A chapter on culture would be incomplete without at least a mention of the influence of national cultures on service delivery. Hofstede (1980 and 1991) conducted a major cross-cultural study of IBM employees to identify characteristics of national cultures. He identified four dimensions which can be used to rate national culture:

- *Power-distance.* A high power-distance rating would suggest that employees are relatively passive, have a liking to be directed, and inhabit a culture that generally expects superiors to wield power. The corollary to this is that superiors frequently exhibit low trust of subordinates. Many Asian cultures have high power-distance ratings.

Low power-distance rankings encourage greater mutual trust and an expectation that subordinates will be involved in decision-making. The UK, some of Western Europe and the USA fall into this group.

- *Uncertainty avoidance.* This dimension evaluates the extent to which the culture encourages risk-taking. Cultures with high uncertainty avoidance adopt strategies such as working long hours and enforcing strict obedience to procedures to deal with difficult conditions. Much of the Japanese work ethic exhibits this tendency.

  Low uncertainty avoidance encourages a more entrepreneurial spirit with less concern for following rigid procedures.

- *Individualism–collectivism.* The UK, along with the USA and Canada, places high regard on the achievements of individuals, whereas some cultures value loyalty to extended family or tribe more highly. In the latter case, the emphasis is on belonging, duty and group decision-making.

- *Masculinity–femininity.* The masculinity-dominant cultures place emphasis on acquisition of money, material possessions, and on ambition. Managers are encouraged to press for ever-increasing goals and objectives. Where femininity is dominant, the emphasis is on creating a more collaborative environment.

This work is interesting in that it challenges assumptions that all people are the same. It clearly has implications for the implementation of global operations strategies. Teamwork and empowerment may not translate from one culture to another. It is necessary to point out, though, that the assumption that all people from a national culture rank high on power-distance, low on uncertainty avoidance and so forth is clearly inaccurate. One hypothesis is that at an organisational level, the company culture might be more influential, not least because the company recruitment policies will tend to favour 'people like us'.

14.5 THE MANAGEMENT OF CHANGE AND SERVICE DELIVERY

14.5.1 Strategies for cultural change

There is not sufficient space here to cover all the aspects of the management of change, but we discuss some of the issues as they specifically relate to service delivery. Bate (1996) provides a helpful overview of strategies for cultural change. He suggests four basic approaches:

- *Progressive.* This approach is used when there isn't time for a consultative approach. Senior managers have to implement change rapidly, frequently upsetting staff in the process. This approach (also termed Aggressive) is effective in implementing rapid major change, but is poor in gaining commitment and ownership of the result.

- *Consultative.* This approach is characterised by a great deal of communication and involvement. It is excellent for gaining commitment, but poor at implementing a radical solution.

- *Educative.* Here, the organisation provides material and training to explain why the change is necessary. It is based on the view that if people can (rationally) understand the need for change, they will be happy to support it. Education and training have been shown to be effective (we would say that!), but one problem is that people do not react to change rationally. The other common issue with this approach is that the company 'road-show' is often seen as playing mind-games with the employees. Hence this is also termed the Indoctrinative approach.

- *Corrosive.* This is akin to the organisation's grapevine. Senior management 'lets loose' the key messages at key points throughout the organisation. This approach is much favoured by those who must attempt to manage groups of professionals, who resist any form of direct control.

Most change processes will contain elements of all four approaches. It is important to note that if, in the early process of change, it has been necessary to employ the Progressive/Aggressive approach, managers must be alert to the danger of disaffected staff displaying unhelpful customer attitudes.

Bate then outlines five parameters to assess the success of the change process:

- *Expressiveness.* This measures the extent to which the change process communicates a new idea. This is what people call the emotional part of 'hearts and minds'. A new mission statement which captures the imagination of the employees will be invaluable here, particularly if this statement is lived up to by senior management.

- *Commonality.* Culture is produced when people speak to each other. This parameter assesses the extent to which everyone speaks the same language and means the same thing. The question here is: 'Is there a sense of solidarity because we know what we are trying to achieve?'

- *Penetration.* To what extent has the change really 'got inside' the organisation? Has it begun to change the way that things are done, particularly at the level of routines and rituals? Has it got to the point where it cannot be ignored?

- *Adaptability.* Is the change process able to deal with the diversity of situations represented in a large, complex organisation? Can those responsible for implementation maintain the essence of the change, making helpful local adaptations? Can it be questioned and rethought in key areas without losing credibility?

- *Durability.* Is it tamper-proof? Will it transcend the departure of the chief executive? Is it clear that this change will not go away?

14.5.2 Pitfalls to avoid

One of the most helpful summaries of the problems of change management is provided by Kotter (1995), who identified the following pitfalls:

- *Not establishing a sense of urgency.* Kotter quotes a key statistic that 75 per cent of managers must accept the need for change if it is to be successful.

- *Not creating a powerful guiding coalition.* For service organisations this must surely include gaining the commitment of customer-facing staff as well as senior management.

- *Lacking a vision.* Too many organisations implement initiative after initiative without a clear sense of how they fit together. A vision, as with the service concept, should be a unifying factor.

- *Undercommunicating by a factor of 10.* A key issue here is that employees usually trust their immediate manager or team leader more than the senior management team, who are often remote and seen as pursuing their own agendas. The first-line supervisor or team leader is central to the implementation of a new service vision.

- *Not removing obstacles to the vision.* It is necessary to ensure that job roles and measurement systems are consistent with the change required, rather than hope that they'll catch up. Any significant change will meet overt and covert resistance which must be faced.

- *Not planning for short-term wins.* Staff need credible evidence of some success within 12 to 24 months. This needs to be managed.

- *Declaring victory too soon.* It is tempting to slacken off the pressure at the first signs of success. Unless the changes have taken root in the rituals of the organisation, it is not completed.

- *Not anchoring the change in the organisation's culture.* Managers need to understand the motivators for their staff. Have they changed in line with the new requirements?

The illustration of Amnesty International in Box 14.2 demonstrates the complexity of change in service strategy when those involved have affiliations to more than one group in the organisation. It is insufficient to present a change as 'being the right thing to do', even if this can be supported with rational arguments. People's loyalties to local groups may be more powerful than logic in many cases.

Box 14.2 Amnesty International

Amnesty International was founded in 1961 by Peter Benenson, a British lawyer, and today it has over 1 million members and supporters spread across over 150 countries. Its objectives are to promote general awareness of human rights and to oppose specific abuses of human rights.

Amnesty has both volunteers and 'professionals' who are paid staff. They are organised into two main groups, the International Secretariat in London and over 50 national sections. The International Secretariat is the research headquarters of the organisation, with specialists in many fields sifting and checking information about alleged abuses before initiating action. The national sections contain the 'grass roots' of the volunteer membership, being responsible for activist campaigning, local recruitment, fund-raising and so forth.

Unfortunately, Amnesty's field of interest is expanding rather than becoming redundant. In many parts of the world there are incidents of human rights abuse. For a number of years Amnesty's work had little co-ordinated international strategy. The approach until the early 1990s was that each of the national sections would be involved to a greater or lesser extent in all aspects of Amnesty's work. This led to a dilution of resources and a somewhat haphazard approach to dealing with abuse of human rights.

The direction of Amnesty is debated in depth every two years at the International Council Meeting (ICM). It was at the ICM in 1991 that the membership of the national sections understood that, in order to meet the increasing challenges, Amnesty would have to act on a basis of international co-ordination rather than simply be an international organisation comprising many national sections.

The impact on the national sections has been that they are no longer left to develop their own plans in isolation. Under an initiative termed 'specialisation' each section must determine its particular strategic focus, taking into consideration its strengths and opportunities. This development of particular strengths for each national section is linked to an international planning process. The International Secretariat in London has the responsibility for determining priority levels for country research and campaigning projects in consultation with the national sections.

The national sections were initially nervous that they would lose 'universality' and would lose touch with what was going on across the world. In reality, many sections probably never had the ability or desire to address all the potential issues in every place that Amnesty was involved. Most national sections contain a number of local or regional groups. This same process of 'specialisation' has been applied within national sections to these local groups, each taking on a different emphasis of fund-raising, public awareness or specific geographical action.

Questions

1 *Is it possible to describe the culture of Amnesty International as a whole? What are the essential differences in culture between the national sections and the International Secretariat?*

2 *In managing this change, what issues should Amnesty International pay attention to at both national and international level?*

14.5.3 Capacity for change

Finally, many change initiatives fail because they are under-resourced. This is a concept that should be understood by operations managers. Change fails because managers do not have the capability to manage it. If this is so, the organisation must recruit or buy this ability. Another common problem is that the organisation does not have the capacity to manage the process and maintain 'business as usual'. Parker and Lewis (1980) studied managers passing through change and proposed that the experience is similar to the bereavement process, illustrated in Figure 14.3.

The transition curve shows the individual's response to a proposed (enforced) change. From a point of relatively high perceived competence, the individual is initially shocked and then fairly quickly moves to the 'denial' state which can be either pretending that the change will go away, or that they can deal with whatever comes their way. This state leads to a downward spiral into reality as they recognise that the new environment will require the acquisition of new skills and new ways

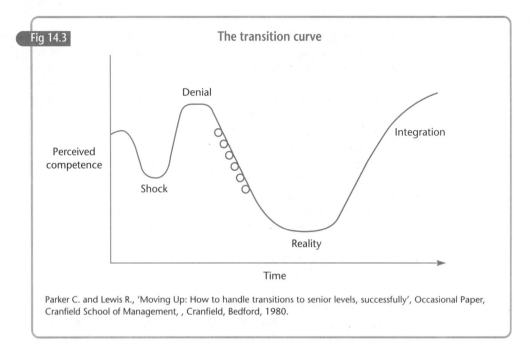

Fig 14.3 The transition curve

Parker C. and Lewis R., 'Moving Up: How to handle transitions to senior levels, successfully', Occasional Paper, Cranfield School of Management, , Cranfield, Bedford, 1980.

of working. Having reached this low point, the individual needs, often by trial and error, to begin to integrate new approaches into their way of working.

Managers going through a change process need time to understand the impact on themselves, let alone those who work for them. The transition curve is generally estimated to require a period of two years to elapse from beginning to end, though this is only an average figure. The implication for operations managers is that they must dedicate resource to managing staff through any period of significant change if 'business as usual' service is to be maintained to an acceptable standard.

14.6 SUMMARY

Understanding organisational culture

- Culture may be considered to be 'tangible' or 'intangible' and is considered to exist at three levels, as artefacts, as espoused values and as basic underlying assumptions.
- The cultural web is a useful way of understanding organisational culture and can also be used to help managers understand how they can influence culture.

Types of culture

- Culture can be characterised as the gods Zeus – the club culture; Apollo – the role culture; Athena – the task culture; and Dionysus – the existential culture.
- Each has a different impact on the service delivery system.

National cultures

- National cultures can be characterised along four dimensions: power-distance, uncertainty avoidance, individualism–collectivism and masculinity-femininity

The management of change

- There are four main strategies for change: Progressive, Consultative, Educative and Corrosive.
- The pitfalls to avoid include:
  ➣ not establishing a sense of urgency
  ➣ not creating a powerful guiding coalition
  ➣ lacking a vision
  ➣ undercommunicating by a factor of 10
  ➣ not removing obstacles to the vision
  ➣ not planning for short-term wins
  ➣ declaring victory too soon
  ➣ not anchoring the change in the organisation's culture.

14.7 DISCUSSION QUESTIONS

1. Give examples of service organisations that fit the 'gods of management' model. What are their strengths and weaknesses in service delivery?

2. What influence can operations managers exert on organisational culture? How important do you think performance measurement is as a component of culture?

14.8 QUESTIONS FOR MANAGERS

1. Do you understand what the principal basic assumption is of your organisation? Does it support your service concept or is the reason for poor performance the fact that your organisational culture is lagging behind your strategy?

2. Can you express the paradigm of your organisation? In what way do you think your interpretation differs from other managers in your organisation?

3. What aspects of your organisation's cultural web can you influence? What action is required to support your organisation's competitive strategy?

4. Which of the 'gods of management' fits your organisation? Is this the type of organisation you want to work in?

5. What lessons can you learn from Kotter's list of reasons for failure in managing change? How do they relate to your experience of change?

14.9 SUGGESTION FOR FURTHER READING

Handy C., *Gods of Management*, Arrow Books, London, 1995.

14.10 REFERENCES

Bate P., *Strategies for Cultural Change*, Butterworth Heinemann, Oxford, 1996.

Handy C., *Gods of Management*, Arrow Books, London, 1995 (3rd edition; first published by Random Century in 1991).

Hofstede G., *Culture's Consequence: International differences in work-related values*, Sage Publications, Beverly Hills, Calif., 1980.

Hofstede G., *Cultures and Organisations, Software of the Mind*, McGraw-Hill, New York, 1991.

Johnson G. and Scholes K., *Exploring Corporate Strategy* (2nd edition), Prentice Hall, London, 1988.

Johnson G. and Scholes K., *Exploring Corporate Strategy* (3rd edition), Prentice Hall, London, 1993.

Kakabadse A. and Kakabadse N., *Essence of Leadership* International Thomson, London, 1999.

Kotter, J.P., 'Why Transformation Efforts Fail', *Harvard Business Review*, March–April, 1995.

Morgan G., *Images of Organization*, Sage, Newbury Park, Calif., 1986.

Oswick C., Lowe S. and Jones P., 'Organisational Culture as Personality: Lessons from psychology?', in Oswick C. and Grant D. (eds), *Organisation Development, Metaphorical Explorations*, Pitman Publishing, London, 1996, pp. 106–120.

Parker C. and Lewis R., 'Moving Up: How to handle transitions to senior levels, successfully', Occasional Paper, Cranfield School of Management, Cranfield, Bedford, 1980.

Schein E.H., *Organizational Culture and Leadership*, Jossey-Bass, San Francisco, 1985.

CASE EXERCISE

Security Alarm Systems Limited

Security Alarm Systems Limited (SASL) is a medium-sized company supplying security alarm systems to both organisations and domestic customers. Its main markets are as follows:

- national retail organisations requiring a standard security system across a network of high street branches or outlets in out-of-town retail parks
- manufacturing companies
- other commercial properties such as office facilities
- luxury domestic premises
- standard domestic premises.

For the first four of these categories, the system can be linked to SASL's central monitoring unit, to facilitate rapid response to alarm activation. In some very sensitive cases, security systems are linked directly to the local police station. These frequently lie in the luxury domestic category, the home of a public personality or an extremely wealthy person.

The industry consists of a few companies providing service nationally. All but one of these restrict their operations to the UK. The exception is the largest company in the market, Intruder Systems, which is a subsidiary of a company based in the USA. There are large numbers of companies that supply and service alarm systems on a local or regional basis. These are often set up and staffed by ex-employees of the national companies.

SASL is organised into four regions, Southern England, Northern England, Midlands and Wales, and Scotland. Each region has a general manager overseeing a number of local depots. A typical depot comprises a depot manager, sales consultants, system installers, service engineers and support staff. There is a small headquarters, which is located in the

Northern region and contains the executive team (managing director, sales and marketing director, finance director and technical director), credit control and a team of engineering experts. This central team of system specialists is available as a resource to the sales consultants, particularly assisting them in the design of more complex systems.

Alfred Higgins, an expert in closed-circuit television, is annoyed that the company's salesforce does not sell more complex systems, preferring to stick to older technology that they can understand. He says, 'We could charge higher prices for state-of-the-art technology, but many of our sales consultants were originally service engineers and have received very little product training since changing roles.' Higgins also claims that the engineers see a move into sales as an escape from the unsocial hours of service, and a chance to get a company car rather than the service van.

The usual sales procedure is as follows. In response to a customer enquiry, the sales consultant will make a visit or 'survey' to assess the requirements and to present SASL's service portfolio. If the system is a small one, as for example in a typical family home, the sales consultant will provide an initial estimate of price and delivery time during the visit. For larger systems, the sales consultant will develop a more detailed quotation, frequently drawing on the expertise of the central specialist team for details of more complex control systems or CCTV (closed-circuit television) application. SASL does not manufacture any equipment, but is attempting to build stronger links with component suppliers. Better information about component quality would be useful, but is currently held only at depot level.

If the quotation is accepted by the customer, the file is passed to the installation engineers. SASL believes that there are fewer problems with commissioning systems if they retain control over this activity, although others, notably Intruder Systems, have out-sourced this work. Security systems are normally sold with a maintenance contract, renewable annually. There are various formats for these contracts, ranging from full service and support contracts through to service being charged as costs are incurred. Full service contracts should be most profitable for SASL, though poor organisation means that margins are reduced, and there are significant differences in the depots' abilities to sell these premium contracts.

The local depot structure of the company has provided a good platform for responsiveness, both to sales enquiries and to system problems. This continues to be valuable for domestic customers and for small manufacturing units where the customer deals solely with the local depot. However, this is proving to be less helpful when dealing with national retail chains where negotiations are normally conducted with a central purchasing department and possibly the customer's own security manager. Joanne Walters, the Birmingham Depot Manager, says, 'I visit my main customers at least once a year. If there are any problems, I use my discretion as to whether to give a credit note for repairs when we are slightly late in fulfilling preventive maintenance schedules. Customers seem to be quite happy if you apologise and give them some money off.'

Response times to system faults are within the British Standard requirement of four hours, but this is largely achieved at the expense of planned maintenance. This sets up a vicious circle, with system breakdowns occurring more frequently as a result. There are frequently differences in operating procedures between depots, with most local managers having been promoted from the depot's service engineers.

Two of the four regional general managers are long-service SASL employees, both promoted from service engineer, through depot manager, to regional general manager. The General Manager, Scotland (George MacLeod), has recently moved from Intruder Systems whilst the General Manager, Southern England (Fred Harvey), came to SASL from another competitor, Securiguard, three months after SASL appointed his previous boss, Andrew Porter, as managing director.

SASL has a good reputation for responsiveness to customers, but Porter is worried that quality inconsistency will limit the company's growth. He is also worried that the company's productivity is lagging behind the industry standard. As a result, Porter has decided to strengthen the headquarters team with the appointment of an operations director whose brief will be to develop consistent processes to be implemented across the network, to increase service quality and productivity. Porter's vision for SASL is that it should be positioned as providing security solutions, advising its customers on all their requirements, rather than limiting itself to supplying and servicing equipment. Andrew Porter has asked Fred Harvey to lead a taskforce to investigate the best performing depots with a view to implementing best practice. It is no secret that Porter favours the appointment of George MacLeod as operations director, although the post will be advertised externally.

SASL, under Andrew Porter, is considering withdrawing from provision of security systems to homes, to concentrate instead on its existing commercial base whilst developing a capability to install and support large security systems. The company has recently completed a major installation in the headquarters of a top financial service company which required installation engineers to be seconded from all four regions to London to ensure that work was completed on schedule.

Joanna Harris, the Sales and Marketing Director, has developed a marketing plan, a first for SASL. It is based on the assumption that in two years' time over 25 per cent of the business will relate to large projects requiring a nation-wide response. This figure is predicted to grow to nearly 40 per cent in five years. This compares with the current level of less than 10 per cent.

'The challenge for SASL,' said Andrew Porter, 'is to reverse a slow decline in our profitability. This will mean significant changes for the organisation as a whole, and particularly for those who have been with SASL for more than ten years, and who remember when it was the acknowledged market leader.'

Questions

1 *What problems does Andrew Porter face?*

2 *How should he deal with them?*

15

Operational Complexity

15.1 INTRODUCTION

In this final chapter we will explore what we think is the fundamental problem that underlies all situations and decisions facing operations managers – complexity. The previous chapters have broken operations management down into handy chunks to enable us to develop each in turn. The reality faced by operations managers is very different. All of these aspects of operations management – people, processes, culture, improvement etc. – are invariably and inextricably interwoven so that decisions or actions in one area will have consequences in all others.

The objectives of this chapter are:

- to define complexity
- to explore the operational consequences of complexity.

This chapter explores the consequences of complexity to try to give a feeling of the nature of operations managers' work. We hope this will provide some insight as to why operations management as a subject, both academic and practical, is both exciting and frustrating.

15.2 WHAT IS COMPLEXITY?

Complexity is both the source of many operational problems and difficulties and at the same time it is the source of inspiration and challenge. Without complexity operations would be an uninteresting, mundane activity that could be assigned as a clerical activity.

The *Concise Oxford Dictionary* tells us that complexity means 'complicated, due to the number of interrelated parts in the system or network'. It also defines a complex as a preoccupation or an obsession with something. Many operations managers we have met have a complex about complexity.

15.2.1 Dimensions of operational complexity

There are several factors that influence the complexity of an operation. The illustration on Oxfam, the international relief organisation, in Box 15.1 is used to describe seven dimensions of operational complexity (see Figure 15.1).

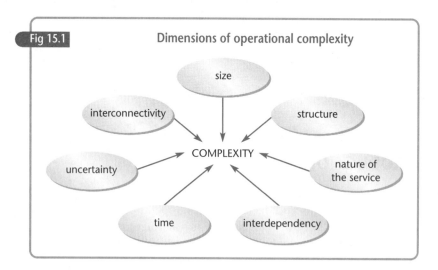

Fig 15.1 Dimensions of operational complexity

Box 15.1 Oxfam

Oxfam is a major international development, relief and campaigning organisation dedicated to finding lasting solutions to poverty and suffering around the world. Oxfam GB, which is affiliated to Oxfam International (an alliance of 11 organisations), works closely with communities through a network of local partners to help provide safety, dignity and opportunity for many disadvantaged people around the world.

The Oxford Committee for Famine Relief began as one of many relief agencies that sprang up during the Second World War. It continued after the war and extended its remit to provide for the relief of suffering whatever the cause might be. Oxfam, as it soon became known, set up collection points for donations and opened its first charity shop in 1948. Oxfam's current network of more than 830 charity shops is supported by about 22,000 volunteers and is a key source of income. The shops sell donated items from the British public and Fair Trade goods – food and handicrafts from around the world, giving small-scale producers fair prices, training, advice and funding support. Orders for items can be made by mail or over the Internet. Oxfam has also teamed up with Yahoo! to provide free access to the Internet in the UK and at the same time raise funds. Together with donations for general use, institutional income and money raised for particular emergencies (restricted funds), Oxfam generated a total income of around £124 million in 1998/99. Oxfam employs around 3,000 staff in total, with about half of these based overseas – mostly local staff from the countries concerned.

Oxfam is perhaps best known for its work in emergency situations, providing humanitarian aid where it is needed. Oxfam has a particular expertise in providing clean water and sanitation facilities. Around 80 per cent of diseases and over one-third of deaths in the developing world are caused by contaminated water, and this can escalate in crises. Yet much of Oxfam's work continues out of the spotlight of disasters and the charity provides continuing help, working with poor communities through a range of programmes concerned with:

- building livelihoods: e.g. agricultural support, providing seeds and tools so people can grow their own food, building flood-prevention barriers, helping people secure access to markets, credit and land

- improving health and education: providing access to clean water, developing schools

- participation in processes: e.g. enabling poor or vulnerable people to gain control over their lives, to have a say and be listened to instead of ignored, bypassed or exploited

- gender issues: e.g. working to remove barriers to girls' education.

Oxfam also speaks out on behalf of disadvantaged communities, pressuring governments and decision-makers on a range of issues including trade, Third World debt, education, land issues, workers' rights etc.

Whether the disasters are natural (such as earthquakes and storms) or political (such as riots and wars), disasters become emergencies when the people involved can no longer cope. In poor countries disasters leave people homeless and vulnerable to famine or disease and they may become ill or die within days if they do not get aid. In such situations Oxfam, through its network of staff in local offices in 70 countries, is able to advise on the resources and help that are needed and on where they are needed. Indeed local teams are often able to provide warnings of impending disasters, giving more time to assess need and enable a multi-agency response.

The emergency programmes are mainly run by Oxfam's regional and country offices. The organisation's headquarters in Oxford provides advice, materials and staff, often deploying emergency support personnel (ESPs) on short-term assignments when and where their skills are required. Shelters, blankets and clothing can be flown out at short notice from the emergencies warehouse in Bicester. Engineers and sanitation equipment can also be provided including water tanks, latrines, hygiene kits and containers such as the 'Oxfam bucket', which is light, easy to carry and transport, and has a sealable lid.

Every emergency is different, with differing security situations, aid needs, logistical problems and access issues. The responses of other agencies such as governments or other relief agencies will also depend on the nature and location of the disaster. Oxfam relies on its local team, with support from HQ as necessary, to assess each situation and decide whether the organisation can make a difference. Sometimes they are unable to respond: the security situation may be too difficult or governments are responding with all that is needed. Local, regional and head office managers have to weigh up all the factors to decide upon the degree and nature of response.

When an emergency is over, Oxfam often continues to work with the affected communities through their local offices, to help people rebuild their lives and livelihoods.

Questions

1 *What, in your view, makes Oxfam's operations so complex?*

2 *What might be the conflicts between the various stakeholders that Oxfam has to try to deal with?*

Interconnectivity

Strictly speaking, complexity is about interconnectivity, created by the many possible interrelationships between different variables. Oxfam has to manage the relationships between its fund-raising activities through the charity shops and network of volunteers, its head office and its network of local offices and regional offices. It also has to manage its relationship to the communities that it is trying to serve, and co-ordinate with the activities of other relief agencies and governments. These two very different activities also need to connect, as Oxfam's ability to overcome poverty and suffering depends upon its ability to raise funds.

Size

Complexity is usually relative to size. The greater the size of an operation, i.e. the more elements it has, the greater the number of interconnections. Indeed as elements increase linearly, the interconnections will grow exponentially. Oxfam is a large organisation with nearly 3,000 staff and about 22,000 volunteers with offices in 70 countries around the world. This size creates many possible interconnections that the organisation attempts to manage through its regional structure.

Structure

Some operations will have more complex structures than others. Simple structures may have more common routines and straightforward requirements with fewer suppliers, for example. The structure of Oxfam creates a degree of complexity. Oxfam is a global organisation with offices in around 70 countries. Co-ordinating such a structure that is dependent upon volunteers and is focused upon both disasters and ongoing programmes is no simple task.

Nature of the service

The nature of Oxfam's service is also a source of complexity. We may see one of Oxfam's services through, for example, the work of its charity shops, or its clothes and handicrafts. However, their core services are much more complex: the provision of relief when disasters strike, together with attempts to find lasting solutions to poverty through its ongoing programmes. There are few organisations with such intricate, complicated and burdensome services.

Interdependency

Some operations may be large with complex structures but if there is little interdependency between the parts, the task will be easier to manage. The many elements of Oxfam's operations are very dependent upon each other. Fund-raising is needed to provide non-restricted funds, the disasters provide leverage for raising restricted funds, the central emergencies warehouse has to stock the items that may be needed to respond appropriately to unknown disasters. Oxfam has a flexibility in staffing that allows a flexible and focused response to emergencies, yet at the same time its local offices both provide support for its ongoing work and also help predict and prepare for disasters. Oxfam is also critically dependent on the goodwill of its volunteers: employees and volunteers give a significant portion of their time and earning potential as a gift. This fact has serious implications for people management; in addition to addressing internal efficiency, operational decisions must respect this 'gift relationship' between the organisation and its workers.

Time

Many tasks undertaken by operations managers are by their nature time sensitive and usually require speedy action or resolution. Although it would be good to be able to hit a 'pause button', this is a luxury not afforded to many operations. Oxfam is often faced with situations where people are dying and will continue to die if help does not get to them within hours. Speed of response, co-ordination with other agencies and preparedness are essential ingredients that help them deal with disasters.

Uncertainty

Service is not a physical product and likewise service operations are not a machine. The interplay between human actors, both staff and customers, creates a dynamic whose outcomes for the customer as well as time required and costs involved are to some extent uncertain. Oxfam faces great environmental uncertainty – not only is it difficult to predict earthquakes and storms as well as the timing of political events, it is impossible to predict the scope and scale of any emergency and the precise needs of communities. Through contingency planning and its staff on the ground, Oxfam can try to manage the impact of these uncertainties. However, when a disaster strikes, nothing can detract from their ability to co-ordinate their efforts into a multi-agency response.

15.3 OPERATIONAL CONSEQUENCES OF COMPLEXITY

Complexity to some extent is a fact of life that faces most, if not all, operations managers. Whilst the previous section attempted to identify the nature of complexity, the reality is that it leads to a number of operational problems. Unfortunately, in many cases there are no remedies, or tools or frameworks, that can help us. We would suggest that the operational consequences of complexity can be summarised as follows:

- things don't work as expected
- things fall down holes
- things are misunderstood
- things are missing
- things have to work.

Things don't work as expected

One problem that operations managers face is that any decision they make and any action they take will have a range of consequences. Changing employee shift patterns may have an effect on morale and commitment, which may have an impact on staff satisfaction and retention and costs of recruitment. It may also impinge upon customer satisfaction and then income and profit. Buddhists, although referring to life rather than just operations, call this the law of interconnectivity. They argue that all events and actions are interconnected and interrelated with all other events and actions. Indeed the doctrine of kamma is based on the principle of causality, the laws of cause and effect (Plamintr 1994).

In Chapter 11 we developed a structure and suggested methodologies for attempting to understand the links between the many possible operational levers and business outcomes. The reality, however, is that there are just so many interconnected variables with differing relationships, which also change over time, that it is impossible to fully map them or control them all.

Operations management will always, to some extent, be an art. We have to make judgements, based on a combination of scientific knowledge about the relationships between variables, together with experience and intuition. At best we will improve operational performance, at worst we will prevent entropy, the natural tendency of things to move toward greater disorder or disorganisation (Flood and Carson 1993).

Things fall down holes

Because of the complexity of many operations things do go wrong and things fall down holes. Even the most efficient bank with the best systems in the world will still occasionally lose a loan application, for example. Even the best public service organisation will occasionally omit to change someone's address despite having the information. Operations managers cannot therefore be perfectionists – that is not to say that they should not strive to attain perfection, just that it is something that will always be out of reach. Service recovery (Chapter 12) is therefore not an add-on extra but a cornerstone of service operations. The best service operations are those that take recovery seriously and have good systems in place that not only deal with the immediate problem, including the customer, but work to improve the processes.

Things are misunderstood

Service involves people. These are the stakeholders, individuals or groups, who have some form of interest in, or claim over, the organisation. They may be people internal to the organisation such as managers, staff, officers and board members, or external to the organisation such as customers, suppliers, political masters, trade unions, local communities and the general public. Most organisations strive to match the varying and sometimes conflicting needs of their stakeholders, though few have the resources to satisfy them all. Stakeholder impact analysis helps managers develop appropriate strategies by identifying stakeholders, identifying their varying needs and concerns, and identifying their relative importance to the organisation (see, for example, Macmillan and Jones 1986; Hill and Jones 1998).

At an operational level we have to deal with the results of these mismatches on a day-to-day basis. They manifest themselves as misunderstandings, misrepresentations and mistakes, brought about by the differing values, mores and expectations of the various stakeholders. They may be nothing more than low-key grumblings at best, or may escalate into disputes resulting in loss of face, loss of office, loss of business, or at worst outright hostility.

Professor Roy Staughton has developed a process that identifies the key elements of a relationship, documents them and brings the two parties together to understand and then work on their differences. The results can be dramatic, as can be seen in the BRE illustration in Box 15.2.

Box 15.2 The BRE

Roy Staughton, www.shape-international.com

The BRE is the UK's leading centre of expertise on building and construction and is a main contractor for the UK Government's Energy Efficiency Best Practice Programme. Employing some 370 professional staff, it has internationally renowned expertise in construction research, testing and consultancy. Originally an Agency of the Department for the Environment, Transport and the Regions (DETR), it is now owned by the Foundation for the Built Environment, a non-profit distributing company with a mission to champion excellence and innovation in the built environment.

Amongst its portfolio BRE carries out significant research and consultancy for the DETR, generating reports, papers and discussion documents and preparing good practice guides and case studies from projects which typically run for 12 to 24 months. Following privatisation, BRE had an ongoing contractual relationship with DETR, giving it a degree of protected status for its work for five years. From 2003, all DETR contracts will be awarded on the basis of open tender.

During 1998, the Managing Director of BRE identified the need to develop the relationship with the former owner and still predominant customer. Its ongoing contractual relationship was time limited and major competitors were known to be preparing aggressive sales positions. Loss of a significant proportion of the business would prove disastrous. The relationship, which had its roots in a common past, had in his view polarised somewhat into a classic buyer–seller stand-off and he was having misgivings about the future relationship. He realised that relationships with his erstwhile colleagues were coloured by the past and that the trigger to improve things had to come from him.

He felt that his staff were adjusting too slowly to the changed circumstances and that the civil servants at DETR were also inexperienced and risked becoming caricatures of traditional buyers in the auto industry – heavy-handed, dictatorial and repeatedly saying 'I am the customer – this is what I want". Being concerned at the somewhat 'emotional' characterisation of BRE's performance, he sought something far more professional and business-like for both parties.

His engineering background influenced his view of the way forward. He wanted to be able to measure the relationship in some formal tangible way, even though he recognised that elements of it would be what he described as 'all soft and fluffy'.

DETR agreed to explore their relationship with BRE in a structured and simple way using The Shape Template Process™ . The first phase of the process elicited individual perceptions of what made a difference to the relationship. These were captured in the words, language and images of the key players and represented in simple visual outputs – Templates. Soundings were taken from several levels across each organisation as preparation for the second phase which encouraged contributors to share their perceptions with their colleagues.

When the contributors from BRE came together for phase two, it soon became apparent that their views weren't as one. There was little consistency around what really influenced the relationship or how well BRE was performing against the identified characteristics. Where they agreed on the title of an issue, key players frequently found that their perceptions of actual or required performance levels were some way apart.

Eventually, with facilitation, a common view of the relationship was developed and represented on a joint Template. Agreed characteristics of the relationship were weighted to reflect importance and scored twice: first to reflect how each characteristic was perceived and second to capture what a satisfactory perception might be. In the third phase, participants from both organisations came together to exchange Templates, share their perceptions and jointly develop a set of metrics – key characteristics of the relationship – that would capture the essence of their dialogue and be used to encourage and monitor the health, status and improvement of the relationship over time.

The MD and his team were rather taken aback to learn that they had quite different perceptions of the relationship from those held by their customer. The BRE team had identified eight key characteristics which they felt would be instrumental in improving the relationship and had placed 'timeliness' on top of their list, followed by 'meeting project objectives' and 'understanding of customer objectives'. The DETR view made fascinating reading for the MD. Their-top rated items were 'professional competence of BRE staff', 'quality of BRE outputs' and 'responsiveness of BRE staff'!

With facilitation the two organisations were able to agree on a set of ten metrics – some hard, others soft, together with agreement against each on where the relationship stood and where the participants would like it to be. Review structures were set up to explore and report on ways of improving performance, and consequently perceptions, against these crucial measures of the well-being of the relationship. Periodically, the participants come together to review progress and identify actions required. The MD feels that the greatest contribution to improving the relationship has been the move from assertion and emotion to a measured and focused assessment of performance where continuous improvement has been transparently achieved.

Questions

1 *What were the causes of the misunderstandings between the BRE and DETR?*

2 *What do you think are the key characteristics of a good relationship and how did the relationship at the start of 1998 compare with those characteristics?*

Things are missing

All managers are blessed with 20–20 hindsight when outcomes are known and certain. Complexity, including a lack of certainty, means that most managers have imperfect knowledge about a situation and its outcomes. Information is usually incomplete, understanding about interconnectivities is limited, and resources are rarely in abundance. As a result operations managers need to accept the imperfect world, accept that things will always be missing and press on regardless. That is not to say that they should not strive to improve their knowledge but that if they wait until they know everything, they will never make any decisions.

Things have to work

Despite all of the above problems, the operation has still got to work. People have to be fed, moved, cared for. If ambulance staff or fire-fighters go on strike, governments have no option but to bring in other agencies, such as the army, to provide some sort of cover. At the other end of the scale a restauranteur whose chef walks out or whose oven breaks down still has to deal with the guests who are booked in for their meals.

As a result operations managers have to be adept at contingency planning. Even 'bodging' is an acceptable way of getting out of a problem in the short term.

15.3.1 Overcoming the problems caused by complexity

At the end of the day, despite the complexity of the task, operations managers have to do their best to make things work smoothly and efficiently, provide good service to their customers and also meet their organisation's business objectives. In order to try to deal as well as we can with the problems caused by the natural complexity of the operations task, our advice is to:

- obtain as much evidence as you can but with a view to making timely decisions
- expect things to go wrong and plan for it
- assume that no one understands your thoughts so take every opportunity to share them
- encourage discussion about your service concept or concepts, their delivery and development
- don't use complexity as an excuse
- understand that you and your colleagues will need to be more flexible in adopting varying approaches to deal with diverse people and processes
- strive for utopia but accept imperfections
- be innovative

and, most importantly,

- enjoy it.

15.4 SUMMARY

Complexity

- Complexity is the source of many operational problems and also the source of inspiration and challenge.
- Complexity means 'complicated, due to the number of interrelated parts in an operation'.
- The dimensions of operations complexity are interconnectivity, size, structure, nature of the service, interdependency, time, and uncertainty.

Operational consequences of complexity

- The operations consequences of complexity are that:
  ➢ things don't work as expected
  ➢ things fall down holes
  ➢ things are misunderstood
  ➢ things are missing
  ➢ things have to work.

15.5 DISCUSSION QUESTIONS

1. How do the operational consequences of complexity apply to an activity you have organised and how did you try to minimise them?

2. Why do you think complexity both fascinates and frustrates many operations managers?

15.6 QUESTIONS FOR MANAGERS

1. What are the dimensions of complexity on your operation? How do you try to minimise their effect?

2. What are the consequences for your operation of the complexity you face?

15.7 SELECTED FURTHER READING

Berry L.L., *Discovering the Soul of Service*, Free Press, New York, 1999.

15.8 REFERENCES

Flood R.L. and Carson E.R., *Dealing with Complexity* (2nd edition), Plenum Press, New York, 1993.

Hill C.W.L. and Jones G.R., *Strategic Management Theory* (4th edition), Houghton Mifflin, Boston, 1998.

Macmillan I.C. and Jones P.E., *Strategy Formulation: Power and politics*, West, St Paul, Minn., 1986.

Plamintr S., *Getting to Know Buddhism*, Buddhhadhamma Foundation, Bangkok, 1994.

Index